POLITICS AFTER T.

Religious Nationalism and the Reshapi

CH00547845

In January 1987, the Indian state-run television began broadcasting a Hindu epic in serial form, the Ramayan, to nationwide audiences, violating a decades-old taboo on religious partisanship. What resulted was the largest political campaign in post-independence times, around the symbol of Lord Ram, led by Hindu nationalists. The complexion of Indian politics was irrevocably changed thereafter. This book examines this extraordinary series of events. While audiences may have thought they were harking back to an epic golden age, Hindu nationalist leaders were embracing the prospects of neoliberalism and globalization. Television was the device that hinged these movements together, symbolizing the new possibilities of politics, at once more inclusive and authoritarian. Simultaneously, this study examines how the larger historical context was woven into and changed the character of Hindu nationalism.

ARVIND RAJAGOPAL is Associate Professor in the Department of Culture and Communication, New York University. He was a Member of the School of Social Sciences, at the Institute for Advanced Study, Princeton, in 1998–99.

POLITICS AFTER TELEVISION

Religious Nationalism and the Reshaping of the Indian Public

ARVIND RAJAGOPAL

CAMBRIDGE
UNIVERSITY PRESS

PUBLISHED BY THE PRESS SYNDICATE OF THE UNIVERSITY OF CAMBRIDGE
The Pitt Building, Trumpington Street, Cambridge, United Kingdom

CAMBRIDGE UNIVERSITY PRESS
The Edinburgh Building, Cambridge CB2 2RU, UK   www.cup.cam.ac.uk
40 West 20th Street, New York, NY 10011-4211, USA   www.cup.org
10 Stamford Road, Oakleigh, Melbourne 3166, Australia
Ruiz de Alarcón 13, 28014 Madrid, Spain

First published 2001

Printed in the United Kingdom at the University Press, Cambridge

Typeset in Baskerville 11/12.5pt [VN]

A catalogue record for this book is available from the British Library

Library of Congress Cataloguing in Publication data
Rajagopal, Arvind
Politics after television: religious nationalism and the reshaping of the Indian public
by Arvind Rajagopal
p.   cm.
ISBN 0 521 64053 9 (hardback)   0 521 64839 4 (paperback)
1. Television in politics – India.   2. Elections – India.   3. Mass media – Political aspects –
India.   4. Nationalism – Religious aspects – India.   5. Immigrants – United States – Hindu
influence.   I. Title.
HE8700.76.I4 R34 2001
306.2'0954 – dc21   00-028954

ISBN 0 521 64053 9 hardback
ISBN 0 521 64839 4 paperback

Contents

Acknowledgments

Todd Gitlin, Robert Bellah, and Robert Goldman have been critical for their mentorship and counsel. Linda Hess planted the seed that grew into this book. To Arjun Appadurai, Nicholas Dirks, and Susanne Rudolph I express my thanks for their critical encouragement. My thanks to Janaki Bakhle, Tanya Fernando, John Foran, Akhil Gupta, Daniel Hallin, B. Kailasam, Aisha Karim, Riyad Koya, Philip Lutgendorf, Purnima Mankekar, Manjunath Pendakur, Steven Pierce, Philip Schlesinger, Anand Swamy, and Jyotika Virdi, who have generously helped in various ways during different stages of this work. I owe Rajeswari Sunder Rajan more than most, for her inspiration and support. Carin McCormack's eye for the architecture of an argument has left its mark on this book.

I am extremely grateful to K. Narayanan for his encouragement and help. Venkitesh Ramakrishnan offered valuable information, and much assistance in meeting people in Uttar Pradesh (U.P.), as did Radhika Ramaseshan. Geeta Bakshi was enormously encouraging in my attempts to gain insight into the workings of Doordarsham. Amar Kanwar, Rahul Roy, and Saba Dewan, as well as Sabina Gadihoke and Sabina Kidwai and the other members of the Media Storm collective, graciously allowed me to view film footage. Thanks to Amar Singh Sachan, Anupama Chandra, Jyoti Mudgal, Kewal Kapoor, Natasha, Niti Anand, Sanjay Kumar, Shahana Bhattacharya, and Usha Bharadwaj for their help with transcription and translation. S. Ravindran helped with the interviewing process in U.P. My appreciation again to Sanjay Kumar for his companionship and quiet encouragement while I was writing. Cara Landry has given me more than I can easily acknowledge. E. Deenadayalan and Nirmala Karunan provided a home away from home when I needed it most, as did Ravi and Srilakshmi Rajagopal, Priya and Asha Jain, and Radha Kumar, and M. K. Srinivasan. Dr. D. L. Prasanna Rao and Manjula Rao dealt cheerfully with the conversion of their basement into an utterly chaotic workspace during the closing stages of this project. For that and much more I am grateful. My gratitude to the scores of people who allowed my repeated intrusions into their lives, and unselfishly gave of their time and friendship.

Robert P. Goldman granted me the opportunity to give a senior seminar at Berkeley, where some of the early ideas in this project were first formulated. For the title of the seminar, which appears here as the title of chapter two, I thank Satish Deshpande. I am indebted to Thomas Adler, William Shafer, Charles Stewart, and most of all to Cynthia Stohl for their help in securing leave while I was engaged in writing this book; to my colleagues who bore the brunt of the teaching in my absence, I owe a further debt of gratitude.

Portions of this book were presented, in earlier versions, at Aalochana, Pune, the 1995 American Ethnological Society meetings in Austin, Texas, the 1995 American Sociological Association meetings in Washington, DC, the University of Chicago, Cornell University, the University of Hyderabad, the University of Iowa, the Nehru Memorial Museum and Library in New Delhi, and the University of Wisconsin, Madison.

My gratitude to my parents for their never-failing affection and support.

And, finally, this book is for Anupama Rao, who has sustained me in numerous ways throughout this project, with inspiration, fierce criticism, and unending challenges. She has been just the reader I could have hoped for, imaginative, generous, quick, and insightful, and more than the friend I ever deserved. Without her nurturance, the writing of this book would have been far more difficult and painful, and indeed it might not have occurred at all.

This book has developed over the course of several years, and some of my earlier essays foreshadowed some of the arguments in it. Portions of this book appeared in earlier versions in "Ram Janmabhumi, Consumer Identity and Image-based Politics," *Economic and Political Weekly*, vol. 29, no. 27, 1994, pp. 1659–1668, and "Communalism and the Consuming Subject," in the *Economic and Political Weekly*, vol. 31, no. 6, 1996, pp. 341–348 (chapter one); "Mediating Modernity: Theorizing Reception in a Non-Western Society," *Communication Review*, vol. 1, no. 4, 1996, pp. 441–469 (chapter two); "Communities Imagined and Unimagined: Contemporary Indian Variations on the Public Sphere," *Discourse*, vol. 21, no. 2, 1998, pp. 48–84 (chapter three); and in "Hindu Immigrants in the U.S.: Imagining Different Communities?" *Bulletin of Concerned Asian Scholars* (Oakland, Calif.), 1997, pp. 51–65 (chapter six).

Introduction

This book is about the work and influence of the media on the career of Hindu nationalist mobilization in India during the late 1980s and early 1990s. It examines the unfolding of the Ram Janmabhumi, or Birthplace of Ram movement, which brought the Bharatiya Janata Party (BJP, or Indian People's Party) into political prominence. It discusses, among other things, the pre-publicity given to the movement's chief symbols via a national broadcast of the Ramayan, a serialized Hindu epic; the promotion carried out by Hindu nationalists through publicity images and through fashioning political participation on consumer choice rather than ideological commitment per se; the attention given the movement by a language-divided print media; television viewers' own readings of the Ramayan serial; and the structured misperceptions of non-resident supporters in the U.S. In arguing that Hindu nationalism's recent salience depended on and worked itself out through the media, I neither uncover nor confirm any simple causal mechanisms of media effect. Instead, I argue that the media re-shape the context in which politics is conceived, enacted, and understood. Hindu nationalism represented an attempt to fashion a Hindu public within the nexus of market reforms and the expansion of communications, rather than religious reaction as such.[1] Focusing on the moment of its emergence clarifies the historical conditions for the transition to a new visual regime, as it were, and at the same time shows the extent to which this emergence cannot be explained with reference to purely material circumstances.[2] That is, it illuminates the power of a given cultural form, and the ways in which this rests on a series of contingent events.

I suggest that Hindu nationalists in recent times represented an attempt to create a populist language of politics, appealing to authoritarian rather than democratic values.[3] It attempted to restructure the forms of public affiliation through a logic of commodification to expand admittance beyond elite groups. Hindu nationalism's rise was concurrent with the unraveling of a consensus that had prevailed during the post-independence years. In the assumptions underlying this consensus, now dubbed "Nehruvianism" after its chief architect, Jawaharlal Nehru, there was a clear hierarchy ordering the realms of politics, economy, and society. Developmental policies conceived in the political realm were going to spur economic growth, thereby modernizing society. Influence was assumed to flow in one direction, from top to bottom. As developmental plans began to bear fruit, however, such an orderly vision of progress became increasingly difficult to maintain. As market reform found its enthusiasts in India, political opponents eventually began to contest the benign (or not-so-benign) authoritarianism through which economic policy was legislated, and which had survived more than four decades of democratic elections. At the same time, new electronic media set up circuits of communication across the realms (of polity, economy, and culture) that state planning sought to compartmentalize. This allowed Hindu nationalism to fashion a range of different rhetorics outside the political sphere proper, and to suggest a homology between forms of consumption and voting behavior, and between cultural identification and the requirements of electoral affiliation. Thus Hindu nationalists worked through commodity images and the partial, shifting affiliation of the novitiate and the sojourner as much as it relied on the commitment of the dedicated convert. In the process, Hindu nationalism sought to bypass the more slow and arduous process of extending its traditional base and of working through the contradictions between its own political positions and those of the different social groups it embraced. Instead, access was declared open to all who would consent to utilize the language being offered. A highly particularistic set of rituals and symbols was brought into a more abstract sphere where they each served to assert *Hindutva*, "Hinduness," without regard to their varying, context-dependent meanings.[4] Paying attention to the language of politics offers a way of contesting the stereotype of Hindutva as a separable and aberrant phenomenon somehow existing apart from the mainstream of national politics. At the same time, it draws attention to the wider cultural and political-economic context within which Hindutva gained influence. As communication systems expand, political participation expands as well, and demands meaningful explanation beyond notions of ideological domination or, for that matter, primordial resurgence.[5]

Hindu nationalism, in fact, became politically conspicuous in the context of economic liberalization and in relation to it. The rhetoric of market reform and that of an insurgent cultural politics went public together, and interacted to express a new historical conjuncture. Both militated against a *dirigiste* status quo and promised radical change if hidden social forces were emancipated, whether of the profit motive or of a long-suppressed Hindu religion. Both drew on market forces energized in the process of liberalization, on the support of middle classes asserting their newly legitimated right to consume and of business groups seeking a successor to a developmentalist regime in eclipse. The onset of liberalization was not a purely economic process, but involved a shift in perception over time (roughly, 1987–93) and a new set of criteria of judgment. Earlier, it had been self-evident that state investment was required in a poor, developing economy, and that the private sector could neither be the main source nor the leading beneficiary of developmental efforts. Now the inefficiency of state intervention and the anodyne character of private enterprise became obvious. There was no causal relation between economic reforms and Hindutva, nor any inherent shared logic. Rather, there was an opportunistic alliance between them, as aspiring middle classes and business elites and a party till recently at the margins of political life sought to maximize their presence. Hindu symbolism had not been absent from public life by any means, but its presence now took on a different, and to many, sinister, meaning, signifying a claim to rule public space and brooking no challenges to its dominion.

Liberalization and Hindu nationalism shared their technologies of transmission for expanding markets and audiences respectively. If their messages and their adherents overlapped or crossed over, it was not necessarily out of conscious design, although design was not absent. Rather, it signaled the influence of the means and methods of communication at work, promoting popular participation without requiring popular control. In a sense, new means of communication generate a new kind of power, one that becomes more intelligible when we examine the work of television as a socio-technical apparatus.

TELEVISION'S POWER: THEORETICAL PREMISES

In this section, I propose to try and understand the workings of television, first as a medium per se, and then in terms of its influence in a country like India. In most critical accounts, television is understood in terms of its ideological power, by virtue of the ruling order it springs from, and in terms of the ideas it helps circulate. A certain abstraction characterizes these arguments, so that domination occurs without viewers being aware of it, and despite the fact that viewers' own experience of television (including that of critics) does not imply such an outcome. Any adequate analysis of television must address this omission.

As a medium, television's work is parallel to and interlinked with that of the economy. Both disseminate information to help circulate goods as well as to socialize members of society.[6] Television is thus active in the material and symbolic reproduction of capitalist relations. Todd Gitlin has pointed out that just as, under capitalism, the surplus value accumulated in social labor is privately appropriated, men and women are estranged from the meanings they produce socially; these are privately appropriated by mass media and returned to them in alienated forms.[7] But the sense of exploitation that inhabits the workplace is absent before television. There is a sense rather of viewing as an autonomous act, done on one's own time. This experience of autonomy is an indivisible part of television's effect, and must be incorporated in any understanding of the medium's power.

Raymond Williams' work on the medium as both "technology and cultural form" points to its dual character, and offers the concept of "flow" as a means of specifying television's distinctness.[8] At one level, the term refers to program composition as a sequence of unrelated items, governed by broadcasting rather than audience interests. As Williams points out, within the flow of television programming is embedded another flow, that of advertising, that appears on no published schedule and yet is the motor of the entire process; audiences are the creation of an economic process designed to serve sponsors.[9] We can extend Williams' metaphor to what is perhaps the most distinctive aspect of the technology, namely its ability to tether diverse temporal flows together.[10] Television audiences across society "tune in" to programs, their time of viewing flowing alongside but separate from the time of the image.[11] Although they inhabit the same space in clock time, as lived duration they are not the same. Thus the packaging of audiences for sale to sponsors and the use of ratings to signal popularity may both occur without the knowledge or consent of viewers, and indeed are thereby more effectively achieved. At the same time, viewers can entertain programs at their leisure, unconstrained by any authority the messages might claim for themselves.

Television yokes together different temporalities in one communicative event. Electronically mediated messages from diverse and far-ranging sources, often at best partially related to viewers' own experiences, tend to lack the relatively deeper, more situated meanings of oral or print culture. This indexes a thinning of time, hence meaning, experienced as a reduction of social control, and as relative freedom. Yet the experience of communication, as Marshall McLuhan correctly describes it, is of participation and sociality, and a tactile sense of being "in touch," regardless of the content communicated.[12] The existence of an ongoing stream of communication shared by others engenders a sense of intimacy across social boundaries, as Claude Lefort has suggested.[13] Thus on the one hand, television offers respite from the compulsions of actually existing social relations, creating a space of temporary immunity from the inhibitions and proscriptions they would impose on any member. On the other hand, it evokes feelings of closeness and reciprocity to unknown participants who may exist only in imagination.

There is a contradictory character to this process. Although television operates within the logic of capitalist exchange, the implicit logic of audiences' own transactions, I suggest, is better understood in terms of anthropological discussions of gift exchange; the experience of communication is one of connection more than of alienation. Communication systems, in fact, impute the sense of an intimacy across society, and presume the existence of an ongoing social connection independent of audience response. The terms in which this connection is experienced, however, do not entail the costs or obligations through which social interaction otherwise occurs. It thus represents a distinct kind of gift exchange. The indefinite time interval between the reception of programming and viewers' own "counter-gift," of talking back to others, to the medium or its sponsors, infuses this gift with the sense of being truly "free," and imposing none of the compulsion customary with gift exchange. This temporal structure serves as an instrument of denial, as Pierre Bourdieu has shown, allowing a subjective truth (of sociality) to exist alongside a contrary, objective truth (of the absence of reciprocity, i.e., of the impossibility of talking back to a monological medium).[14]

Gift and commodity exchange are always implicated in each other; neither ever exists by itself in a pure sense. No commodity transaction is purely instrumental; there is always a sense of reciprocity involved; similarly any exchange of gifts always has an element of calculation in it. Television does something distinct to this entanglement. It invokes the logic of the gift within the private space secured by commodity exchange. The experiences of gift and commodity exchange can hence be separated, and thereby imagined as separate as well. As Marcel Mauss argued, the symbolic existence of a gift economy remains crucial as the underpinning of a capitalist economy.[15]

The private space of reception enables the imagining of a "free" engagement with media messages, and the latter thus become open to imaginative reconstruction. Audiences can thus imagine new communities of sentiment, in fantasies of complete acceptance where the disciplining presence of other minds can be made to retreat, so entailing none of the usual costs of social membership. At the same time, this newly crafted autonomy provides them the critical distance with which it is possible to reflect on society itself as an external object of thought, independent of their own place in it.[16]

As Arjun Appadurai has argued, the imagination has an unprecedented provenance in contemporary society, due in part to the media.[17] I suggest that we can locate the present-day salience of the imagination, as well as the forms it takes, in the context of media and markets, and at the intersection of commodity exchange and the affective economy of the gift. Pre-existing understandings are of course inadequate to grasp the ways in which social relations are transformed by new and widening circuits of exchange. Moreover, if audiences feel independent of prevailing constraints, they can imagine themselves within altogether new kinds of associations that arise from, but do not in any simple way reflect, the market conditions of their existence. If media and markets have typically been conceived as advance guards of modernization and secularism, my analysis here indicates why their political outcomes might lead in unpredictable directions. Crucially, any elite-led process of development must confront the irreducible and indeed mushrooming existence of popular affiliations that a medium like television provokes, and acknowledge the new "communities of sentiment" it may give rise to.[18]

Any critical analysis of the work of television therefore entails sifting through historical assumptions that may carry over when transposing a theory from one society to another. In theories of media and politics, assumptions about the character of politics in a modern, democratic society are most prominent, in this respect. Whether politics pertains to the realm of civil order or to that of the state, it exists to a great extent through the means of communication. With electronic media, the institutionalized production and circulation of images and symbols displaces and transforms the boundaries of the political sphere, and reshapes the flows of information society depends on. This is partly a result of the particular technical characteristics of electronic media, but principally, it appears as a feature confirming principles of modern democratic society.

Among the shifts and transformations understood as constitutive of modernity is the decline of a sphere of transcendental authority, of the rule of kings by divine right and of the claims of a supramundane religious realm over temporal life. A secular discourse of politics takes its place, deriving its strength not from theological sources but from society itself. In the West, politics is thereby held to be excluded from the sphere of the church; if we consider democracy as the political form emblematic of modernity, it is thereafter determined by appeals to the history, culture, and needs of the people. Normatively, the space of politics merges with the space of the social. It is customary to locate the emergence of the mass media in the context of this shift from theological to worldly authority, operating as an institutional under-pinning of modern society, and helping to secure a certain ideological unity across it.[19] The growth of literacy and of reading publics in the wake of the print media, succeeded by electronic media and the enormous expansion of communication, secure the establishment of a secular, democratic society, in the standard rendition of this argu-ment.[20]

What if the media are introduced before the rationalization of politics and the "disenchantment" of society? In a country like India, the classic assumptions of liberal politics have been refashioned first by the colonial and then by the developmentalist state. The colonial state suppressed the growth of literacy and maintained a limited English educated middle class for administrative purposes. With independence, a tacit divide continued between a literate elite and mass audiences, with the press catering largely to the former, and the film industry winning a large popular following. The broadcast media, which were under state monopoly, formed a tentative bridge across this divide, and aired mainly Indian films and clips of film song sequences. Institutional constraints (chiefly, the difficulty of attracting audiences with bureaucratic staff) combined with political restrictions (e.g., the absence of competition, foreign or domestic, and the attempt to minimize religious programming) preser-ved the gulf between elite and mass media, and made it difficult for broadcasting to realize its promise of fostering popular education or participation in any significant way. The arrival of satellite tele-vision and the dismantling of state controls, however, brought market forces and the power of television together by 1992. By this time, political opportunism had brought religious programming onto state-controlled television and created what did emerge as a distinctive Indian programming genre, namely, mythological soap operas, the successor to the government's failed experiment in developmental soap operas.[21] Meanwhile, unlike in the West, print audiences were expanding, not diminishing, even as television audiences grew. Thus as Hindu nationalism sought to gain momentum, it could appeal to a base of educated intelligentsia even while generating popular participation through audio-visual and direct mobilization.[22] Here we have a model of politicization that cannot be dismissed as aberrant and/or fundamentalist, but requires explanation in its own terms, acknowledging the complex consequences of what Trotsky called combined and uneven development, while tracking the movements of capital and images and assessing their effects.[23]

Attempts to illuminate the forms of politicization while factoring in the context of uneven development are, regrettably, rare in media studies, and any suggestions I can offer are necessarily provisional and incomplete. In that spirit, and by way of offering a set of coordinates for my project's methodological underpinnings, I will cite the work of Pierre Bourdieu and Antonio Gramsci, intellectuals who have rather different understandings of their work but nevertheless converge in some important respects.[24] Bourdieu exemplifies the social scientist in his value-neutrality, proceeding by way of objectifying objectivism, and academicism itself, while Gramsci is insistent that socio-political analysis acquires significance only when underwriting "initiatives of will" aimed at "points of least resistance" in tactical political operations.[25] But they share a certain agnosticism towards the ruling pieties of their vocations (sociologist and Communist Party theoretician respectively), rejecting the notion that a given mode of thought determines the forms of being it claims to represent, and so exercise a more grounded and pragmatic approach in analysis. Thus Bourdieu's formulations on practice, and on the rules of transformation of practice as it moves from one social realm to another complements Gramsci's emphasis on the fluid, shifting, and internally contradictory nature of political regimes, class coalitions, and of consciousness itself. Bourdieu assumes the existence of relatively autonomous fields, and frames the concept of capital as something like the energy of a social physics. Hence capital infuses and empowers the social metabolism, taking dissimilar forms in different fields but serving in each field as the site of its distinctive form of power:

The theory of strictly economic practices is a particular case of a general theory of the economy of practices. Even when they give every appearance of disinterestedness because they escape the logic of "economic" interest (in the narrow sense) and are oriented towards non-material stakes that are not easily quantified, as in "pre-capitalist" societies or in the cultural sphere of capitalist societies, practices never cease to comply with an economic logic. The correspondences which are established between . . . the different kinds of capital and the corresponding modes of circulation, require us to abandon the economic/ non-economic dichotomy which makes it impossible to see the science of "economic" practices as a particular case of a science capable of treating all practices, including those that are experienced as disinterested or gratuitous, and therefore freed from the "economy," as economic practices aimed at maximizing material or symbolic profit.[26]

Universalized commodity production and exchange permits us to see through the fiction of social groupings and cultural standards that constitute themselves as autonomous and aloof from worldly corruptions, and to point to the "bottom line" calculations that cut across their various manifestations. However, as Bourdieu argues, to depend exclusively on an economistic approach misses the real and important differences between social fields, which constitute their diverse forms of capital *as* capital, and ignores the transformations allowing the movement of this capital from one field to another. He therefore distinguishes between economic and symbolic capital, with the latter itself taking many different forms. Symbolic capital, he suggests, depends for its value on being perceived as not economic, as a form of social esteem that derives from other sources. The labor through which symbolic capital is accumulated, Bourdieu argues, includes that of disguising the potential for its conversion into economic capital, and without this additional labor, symbolic capital would lose its distinctive character.[27]

While Bourdieu provides an elegant model for framing key aspects of the social process at work here, there is the risk that his analysis merely replicates the work of capital in homogenizing and unifying diverse cultural domains.[28] One way of resisting this homogenization is to point to the multiple forms of exchange, affective and instrumental both, that co-exist, e.g., of gift and commodity. To stay here with Bourdieu's own terms of analysis, however, we may observe that he ignores the two-fold nature of value constitutive of capital. As Marx has argued, value can be understood as being comprised of use value and exchange value.[29] The former is specific to the purposes for which a commodity is employed and hence non-transferable, while the latter signifies the social relation of equivalence established between commodities, that enables the circulation and the accumulation of capital. Considering value only at an abstract level omits a consideration of the diverse concrete needs represented in specific uses, without whose interpretive elaboration we cannot understand how exchange value, i.e., capital, is accumulated.

Here Todd Gitlin's emphasis on the similarity between meaning and value is insightful. Meaning, like value, can be understood as having a two-fold character. Without inquiring into the specific meanings of an event for the different actors in a circuit of communication, any account of the messages in circulation would be incomplete. The inseparability of communicative and economic processes is emphasized in such an approach. There is no economic process without representations of itself; indeed this is what renders relations of production as social relations.

Stuart Hall's schema of "encoding/decoding," modeled on the circuit that the commodity itself travels, offers a powerful model for thinking about media communication. It points to the complex series of transformations, of (message) production, distribution, consumption, and reproduction which, taken together, represent an entire social process at work. Arguing that the media message is a commodity, but a distinct form of commodity, Hall points out that it is produced within a shared context of social understandings by broadcasters, consumed by audiences, re-incorporated and reproduced as part of a collective pool of ideas and meanings. Meanings "preferred" by broadcasters tend to be "negotiated" in audience readings, and subsumed in their larger world-view; "oppositional" readings however resist such an easy incorporation, and potentially complicate this process of reproduction, Hall has argued.[30] A limitation here, however, is (what has been called) Hall's conveyor-belt approach to communication, with the "preferred meaning" of the broadcast message moving serially through the different stages of the circuit. Such an approach assumes that the moments of encoding and decoding are or should be homologous, whereas in fact the difference between them is characteristic of mass communication.[31] The underlying problem is Hall's assumption that the circuit of production/communication is reproduced; this renders meaning ornamental to an inexorable process of system maintenance. But this is not possible if we consider the circuits of use and exchange value both (rather than that of exchange alone), involving meanings "preferred" by broadcasters as well as "non-preferred" meanings, and the interaction and resultant of these circuits. Other social processes are set in motion that complicate any narrowly defined process of reproduction.[32]

Furthermore, the power of commodities in capitalism rests not simply in their value, but depends also on the labor required to turn this value into profit, finding buyers for the product at a good price, and securing a process of accumulation while engaging with the competition, and so on. Similarly, the power of communication is determined ultimately in its effects or end-results. This entails tracing the contingent links through which ideas are twisted and transformed as different groups vie with each other for dominance. Accumulation would be a contingent process, varying across time and space. It would then be necessary to trace the specific paths taken in the circulation of messages/capital to understand the outcome of a given historical event.

Television stitches together a plurality of fields through a currency of images, instituting a system of representation that cuts across society. Within it, the distinct symbols of each social field can be "realistically" portrayed in all their uniqueness, while ignoring their constitution within a newly homogenized system of representation. It thus permits the unobtrusive accumulation of economic as well as symbolic capital on an unprecedented scale. At the same time, in the case of the Ram Janmabhumi movement, the medium itself served as a figure of the campaign, as it set up new circuits of accumulation between different social fields. Hindu nationalists sought to make the most of differential rates of exchange, and, like television, converted the diverse currencies so gathered into the singular one of popular appeal.

Daniel Lerner's influential *The Passing of Traditional Society* (1958) noticed the affective potential of the media and departed from strictly rational/informational conceptions about it. Lerner championed the use of electronic media as a means of stimulating empathy, to promote modernization. The media "simplify perception, but complicate response," and are therefore great teachers of "interior manipulation," he wrote. Individuals can thus identify with those in hitherto distant or unfamiliar roles, and form bonds of association based on new sets of symbols, he argued, thereby leading the way out of traditional society.[33] Lerner's argument is valuable in spelling out the pedagogical assumptions behind a widely influential developmental approach.[34] But if electronic media work by mobilizing desire and creating new forms of association, there is surely no guarantee that desires, once stimulated, will flow in obedient fashion. If the sources of power thereby appear closer to people, this heightens the possibility that they may be conceived differently, and thereby politicized. Hence television offers a means of swift mobilization; on the other hand, the numbers mobilized can more readily be adduced to different agenda, through co-optation. In this sense television is both a sign and a cause of the altered scale and quality of contemporary politics, between its participatory character at an experiential level, and the authoritarian features it discloses in a larger view. The Ram Temple movement, an event that brought together diverse arguments and tendencies symptomatic of a broader shift in politics, illustrated both these features. Here television helped to define a context and to make evident certain latent opportunities in the political field; it was, however, through print and other forms of communication that the bulk of the movement actually worked itself out.

THE RAM TEMPLE MOVEMENT, THE BJP, AND A FISSURED PUBLIC

The Ram Janmabhumi movement aimed to destroy the Babri mosque in Ayodhya, in Uttar Pradesh (U.P.), claiming the sixteenth-century structure was erected on the ruins of a temple supposedly built to mark the birthplace of the god-king Ram. Ram was claimed to be a national symbol, and Hindus were declared to be an oppressed community, a majority denied its rightful status by politicians pandering to minority votes, chiefly of the Muslims.

The power of religious symbolism to sway multitudes was not simply a matter of superstition. It reflected a specific series of compromises made between the nationalist movement and religious orthodoxy. In the nineteenth century, the efforts of social reformers were aimed at restoring national vigor and self-confidence, cleansing social customs of their prejudices and superstitions. Convinced that left to themselves, orthodox Hindus would be resistant to change, they advocated the abolition or emendation of a range of practices. Issues such as the age of consent, widow re-marriage, caste reform, and the stranglehold of a corrupt Brahmin priesthood, provoked passionate debate among educated classes. Raja Rammohun Roy, Keshav Chandra Sen, Mahadev Govind Ranade, and many others looked to the colonial state to accomplish these reforms, arguing that even if the majority did not favor them, over time they would come to see the wisdom of the reformers' ways. By the last two decades of the nineteenth century, orthodox Hindus began to organize against the attacks of reformers, and membership of educated Hindus in *sanatan dharmi* organizations and the Arya Sabha rose greatly.[35]

Bal Gangadhar Tilak's switch on the issue of age of consent, from recommending reform to passionately defending Hindu society's right to regulate itself, was a forerunner of things to come in this respect. The bill in question proposed raising the age of consent for marriage from ten to twelve years of age. The bill passed in 1891, but preceding it and even more so subsequently, there was furious controversy over the indignity of the colonial state adjudicating over domestic affairs. If Indians were to aspire to self-rule, they had to demonstrate the ability to put their own house in order, an influential section of nationalists argued, and their arguments carried the day. This in turn was related to two other crucial issues. The first was that of the image of the Indian nation held by reformers. Bipin Chandra Pal succinctly expressed the dilemma: "In the name of India we loved Europe . . . We loved the abstraction we called India but, yes, we hated the thing it actually was . . . Our love for our people was something like the pious love of the Christian missionaries for the heathen."[36] Like Bankim Chandra before him, he and others concluded that it was necessary to embrace indigenous religion and culture, which to them meant Hindu religion and culture, rather than hope to mold India after an alien image. Finally, and most decisively, this would bring the nationalist movement closer to the people, and help overcome the lack of social solidarity that beset attempts at mobilization.

Between the late nineteenth century and the post-World War I period when M. K. Gandhi joined the independence struggle, the national movement and the reform movements parted company, as issues of reform ceased to be publicly debated by nationalist politicians. Partha Chatterjee has argued that in fact the question of reform became nested within the national movement, as the nationalists declared sovereignty over their social and cultural affairs in preparation for independence. Social reform retreated to the indigenous realm, beyond the colonial public sphere, in his view, enacting an outside/inside division that became the basis of nationalist difference.[37]

The shift from "outside" to "inside," in Chatterjee's terms, indexes a compromise with Hindu orthodox opinion by the social reformers in the nationalist movement. The cooperation of social conservatives and of religious orthodoxy was meant to secure the nationalist coalition and shore up its mass base as the Congress Party, led by English-educated moderates, fought for independence. But as reform shifted from a goal to a theme of mobilization, undertaken on an individual rather than a political footing, the authority of orthodox opinion was mitigated but not fundamentally challenged. Gandhi epitomized this equivocation, denouncing untouchability but upholding an idealized *varnashrama dharma* (caste order), and using traditional themes to mobilize for the nationalist movement. The urban, well-to-do lawyers leading the Congress Party lacked the cultural means to communicate with the rural majority and widen the base of their movement. This compromise, evolving roughly between 1890 and 1915, and crystallizing in the political strategies honed by Gandhi, was crucial in forging the party's mass support. Following World War I and until the time of Independence in 1947, there was an escalation of religio-cultural symbology in the party's strategy.[38]

Chatterjee's argument rehearses the Indian political compromise without critique. He refers to one phase of nationalism's career in the colony arising from a bargain between political elites rather than to an enduring form of postcolonial nationalism. What it led to was a division of the language of politics between elites and the majority, the one modern and forward-looking, representing the future of the nation or the best part of it at any rate, standing in a pedagogical relationship to the indigenous political languages of the majority.

The achievement of independence was of course an enormous triumph for the Indian people, and a public endorsement of the superior virtues claimed vis-à-vis the West. The state's post-independence focus on economic development emphasized the prevailing belief that social change would follow in the wake of planned economic development. The compromise with orthodox opinion meant that an unreconstructed brahminical vision of Indian culture remained available for political appropriation, as representing the civilization's genius and its best promise of future glory. It is against this historical background that the appeal of the BJP's vision of Hindutva, "Hinduness," and the political opportunity it represented in the wake of Congress failure, becomes clearer.

Although it was spearheaded by the Bharatiya Janata Party (Indian People's Party, or BJP), the power of the Ram Janmabhumi campaign was such that no major party dared oppose it. Even the BJP's major political opponents would only say that a Ram temple should be built without disturbing the mosque. The Congress Party, ruling with little interruption since India's independence in 1947, chose to support rather than confront the movement, and offered the BJP little hindrance in its attempt to shape a Hindu nationalist agenda. With the Ram Temple issue, which led to the BJP increasing its Parliamentary seat total from two to eighty-eight in the 1989 general elections, big business and the professional middle classes began to look upon the party as a possible replacement and successor to the moribund ruling party.

A range of different perceptions, cultivated and nurtured by publicists, came together in the demand to demolish the mosque and construct the temple. There was first of all the experience of the Partition, in 1947, which resulted in gruesome Hindu–Muslim riots that took over a million lives and became perceived by conservatives as proof of the immiscibility of Muslims in the Indian nation and the need for vigilance against the threat of Muslim treachery, of further separation, of conversion of Hindus, or of other anti-national activities. There was in addition: the anger of aspiring lower middle classes at a sense of exclusion from the political process and from the social mainstream; peasants and small farmers responding to the call to the faithful; upper castes perceiving a conservative means of political assertion that did not challenge the caste hierarchy; sections of the intelligentsia finding in the movement an echo of their own frustrated ambitions for national greatness; non-resident Indians abroad, thinking that a strong nationalist party would bolster the country's reputation abroad, and hence their own expatriate situation; and businesses seeking a strong nationalist party to replace the Congress, and to become, in a sense, what the Congress had never been, namely an ideologically based party articulating a distinct and explicit consensus.

The Ram Janmabhumi movement was a complex and many-layered series of events, not submissible to a single mode of explanation. One of the things it made evident however was precisely the kind of social contradictions brought to the forefront by television; at the same time of course it highlighted the need to be able to manage such contradictions. The unprecedented event of the broadcast of the Ramayan, a Hindu epic serialized on the state-run television system, and the astuteness of the BJP, which was eventually able to perceive the opportunity presented in the serial's enormous success, were important here. Drawing on myth and devotionalism to portray a golden age of tradition that was yet ahead of the modern era in statecraft and warfare, the show which ran from January 1987 to September 1990 adroitly made appeals to diverse social groups, under a symbolic rubric that could be tied to the banner of Hindu assertion.

If inhibition and prohibition earlier joined to limit religion's use for systematic political mobilization, what was offered now was an extra charge in bringing together previously separated realms. The affinity of these spheres, that in their different ways envision the good society, appeared stronger at a time when politics itself seemed corrupt and exhausted, and the objectionable character of much religious tradition seemed either a faint memory or altogether a new idea. At the same time, bringing politics and religion together meant joining political constituencies whose differences had deepened and extended with uneven development. Any mobilization would then proceed by working through the deep contradictions between these groups, rather than in any simple addition of electoral weights. I use the term "split public" (see below) to understand the friction between realms newly joined through the media, but preserved due to uneven social development, wherein political discourse occurs through a set of structured misunderstandings.

To be sure, the Ramayan broadcast did not initiate Hindu nationalist sentiment. A key location for the latter was in the indigenous language press, notably the Hindi press, carrying on debates older than the Ram Janmabhumi movement but gaining intensity during it, of the inseparability of Hindu religion from the Indian nation, and of the inadmissibility of any challenges to that idea. The historical cleavage between English as the language of command and the indigenous languages was accentuated with independence and the new elite. The usage of English became the shortcut and compensation for the absence of a cultural policy, stringing a high wire above the particularist thickets of region, caste and religion. To summarize a complex argument here, the English language, by virtue of being subsumed as the Nehruvian language of command, continued a colonial practice of aloofness and unfamiliarity with local traditions.[39] This was a lack that had to be made up in the indigenous languages, and it led to a division with obvious political dangers, as a nationalist intelligentsia, arguably the dominant intelligentsia, was only poorly capable of dialogue with sentiments emerging in the course of debates amongst the majority population. The BJP perceived and was able to utilize this deep cultural fault line, building sympathy for their cause through a compliant Hindi language press and allowing friction to be generated in the English language press through their militant postures. With an intricate sense of existing cultural fields and their patterns and limits of reach, Hindu nationalists strategically crossed certain boundaries and maintained others, gathering and distributing the energies from particular fields in other, designated zones across society for an orchestrated total effect.

There was no simple mechanical system of support provided in the Hindi language press; rather their contribution to the Ram Janmabhumi movement depended on a structured set of mutual misperceptions between English language elites and those who dwelt predominantly in regional language environments. Both sympathy and fear worked to help the movement, support being extended through a vocal upper-caste intelligentsia who (among other things) felt disenfranchised by caste-based reservations for the backward classes, and fear being generated in the English language press at the seemingly imminent threat to secular freedoms – both of these worked in tandem, the former solidifying its base and the latter creating the resistance necessary for its onward movement. In short, the diverse and contradictory constituents of a language-divided public worked themselves out against the shared backdrop of a single (but diversely) imagined national culture, represented by television.

The demand for the demolition of Babri Masjid, coming in the wake of escalating Hindu–Muslim tensions through the eighties, appeared as a serious attempt to relegate Muslims to the position of a disenfranchised and embattled minority. There was a steady increase in the yearly toll of lives taken in anti-Muslim riots through the mid-eighties; this was itself dwarfed by the unprecedented spate of riots in the wake of the Ram Janmabhumi movement.[40]

On 6 December 1992, the mosque was finally destroyed, leading to riots across the country that left 2,026 dead and 6,957 wounded.[41] In November 1993, in elections held to replace the BJP state governments dismissed after the demolition, a lower-caste Muslim coalition edged out the BJP to capture power in Uttar Pradesh, the most populous and historically the most influential state in shaping national politics.[42] The BJP won in only two of the four other states, losing in its erstwhile strongholds of Madhya Pradesh and Himachal Pradesh.[43] The election revealed the upper caste-based limits of the Hindu vote, and for the time being put paid to the idea that a party banking on the faith of the Hindu majority could capture power unaided.

Contemporary Hindu nationalism came to prominence in the context of economic liberalization, as the political ideology of aspiring elites converged with the electoral expediency of a beleaguered government and its beneficiary classes. We can conveniently date the process of liberalization from about 1985 onwards, gathering pace after 1991 in the wake of IMF-induced reforms and the attendant dismantling of government controls over the economy. With the ruling party alternately cultivating the Muslim and the Hindu vote in a vain effort to retain its hegemony, the stage was set for its hijacking by Hindu nationalists, who had nurtured visions of Hindu unification for decades. Having stumbled onto an issue that proved an electoral windfall, the BJP deftly redefined its success as part of an inexorable tide of change. If Hindutva was the religious and cultural aspect of the program, liberalization became its economic aspect and was declared integral to the BJP's vision. The BJP had, with the Congress Party, endorsed state-led economic development as recently as the 1984 elections, but performed a complete about-face by the 1990 elections. "Nehruvianism" simultaneously became the name for the entire post-independence era and an indictment of the secular developmental ethos of the Congress Party. It derived its name from one of the chief architects of Indian independence, Jawaharlal Nehru (Prime Minister from 1947 until his death in 1963). Although liberalization itself had been introduced and indeed promoted by Congress prime ministers, Rajiv Gandhi and P. V. Narasimha Rao, the BJP insisted, plausibly, that a different party would be needed to oversee a break from the past. Liberalization would have to mean the undoing of Nehruvianism, and the BJP offered itself for the task (see chapter one).

In an era of liberalization and the rollback of state-led development initiatives, market forces were offered as the answer to crises of accumulation and growth. But liberalization itself retained the need for a strong interventionist state, whether to maintain market discipline or to defend the interests of those who now dominated the market. It was the legitimacy of public institutions and public spaces that was under attack, as private business was fashioned as a cure-all. The inability of laissez-faire capitalism to deliver on its promises, and the shedding of the state's progressive aspect in favor of its more authoritarian functions, combined to accentuate a crisis of legitimation. Religious nationalism emerged as a potential answer, as both a diffuse protest against injustice and simultaneously an attempt to shape or harness this protest to a new conservative orthodoxy.

The religio-cultural component of the BJP program, Hindutva ("Hinduness"), appeared in various ways: as increasing the stakes in a political marketplace already structured in terms of religion and caste; as the conspicuous consumption of newly rich classes; as the efforts of caste groupings to improve their position in an aggressive form of Sanskritization; and, most conspicuously, as cultural renewal through what was held to be purifying violence directed at Muslims.

With a portion of the urban middle classes, the Hindu nationalist used religious appeals to distinguish itself from the unscrupulous majority of politicians in returning to politics a long-awaited *dharma*, a sense of duty and righteousness. Although the Hindu nationalist criticized erstwhile secular policy for excluding Hindu religion and culture from public life, its own appeal depended on the history of such a separation. At the same time, the introduction of religion into the center of political debates was seen as a scandal by those on the secular side, and portrayed as such in the English language news media for instance. Adroitly shuttling between different positions, BJP leaders, in speeches in the capital, pointed to a popular upsurge of religious feeling which they did not themselves participate in, perhaps, but which they claimed to be the spokespersons for. Not the aura of spirituality but the more banal, but nonetheless effective, accumulation of popular support counted for it here.

The Hindu nationalists responded to the power vacuum growing in the wake of the Congress's decline with a sensational campaign that was both ideological and issue-based, and anointed itself as the Congress's heir-apparent. The alarm this provoked from the secular press and the left parties was deflected by the party's publicists to heighten the drama of the party's ascent to power, with the left's enmity becoming an inverse measure of the BJP's virtue. The BJP's newfound opposition to the regulation of market forces won the interest of business classes and brought the party a degree of support it had never previously achieved. The dispersed presence of religious nationalism in publicity images rather than as exclusively the preserve of a political party, perhaps allowed the party to endure changes in electoral fortunes, insofar as the images served as forms of cultural expression within a market-driven regime. There occurred something like a chemical interaction that altered the composition of both religion and nation, the former becoming more public and hollowed out, the latter more private and shrunken. Here the multiple meanings carried by the imagery became relevant: the proximity of religious symbols with prevailing lived cultures could render them into durable prisms through which social change was refracted and understood.

The repeated use of religion in electoral campaigns, however, would inevitably depreciate the symbolic capital accrued from Hindu themes. The sensation created in championing a Hindu god was in no small part due to the unprecedented nature of the campaign. Especially with the urban middle and upper classes, critical in the formation of public opinion, the appeal could not last indefinitely. In this respect, a statement such as "I am tired of Ram – I want a new name," made by a fifteen-year-old schoolgirl in conversation, reflected one end of a predictable array of responses to the extended use of the Birthplace campaign.[44] She was no heretic. This was, rather, her opinion of a personal relationship that, in her view, had reached the end of its course, and now needed reinforcement. Her statement suggested that the social basis of the new visual regime might lie in the success or failure of political campaign strategists and media managers rather than in the lifeworld of faith and ritual. Without something like the nurturing given to commercial brands, with "re-launches" being used to extend their "life cycle," the public stitched together through the electronic media was liable to decompose into its several parts.

VARIETIES OF NATIONALISM

One of the more remarkable assumptions in politics in the post-World War I era was that while the word "nation" could qualify other words, it could itself bear no qualifiers unless they referred to distinct contenders for the description. Thus, national socialism and national democratic parties, or else, Italian nationalism, Sri Lankan nationalism, and so on. The idea that there might be different views on how the nation ought to be formed was a suspect one. That there was only one kind of nationalism that was desirable, indeed legitimate, was a deep and unspoken belief amongst scholars.[45]

If "communalism" usually referred to the identification of political interest with religious community, what was striking with the BJP and its affiliates was the volatile nature of this identification, and the consequent difficulty of drawing a sharp and consistent distinction between "communal" and "secular" events. "Communalism" was then understood to comprise certain kinds of extraordinary events and activities, e.g., Hindu–Muslim riots, or attempts to render Hindu identity politically dominant, against a background itself believed to be neutral, i.e., "secular." A hitherto taken-for-granted consensus about what divided "communal" and "secular" unraveled through an excess of exhortation, so that those who thought they were secular themselves were no longer clear about how the boundaries were to be constituted. What I am seeking to clarify here then are the circumstances in which the problem of "communalism" itself came to be posed, and the way in which this was part of a larger political configuration requiring understanding.

The conceptual opposition of the terms, one good, the other bad, and the urgent character of the problems they have been used to refer to, often obscure the fact that they are less useful in understanding events than as markers evoking appropriate political responses.[46]

Communalism is usually described as an intermixing of traditional and modern categories; often, scholars settle on one or the other term. The unyielding dualism of this classification offers little purchase on the phenomenon, however, and its fluid and multiform movements bypass such a polarity altogether. Classifying it as either "modern" or "traditional," moreover, says nothing about its precise meanings, and risks ignoring the content that renders the subject noteworthy.

Nationalist historiography has understood communalism as a product of British divide-and-rule policies.[47] The localized and fragmentary nature of indigenous conflict, and the changing composition of warring camps, was overlaid with perceptions of an implacable hostility based on religious identity. The inability of India to govern herself and the necessity of British rule thus appeared as a logical conclusion to this observation. Nationalist politics reproduced this construction, especially with the Congress Party's entry into mass politics after the First World War, and its wish to avoid the violent outbursts that invariably accompanied its efforts at political mobilization. For the duration of the freedom struggle, nationalist politics was defined as secular, in the sense of being above and beyond existing communities, rather than as working through their contradictions. Once a unified anti-imperial front was no longer necessary after independence, the difficulties of such a view returned to roost.[48]

In debates conducted during the framing of the Indian Constitution, for instance, members used the term "secular state" but argued around it, avoiding debates about how precisely it should apply to the Indian State. The question of whether the state should be considered outside religious communities and equally indifferent to them, or whether it should somehow embrace the diversity of religions prevailing, and relate to them equally without prejudice, was thus sidestepped. The Indian State saw its mission as a modernizing one, and was thus unavoidably committed to intervening in the affairs of religious communities, even if only to eventually transcend the need for intervention. At the same time, the presence of a Hindu majority and the legacy of violence against Muslims during the Partition rendered the adjudication of minority religions a delicate matter, to say the least. The precise meaning of secularism was thus too contentious at this point to be legislated upon, and remained as a political problem, if for a while a dormant one.[49]

Partly as a result of the challenge posed by the Hindu nationalist, and partly due to critiques of the nation as a naturalized entity, scholars have also challenged the unquestioning identification of nationalism with "secularism," and the positive valence placed on both, pointing to the hybrid origins of the former and the uneven practice of the latter.[50] Secularism was understood variously: in the electoral system, as prohibiting religious language; in public institutions, as fostering fair and inclusive treatment of different religious groups; and in the courts, as protective of religious sensibilities from various kinds of offenses.[51] The necessity of negotiating through religious differences forbade any non-controversial claim to neutrality.

The BJP itself insisted that secularism required stewardship by "the majority community," *viz.*, the Hindus, and presented this view as a political solution. Without an explicit politicization of cultural identity and of the means of managing diversity, the invocations of national identity had become part of a particular rhetoric, deeply meaningful to educated classes perhaps but little more than a bland and easily endured invocation for others. With the escalating rhetoric of Hindu nationalism, and the identification by the BJP of Muslims as the enemy within, what became evident was the sinister form of politicization of Muslim identity. To assert Hindu identity was merely a cultural matter, giving voice to what had been unmarked and taken for granted. Secularism was, in this sense, folded into Hindu culture, and to dispute such an understanding was "pseudo-secular." Muslim assertion was therefore disruptive and threatening in this account, implicitly anti-national and requiring to be closely monitored.[52]

Recent critical analyses of communalism can broadly be classified into political-economic and cultural perspectives. In the first category, we can distinguish at least two variants. In one view, communalism is the expression of aspiring middle classes competing for scarce resources, using pre-existing categories and primordial ties for modern purposes.[53] This somewhat utilitarian definition does not address the meanings of the phenomenon, nor indeed the variety of its manifestations. Another, more prominent argument, understands Hindu communalism as the South Asian equivalent of German or Italian fascism, as an attempt by ruling classes to resolve the crises of a stagnant economy and a deadlocked polity by force. Here arguments based on the European example stress the contradictions of uneven development and the enlistment of large sections of working and peasant classes through feudal or semi-feudal appeals. The analogy risks obscuring the many differences in the South Asian context, however, with the invocation of fascism usually serving as a call for united opposition rather than a tool for analyzing the precise forms of its materialization.[54]

Perhaps the most recent scholarly approach understands communalism as a "critique of modernity." In this view, communalism represents the misunderstood response of beleaguered communities resisting the violent transformations modernity, specifically the nation-state, wreaks on them. In its totalizing wish to cancel out its "others," the state refuses to recognize its reflection offered up in communal resistance. It is the secular state that stamps out traditional tolerance and engenders violence, the argument goes. But the view that tradition and modernity can be located in spatially distinct zones and distinct political agenda takes as literal historical truths terms that emerged together in Enlightenment polemics. The deft switching of the usual valence presents a sanitized, indeed modernized, version of traditional culture as a defense against the discontents of the Enlightenment, in a schema removed from all real conflicts.[55]

In my own attempt to make sense of communalism, Antonio Gramsci's account of the workings of Italian fascism, and his failure to arrive at any definitive demarcation of that term's embrace, are instructive. The word "fascism" is itself mostly absent from Gramsci's lexicon due to prison censorship, a fact that, paradoxically, may have worked to his advantage. Deprived of the word, he could thereby enact a certain disbelief in any conceptual unity it might bestow, and so attend to the minutiae of events under its rubric. In the process, he conducted an empirically rich, non-reductive analysis of Italian society. In a similar vein, I allow the contradictory and often mutually incoherent character of "communal" phenomena, indexed by my use of the term "Hindu nationalism." I offer instead interpretations of specific events, discussing their significance in their particular settings.

To offer a definition of Hindu nationalism requires steering between two tendencies, of isolating the variety of phenomena so described from the historical context and of reducing them to that context. The challenge is to capture the balance between its determined and determining features.

In my view, recent manifestations of Hindu nationalism (e.g., between 1987 and 1993) lay at the intersection of the efforts of Hindu nationalist, to mobilize and consolidate a Hindu vote, and the increased assertiveness of a variety of new claimants to political power. This occurred in the context of a wider cultural prominence of Hindu religious themes and symbols, due among other things to the expansion of communications and the consequently greater circulation given to religion. I understand Hindu nationalism as distinct in the quality of its aggressive and sectarian effects, but suggest that this is a dimension of the increased political assertiveness manifested in the 1980s and 1990s rather than comprising its entirety. The question then is to clarify the relation between Hindu nationalist and other forms of politics, rather than to isolate the former as uniquely aberrant.

OVERVIEW

Why politics *after* television? Television profoundly changes the context of politics. But to thereafter treat it as center and source point of influence is misleading. A critical theory of the media cannot have the media as its center, as Oskar Negt has written.[56] There is an institutional break between production and reception, and between the dispersed regions of message interpretation and the indirect modes of its use. Accordingly, no law-like patterns of influence are likely to be discerned. Different effects may ensue at different locations, harnessed together discreetly if not altogether invisibly, as they rise and fall with the cadences of media narratives, journalistic routines, public relations promotions, and marketing campaigns. Television's influence has, then, to be presumed rather than discovered, *contra* media effects research, as the backdrop, stage, and vehicle of social interaction.

The consolidation of the mass media is paradoxical in this regard, being proof simultaneously of the material basis of culture as well as of an irreducibly ideational aspect to social phenomena, hence of the limits to causal explanation in accounting for historical outcomes. I attempt to provide a social and historical context for my focus on the media through the notions of "electronic capitalism" and "split public."

The term "electronic capitalism," which takes as its precedent Benedict Anderson's formulation of "print capitalism,"[57] indicates the link between media and the social relations within which they exist. One way to chart the relationship involved here is to point to the fundamental unit of the commodity. Just as the commodity preserves a certain in-built openness to difference, with a plurality of use-values co-existing alongside a quantifiable exchange value, the commodified image as well accommodates and subsumes the variety of interpretive stances within a heterogeneous society.[58] The distinctness of electronic media is in the way they can implode a diversity of user contexts and a range of understandings in the singularity of a communicative event. Electronic capitalism foregrounds, in unprecedented fashion, the plurality of world-views that co-exist, even while rapidly creating circuits of communication across them. This then changes the constraints within which politics takes place. If with the relatively small audience for print, the normative fiction of a bourgeois public could be preserved in some sense, the fissured character of this public becomes undeniable with electronic media.

Analyses of politics tend to homogenize the realm of politics and, in practice if not in principle, focus largely on elite politics. Habermas's model of the public sphere has this problem as well, as several critics have pointed out.[59] To focus on the relative autonomy of elite and subaltern publics, however, can be deeply misleading, as it may attribute a spurious sovereignty to the latter, and thus fail to explain its political constitution *as* a subaltern public.[60] It is preferable to think in terms of a split public, inhabited by different languages of politics, so that the salient question is of the *terms of translation* between them, in the reproduction of a structured set of misunderstandings. With the introduction of a new medium like television, differences that were previously mediated through the print media now achieve a new level of salience, so that the relationship between the public's several parts must now be reworked. The ways in which this reworking occurs represents the trajectory of a society's political development and will obviously express its particular historical circumstances.

In India, the contradictions of a split public are brought to the fore with national television. Serialized epics portrayed on television allow the collective sharing of an idealized past, one that achieved a certain verisimilitude but whose veracity was open to question. The absence of this past was crucial to its collective enjoyment, and can be broadly understood at two levels, socio-cultural and technological. At the first level, the indefinitely transitional status of a postcolonial society oriented towards a modernity that seemed forever beyond reach entailed the awareness of an absence in its lived structures. Turning back to a past that showed the symptoms of modernity long before its time, the broadcast of religious epics compensated for this absence and offered it up as a viewing experience. The apparatus of television was well suited for such a purpose, designed as it was to bring images seemingly from nowhere to everywhere all at once. The liminal character of the technology, seemingly both public and private and so not quite either, helped evoke the sense of a bygone past; the ubiquitous "recognition" of this fiction anointed it as a kind of *de facto* truth. It was against the perceived truth of a golden Hindu past, declared week after week, that the opportunity of religious nationalist mobilization was eventually seized. The collective perception of a desiring public became an indelible one, I argue, in the wake of the television epics which lasted from January 1987 to September 1990, to say nothing of the reruns, which remain an ongoing feature. It was against this collective fantasy that the Birthplace of Ram movement gained its strength.

The contradictions of a public split by divisions of language and caste, mediated in complex ways by a linguistically split media, allowed the movement to escalate; the same contradictions that gave rise to the movement eventually brought it down. Retailing Hindutva, or "Hinduness," was a means of negotiating with this split public, offering discrete forms of Hindu affiliation via multiple modes of participation consumption, and so cutting across divides of class and caste. At the same time, it reflected the production of a new and contradictory mode of public affiliation, simultaneously more individualistic and modern while being aggressive, exclusionary, and hostile to individual expression. The themes of mobilization evoked libidinal ties and primordial belonging, but the methods through which it proceeded and the forms of identification it sought often pointed in a different direction. Ultimately, the contradictions of caste erupted through the myth of a consolidated Hindu community and, in the short run, relegated the Hindu nationalist party to a regional force reflecting the political balance of castes in a few northern Indian states, relative to the rest of the country. Commodity images of Hindutva, however, became absorbed as part of the symbolic apparatus of liberalization, providing the semblance of a self-sufficient indigenous modernity unruffled by the developmentalist state's retreat, and coming into its own, paradoxically, amidst globalization.

In tracing the contingent character of the Hindu nationalists' efforts to gain prominence, no single research site could yield the necessary material for this study. My inquiry moves across a range of discursive locations and registers, relating to the subject of Hindu nationalism on Indian state television, its audience, the Hindu nationalist, English language and vernacular newspapers, and U.S.-based expatriates. I investigate the circumstances of production and the burden of each of these discourses, the tensions and contradictions inter-animating them, and the competing and overlapping ways in which they were deployed. Neither a single structure of meaning nor an unvarying set of interests characterizes these several discourses, yet understanding their complex connection is crucial in coming to terms with the recent career of Hindu nationalism.

Through ethnography, personal interviews, and information culled from newspapers and periodicals, government reports and privately produced pamphlets, I constructed an archive for my purposes. My fieldwork was conducted in June–July 1988, March–August 1989, June–July 1992, September 1993–June 1994, and September 1996–March 1997. Between March and May in 1989, I engaged in fieldwork at the state-owned television system, the Delhi Doordarshan Kendra, and conducted interviews with producers, program executives, and audience research officers, as well as with senior administration and television producers commissioned by Doordarshan. I also obtained clippings from the Indian Institute of Mass Communication and the Centre for Education and Communication in New Delhi, and subsequently from the Centre for Education and Documentation in Mumbai.

In conducting my reception study, I interviewed 169 people altogether, in Delhi and in a small town, "Kaynagar," a few hours away, in June and July 1988 and between March and August 1989. I selected interviewees on the basis of their residence in low-, medium-, or high-income neighborhoods. In New Delhi, I chose a range of older and newer neighborhoods, a resettlement colony built in the 1980s, whose residents were recently uprooted by the construction of the Indira Gandhi International Airport, a colony whose residents were driven out from Old Delhi during the urban "beautification" programs of the Emergency (1975–77), a government housing colony itself segregated for Class I, II, III, and IV government servants, and two medium- to high-income South Delhi neighborhoods. In addition, I analyzed viewers' letters: I received seventy-three letters in response to a solicitation published in *The Times of India* (New Delhi) and in the Hindi language daily *Navbharat Times* (New Delhi), requesting Ramayan viewers to write and tell me the reasons they liked the show. Ien Ang bases her study *Watching Dallas* (1985) on an analysis of letters collected in this way. I also analyzed files from the Audience Research Office at the Delhi Doordarshan Kendra containing 328 letters to Doordarshan from viewers of the Ramayan serial.

Interviews were also conducted with members of the English and Hindi language press in New Delhi and in U.P., as well as with members and leaders in the Hindu nationalist movement in New Delhi, in Faizabad, Lucknow, and Varanasi, in 1992, 1993–94, and in 1996–97. Interviews with the press in 1997 were conducted with the help of a research associate. I made field trips to Ayodhya in July 1992 and in January 1994. Finally, in studying the VHP of America, I interviewed participants at the VHP's "Global Vision 2000" conference in Washington, DC in August 1993, and conducted interviews as well with members of the Hindu Students' Council and the VHP in the fall of 1994 in the greater Chicago area and elsewhere.

Tracing the different sites through which a given circuit of communication travels, and analyzing the social relations specific to each site and the kinds of transformations wrought across them, is essential in understanding the work of "the media." In such an approach, the researcher is forced to depart from a media-centric perspective, to go beyond the mere invocation of historical context, and instead actively to examine the inter-animation between media and the world. The most zealous scrutiny of media texts, uncovering deep structures of meaning, must remain in a kind of suspended relation to history if they impute rather than investigate the mobilizations of the text by historical actors, and if they evoke rather than explore and assess the significance of the technology of communication and the way it is implicated in the larger sociopolitical context.

In the first chapter, "Hindu Nationalism and the Cultural Forms of Indian Politics," I argue that the utilization of the market and the media, in publicity and mobilization, signaled a re-definition of Hindu nationalist identity that could render it compatible with an authoritarian populist market regime. The attempt to devolve power from the state to the private sector is thus complemented by efforts to effect discipline through decentralized, coordinated initiatives, as authority is dispersed to police an expanding market economy and manage its contradictions.

The second chapter, "Prime Time Religion," discusses the televised serial, the Ramayan, based on the well-known Hindu epic, whose success prepared the environment for the Birthplace of Ram movement. The serial reformulated the epic in a revivalist manner, projecting a proto-national security state back into the Vedic past. The third chapter, "The Communicating Thing and Its Public," continues a discussion begun in the previous chapter about the problems of theorizing popular culture in postcolonial societies, devolving on two issues, the problem of genre and that of religion. Based on interviews with viewers of the Ramayan serial, I argue that no single ideology linked those who watched the show; rather, there were themes and symbols that resonated with most of them, although not in the same ways. Not only does this suggest how popular culture may work to favor religious nationalists, it also emphasizes that the broadcast's outcome was far from inevitable. The opposition of "communal" and "secular" sentiments is, rather, a discursive one, susceptible of mediation between what is otherwise an unyielding polarity.

The fourth chapter, "A 'Split Public' in the Making and Unmaking of the Ram Janmabhumi Movement," argues that the Hindu nationalist utilized the cultural fault lines between the English language and vernacular press to gain publicity, with the criticism and fear from the former indirectly reinforcing the sympathy offered by the latter. The English language press thus unwittingly provided the opposition necessary for the progress of the Hindu nationalist movement. Ultimately, the movement itself appeared to have been taken in by the publicity; at any rate, the kind of power claimed by the movement was rendered unlikely by the very means of its advancement.[61]

The fifth chapter, "Organization, Performance, and Symbol," traces the departure of Hindu nationalists from an ascetic, brahminical Hinduism to an opportunistic use of a range of diverse elements from Hinduism. I demonstrate that a mystification of religious sentiment characterized most erstwhile discussions of Hindu mobilization in the late 'eighties and early 'nineties. The sixth chapter, "Hindutva Goes Global," points to the international context within which nationalist groups mobilize, and highlights the deep and systematic differences between expatriate and indigenous constituencies that they coordinate in "Hindu" assertion.

CHAPTER I

Hindu nationalism and the cultural forms of Indian politics

The Ramayan epic was serialized on national television in India from January 1987 to August 1989. During the broadcast, the Ram Janmabhumi (Birthplace of Ram) movement, which aimed to demolish a mosque, Babri Masjid (Babur's mosque) in Ayodhya and build a Ram temple in its place, grew in importance. The Ramayan serial overlapped with the most crucial phase of the Janmabhumi movement, when it changed from an ominous but still relatively obscure campaign into the dominant issue before the country, one that made and unmade prime ministers and ruling parties.[1] The Ramayan achieved record viewership in virtually every part of the country (something no serial before it had done), and made Sunday mornings "belong" to it; any public event scheduled for that time courted disaster. With such publicity given to its pre-eminent symbol, the god-king Ram, the Hindu nationalist Bharatiya Janata Party was emboldened to declare, by the middle of 1989, that the Ayodhya movement "had reached a state and status in Indian public life when it was no more possible to ignore its effect in politics, including electoral politics."[2] The issue was officially declared to be political, with the BJP making it their number one priority that "a grand temple to Lord Ram" would be built at the site of the mosque.

In the launching of one procession from Delhi to Ayodhya, Ram's birthplace, volunteers dressed to look like the television versions of Ram and his brother Lakshman, with their bows strung, posed for photographs in front of a pile of bricks intended for the proposed Ram temple, dubbed Ram *shilas*, using the Sanskrit *shila* for brick to underline that this was religious, not political work. Participants shouted slogans like *Saugandh Ram ki khaten hain, mandir wahin banayenge* (We swear by Lord Ram, we will build the temple there) and *Jis Hindu ka khoon na khaula, woh khoon nahin, pani hai* (the Hindu whose blood does not boil does not have blood but water). B. L. Sharma, general secretary of the Delhi unit of the Hindu nationalist Vishwa Hindu Parishad, declared, "The Hindu is up in arms, the storm has risen, and nothing can stop it now."[3] One VHP activist rallying volunteers declared, after a clash with police in Ayodhya: "What you are seeing today is a replay of the battle scenes you have witnessed on the television screen in the Mahabharat epic.[4] Only this time the fight is for who will win the throne of Lucknow and Delhi."[5] Ashok Singhal, who led the mobilization, noted about the Ramayan serial, in an interview, "[I]t was a great gift to our movement. We owed our recruits to the serial's inspiration."[6] Mahant Avaidyanath, President of the Ram Janmabhumi Mukti Yagna Samiti (Committee to Liberate the Birthplace of Ram), speaking at a VHP meeting in Bangarmau, Unnao District, in U.P., observed that Ramanand Sagar had spread *prachar prasad*, auspicious publicity, for Lord Ram, and the VHP wished to do the same all across India.[7] Sequences in the serial itself seemed to make explicit reference to the VHP's campaign, with Ram uttering prayers to a parcel of earth from his birthplace, a novel interpolation in the story.[8]

Battle scenes in a tele-epic were seen as models for Hindu militancy, and at the same time the serial itself began to echo themes from the movement (see chapter two). A historical conjuncture was in formation, one that had a kind of transparency: there was, for a while, the feeling of a great clarity about the character and causes of social problems and the nature of their solution, and these were similar in their simplicity and attractiveness. What drew little attention, amidst this great clarity, was the new prominence of the media itself, which as facilitator rather than unmoved mover, enabled a new order of social connectivity, in a visual regime that now extended across the nation. Ordinary citizens now perceived their actions as having implications for society at large, suggesting a new dimension to their perception, and a different quality to the power they wielded. Such widespread changes invested claims by the BJP and its affiliates about the re-birth of a Hindu public with an ominous force.

A new public language was emerging, more intimate to a section of the population and intimidating to the rest, that resonated with themes of collective empowerment, albeit in disquieting ways. This was of course not due simply to the broadcast of some television programs. Merely focusing on the media itself does little more than confirm our own fascination with its power. The media neither cause nor reflect events, they participate in them. To an important extent, television, like the media in general, exteriorize and consolidate the social functions of communication and representation, leading to a quicker, more efficient network of signs and messages, and in turn changing the context for social communication in general. Communication now occurs at personal and societal levels simultaneously, in interlinked circuits. The things people use, as well as the ideas and images they receive, are increasingly part of a single circuit of consumption, enabling a new and more mutable style of collective representation. The quality and extent of popular consent and participation thus become immediate and pressing issues, changing the way in which politics is conducted.[9] The Ram Janmabhumi campaign made the most of the resulting volatility, drawing large numbers into a nationwide movement by combining symbols of Hindu religion with themes of popular empowerment and aggression against a stereotyped enemy, notably Muslims. The temple movement came to focus a wide-ranging set of political and economic claims by the Hindu nationalist party, in a determined and powerful challenge to the state to fulfill its obligation to society.

I will anticipate my argument here, and at the same time outline the chronology of events analyzed. The Ram Janmabhumi campaign, I suggest, can be seen as part of the third of three successive phases, each marking a growing crisis of the Indian State. They can be distinguished in terms of attempted resolutions to this crisis that recast the relation between political authority and citizen-subjects, through the systems of communication and the language of politics available. The first phase is that of "Nehruvianism," beginning in 1947 and decisively concluding with the imposition of a National Emergency in 1975. Nehruvianism, a term retrospectively applied to the first decades of the post-independence period, is the name for the consensus undergirding the Indian developmental state, referring to a particular distribution of political power and its legitimating vision of secular, autarkic growth. During this period, the work of the economy was seen to stand for and be capable of resolving any problems that arose in the sphere of culture; technocracy was in fact the form of politics. Planning and policy were conceived from the "commanding heights" of the state, functioning for the most part at a remove from the ordinary language of people. Consequently the National Emergency in 1975 sought to close the gap between state authority and the people (including their representatives in opposition parties, labor unions, and other organizations), and to find an authoritarian solution to the problem of inducing political consent. Thus censorship was imposed on the press, and experiments to set up a nationwide television system commenced. The institution of the Emergency pointed to the beginning of the breakdown of the Nehruvian consensus, although the restoration of democracy a mere two years later delayed recognition of this fact, and allowed the appearance of continuity. The experience of the Emergency suggested that consent could not be commanded and that force was no compensation for the lack of effective communication. This lesson was taken in not only by the ruling Congress party, but also by the Hindu nationalists who came to focus on popular mobilization, using the rhetoric of democratic politics and empowerment.

The phase of liberalization which began piecemeal in the 1980s, and then more decisively in 1991, was in many ways an acknowledgment that the inefficiencies of the economy had reached crisis proportions, and required not merely technical but political management. The press, largely captive to business interests, attacked state-led development as a wasteful and inefficient system nurturing stagnation and corruption rather than productivity. With scant regard for the historic dependence of indigenous big business on the state, privatization and laissez faire were euphorically endorsed as providing the answer to problems of the economy and, implicitly, as the guarantee of a more stable polity. There was a retreat from the certitude of the developmental state that had presumed knowledge only markets were now considered capable of, of how to match demand and supply while increasing both. The market's wisdom was enigmatic, however, appearing as a set of self-evident principles whose outcomes were in fact unpredictable. The difficulty was two-fold and rested in the state's inability to induce either a properly productive economy or the consent of its people, and these were now seen to be inter-related problems. Both the pedagogical role adopted in state policy, e.g., in broadcasting institutions, and the developmental role in economic planning, indicated an incongruity between a top-down mode of governance and a system of communication which called for a more reciprocal interaction. The problem of consent became an increasingly urgent one for the economy itself, in terms of incentives to produce and the willingness to consume.

It was in this nexus of circumstances that there arose a receptivity to the idea of a break from the past, one that Hindu nationalists capitalized on, although they did so, paradoxically, by claiming to return to a deeper, purer past. With a sophistication in communication far ahead of its competition, the BJP and its affiliates identified the opportunity presented by the growing numbers of "non-committed voters" due to the waning influence of the Congress Party. Crafting a range of appeals that converged in the single-issue temple campaign, Hindu nationalism promised a pro-business government combined with strong nationalist discipline, in a solution whose hostility to the poor and to minorities may actually have enhanced its credibility with large sections of the middle classes. Hindu nationalism worked at two levels, on the one hand offering the cultural and ideological accompaniment to liberalization for middle and upper classes, and at the same time translating it into a religio-mythic narrative that would win popular consent (see below). The promotion of a 'Hindu' public, partial and contradictory as it was, was seen to be capable of addressing the crisis of political legitimation, so that both the Congress and the BJP would have to draw on it. Meanwhile this Hindu public helped distract attention from the limited and class-biased character of economic reforms that were being carried out.[10] The alliance between economic liberalization and Hindu nationalism was opportunistic and unstable, but nevertheless, in the context, developed a considerable force and momentum. Individual actions were declared to have a national relevance and a capacity to affect the body politic as a whole; participation in the temple campaign meant participation in making India Hindu (again). There was a homology between these arguments and those being made for the economic sphere. Production and consumption by individuals were deemed to be salient for the wealth of the nation as a whole, and indeed to be its aim and basis; similarly, the action of individuals, e.g., in Hindu nationalist processions, was the means of national self-realization. The motto publicized during the Emergency, "Be Indian, Buy Indian," was perhaps ahead of its time in its association of buying and national identity. Whether Indian goods were purchased or not, the definition of buying as patriotic came, during the early period of liberalization, to have an expanded, if ironic significance, as consumer expenditure was subsidized at the cost of a rising national debt.

In attempting to understand the influence of the economic crisis on ideology, it would be misleading to think that an empirical description of the economy alone would clarify matters. The conventional Marxist model of an economic base anchoring an ideological superstructure is only of partial help, I suggest, in comprehending the two-way interaction between these realms. Rather, the economy and ideology each has a specific form of materiality, in Balibar's terms, arising from their mode of production and mode of subjection respectively.[11] Each tells the story of the other, ideology that of the economy, and the economy that of ideology. The economy provokes ideology's effects, just as in turn, the kinds of subject positions, the narratives of economic action, the relationship of classes one to the other, portrayed in ideology turn out to influence and impel events in the economy. Thus, for instance, Nehruvianism told the story of state-led modernization, and in doing so expressed the paternalism of the developmentalist economy. In fact, the existence of a protected private sector, growing under the control of a license-permit raj, pointed to a more authoritarian and inegalitarian economic model, and so disclosed the elitist character of Nehruvian ideology. Similarly, the ideology of liberalization sponsored the introduction of market reforms and the rollback of an inefficient welfare state, while heralding expansive, unhindered growth. The ways in which economic reforms actually took shape, however, disclosed a system that was no longer merely elitist but, in fact, was rapidly aggravating class inequality, with a more arbitrarily interventionist state serving to protect these class gains. A brief examination of some of the events of liberalization will therefore shed light on the unacknowledged gaps in the narratives of liberalization and assist in the task of ideology critique.

IN THE THROES OF ECONOMIC CRISIS: LIBERALIZATION / "HINDUIZATION"[12]

The Indian economy, in a famous quip by economist Raj Krishna, suffered from a "Hindu rate of growth" for decades after Independence – a "sluggish" 3 to 3.5 percent per annum between 1950 and 1980, which meant, given the rate of population growth at this time, a per capita growth rate of 1.4 percent per annum.[13] Embodied in the phrase is not only the economist's old adage that growth is the chief goal of an economy, but also the self-deprecating characterization of this failure as "Hindu." "Hindu" here was metonymic of India – ancient and out-of-date, too vast to be successfully influenced by mere mortals, and possessing in this intractability its own peculiar distinction. Yet the overriding feature of this distinctiveness was failure – its seeming incapacity to answer the needs of changing times. From being considered the glory of an old civilization, to be "Hindu" had become the unbudgeable burden of a backward nation attempting to be modern.

Yet in a matter of a few years, the meaning of the term changed completely. To be Hindu became a triumphant declaration of strength and vigor, and the symbol of an aggressive culture on the ascendant. Now it was those who had believed the term to signify anything else who were at fault – they were traitors to a great heritage who, by their unbelief, had paralyzed an incomparable civilization. In a criticism symptomatic of the change, BJP economist Jay Dubashi declared, "It was not the Hindu Rate of Growth that failed India but the Nehru Rate of Growth and men like Raj Krishna are as much the guilty men as Nehru himself."[14]

In the 1980s, the average annual growth rate was above 5 per cent, thereby "breaking the barrier of the Hindu growth rate," declared a prominent business magazine.[15] "The last ten years have transformed not only the society and the economy, but also the psyche of the country," it proclaimed. "[R]evered terms of the past are now *passé*: – socialism, controls, state interference . . . One can easily sum up the decade by saying, 'Long live democracy.' Or if one wants to be more specific, 'Long live liberalization' " (*ibid.*). There is journalistic hyperbole here, but the choice of rhetoric is itself revealing. With the lifting of socialism or state interference (the terms slide into each other, as in many such accounts), and the liberalization this implies, democracy springs forth, and psychic transformation proceeds. From being seen as a burden, events seemed to suggest that "Hinduism" too was a part of the repressed truth of society, released by the lifting of state controls and the mobilization of latent popular forces, although those espousing "Hinduness" insisted that much remained to be done.

Liberalization as such, involving structural reforms, was launched after July 1991 at the behest of the international lending agencies, following the government's application for an emergency loan to cover its negative balance of payments. There were severe external constraints placed on the economy, in terms, for instance, of debt service and excise reductions on imports, opening more and more sectors of the economy to foreign competition, generating resources for investment when the state's ability to collect revenue had new limits, addressing demands for full convertibility of the rupee and so on. Although reforms were externally imposed, the business classes as well as the political elites chose to present them as undertaken on their own initiative, and as a triumph of their own decisiveness in turning away from deleterious "big government" methods of running the economy. When it seemed that liberalization offered a means of quick expansion in a rapidly growing market, it was welcomed by businesses. When it began to be clear that foreign competition would enter as a necessary concomitant of any internal liberalization, the mood rapidly became more ambivalent, and the hitherto protected industrial houses began to demand a "level" playing field, something whose absence their prosperity had depended on.

The appeal of privatization built on a widespread disillusionment with the state, acquiring force when the state itself anointed private business as the new agent of progress and change. Although understood as the opposite of "state-owned," "privatization" was justified not so much as a transfer of ownership and control as in terms of a change in the *nature* of control, seeking efficiency through competition. In practice, privatization was used to cover a range of scenarios, from creating a public limited company out of a government unit in Malaysia, to the setting up of a joint-sector enterprise in China, and the introduction of property rights in Hungary.[16] Indeed, privatization could be said to require a more, not a less effective state, one that held its players to a given set of regulations and maintained market discipline, to promote industrial efficiency and enhance production. Privatization's promise of transparency could thus function to screen the specific agenda behind reforms, as a set of procedural norms benefiting a particular status quo. In the case of India, initial evidence pointed to the transfer of public resources to private ownership, and the protection of middle- and upper-class privileges, all enacted at the cost of the majority of the population.

Critics of the public sector were insistent that their privatization was a guaranteed solution to the government deficit. However, one analysis of the macroeconomic impact of public sector enterprises from 1960–61 to 1989–90 showed that their deficit did not increase significantly over the period, and that the growing fiscal drain was actually caused by growing expenditure and subsidies of administrative departments.[17] Simultaneously, those favoring a rollback of the state nevertheless held on to the need for force against the enemies of progress, to break militant unions, for instance, and to crush organized strikes, and so on.[18]

The economic reforms initiated by Indira Gandhi following her return to office in 1980 were taken further after her death by Rajiv Gandhi from 1985 onwards with his "New Economic Policy" (NEP). The NEP was designed to jump-start the stagnant industrial economy and stimulate domestic consumption, through tax concessions to high-income groups and to corporations, new government jobs and substantial salary increases at the upper echelons of the public sector. The second half of the 1980s witnessed a veritable explosion in the economy, with the consumer durable market alone growing at a rate of between 8 and 22 percent per annum in this period. The growth rate of the economy as a whole rose at the same time, averaging above 5 percent. Media pundits, bureaucrats, and politicians alike declared it only the beginning of an extended period of growth, as a sleeping giant awoke to take its rightful place among the world's leading nations.[19] Within a year, the picture changed beyond recognition, and seemingly without warning. The World Bank issued a report in October 1990, advocating 20 percent devaluation in the rupee to help remedy the balance of payments. Non-Resident Indian deposits began to leave the country directly thereafter, with the capital flight totaling $1.33 billion over the next eight months. By June 1991, exchange reserves reached an all-time low of two weeks' supply. The new minority Congress government, led by Prime Minister Narasimha Rao and his Finance Minister Manmohan Singh, soon sought IMF assistance.[20]

The causes of the crisis were not obscure. The extent of growth in the national debt during the 1980s was without parallel in the country's history. Commercial borrowing to serve what one economist called India's "ten per cent socialism," providing extra comforts for the fortunate few, soon reached its limit.[21] Non-essential governmental expenditures had grown unabated. Imports had outstripped exports for the entire duration of the post-independence period, with the exception of two years in the 1970s, with balance of payments crises recurring across the whole period.[22] The gross expenditure of the Central Government had risen from about Rs.178 billion in 1979–80 to Rs.220 billion in 1980–81 to Rs.820 billion in 1989–90.[23] Public and commercial debt had risen steeply to meet these expenditures, since taxes had also been cut and deficit financing had played a considerable role in underwriting the government budget. Interest payments of course led to further increases in public expenditure. The fiscal deficit reached 9 percent of GDP in 1986–87, the highest it had ever reached until then, and the rest of the decade saw no significant decrease from this figure. Import liberalization led to a considerable increase in the import surpluses supporting industrialization. With the decline in foreign concessional loans after the oil crisis of 1979–80, interest rates increased worldwide, and the average interest rate on the Indian debt rose from 2.4 to 6.1 percent between 1980 and 1982 alone. The period of maturity of loans was nearly halved between 1980 and 1989, from 40.8 to 24.4 years. Although these changed conditions meant that incurring external debt was a far more serious proposition than before, loans accumulated uninterruptedly, from $18.7 billion in 1980 to $56.3 billion in 1989, that is, from about 10.8 percent to 21.5 percent of GNP. By 1989, debt service as a percentage of exports of goods and services had risen to 26.3 percent, up from 9.1 percent in 1980.[24]

By 1987, India was seventh in the ranks of debtor nations. And in another four years, it had risen to third place, with a debt total of $70 billion, surpassed only by Brazil ($122 billion) and by Mexico ($101 billion), and total debt service as a percentage of goods and services was of the order of 26 percent that year (1991).[25] At the end of 1990–91, the total internal debt amounted to 50.2 percent of the GDP; taken together with external debt, the total public debt at this time amounted to 62.9 percent of the GDP.[26]

IMF-imposed structural adjustment commenced, with its conditionalities including currency devaluation, opening the economy to imports, effecting cuts in subsidies, and initiating privatization, among other things. Those who had hitherto been the leading apostles of debt-induced growth soon became its most articulate critics, as they championed the new reforms imposed by the international institutions (e.g., Manmohan Singh, the Finance Minister between 1991 and 1996). If liberalization and privatization had already been words in vogue until this time, they attained the status of gospel truths, containing both diagnosis and cure.[27]

On 1 and 3 July 1991, Prime Minister Narasimha Rao's government devalued the rupee in two steps and promised to make the currency convertible within three to five years. Major reforms in trade policy were also made soon after. Twenty days later, the asset limit for firms listed under the Monopolies and Restrictive Trade Practices Act was scrapped, along with industrial licensing for most projects, and the foreign equity limit was raised to 51 percent. The industrial policy was announced the same day that the union budget was presented in Parliament. In the annual budgets that followed, additional measures were announced to reduce the fiscal deficit, including divestment in state owned enterprises, promotion of foreign direct investment and portfolio investment by the state, and private sector participation in infrastructure (core) sectors like power, telecommunications, and roads.[28] In addition, the measures included the abolition of import control through licensing for capital goods, raw materials and intermediates, the reduction across the board of all import duties, and the liberalization of gold and silver imports. Divestment of up to 49 percent was allowed in select public sector enterprises, support was to be withdrawn from loss-making units, and a National Renewal Fund was announced, to help workers affected by industrial restructuring.[29]

Under the guise of divestment, public property accumulated over four decades of independence began to be given away at prices far below their real cost, in an extraordinary and little-publicized raid on the treasury. Only investors capable of making bulk purchases of 20 to 50 million rupees were eligible to participate, ensuring that most people were excluded.[30] According to the Comptroller and Auditor-General of India, the first sale of shares of ten public sector units alone involved a loss of almost 400 percent per share on an average.[31] Thus shares of the Steel Authority of India (SAIL) with a market value of Rs.200 per share were sold at Rs.15, and Hindustan Petro Chemicals Limited (HPCL) shares valued at Rs.800 in the open market were sold at Rs.250. A former state Finance Minister, Ashok Mitra, estimated in 1992 that one lot of public sector shares that was sold in this fashion for Rs.30.38 billion could have fetched about five times as much if a fair market price had been sought.[32]

There were additional signs of the disparity between the triumphal rhetoric at this time and actual economic conditions. Amid all the austerity measures, and predictions that hundreds of thousands of workers could be laid off in public sector units, those at the managerial and executive levels faced no threat, and government servants themselves were nowhere affected. It was not only the urban middle classes who were protected from the brunt of rising prices. While announcing the removal of subsidies of fertilizers, farmers were assured that they would be compensated by excise reductions. Meanwhile, there was no mention of remedial measures for tackling the problems of the growing unemployed, including the educated unemployed.[33] Although the 1970s were a period of relatively low growth, the increase in employment was nearly twice that of the subsequent high growth decade of the 1980s. The average annual increase in employment declined from 2.82 percent between 1972–73 and 1977–78 to 2.22 percent from 1977–78 to 1983–84, and fell further to 1.55 percent from 1983–84 to 1987–88. The agricultural sector as well saw a decline in the growth rate of employment, from 2.32 percent in the 1972–78 period to 1.20 percent in the 1983–88 period.[34]

Apart from the layoffs in government-owned organizations, private companies had been closing down industrial units, paying no heed to the Industrial Disputes Act that forbade such summary initiatives. Most large private companies, especially those controlled by multinationals, had been reducing their workforce for several years past, by offering "voluntary retirement" with improved benefits.[35] According to one estimate, nearly twenty million people were affected by the setback in poverty alleviation as a result of the reforms, and the number of registered unemployed rose by more than 5 percent, or 1.7 million, between 1990–91 and 1991–92 to 36.6 million in February 1992.[36] One study determined that the proportion of household consumer expenditure devoted to food actually decreased between the early 1960s and the 1990s.[37] And the per capita availability of total foodgrain for consumption (defined as net output adjusted for net imports and net changes in stock) declined from 510 grams per days in 1991 to 465 grams per day in 1993.[38]

One economist, remarking on the absence of criticism of the harsh measures being taken at the IMF's behest, wrote:

We have already been more than accommodating in not only conceding to, but indeed adopting virtually each one of the conditionality requirements, with scant regard for [their] demonstrably harmful effects . . . and for the poor in particular. Yet there has been a tide of support for the IMF-dictated path of adjustment among the media, academics and other people that has seldom been witnessed before. Emboldened by the support of this influential group, the government has gone about implementing a broad package of reform measures to give the right signals to the IMF.[39]

This was no abstract economic process, but one with political assumptions and consequences. Yet there was a powerful consensus amongst elite groups, including those more often critical of government actions. What led to the apparent disenfranchisement of liberalization's critics was not any obvious success of the economic reforms as such. Rather, the terms of reference for understanding the economy and its relation to politics had shifted. It was as though a different set of conceptual coordinates had to be brought into place to comprehend how a planned economy might have been undertaken in the first place.[40] The ends liberalization aimed at, e.g., deregulation, opening the domestic market, and increasing consumption, involved political outcomes that eluded any purely economistic analysis. Understood as a historical conjuncture, liberalization brought together a broad range of ostensibly unrelated tendencies, in a changing combination whose unity lay in their contribution to the growth and development of the market: the dismantling of economic controls, the expansion of communications, including the institution of national television, and the changing political balance of forces.[41] The end of the era of one-party dominance and the gradual loss of legitimacy of the planned economy was accompanied by a change in the terms of reference, so that the value of terms such as "public" and "private" appeared reversed. Now the private sector seemed to be the great reservoir of hope for growth, and the public sector the impediment to realizing this hope; earlier, investment in the public sector had symbolized the national will to modernize. There was obviously nothing inevitable about the transformation in perspective, although it did follow market-oriented shifts in the West. A look at the broader historical circumstances preceding the shift helps illuminate the changes in political language that emerged.

Two streams of discourse, on economic liberalization and "Hinduness," came to prominence in close succession in the mid-1980s, each reinforcing the resurgent rhetoric of the other, while also periodically clashing, in their laissez-faire and communitarian resonances. With the prying loose of voters from the Congress Party's decades-old hegemony on the one hand, and the efforts of businesses to secure dominance with market liberalization still nascent on the other, voters and consumers both became subject to intense recruitment. Communal mobilization occurred at the nexus between these strategies, which were united in their technologies of communication, and in their credo of opening out to the world. BJP leader Pramod Mahajan defended this nexus between marketing and political mobilization: "I think it is time we stopped shying away from words such as 'sell.' We must realize there has been a major revolution in communication. If we maintain that a good ad campaign can't sell a bad product, conversely people will never purchase a good product if they don't know about it."[42] Mahajan's assumption of the necessary equation between buying and voting pointed, in its own way, to a re-politicization of the electoral process in the wake of the Congress's decline. The euphoria over liberalization, the growing assertiveness of its beneficiary classes, and the spread of a consumerist ethos, required a new set of ideas to replace a political world-view that now became associated with stasis and quietism. The Hindu nationalists' appeals echoed and reinforced those of an expanding market economy, both expressing the cultural and political assertion of newly rich classes.[43] Understanding the spread of Hindu nationalism, then, requires inquiring how a sectarian ideology could metamorphose into a "good product," and how the political project of the BJP could be advanced in the process.

The remainder of this chapter illuminates the circumstances in which such a shift of political language occurred, such that Hindu nationalism became simultaneously an ideology aspiring to hegemony and an array of consumable objects, and how these developments in turn enabled the rise of the BJP and forged the nature of its appeal.

PASSIVE REVOLUTION AND THE UNRAVELING OF A FRAGILE
CONSENSUS

A variety of factors had allowed majority governments to rule in a heterogeneous polity like India, although no party acquired an absolute majority. These factors included the fragmentation of the electorate along class and caste lines and the imperatives of securing power in such a context, as well as the nature of the Indian electoral system itself.[44] This led to what has been described as centrist politics, which meant in practice that compromises were made with erstwhile ruling classes in most regions of the country. From an independence movement, the Indian National Congress shifted to being a party of government, beginning with the compromise and consent of a range of class interests, and developing over time into little more than a mechanism for fighting elections. In the two decades following Independence, most power was handled by state-level bosses who ran traditional party machines based on patronage. It was through the state leaders that new political aspirants challenged Indira Gandhi in 1967 and 1969, and it was their candidates whom she defeated in 1971 and 1972. Thereafter, she attempted to prevent independent centers of power from developing. State and local level leaders were liable to be dismissed if they functioned independently; after 1971, appointments were made from the center rather than through the Congress Committees. The older functions of the Congress Party, including generating local support, negotiating between local interests, and acting as a grass-roots conduit of information between center and branch, declined. In their stead, Mrs. Gandhi increasingly resorted to the bureaucracy to replace these functions, including the government intelligence bureaus, the Central Reserve Police Force, and sundry paramilitary institutions. Over time, the consensus it represented dwindled, although the halo achieved with independence could not be erased so easily; rather, it drew out the party's atrophy.

There was a contradiction between the economic and the political priorities of the government, between the goal of increasing economic growth, and that of ensuring its political survival by improving the income and consumption of the majority. Since economic growth did not generate sufficient revenues for redistribution by the state, raising mass consumption and purchasing the electorate's temporary allegiance effectively undercut investment in development. The government's inability to limit income tax evasion and various forms of corruption, and its unwillingness to impose direct taxes on agricultural income, remained as limits on revenue collection. The flexibility of the government in responding to crises steadily diminished over time, and if the accumulation of power at the top compensated for a rigid and unresponsive bureaucracy, the translation of this power into effective decision-making diminished in tandem. What followed has been described as a structural crisis of the Indian state.[45]

That the BJP came to stand out as having a "fresh" appeal to voters reflected a deep-rooted problem of political rhetoric.[46] The BJP, after all, claimed to be returning to the culture of the people, long scorned by the colonial elite and their imitators in the Nehruvian Congress. Hindutva's rise can be seen as a partial and contradictory vernacularization of political language, where concepts existing at a remove for the majority, such as those of nation and citizenship, were rendered into local vocabularies, and in the process underwent a shift of meaning.[47] The language of Hindutva represented a very specific kind of vernacularization, deploying a range of localized narratives and themes that were subsumed under a strictly limited set of Hindu symbols and political demands.[48] The party's own aims were to increase their support rather than actually re-orient politics towards the grassroots, no doubt. Nevertheless, a language that distanced itself from politics as usual and that expressed itself in a simple idiom of faith, divisive as it was, signaled at the same time the availability of a political choice and a widening of the space for popular participation. The invocation of terms that were part of the daily lexicon, but little used in national politics, effectively drew on the performative character of language and helped the BJP bring a wider circle into the stream of national politics.

The limited, makeshift nature of this politicization, on a continuum with the broader process of social and political change, can be understood in terms of Gramsci's notion of a "passive revolution."[49] The term refers to the relatively non-confrontational approach to change required of a ruling elite that lacks the power to carry out a Jacobin, i.e., for Gramsci, classical bourgeois revolution. With the resulting lack of mass participation in the political process, the state proceeds on a more limited, reformist basis, working through molecular transformations below the surface, to advance the bourgeoisie's power. For instance, Gramsci cites the case of Italy, where the aspirations of the great mass of the urban and rural petty bourgeoisie were raised, enlisting their services in the reinforcement of traditional ruling classes' hegemony. Similarly, in India, the promise of averting any fundamental social transformation is the necessary compromise the state makes with the old ruling classes, so that the state becomes at once the guardian of tradition and the apostle of modernity. Whether such arrangements themselves succeed or not, they form a framework of perception that helps bring the state's class allies together.[50] In other words, the precise character of consent influences the character of politics. Nehruvianism, held to represent the consent of the majority, in fact involved only a small minority, comprised of the educated middle and upper classes.

Nehruvianism, vociferously criticized by the BJP and by other advocates of liberalization as responsible for the waste and inefficiency of a planned economy, did not in fact possess the coherence attributed to it.[51] The failures of the economy could indeed have been attributed to too little rather than too much planning, and to the inappropriate character of existing plans. In fact, there were limitations built into the way in which economic growth was being managed, which when taken into account presented a very different picture from what was most prominent in debates of the late 1980s. The regulatory power of the state in India was less than in many western countries that were described as having planned economies. The proportion of national income collected through taxation and other state measures was relatively small, as was the area of economic activity directly under the state, and the extent to which the state was engaged in redistributive measures. To quote D. R. Gadgil, who played a prominent part in the early economic debates, "Planning in India has yet to be looked upon as an uncertain, though pretentious, enterprise in which the volume and the quality of effort by government are too inadequate to make any large and consistent impression on the total situation."[52]

The heterogeneous and unevenly developed society and the considerable expanse of the country, Gadgil argued, rendered it difficult for government policy to be coherent or unified. In fact, the modalities of industrialization were ad hoc, and never existed as a theoretical framework, or as a systematic plan of economic development. Thus for instance the approach of heavy capital investment in an industrial infrastructure was bound to cause severe hardship in a predominantly rural economy. At the same time, it entailed an increase in the concentration of economic control in an already highly unequal society. Although some of this control was in government hands, the greatest part of industrialization was achieved by capitalist business. This was capitalism with a difference, however, since any success achieved by private industry depended on state planning, and was protected at public cost. With capital formation centered in the private sector, those industrialists permitted to operate were also afforded a large margin of savings over and beyond their regular profit levels. In effect, as Gadgil wrote, "[T]he existing group of capitalists is assured of a monopoly of large expansion-opportunities in the future and a continued and an increasingly concentrated hold on the industrial economy."[53] Emphasizing "production before distribution," in the phrase of the time, assumed that more production would eventually lead to better distribution (of wealth produced). In effect this legitimated private ownership and concentration, and relegated the question of living standards for the majority to the sidelines.[54]

Few advocates of liberalization, however, criticized this elitist bias, or the implicitly trickle-down emphasis of the Nehruvian planned economy approach.[55] State planning itself was rejected, often without acknowledging the enormous gains made since Independence, as hampering economic efficiency and curbing the growth of Indian business.[56] Laissez faire would restore to the private sector the efficiency that it was truly capable of, in this argument, and generate enough wealth to go around. There were at least two important and related flaws in the argument. It assumed that the private sector in India was autonomous and that its growth had been self-propelled, rather than acknowledging the pampered entity it actually was. Secondly, the case for a "minimalist state" was not in fact to be taken literally, since tighter and more efficient controls over the economy were required, for instance to allow businesses to close down industries when they chose, and to discipline labor in the process. There was thus a restructuring of the character of state power and of the mode of governmental intervention. As T. J. Byres has written, "The state, then, beneath the cloak of privatisation and deregulation, would become, in particular respects, more intrusive than it was previously."[57]

Economic liberalization, however, also meant a delegation of a larger share of power to the "fortresses and earthworks" of civil society,[58] to private business and market forces. The prominence of Hindutva pointed to the political advantage in offering a cultural component to this "solution," in the attempt to widen the base of the erstwhile consensus. But any attempt at politicization would inevitably be difficult and conflicted, and test the preparedness of leadership and of existing institutions to withstand the pressures released in the process. The choice of Hindutva in particular was a deeply problematic one.

On 26 June 1975, Indira Gandhi declared a State of Emergency, allegedly to prevent a conspiracy from undermining the progressive measures being undertaken by her. A national railway workers' strike and broad-based popular campaigns in one of the more urbanized and developed states, Gujarat, and in one of the most backward, Bihar (campaigns which were both escalating into nationwide opposition movements) formed the background to the decision. Individual rights were revoked, including the right to move courts and the right to trial; over 100,000 arrests of political leaders and dissidents were made during the eighteen month period before elections were called.[59] Side by side with political repression were measures to promote economic growth and equity, such as the Twenty Point Program, heralded as a "direct assault on poverty."[60] It gave priority to implementing laws on land ceilings, housing for landless labor, abolition of bonded labor and of rural indebtedness, and providing higher minimum wages for agricultural workers. Special teams were instituted in the large cities, to undertake house-to-house searches for undisclosed or undervalued property. Widely publicized campaigns against tax evasion and smuggling were launched, and within twelve months over 2,100 alleged smugglers were jailed and property worth over ten million rupees seized.[61] Labor "peace" was achieved, with a dramatic decrease in strikes and lockouts of about 75 percent.[62]

The government's aim appeared to be to stop at source all conceivable political opposition. Elections were suspended and press censorship instituted. A constitutional amendment was passed in Parliament, the Forty-fourth Amendment Bill, that gave Parliament unrestricted power to amend the Constitution and made citizens' fundamental rights subordinate to a new code of "Fundamental Duties."[63] The Youth Congress promoted by Sanjay Gandhi, son of the Prime Minister, attempted to generate a measure of grassroots support, but it was perhaps better known for its promotion of harsh measures such as forcible sterilization and slum demolition.[64]

The Emergency sought to divert energies dammed in the political process and harness them for economic production and national unity. Thus the ubiquitous billboards and posters in towns and cities contained slogans and exhortations such as the following: "Discipline makes the nation great," "The 20 point program is the nation's charter," "Rumor mongers are the nation's enemies," "Efficiency is our watchword," "Produce more for prosperity," and "Less Talk, More Work."[65] The stern, admonitory character of the publicity presumed the existence of a willing and obedient citizenry; the profuse deployment of police and other repressive measures suggested the absence of such a population. Taken together, they indicated an inability to transcend the political crisis that the Emergency was meant to resolve, and they gave a hint of where at least one crucial problem might lie. There was perhaps an overly abstract conception of the audience of these messages, as citizens predisposed to discipline, hard work, and national pride. But as Indira Gandhi herself said, in a 1976 interview, "One thing that people outside simply can't understand [is] that India is a different country."[66] No doubt. Her confidence that it could change easily was then perhaps misplaced. Lee Schlesinger provides a lapidary anecdote about some flawed propaganda during this time:

Many of the posters and slogans were stilted translations of the Prime Minister's idiomatic Indian English; she said that the only magic is hard work, clear vision, iron will and strict discipline. The "only magic" came out in Marathi as precisely that – *ekatz jadu*. The urbane and poetic section of the populace may construe the metaphor properly, but for most the jadu sign said something confusing about trickery, perhaps expressing a truth about the government efforts which escaped the government translators. Of course, in many cases the meaning of the posters could be grasped without knowing all the words, but considering the posters as symbols of or for the Emergency, it is clear that in addition to whatever content, i.e., policy, may have been symbolized, one facet of the gap between the state and the citizen – namely, the entrenched inability to communicate effectively – was perhaps effectively communicated.[67]

The Emergency represented an authoritarian attempt to resolve the political crisis of the state, and overcome the economic stagnation resulting from the inability to mobilize labor and curtail revenue losses, to ensure investment and growth. The experience made clear the limits of an autarkic, extra-political solution to the interlinked problems of polity and economy, of the non-viability of forcibly jumpstarting a vigorous productive process. Liberalization represented a second attempt, working this time at different levels, through deregulation, privatization, and expansion of the consumer economy. It was presented as the need of the hour and a genuine response to prevailing problems. In fact, as K. Balagopal has argued, it was overdetermined. Its apparent causes were epiphenomenal: a balance of payments crisis, an IMF bailout, and structural adjustment serving to augur a new dispensation rather than manifesting as its true roots.[68]

What the Emergency led to was the closure of those channels of communication that could have corrected official misperceptions, such as free speech, elections, and a free press. It confirmed for sections of the elite that democratic freedom aggravated rather than solved the country's problems, since trains now ran on time and workers were afraid to strike. But the real political lesson distilled in the end was the opposite. The defeat of the Congress in the elections, held in March 1977, proved that Indian difference notwithstanding, democracy and political awareness were now too deep-rooted to be wished away from the polity and that there was no possibility of working around these facts. Events leading up to the Emergency, as well as its aftermath, showed the indispensability of popular mobilization and the rewards of maintaining effective communication on terms that ordinary people at the grassroots could understand.

The historic consensus represented in the Congress continued to unravel. Moving away from its radical rhetoric of the Emergency days, but still unable to articulate a plausible unifying vision, the party began to make sectional appeals to portions of its coalition. In doing so, the Congress offered a political opportunity to its opponents to capitalize on the ensuing resentment of excluded sections. Alternative parties tended to be short-lived though, as leaders fell out with each other, and popular movements often failed to secure lasting means of political representation. Opposition parties succeeded mainly at the regional level and in the south; at the national level, diverse parties routinely submerged their differences in their attempt to dislodge the Congress, but with only occasional success.[69] Partly due to the limited size of opposition parties and the failure of an alternative political formation to cohere, the Congress became a familiar lesser-evil, an option that for all its corruption and ineptitude was always available to muddle through until the next election. It operated on the basis of expediency, and its continued survival was again a matter of expediency on a larger scale.[70]

Rajiv Gandhi, Prime Minister from 1985 to 1989, was the transitional figure who heralded a change. His policies, modeled after Reagan and Thatcher, signaled a dual emphasis on both market forces and "national culture" in some sense.[71] The difficulties of creating a state-sponsored national culture in a "secular" society, where there were limits to the overt emphasis on religion, together with the anglophonic character of state technocracy, tended to result in official propaganda indifferent to its reception.[72] With his accession to power, Rajiv Gandhi attempted to mark a distance between himself and his predecessors, coming into office as a "clean" Prime Minister, one who had only entered politics "to help Mummy out." Along with reforms that announced a move towards supply-side economics and declarations that India's middle classes were the vanguard of change, there was a determined attempt to crystallize some conception of the national-popular for the first time, leavening a high-tech, Westernized orientation with native idiom and vernacular traditions. Rajiv's wearing a sacred thread *above* his vest during the nationally televised funeral rites for his mother was a hint, for those attentive to such symptoms, that the public culture of the new regime would bring with it something quite old, but worn in a distinctly new fashion. His close association with the Congress combined with his political inexperience allowed him to open the party to new forces, through publicity and a new level of attentiveness to the public, in the attempt to extend its lease of life. The Congress eventually proved unable to withstand these forces of change, or was too advanced in its life cycle to be resuscitated by them. It was the BJP that was able to capitalize on these emergent tendencies, its distinctive combination of political and cultural mobilization allowing it to take advantage of the crisis of the ruling party and of the energies released with liberalization.

During Rajiv Gandhi's prime ministership, cultural sponsorship concentrated on the spectacular form, to reach beyond the educated minority as well as to highlight the ruling party's imprimatur. A guiding precedent was perhaps the 1982 Asian Games, which, for the first time in India, was broadcast in color and won large domestic audiences. There followed a host of other events, with the sponsorship of cultural extravaganzas such as *Apna Utsav* (Our Festival), the Festival of India in the U.S. and in France (and their transmission back to India in various ways), and the initiation of "national epics" on the recently inaugurated national program on television. Suddenly, what had until then circulated mostly in regional language mythological films became a nationwide spectacle, recast both as an object and a medium of public commentary. The mid-1980s also saw the burgeoning of other media and media-related businesses: the advertising industry alone quintupled its revenues over the decade. Television for its part created for the first time a single cultural platform that could be "shared," in some sense, right across the country; and in the early, crucial years before the arrival of satellite television, the state served as undisputed ringmaster of the show.

Rajiv Gandhi's confidence that he could bring a sea change in Indian politics by virtue of his sincerity and good intentions perhaps took for granted the security of his dynastic inheritance of state power. He quickly won the admiration of the press and of urban middle classes with his promise of consumption-led growth and his criticism of the public sector.[73] At the same time, his government authorized moves that represented significant changes of policy, e.g., the broadcast of Hindu serials as a staple of the national program, the overruling of a Supreme Court judgment on Muslim women's right to divorce with a controversial bill that addressed the conservative Muslim constituency, and the opening of a mosque (Babri Masjid) that was the subject of a decades-long dispute in order to placate the Hindus angry over the Muslim Women's Bill. It was left to Rajiv's successors to deal with the consequences of his naïveté. The Hindu nationalists were much less constrained in their appeal to religious sentiments and by virtue of their oppositional status, more sensitive to the need for a popular mobilizational component to any such significant political shifts. Aided by upper-caste reaction against government-mandated reservations to Backward Classes, the BJP changed from a politically marginal to a national force, one whose agenda other parties were now forced to contend with. Underlying this relatively abrupt change was a more extensive transformation of the Hindu nationalists over the 1970s and 1980s.

THE HINDU NATIONALIST COMBINE[74]

We can map the development of the Hindu nationalists in three phases, in tandem with the three phases noted in post-independence Indian politics, of quietism and consensus, succeeded by a period of politicization immediately before and during the Emergency.[75] The third phase, beginning in the mid-1980s, saw the attempt to capitalize on the limited and increasingly contested character of the prevailing consensus. An alternative, Hindu nationalist program was championed, one that was aggressive and exclusionary, and presumed the unity of divergent and unequal caste groups. The failure of the ruling party to seriously oppose this program said much about the Congress's own compromise with the Hindu nationalists and the scant hindrance provided to the latter's campaign. The ability to make use of this advantage, however, resulted from changes the Hindu nationalists underwent over a number of years.

Three principal components can be identified in the Hindu nationalists, namely the Bharatiya Janata Party, its political party, begun in 1980 (its predecessor, the Bharatiya Jana Sangh, or the Jana Sangh for short, which like the party it begat also translates as the Indian People's Party, was founded in 1951); the Rashtriya Swayamsewak Sangh (National

Volunteer Corps, or RSS), founded in 1925, which provides ideological direction and serves as a seedbed of leadership, and controls a grassroots cadre who number several hundred thousand;[76] and, finally, the Vishwa Hindu Parishad (World Hindu Council, or VHP), founded in 1964 to spread Hindu values and strengthen links among Hindus in India and abroad.[77] There are numerous others, but these are mostly offshoots of the RSS, led by RSS members and coordinating their actions with it.

I have noted that the political history of the Hindu nationalists is in many respects intertwined with that of the Congress Party, with many rank and file members of the Congress espousing a larger role for Hindu culture in public life. The first major mobilization of the Indian National Congress, indeed, had been to demand a ban on cow-slaughter in the 1880s; the issue had enabled the party to gather support beyond urban professionals for the first time and helped to create a broad base in the Hindi heartland.[78] The entry of Gandhi had again allowed the party to transcend its middle-class limitations and appeal to peasants and farmers in a language that yet drew heavily on Hindu themes. Within the Congress itself, rank and file support for the Deputy Prime Minister, Vallabhbhai Patel, on accepting RSS volunteers into the Congress appeared to suggest a substantial degree of sympathy for Hindu nationalists' views.[79] Hindu nationalist leaders for years advised members to seek affiliation with the Congress Party and other parties as well, to avoid "political casteism."[80]

That a Congress government at the center should have overseen the December 1992 demolition of the Babri Masjid also points to the difficulty of rigidly separating the Hindu nationalists as a political and ideological formation.[81] BJP General Secretary Govindacharya's concise formula for the relationship deserves emphasis: *BJP minus Congress equals RSS.*[82] It was the "cultural" arm of the Hindu nationalists, the paramilitary volunteers of the RSS, that constituted the decisive difference between otherwise closely related parties. Understanding the Hindu nationalists therefore requires specifying how particular "cultural" activities, occuring beneath the gaze of official politics and its attendant censors, allowed the Hindu nationalist party to extend and transform the political terrain as such, from the late 1980s onwards.

The principal organizational basis of Hindu nationalist politics has been the RSS, founded by Dr. K. B. Hedgewar in Nagpur in 1925, developing over time into a *sangh parivar,* an extended "family" of affiliated organizations. Accounts of the RSS often veer towards an ahistorical portrayal, depicting it as having an unchanging ideology since its inception. The author of a critical study on the subject observed in 1979:

> The total thought content of the RSS can be summed up as follows: "Hindus have lived in India since times immemorial; Hindus are the nation because all culture, civilization and life is contributed by them alone . . .; the Hindus must develop the capacity for massive retaliation and offensive is the best defense; lack of unity is the root cause of all the troubles of the Hindus and the Sangh is born with the divine mission to bring about that unity." Without any fear of contradiction it can be stated that nothing more than this has been said in the RSS *shakas* [branches] during the past 54 years of its existence.[83]

Many writers have tended to assume more or less similar notions, and to accept the RSS's own assertion of an unwavering conviction in its core philosophy of conservative Hindu nationalism.[84] Behind superficial continuities, however, are important changes in the RSS's strategy, corresponding to a changing political context, although these are not necessarily acknowledged in its publicity. Thus for instance, prior to 1983 the emphasis of the VHP and the RSS was on the "threat" to Hinduism from conversions and the need to keep lower castes within the fold.[85] By the mid-1980s, Babri Masjid became the key issue, one that was declared to have angered Hindus through the ages. There were two crucial changes underlying this new emphasis. There was a shift away from a sectarian view of organizing, with indoctrination as its aim and daily drill as its chief method, to a far more pragmatic approach that emphasized mobilization over indoctrination, and political effect over organizational discipline. This was complemented by a move away from a relatively secular nationalist belief that religious ritual and idol-worship would impair the quality of recruits' loyalty, to an opportunistic utilization of a range of elements from popular Hindu practices and traditions. Implied in these changes was a change in the RSS's orientation to politics, from a view where its ideology was pre-eminent to one dominated by the goal of gaining political power.

The first period of Hindu nationalist development, the time of Congress dominance lasting until the early 1970s, was a long period of gestation and growth. During this time, the RSS, under the leadership of Madhav Sadashiv Golwalkar, concentrated on its "cultural" task of "Hinduizing society," according to its understanding of Hinduism, extending its particular brand of nationalism as it expanded across the country. It was under Golwalkar that the RSS expanded from a relatively small regional youth association to a nationwide organization with over 10,000 branches. A more activist orientation at this early phase might well have opened the fledgling organization to pressures that would have inhibited its growth. The quietist character of Nehruvianism provided the context for the insular and predominantly cultural emphasis of the RSS during these years. Not only did the organization eschew overt engagement in politics, but religion and ritual as well were adapted in rather austere terms, with the emphasis on an abstract, brahminical conception of Hinduism, invoking prayers to the sun and to the *bhagawa dhwaj*, the saffron flag that was the RSS's standard.

Golwalkar had warned against the ephemeral character of political power, and had urged a cultural role as the best way to forge a durable presence for the sangh, influencing the political sphere from above instead of from within. The RSS for its part had kept clear of the independence struggle, and had played no part in anti-colonial politics. Thus the Hindu nationalists as a whole had had no real experience of politicization and remained uninvolved with any popular movement until 1973. Golwalkar's successor, Madhukar Dattatreya ("Balasaheb") Deoras, envisioned a more hands-on approach: if the goal was to shape politics, joining a political party was surely the best way to do that. His accession to leadership coincided with the advent of a tumultuous popular campaign, at which time he decided on involving the RSS headlong (see below).

The political wing of the Hindu nationalists at this time was of course participating in electoral politics, but its position was a minor one. In relation to other Hindu nationalist parties, the Bharatiya Jan Sangh was a liberal constitutional party.[86] But the party had tended to stay close to its North Indian petty bourgeois constituents' concerns and had never managed to plausibly cast itself as a national party.[87] The issues that defined its character and made it an alternative to the Congress centered on hostility to Pakistan and to regional languages vis-à-vis Hindi (as a national language), and on problems relating to Partition. All of these issues marked the Jan Sangh as essentially a regional party. Its upper-caste bias in the way in which it defined Hinduism as well confirmed the limited social basis of the party.

The second phase of Hindu nationalist development began with events leading up to the Emergency, with the 1974–75 student campaigns in Bihar, and the *nav nirman* (new society) student-led movement in Gujarat against political corruption.[88] The RSS student organization, the Akhil Bharatiya Vidyarthi Parishad (All India Students' Organization), entered aggressively into politics at this time. The movements in Bihar and Gujarat formed the first experience of mass politics for the sangh. In Bihar, the RSS gained enormously by merging with Jaya-prakash Narayan's "Total Revolution," having for the first time an opportunity to enter the mainstream opposition. "J. P." was of course a socialist and not in agreement with Hindu nationalist philosophy, such as it was; what he approved of in the RSS was its commitment to social welfare. The RSS for its part perceived such work not as humanitarian so much as promoting the larger cause of a Hindu society.[89] But J. P. was sufficiently impressed with the RSS to ask for their continued support, upon his arrest during the Emergency. Until this time, the obscurantist philosophy and the limited electoral constituency of the party made a broad-based popular engagement unlikely. The absence of a coherent socio-economic policy combined with its stress on issues such as the banning of cow slaughter ensured the party's marginality. The RSS's avoidance of any confrontation either with the British or with the Congress had in practice dictated the terms of the Jan Sangh's position, one that was peripheral to the main battles of the day. But during the Emergency, the reliance by the Opposition leadership on the RSS gave the latter invaluable experience in terms of opening the organization to a more democratic engagement with the people, forcing an explicitly political relationship to the state and to the ruling party.[90]

Events in Bihar and Gujarat were followed by the imposition of the National Emergency and a ban on the RSS, forcing the organization underground. The RSS became a key political actor in the opposition movement and the strongest organized force in the Lok Sangharsh Samiti (People's Struggle Committee) set up by non-Communist parties to demand the resignation of the Prime Minister, Mrs. Gandhi. The RSS's experience in rallying the opposition, and in coordinating effective communication at the grassroots level, for the first time gave the cadre the experience of direct contact with democratic forces and brought the organization out of its self-absorption.[91] With the victory in 1977 of the opposition coalition, the Janata Party, over the Congress, the Hindu nationalists for the first time had the opportunity to occupy office at the center, thereby bringing to an end its nearly three decades of political marginality. In addition to opening up the Hindu nationalists to new ways of thinking, then, the culmination of this period also had the effect of winning it a measure of respectability.

Highlighting the experience of the Emergency in the seventies helps to frame the subsequent career of the Hindu nationalists. It provides a mediating link between the more parochial and self-involved past of the RSS and its affiliates, and their more dynamic and militant public phase during the temple campaign and after. It helps explain how, for instance, the Jana Sangh, which had hitherto never been able to rise above its base in the urban, middle- and lower-middle trading classes was able for a period to gain widespread acceptance and to envision a national audience for itself.[92] With much of the leadership in jail, the RSS's tendency to avoid confrontation and to ingratiate itself with ruling power was thwarted, and there ensued, willy-nilly, a politicization of the rank and file, which in turn created a powerful second tier of leadership.[93] The politically quiescent phase of the Nehruvian consensus was decisively superseded, and the RSS was able to emerge from it with a large and committed grassroots cadre capable of sacrifice and hardship, and to acquire, for some time, an aura of martyrdom and respectability. The importance of going beyond their own membership and mobilizing large numbers on issues proven to evoke a popular response registered itself powerfully.

At the same time, the Jan Sangh tasted power at the center, and leaders such as L. K. Advani and A. B. Vajpayee gained visibility as senior cabinet ministers, of Information and Broadcasting and of External Affairs respectively. The Bharatiya Janata Party, formed in 1980 after the break up of the Janata as successor to the Jan Sangh, was in important respects a changed party. The Janata Party's emergence represented the first unification of the anti-Congress opposition, despite many previous attempts, and signaled a moment of some transparency in Indian politics. But the lack of unity on more substantive issues than opposition itself and the faction-riven nature of the party made it short-lived. The government did not last its full term, and the Indira Congress was returned to office in 1980.

By the late eighties the BJP seemed to be poised to break through the political deadlock of the years following the Emergency and to forge a powerful new hegemony. Its espousal of Hindu identity without mention of caste, and its credo of growth without the specter of distributive justice, were both welcome to ruling upper castes. Its record of violence was regrettable, no doubt, but if the truth were told, there were many who saw this as an omen of greatness, and a sign that the party was prepared to do as it said, unlike the Congress of course. If the decades-long national movement that had coalesced into the Congress party was ossified, there was now an effort to jump-start a new movement to reinvigorate the nation and revitalize the party, only this time it would not be the Congress Party. But it was as an unredeemed aspect of the Congress legacy that the BJP presented itself. Earlier, the figure its predecessor the Jan Sangh invoked was Bal Gangadhar Tilak, who used the Ganapati festival in Maharashtra to stimulate Hindu, in his view synonymous with national, mobilization. Now it was Sardar Patel whom the BJP claimed, a conservative leader whose tolerance of Hindu orthodoxy was reinterpreted as implicitly Hindu nationalist. His untimely death in 1950 was alleged to have allowed Pandit Nehru's "pseudo-secular" suppression of Hindu culture in favor of Muslims and other minorities to flourish unchecked. The Ram Janmabhumi movement was declared to be modeled on Gandhi's Salt March of 1930, one that would finally cast off the last shackles of colonial dependency (namely, "pseudo-secularism") and assert the nation's true identity.

This rhetoric characterized the third phase of Hindu nationalist development, from 1980 onwards, and especially after 1983, which combined the Hindu nationalists' experience of popular communication and grassroots mobilization with a rhetoric of popular empowerment with its ideology of Hindu nationalism. The political context was one in which the Congress Party itself, under Indira Gandhi, had begun explicit appeals to the Hindu vote, following the declining power of populist and socialist campaigns. The importance of effective communication had been proven by her disastrous rout in the 1977 national elections, which occurred against all the information Mrs. Gandhi had had available to her. In seeking a more participatory language of politics, the symbols and images of religious faith seemed to offer an easy solution. When the newly constituted Bharatiya Janata Party followed suit, it did so at first through its proxy organizations, in ways that were more bold and through means that made no secret of their aggressive intent. The decision to pursue such a stratagem indicated a shift in thinking within the Hindu nationalists.

If the Congress "core" constituency was upper castes, Harijans, and Muslims, the BJP, like its predecessor the Jana Sangh, had a vote base that was largely a sub-set of the Congress's, comprised predominantly of the small industrialists, traders, and lower rung professionals, most belonging to bania (trader) castes. Although the party was virtually wiped out in 1984, with only two seats in the lower house of Parliament, the Lok Sabha, the percentage of votes it received was actually more than in the previous election, when it had ten seats, and about the same as in 1971.[94] Amidst its furious denunciations of Congress opportunism and Nehruvian ideology, and its claim to be breaking new ground, the BJP essentially attempted an aggressive reworking of the Congress's upper caste hegemony, repudiating its claims to benevolence and offering itself as bearer of a revitalized tradition equal to the challenge of globalization. If indigenous corporations were nervous about cutting loose from the protected economy of the license-permit raj, the proposal of a disciplined party with an efficient and well-drilled cadre to undertake a molecular re-invigoration of society was difficult to resist. It promised all the prerequisites of liberal industrial society with few accompanying burdens such as welfare and high taxes. Although the BJP's economic policy had been ill defined and in general uncritical of the Congress (as late as 1984 the party's manifesto had argued for "Gandhian socialism"), the party was now presented as having always been committed to liberalization. Thus its attraction to big business was hardly surprising, since it was crafted with precisely such an end in view.[95] For an older generation reared on Nehruvian idealism, to say nothing of the hopes of Rostowian "take-off," the BJP appeared as the nation's last chance at making something of itself.[96]

It was paradoxical, however, that the BJP presented itself as an opponent of the Congress in political terms while not taking issue with the most significant political developments of the period. Although the record of the BJP's economic resolutions reveals incisive criticisms of the way liberalization was being pursued, arguing against multinationals and for indigenous production ("swadeshi," and later, for a "calibrated globalization"), the party unconditionally supported the Congress's economic reforms, at least until March 1992.[97] The thrust of its opposition was to present an overarching cultural and political alternative to the Congress, as the leadership India required but could not provide. The Congress leadership could not have responded to the Hindu nationalists' mobilization in adequate terms, even if it were willing to do so; substantial sections of its membership were too close to the BJP, and the Congress Party lacked the grassroots cadre and the organizational strength the latter had. The interaction between the Congress and the BJP is an intricate story, pointing to the shared social bases and overlapping histories of the two parties, and the difficulty of articulating a clear space of opposition between such entangled lineages. It was in the extra-political domain that the difference between them could be most clearly articulated, in the space of civil society, and through the means of violence.

Until his death in 1973, Golwalkar had held the use of religious ritual to be potentially divisive, and as capable of interfering with the RSS's object of maximizing recruitment. It was the nation itself that was sacred, he argued; nationalism subsumed and transcended religion. In this respect he followed the Hindu Mahasabha leader V. D. Savarkar, who defined Hindus as those who regarded the country as their father-land and holy land both. Beyond this no requirements were to limit their numbers: no "theological tests" could specify, for Savarkar, who was a Hindu.[98] Golwalkar for his part disdained idolatry. "People go to temples and try to concentrate on the idols taking them to be emblems of the Almighty," he wrote. "But all this does not satisfy us who are full of activity. We want a 'living' God."[99] Golwalkar can be distinguished here from his predecessor, RSS founder Dr. K. B. Hedgewar, who used to carry a figurine of Hanuman with him and who had activists end their daily prayer with an invocation to Lord Hanuman: *Jai Bajrang Bali Balbhim ki Jai* (victory to Hanuman, victory to Bhim). After Golwalkar assumed power, this was replaced with a more "nationalist" slogan, *Bharat Mata ki jai* (victory to Mother India).[100] He defined the sangh's own ritual as distinct from other Hindu forms of worship:

[I]n our various sects, each individual has a definite emblem in keeping with his particular sect. He dresses and adorns himself in a particular manner, recites a particular mantra and follows a particular code of discipline. A Shaiva, a Shakta or a Vaishnava, each has his own method of worship, his own ritual, his own codes and conventions regulating his life. We too have evolved a tech-nique, an emblem, a "mantra" and a code of discipline in keeping with our ideal of a unified and disciplined national life. The great and inspiring emblem that we have chosen is the immortal *Bhagawa Dhwaj* which brings before our eyes the living image of our ancient, sacred and integrated national life in all its pristine purity . . . crossing all superficial barriers of province, sect, creed, caste, language and custom . . . Some worship Sri Rama as their Chosen Deity whereas some others look upon Sri Krishna as their God and so on. Therefore the Sangh has kept a symbol which is at once universal and all-absorbing in its appeal.[101]

Preaching . . . a particular form or name of God and criticising all others will only harm the great mission of consolidating and rejuvenating the entire Hindu people.[102]

It was all very well to choose a new symbol. But if the very notion of "Hindu" was "too fine to be defined," on what basis could Hindus unite?[103] It was at the level of practice that Golwalkar sought the answer to Hindu unification, rather than through ideology or symbolism. Self-less devotion to society would actualize Hindu nationhood. To live with no thought for oneself and to devote all one's energies to the betterment of others would bring about a harmonious nation. And the crucible of national reorganization, the nerve center of the apparatus that would overcome the forces of disunity, was the *shakha* (branch), the basic unit of membership and activity.[104] What chiefly distinguished the sangh was its insistence on *sangathan*, organization, through the discipline of daily drill, as both means and end to their activity.[105] These changes arose in the third phase of its development, through a hitherto relatively obscure Hindu nationalist organization, the Vishwa Hindu Parishad.

The Vishwa Hindu Parishad (World Hindu Council, or VHP) was founded in 1964 to spread Hindu values and strengthen links among Hindus in India and abroad. It was at the forefront of the Hindu assertion that began in the 1980s, spearheading the Ram Janmabhumi movement for instance. In contrast to the RSS, the VHP worked using the leadership of traditional religious figures, inserting popular Hindu symbols and practices into its political mobilization. It presented itself as a purely cultural organization, without political interests, while the BJP was supposed to remain respectful of the strictures on political parties, of avoiding the use of religion for electoral campaigning. But it could be the same figure wearing one costume in the capital and another in the villages, or even the same figure in the same outfit speaking a different language. Thus there was a systematic coordination between parliamentary and extra-parliamentary wings of the Hindu nationalists, with statements made by the one designed as counterpoint to the other. BJP political leaders, for instance, could moderate the militancy of the activist wing for the benefit of the national press. Contrarily, the same political assurances could be reinterpreted by RSS cadre at the grass-roots as necessary lies for a genuinely subversive cause.[106] What made the Hindu nationalists distinctive was their ability to slide across different sectors of society, and to dispel the perception of any one branch as "communal" by dispersing the question into a host of subsidiary functions and organizations, cultural, religious, and political. But it was in their joint operation that Hindutva actually took shape.

In its promotional literature, the VHP described itself as the organizational representative of Hindu society as a whole. It declared its interest in ensuring that every village, town and district in the country had the guidance of saints and the discipline of ritual. It sketched an idealized portrait of the past, one in which a thoroughly spiritual, yet highly scientific culture pervaded Indian society.[107] There were no divisions between the various castes, sects, and faiths at the time, and a feeling of selfless unity prevailed, it is claimed. The present generation had lost sight of the fundamental truths of Hindu culture and philosophy, evidently, having immersed itself in a self-seeking and materialist,

Westernized culture. The only way to rectify this, then, was through religious ritual, guided by traditional Hindu sages and gurus.[108] Such measures could restore Indian society to its erstwhile high status, when a culture that was both scientific and spiritual prevailed.[109]

The claim of the VHP to represent all of Hindu society was mediated and reinforced through the image of saints and ascetics. The coming together of those who have always been Hindus' traditional leaders under the aegis of the VHP confirmed the representative nature of the organization.[110] Religious ritual is presented as the ready cure for the ills afflicting present day society, recuperating an age-old remedy that Western education and loss of faith had condemned to neglect. The understanding of ritual was abstract and benign, in striking contrast with a more traditional viewpoint, according to which ritual is as ambivalent as any other technology in its outcomes. Because ritual had not been overseen and managed suitably in the past, it had been allowed to lapse into disuse, it is asserted, bringing ill fortune upon society. The VHP now undertook to make good this drawback, and coordinated and conducted rituals on behalf of Hindu society at large.[111] Hindu ritual, from being a medium of communication within a highly particularistic and heterogeneous universe, was thus recast into a symbolic affirmation of a Hindu public. It was a contradictory and incoherent public, to be sure, one that was incipient and far from coming to fruition, staggering as it did from one election to another. It did index, however, a connection the Hindu nationalists were able to establish between religious identity and a long-denied participation in the polity, so that the exercise of faith could become not only an act of consumption but an assertion of political will.[112]

In these and other ways (see chapter five), the VHP expanded on an array of practices of worship G.-D. Sontheimer has called "folk Hinduism," coexisting in interaction with but distinct from other components of Hinduism.[113] The VHP's resolve to utilize ritual may have been reinforced by the observation of its numerous overseas branches that temples were focal points for Indians abroad, across differences of caste, region, and sect. The first large-scale domestic experiment was the Ekatmata Yatra (Unity Journey) in 1983, where pictures of "Bharat Mata," a mother goddess figure representing India, were taken in processions across the country. Water from the Ganges mixed with water from local rivers was sold along the route, to symbolize the oneness of Hindu faith and of the nation. The response to the effort "demonstrated beyond doubt that the Hindu Society is quite alive and kicking," in the words of the former VHP General Secretary.[114] The Yatra represented the VHP's first mass contact program, and simultaneously its attempt at rewriting the language of religious affiliation. Older notions of the purifying power of sacred water were intermingled with the demonstration of a congregated activity and, by imputation, a common sentiment. The effort was declared to have "changed the mood of the entire Hindu society."[115]

Perceiving the Ekatmata Yagna as a success, the VHP began to pursue Hindu festivals and ceremonies seriously as potent instruments of assemblage, widening their celebration "to mass and collective level" and beyond existing family level observances.[116] Not only ordinary people, but traditional scholars and spiritual leaders too could be drawn into the movement through these means, as they came to "realise the immensity of the Hindu awakening endeavour undertaken by the Parishad."[117] Religious ceremonies, it was noted, were also useful in making contact with up-and-coming opinion leaders in society, professionals, businessmen, and others, and thus served as extremely useful sites of publicity.[118]

Eventually, the Janmabhumi movement culminated in the demolition of the Babri Masjid, and the BJP governments were dismissed in four states and in Delhi, in retaliation for the communal violence the movement had engendered. In the wake of these events, Prime Minister Narasimha Rao, speaking on the subject of reforms, commented, "We have certain hard decisions to take. But there is one limitation. Hard decisions cannot be taken by a soft state."[119] It was as a party capable of leading a hard state that the BJP tried to present itself. Obedient to the changes signaled in the era of Reagan and Thatcher, the BJP declared a laissez-faire economic philosophy, with its strong nationalism as guarantee of a superior political will. Here is Jay Dubashi on the need to emulate Thatcher:

Leadership does not mean giving people or promising people what they want; it means leading people where they do not at first want to go. This is what Margaret Thatcher did in Britain, and that is why she has been in power for ten years, the longest such period in this century . . . She said this is what I am going to do: I am going to cut down on useless employment even if people will be thrown out of jobs. I am going to denationalize useless industries which, for years have been cheating the taxpayer. I am going to cut the trade unions down to size because they are resisting change. This was her programme, a tough programme which no prime minister had the courage to offer. The Labor Party did the exact opposite; it promised the moon. But in the end it was Thatcher who triumphed and Labor has been eating the dust for the last ten years. Leadership, I repeat, means leading people where they do not at first want to go. Let BJP tell people that this country will never be great unless people make sacrifices, that they must be prepared to accept change, and they can never get anything for nothing. Let the critics say that it is a right-wing party, that it is reactionary and communal. Dogs bark but a party that believes in itself goes on.[120]

The BJP's version of Thatcherism was of course complicated by the caste and communal contradictions entailed in its Hindu assertion.[121] Further, there was a tension between the promise of free markets and that of a strong national state, expressed in the demand for indigenous enterprise, *swadeshi*, which the BJP attempted to balance along with its promises to big business.[122] Its mobilizational strategy consequently shifted in important ways. Previously, the main mode of mobilization was by means of slow and patient work at the grassroots, symbolized by the daily drill of the RSS. Political goals were long-term, and conceived in terms of influence rather than direct control. For various reasons, principally relating to the growing power vacuum at the center, this approach changed to a direct bid for electoral power, with all the vagaries of support it entailed. Apart from ideological indoctrination, Hindu identity began to be retailed, by means of discrete commodified images, such as stickers, buttons, and armbands, and the exhortation of discrete acts of support from token participation at rallies to *kar seva*.[123] Increasingly, particular kinds of consumption were used to inculcate a different relationship between individuals and the polity, signaled by the introduction of nationwide television programming in the mid-1980s, and to define a new style of citizenship commensurate with this shift.[124]

THE NON-COMMITTED VOTER AND THE RETAILING OF HINDU IDENTITY[125]

BJP leader L. K. Advani, for many years film critic of the RSS's weekly, *Organiser*, understood that to affect perceptions about his party it was not necessary to change the party itself: illusion could do the trick. "For the purpose of securing the non-committed vote," he observed, "you must at least create an illusion that you are likely to come to power."[126] The BJP had now arrived at the center of the political stage, he said, perhaps indicating in his dramaturgical imagery a degree of contrivance under-lying the observation. The BJP was the party of liberalization, he asserted, and as such was suited to assume the reins of power.

We witness here the emergence of a new way of conceiving the political terrain. Advani's comment indicated the importance of choosing a winner over articulating a convincing political vision. The development of voting blocs that migrated in search of a better electoral bargain, as it were, was a departure from the relatively settled voting formations of before.[127] The Nehruvian era witnessed a period of one-party dominance, with parties other than the Congress confined to articulating relatively marginal, sectional interests. Party affiliations were regarded as loyalties; even when they changed, their net effect was understood to leave the existing political cosmos largely unchanged. Advani, in many ways an old-fashioned politician even though instrumental in ushering in a new style of politics, indicated a certain disdain for a constituency for whom illusion could publicly be acknowledged as sufficient lure.

The mission of the Nehruvian state had absorbed all questions of politics into itself, so that the decision before voters reduced to choosing which party was most fit to carry the task of development forward.[128] Any curtailment of liberties by the state was, from this perspective, an investment in the future, as modernization progressed under government auspices. To oppose the state could thus be dubbed anti-modern. As the ability of the state to fulfill its mission diminished, the definition of the national agenda became open to contention. The old verities of politics could not, in these circumstances, be expected to last.

It was in the cultural realm that the turbulence of the transition primarily manifested, as the need to make new events intelligible came up against outdated modes of perception. The growth and extension of markets and media appeared to confirm the obsolescence of old forms of state power, and indeed made it harder for the state to function without refashioning its modes of operation. In this context, Hindu nationalism emerged, appealing to more authoritarian forms of state authority even while it relied on decentralized channels of communication and a more popular base of support. It presented itself as a social and political vanguard although its own agendas were in these matters confused, contradictory, and often anachronistic. But the institution of a new visual regime and the availability of a familiar religio-political idiom permitted consent to be mobilized, and simulated as well. The expanded room for popular participation was made through individual acts of consumption, and religion became the medium through which it was articulated. Retail Hindutva was not manifest only in a range of consumer objects, but as well in the variety of consumption styles, and the range of modes of aesthetic appropriation possible.

A cloth trader and RSS member in Berasia, a small town in Madhya Pradesh, offered a synoptic view of the way in which religion was deployed by the BJP from the 1980s. It was a view that those in New Delhi too might have articulated but were perhaps too wary to share with an inquirer from abroad. "There are two kinds of people associated with the Ram Janmabhumi movement," he said. "There are uneducated people, who are affected by religious feeling. And there are educated people, who are nationalist in their thinking. The intention of the Ram Janmabhumi movement is a nationalist intention."[129] The BJP's purpose was to bring the two together, so that the religious-minded could be educated in a nationalist way of thinking, he said.

If the distinction between "educated" and "uneducated" was too crude and simple a way of referring to a diverse class base, what the remark highlighted nevertheless was the variety of discursive registers at which Hindutva publicity worked. Mechanical as the conception of religion appeared to be in Hindutva theory, an examination of the range of rhetorics through which its mobilization in fact occurred suggested a far more fluid and deft approach. Those making visits to Ayodhya when the movement was in progress could pick up pamphlets seldom seen in New Delhi. In them, innumerable battles were alleged to have been fought over the birthplace of Ram, and described in some detail, with estimates of the thousands of Hindus who had died in the cause over the years, at the hands of Muslim rulers.[130] Paintings arranged "chronologically," in a gallery behind the VHP office in Ayodhya, illustrated highlights from these battles. Paragraph-long captions recounted how devotees of Ram (or the Bajrang Dal of those days, one activist explained to me) would strike at night, attempting to rebuild the temple that the forces of the Mughal emperor Babar would tear down by day. This kind of vivid invocation of "detail" immediately linked earlier events to Hindutva's mission of the moment, making claims to historicity while in fact drawing out and creating popular myths about the birthplace. As against the above, there was literature that was more conservative in its style, arguing about the hurt to national sentiment, the importance of Ram as a national symbol, and the status of the deity as a legal person, demanding restitution of "his" temple. Making copious references to colonial records and legislative acts, with citations of volume, section, and page number, such literature projected an aura of erudition, and while it assumed the validity of faith, relied more on evidentiary claims.[131]

Against the simplistic compartmentalization of the educated and uneducated, or the nationalist and the religious, we can observe the awareness of a range of diverse reading contexts, ranging from the legal-political and jurisprudential to the mytho-poetic and the popular. Readers may themselves place texts against different contexts, of course, and thereby accommodate appeals to the fabulous and to faith as well as to argument and to fact. Not only a variety of commodity-objects and symbolic forms of participation, but as well, a range of modes of aesthetic appropriation or consumption styles were accommodated, thus encompassing a remarkable array of forms of commitment to the movement's cause. We have observed that Hindu nationalism came to prominence by enlarging the ways in which public action could register itself. What was the significance of the expanded modes and spaces of political participation, and of the forms in which Hindutva promoted these?

Retail Hindutva pointed to a greater energy and investment in securing popular participation. The counterpart however was the greater chaos of the public sphere, due both to the greater volume of participation and also to the more authoritarian character of the state, as it assumed a more blatantly partial and aggressive role. The increase in mass participation is often a violent process, accompanying a restructuring of the relationship between political power and its strategies of representation.[132] At the same time, in the short term, this increase, as represented specifically in Hindu nationalism, was, I suggest, an attempt to anticipate and co-opt burgeoning popular energies as their presence swells.

If an earlier ideology of modernization involved an explicit imitation of brahminical rituals, lifestyles, and mores, or Sanskritization, four important developments led to a redefinition of this earlier ideology. First, the rise of intermediate (or, colloquially, "backward") castes as a result of the development process itself, reducing the gap between the more well-to-do sections of these rising caste groups and the upper castes; secondly, the reservation system, leading to a sense of entitlement and privilege arising from different caste positions and to a cultivation and assertion of a range of caste identities; thirdly, the development of communication systems that led to a shift away from classical to more demotic cultural forms, as the forms of communication slowly aligned with the more popular character of the audience; and fourthly, the rise of a consumer culture, catering to classes whose fault lines intersected with rather than simply mimicking caste cleavages, so that implicitly trans-caste identities arose.[133] We may say that the Hindu nationalists offered identities formally free of caste and sect, but that in fact could be filled up by prevailing configurations. More specifically, it offered underdetermined identities, resituating prevailing ritual objects and practices for consumption through appropriate publicity campaigns. Existing caste hierarchies could thereby be projected onto it and repro-duced. At the same time the evidence of hierarchy was idealized, so that difference was not necessarily seen as inequality. Older markers of brahminhood could thus be redefined rather than explicitly rejected. This, I suggest, was the cultural façade of Hindu society attempting to "liberalize" without directly confronting the illiberal ordering of caste.

The commodification of ritual objects potentially rendered them more open and available to appropriation by diverse caste groups, while at the same time, upper-caste retention of the means of cultural produc-tion led to new inscriptions of erstwhile hierarchies. Four crucial fea-tures of the restructured language of ritual can be noted. It abstracted objects, symbols, and practices from existing, rooted networks of belief and practice; they often involved purchase, e.g., of buttons, stickers, flags, saffron armbands, small pots of holy water, coupons contributing to public rituals, e.g., the *shila pujan*; these discrete acts were for public display rather than for worship per se; and they were meant to signal membership in a new group, the public Hindus, or the "political Hindus."[134] The assertion of pre-existing identities, albeit in modified guise, was now offered as a right, and as a form of political participation previously denied. In fact Hindu nationalists were creating a new mode of participation, where access did not necessarily depend on caste status. Instead, in a tautologous mode of reasoning, belonging was defined in terms of a Hindu crowd or mass, one whose growing size was seen to be commensurate with the increasing political strength of the participants.[135]

If new identities were being made available, and individual affiliation could be asserted with all the convenience and ease that Hindu national-ists could make available, nevertheless the fixity and durability of membership was not certain. To take the oath to the saffron flag and to dedicate one's life to organizing Hindu society was one thing. To chant slogans and pay a rupee, to walk along with the crowd for a while or to lay a few bricks, was another. The more uncertain character of recruits acquired through new modes of publicity complemented the volatility in the electoral arena. Working with this situation meant accepting this new uncertainty and utilizing what it made available.

In the 1980s, Hindu religious practices came to be defined for the first time as acts of national citizenship, as existing petty commodity production around Hindu ritual practices was selectively reformulated and consolidated into regional and nationwide markets, and private consumption began to signal membership in a Hindu public. New products came to be available, retail Hindu commodities such as buttons, pamphlets and posters, scarves, shawls, stickers, bricks for the Ram temple, bottled holy water, audio and video cassettes, and viewers' consumption of other media products including Hindu teleserials, which were themselves sold on tape. Securing the interest of small traders, whose incentives were built into their activity, complemented the publicity guaranteed Hindutva by its militant maneuvers and a spectacle-hungry press, and thus opened Hindu nationalism up to a wide audience. At the same time, it signaled an important shift in Hindu nationalist strategy, embracing what the RSS leader Golwalkar had earlier condemned as "today's method of more advertisement than actual work."[136] As political propaganda mimicked the language of advertising, and the social landscape itself became a metaphor for the market, the categories of voter and consumer increasingly began to merge into each other.

The category of the non-committed voter thus indexed the growing reliance on mass media in political mobilization and reflected the closer alignment of the electoral arena with the market.[137] The change in the character of "commitment" of voters and its ostensible tilt towards a politics of religious identity was not a purely discursive shift, nor did it reflect a peculiar propensity of the collective. It was rather a historical shift, one that Walter Benjamin's discussion on the transformation wrought by media helps clarify.[138]

Contemplating works of art in the context of mechanical reproduction, Benjamin focused on the means of reproduction as the material basis for tracking and understanding the cultural shift to modernity, and thereby connected questions of media and representation directly to politics. Central to his argument, which is built around changing perceptions of art with mass reproduction, is the loss of what he calls the "aura" of the art object, due to its now infinite reproducibility. With the loss of the aura, the ritual space of the art object is no longer singular or unique, but is desacralized, and the power of tradition must now pass through the filter of mass perception. He relates this loss to the disenchantment of the world, but argues, at the same time, that the rise of new forms of politics can be understood as its consequence. He describes these new forms generically, and disparagingly, as the aestheticization of politics, i.e., the deflection of mass politics from economic transformation to mere self-expression.[139] Writing in the 1930s, he was of course referring to German fascism, and he pointed to the Nazis' skillful uses of new technologies, specifically the cinema, to illustrate his point.

Here it is useful to try and clarify the significance Benjamin attributes to the aura.[140] If aura, described as the "unique appearance of a distance, however close it may be," is only intelligible from a certain separation, reproductive technology appears to abolish that distance. If it does so, it simultaneously abolishes the uniqueness of ritual objects, which can be understood as abolishing the very notion of unapproachability, Benjamin argues.[141] The perception of the artwork's distance does not in fact disappear; rather, its meaning is transformed. From being something apparently fixed, it becomes perceived as variable, and dependent on particular, contingent technologies. Does this mean that this notion of aura, or singularity, disappears, or does its meaning simply change?

If we specify the coordinates within which this transformation of meaning occurs, we can say that the imagined space of communication changes from a vertical to a horizontal one, from one where the aura is endorsed by divinity to one where its meaning is sanctioned more explicitly within society. If earlier the aura existed in the context of tradition and religious belief, it is publicity itself that now largely constitutes the significance of the event. Whereas publicity earlier had connotations of inherited right or priestly sanction, it now refers to the approval of the people, and to the authority of their sanction.

The technology of publicity is thus perceived to be social, even democratic, rather than divine. The institution of a visual regime through television is thus a means of staging this new kind of authority and of giving it form and meaning. But the demystification of publicity does not necessarily result in a unilateral, collective loss of religious belief. Rather, religion may provide an important symbolic system for a community, while the beliefs underwriting it may become more plural and usually more private. Television programs such as the Ramayan serial can thus augur the transition to a more fully market-dominated society, pointing to the harmony of an ideal past while offering a technology for maneuvering through the conflicting interests of a discordant present. As a mode of inducting the masses into public life, however, it is deeply contentious, as the character of religious identities is fought out between aspirants to equality and the upholders of hierarchy, and the mutual toleration of religious groups is tested. If "the state rests on ethical sentiment, and that on the religious,"[142] multi-religious societies such as India clearly face the most prolonged conflicts in resolving the problems that arise in this wake.

Walter Benjamin argued that the logical result of fascism was the introduction of aesthetics into politics: the right of the masses to change property relations was replaced by the opportunity to express themselves. His argument is misleading in its assumption of a transparent revolutionary politics where the true and the good coincide, as opposed to aestheticized politics. The challenge is rather to identify the new cultural forms of politics as they arise, and discern the varieties of agenda they may be made to serve.

The entry of aesthetics into politics expands and simultaneously channels the possibility for self-expression, and works to orchestrate the collective expression of this desire. In Hindu nationalism during this period self-expression was oppositional in its lived meanings, and harnessed the memories of "otherness" in community as means of resistance to oppression. The ceaseless emphasis on mobilization and performance, whether in kar seva or in riots, was both a sign and an outcome of the contradictions coiled within communal politics, between individual expression and a coercive political regime, between the claims to community and the stereotyping of the "other" through which community was realized.

With the meager legitimacy accorded to state institutions, however, coercion and the violence of communal assertion could not issue from centralized apparatuses of government in any direct or explicit manner. In the context of the growing crisis of political institutions, the ideological charge of liberalization and the boost given to private, market forces assisted in the entrepreneurialization of social function. The familiar notion of the edifices of the state at work, then, had now to reckon with the informal character of centralization, dispersed in the quieter, more inconspicuous and so less culpable forces of voluntary initiative. Thus organized and systematic communal violence could be inflicted by scattered and nameless rioters, striking terror all the more effectively for their apparently spontaneous mob action. Thus state extortion of income and bureaucratic rent-seeking themselves became shrouded in mystery as they re-appeared in the guise of a stock market collapse shortly after the mosque's demolition, with a long bullish trend successfully engineered to lure millions from hapless small investors.[143] The seemingly chaotic character of the violence, and the diffuse signs of its origins, testified to a form of governmental power that worked in a distinct fashion. Rather than provoke a call to get the state "off the people's backs" for instance, the sense of lawless violence generated a sentiment in favor of authoritarian solutions.[144]

From its inception, the RSS had aimed at conducting a far-reaching, long-term program of building a universalist national "brotherhood" insulated from the vagaries of the marketplace and the fickleness of electoral democracy. The move to retailing Hindu identity declared an intention to seek and build on far more partial forms of support, with the explicit aim of securing political power. The taste of power at the center during the Janata government, an awareness that the BJP could benefit in comparison to the Congress's relatively timid and spasmodic use of the Hindu card, as well as a keen sense that in the current political conjuncture, there were few strong contenders to oppose its quest for power, were among the factors combining to instigate this important shift.

The harnessing of the circuits of commodity power, however, entailed a certain vulnerability to the rhythms of market cycles, and the need to bolster demand by keeping alive the political promises of Hindutva. As Advani remarked, "For the purpose of securing the non-committed vote, you must at least create an illusion that you are likely to come to power." When the illusion was revealed as such, and the seemingly unstoppable momentum of its political purveyors was checked, the identification of the images and symbols of retail Hindutva with its political proponents could loosen. Liberalization could proceed with its re-organization of public and private spaces in ways that were articulated to the Hindu nationalists' political project but not necessarily identical with it. Late capitalism's attempts to revitalize itself thus demonstrated an eruption of the contradictions of community onto the stage of capital, and an effort to harness these contradictions in furthering accumulation.

I have demonstrated the reliance of Hindu nationalist appeals on consumer images, and I have argued that these appeals depended on and worked through the media. It remains to assess the electronic media's functioning, in terms of the institutional underpinnings of television, and the broad outlines of the symbolic backdrop created by the telecast of the Ramayan serial, against which the movement unfolded. The next chapter examines the imbrication of languages of community and of democratic politics, through the contradictory workings of the televisual form.

CHAPTER 2

Prime time religion[1]

Speaking at a gathering of the Virat Hindu Sammelan (Mammoth Hindu Assembly), one of the guests of honor, Ramanand Sagar, spoke of his work as the maker (producer-director-script writer) of the Ramayan serial.[2] All he had done was to take a cloth, he said, and wipe the dust off the old treasures everyone knew about, but had lately ignored. That had been the extent of his role, he concluded modestly. That was how the Ramayan serial should be perceived, he was saying, as a reminder of a forgotten presence. Its production was therefore a simple matter, requiring no thought or skill, he implied. Sagar's humility notwithstanding, his statement said something interesting about television: even when depicting something as contrived as a pre-historic epic, the medium could be treated as transparent, and as having no effect of its own. The politically charged decision to broadcast a mythological serial on a government medium, at a time when Hindu–Muslim relations had been wracked by violence,[3] and Sagar's own decision to offer an obscurantist rendition of the narrative, at times reinforcing themes of the VHP's own campaign (see below), receded in his homely explanation. The salient event appeared rather to be that of story telling, his modesty reflecting in its own way the importance of the teller, in a society where television was still a recent arrival.

The BJP's mobilization of the Ram temple movement resembled Sagar's presentation of the Ramayan serial, in its denial of its own novelty, and in its assurance that the sense of recognition it evoked was spurred by events of the distant past. To champion the issue now was therefore nothing more than a public-spirited act, and proof of the disinterested character of its publicists. The serial was sponsored by a Congress-led government, in the hope that its flagging electoral fortunes might be revived with an infusion of "Hindu vote," votes inspired by Hindu solidarity and its attendant exclusions. But in doing so the Congress demonstrated an overly mechanistic conception of televisual effect, together with a failure to muster the organizational strength required to capitalize on the serial's popularity, to say nothing of its own waning political credibility. It was the BJP, hardly a significant electoral force when the serial began in January 1987, that seized the opportunity afforded by the serial, and thereafter established itself as a major national party, one that no future ruling party or coalition could afford to ignore.

The serial's broadcast violated a Nehruvian taboo, of the secular and non-partisan status of government institutions, in this case of Doordarshan, the government-controlled television system. The government's avoidance of religious imagery had aimed to secure a modern democracy that ruled irrespective of caste or creed. Beyond a privileged urban middle class, however, the failure of independence to deliver the majority from the indignities of want and from what was perceived as arbitrary rule signaled the exclusion of the majority from effective political life. This gave room for attributing religion's absence to politics itself, i.e., to the corruptions of politics and to the unredeemed nature of the political sphere (see chapter three). Given the essentially overlapping claims of religion and politics, in their envisioning of ethical life based on prescribed modes of conduct, the slippery status of the religious in public life could not, in these circumstances, be indefinitely controlled by state injunctions of one kind or another.[4] The weekly broadcast of popular serials like the Ramayan thus inaugurated a new era not only in television but in politics as well, with the popularity of these serials allowing the ambivalent status of religion to be exploited, and to sanction Hindu nationalist initiatives in the name of the people.

Television was a long time in coming to India. It was only during the 1975–77 National Emergency that experiments were carried out in satellite broadcasting (S.I.T.E., or Satellite Instructional Television Experiment) for nationwide telecasts, and the first moves were made towards systematic testing of the programming aimed at the majority population.[5] The problem of developing attractive programming that served government interests at the same time was, however, not susceptible of quick solution.[6] But a communication channel was developed that bypassed the independent print news media. The experience of the Emergency had proven the impracticality of propaganda conceived without regard to its audience, and served as a reminder that the majority could still withhold its consent. The case of Doordarshan was of course similar.[7] But the need to synchronize different circuits coming together at the institutional locus of television, of economy (through advertising), polity (in terms of the ruling party and different pressure groups contending for airtime), and culture, entailed an immensely complex task in its overhauling.

Meanwhile, external developments competing for the public time that Doordarshan was squandering, i.e., other means of communication such as audio and video cassettes, and satellite television channels, loomed large.[8] Realizing that it would soon be presiding over an empty fortress, rendering its broadcasting monopoly irrelevant, "outside talent" began to be engaged to ensure that at least some programs were watchable. The opening up of Doordarshan began in small, regulated steps on Doordarshan in tandem with Rajiv Gandhi's New Economic Policy, with the introduction of commercially sponsored programming for a few hours every day. The idea of airing "national epics" was conceived in this context, as a way of using the medium to draw on pre-existing culture and enlarge television's audience.

In this chapter, I will discuss the key meanings made available by the broadcast of the Ramayan serial, first in terms of the institutional circumstances in which it was telecast, and in terms of the reformulation of an epic tradition. If television created a new representational field, we cannot tell what representations arose without a discussion of the specific messages circulated, within the historical context of their making. In this sense, the Ramayan became the medium within which a new set of political opportunities came to be articulated; and, as I hope to show, the difficulty of perceiving their novelty was itself crucial in expanding the possibilities presented by the communicational environment.

I have argued that Hindu nationalism came to prominence in the context of economic reforms and through the expansion of the market accomplished by liberalization. The Ramayan serial in a sense joined these events together in the medium of its communication, swiveling between the lost utopia summoned by Hindu nationalists and the brave new world promised by them and by market enthusiasts alike. Audiences then experienced two events traveling in different directions, liberalization, as a portent of things to come, symbolized in the newly visible wealth of consumer goods, and the Ramayan serial, harkening back to a golden age. They were in a sense hinged together by television, as a device that brought past and future together while itself oscillating between time zones in a kind of eternal present.

If a thing must first be imagined in order for it to exist, what television edges closer to the collective consciousness is the machinery of imagination, and the productive character of this machinery, distinct from the phenomena it reflects and transmits. The images and the things they represent and refer to, the products they move, and the persons they are borne and reshaped by, now exist in a circuit coiled across society. There is a two-way process of change here, affecting both the dominant culture television is institutionally located in, and the wider society. But if things are no longer in their "proper" places, how are they now to be understood? If what used to be familiar can now be an effect of the most novel, does the commonsense of social causation change so quickly? If the old retains some of the aura and sanctity of age, to what extent is this a reliable memory, and to what extent is it a trick of perception? It is in tracing and assessing this uncertainty, following the event of television, that we can begin to determine its political effects.

STATE SPONSORSHIP IN THE COMMERCE OF IMAGES[9]

The career of television in the developing world has for the most part begun late, relative to the West.[10] Those who write about non-Western television, not only in scholarly volumes but also in the popular media, are usually familiar with it from elsewhere. The appraisals it receives are those of a knowing eye. The first chapters of its history are already written; the medium comes with a prepared script in a sense that goes beyond the usual arguments of media imperialism. The latter focus on direct control of software or of media corporations, and point to Western interests being served by institutions and images endorsing the West's eminence. What requires notice though is how the imagination is blunted in apprehending a transplanted technology's distinctive history. If the postcolonial developmentalist state is the modernizing agent, the nation is the heterogeneous object of its efforts, at best partially modern. A modernizing state presumes an illiberal form of power, since liberal freedoms cannot be allowed to those who are not yet modern. However, liberal norms tend to dominate discussions of media in postcolonial societies, deriving from a particular interpretation of Western experience.[11] Theory is the rule and practice the exception, Marx has written, in discussions of civil society.[12] Since the fit between civil society in the West and unevenly developed societies elsewhere is partial, such an approach is doubly unequipped to answer the increasingly complex questions posed by scrambled social formations with hybrid genealogies. Overarching these issues and interfused with them is the distinct character of politics in the context of a postcolonial developmentalist state.

The representative (democratic) character of the state in postcolonial societies was sharply qualified by its leading "developmental" role, in those cases where the state did take on such a role. The state assumed the responsibility of organizing a field of meanings to empower its drive towards modernity, so that whatever was residual could be defined as foreign to the national character. If the postcolonial developmentalist state presented itself as modernizing society, it was pre-eminently in terms of economic development; the development of other spheres was presumed to follow from this. Culture was therefore accorded a low priority in developmental activity. Broadcasting, of course, squarely addressed the cultural sphere, but beyond curbing negative publicity, and airing films and film music, little was done. The Minister of Information and Broadcasting once argued that if they stopped showing films, people would shut off their TV sets, thereby conceding that no one watched Doordarshan's own programs.[13] The establishment of the planned economy exemplified the separation of the developmental mission from popular will. Policy experts in the Planning Commission decreed the appropriate allocation of national resources, in a language removed from the euphemisms of liberal discourse, appealing rather to strictly technocratic considerations. At the same time, the social relations of production were often pre-capitalist in nature, involving caste and kin networks, such as the hereditary domination of particular groups. Partha Chatterjee has pithily described the resulting contradiction in terms of "rational planning" complemented by "irrational politics" (in the Weberian sense), which are but two faces of the same process. Moreover the irrational character of the politics periodically required the intervention of the state, which was then legitimized to the victims of such processes as a rescuer from above.[14]

But if rational planning was the norm of functioning for state institutions, in practice it was hardly possible to erect an impermeable barrier from the irrational politics they engaged in. It was rather the *idea* of rational planning that was presented, and whose image had to be protected. The institutions themselves were creatures of their environment, "embedded bureaucracies" whose actors brought with them the values and interests of their class, and thus might compromise policy implementation from the very start.[15] Ad hocism tended to be the means by which implementation proceeded, so that the exercise of authority was arbitrary even if its desired image was rational.

In this context, radio and television helped stage the ceremony of leaders at work, giving off the impression of rationality as it were. Since the ruling party itself best perceived what was rational, it was under their control that the media were considered safe. Meanwhile, communication policy tended to be uncoordinated, with different departments fighting turf battles. Several government departments had their own communication systems, such as the Defense Ministry, the Space Research Organisation, the Ministries of Human Resources Development, Agriculture, Information and Broadcasting, and so on, each operating on its own, and overlapping or clashing with the communications systems of the other. The lack of coordination characterized even departments within the Ministry of Information and Broadcasting, where All India Radio, Doordarshan, the Field Publicity Organisation, the Directorate of Advertising and Visual Publicity tended to compete rather than cooperate with each other.[16]

Sovereignty rather than efficiency was the ground of state retention of its monopoly over the airwaves. The idea of independent broadcasting was always resisted on the grounds that the developmental task of the media could not be ensured without the state at the helm; the position of successive ruling parties on the question of autonomy for radio and TV has wavered between reluctance and refusal.[17] The media were to provide "education, information and entertainment," and under government control they were assumed to be fulfilling those functions. If control over the media was retained for purposes of propaganda, some curiosity about the efficacy of broadcasts might have been expected. However, audience research was disregarded;[18] it was no secret that for years few people watched much other than the films or the sequences of film songs screened a few times a week. But as long as the government retained a monopoly over the broadcasting apparatus, this did not appear to matter. If in the U.S., the media are often held as a mirror to society, it might be said that Doordarshan offered a mirror to the state's official aspect, presenting it as it wished to be seen.[19] In practice, this meant that the political party and the leaders in power at any given time were presented making speeches, cutting ribbons, presiding over parades, and deliberating at meetings. The purely self-referential character of broadcasting was confirmed by the negligence shown towards the issue of viewership. Community receivers were poorly funded and, after the Sixth Plan, ceased to be mentioned at all in Plan documents. Most sets were privately owned, and their number, although steadily increasing, suggested viewing was by a minority: 2.8 million in 1983, 13.2 million in 1987, and between 42 and 47 million in 1994.[20]

The Indian Constitution makes no mention of broadcasting, and there is no enforceable legislation guarding the public interest, one former official declared; as such, there is no broadcasting policy, she concluded.[21] The All India Radio (AIR) Code, adopted in 1968 and revised in 1970, which applies to Doordarshan as well, forbade hostile criticism of various entities, including any state government, political party, religion or community, the judiciary, and friendly countries. Designed for political safety rather than public service, it offered no positive commitments against which broadcasting institutions could be held accountable.[22] Litigation over representations of issues usually appealed rather to the fundamental rights of citizens. In this context, the government view of the character of broadcasting authority was stated in a 1986 court case. In that case, Supreme Court advocate Indira Jaising filed a writ petition challenging Doordarshan's deletion of certain views expressed by her in an interview broadcast on the controversial Muslim Women's Bill, then pending before Parliament.[23] The central government and Doordarshan contended that there was no right to free speech on television, and that Article Nineteen of the Constitution, which guarantees free speech, did not apply to TV programs. This was rejected by Justice Sujata Manohar of the Bombay High Court, who observed that not a single authority in law was cited by the government counsel, G. K. Nilkanth, in support of his "somewhat alarming proposition." Doordarshan was ordered to telecast the program again with Ms. Jaising's comments in their entirety.[24] But court orders notwithstanding, the government counsel's defense suggested a conception of operating procedure far removed from any defense of citizens' rights.

Broadcasting's principal objective, then, was tautologous, i.e., to display and enact government control over a state institution. The Ministry for Information and Broadcasting was thus an important one, invariably awarded to key figures; for some years Mrs. Gandhi retained the position herself, and when the Janata Party came to power in 1977, Jan Sangh leader L. K. Advani assumed the post. At the same time, however, the bulk of funding went for expansion of infrastructure, and programming itself was paid scant regard. Together with numerous problems such as a low correlation between skills and posting, and between performance and reward, this combined to create an organization unequipped to attract audiences.[25] The Director of Audience Research for All India Radio conceded that in the absence of "basic data," broadcasting over radio and television was repetitive in its themes, overly general, and hardly relevant to people's needs.[26] Little serious thought was given to questions of software, and broadcasting was carried on as a purely engineering affair.

One former broadcasting official observed: "Much time is spent in putting up transmitters, building and equipping studios (all on standardized pattern without reference to specialized programme requirements) but no thought is given to the programmes which are to be broadcast from these centres. The entire machinery is upside down."[27] The maintenance of autonomy was thus not only an empty exercise, but given the spread of video, cable, and satellite broadcasting, destined to become irrelevant. It was perhaps inevitable then that independent programming services would eventually be sought.

The attempt to assume a positive role in regard to programming meant not only evolving appropriate cultural forms but also working through the distinct nature of broadcasting media, rather than simply grafting pre-existing ones (such as films) onto a new medium. The first effort in this direction was the so-called "pro-development soap opera," with the 1984–85 serial *Hum Log* (We People) being the prototype, initiated at the instance of then-Secretary of Information and Broadcasting S. S. Gill. Attempting to mix education in entertainment, the experiment had its inspiration in the Latin American telenovela. A Peruvian soap opera, *Simplemente Maria* (Simply Mary), modeled on entrepreneurial and pro-social ideas, had been released in 1969 and had led to numerous imitations in Mexico and elsewhere.[28] The idea of "mixing entertainment with education" was, in the words of one group of proponents, a "win-win" situation, offering the prospect of profit-making along with education.[29] But although *Hum Log* ran for seventeen months, it was as a family drama that it retained sponsors and viewers, with "developmental" messages jettisoned within a few weeks.[30] One more attempt ensued in 1991, *Hum Raahi* (Co-Travelers), which also earned substantial ratings but was described by its script-writer as "just entertainment."[31]

Commercially sponsored programs began to be commissioned, beginning in 1984 and increasing thereafter, in a move that itself appears to have emerged ad hoc rather than as a planned event.[32] Proposals for scripts were invited from independent producers, and a list of preferred topics was made available; programs could be submitted for Doordarshan's approval. This repeats the pattern noted by Pranab Bardhan: as the process of development gets under way, the developmental role of the state shifts to one of regulation. Typically, this is because development strengthens new groups who are able to influence or impede state functioning. Bureaucrats then seek to exercise control through regulation, acknowledging their increasing inability to occupy the commanding heights of the economy.[33] Producers would in effect submit work to Doordarshan's censorship, so that bureaucrats were rendered ringmasters over a substantial portion of popular culture, as talent flowed in from the film industry and financing from commercial sponsors. For a few crucial years, roughly between 1984, when the licensing system for radio and TV sets was discontinued, and 1992, when satellite TV began to make its impact, the state not only had a virtual monopoly over television programming, but for the first time also had access to programmers who could actually win audiences. Politically, this represented a rare opportunity to set cultural agenda. Significantly, it was in this context that serialized versions of Hindu epics, the Ramayana and the Mahabharata, were made, commissioned by the bureaucrat who oversaw the historic expansion of Doordarshan transmission across the country (see below).[34]

It is the effort rather than its success or failure per se that illuminates the intended political role of broadcasting. In this context, mythological serials must be seen as a successor to the pro-development soap opera. This is rarely recognized; more often, the former are understood as a product of political opportunism and mercenary zeal, and the latter are seen as a more or less defunct category. The pro-development soap opera espoused a relationship between political authority and genre explicitly conceded at the level of policy, with television used as a tool to bend minds in the requisite direction. With mythological serials the same candor did not last, nor the same clarity, because a certain expediency influenced the choice. But the concession to local culture could be seen as a virtue. Thus the official proposal for the serialization of the Ramayana and the Mahabharata stated: "Ramayan is not only a great epic of Himalayan dimensions, it is also a repository of our social and moral values . . . The real challenge . . . lies in seeing this immortal epic with the eyes of a modern man and relating its message to the spiritual and emotional needs of our age." It also stressed the importance of the epic's "contemporary relevance for the human condition."[35] This was a contradictory phrase that could underwrite a projection of the present as a timeless condition, as well as filter the epic's account of the past according to latter-day convenience. In the case of the Ramayan serial, both these aspects were to be seen. In a shared past, behind and above latter-day divisions, a glorified image of national identity emerged in saffron colors, as a Hindu heritage that had been prepared for the modern age well ahead of time. Wise kings devoted to their people, animated by the highest spiritual motives, and sponsoring scientific research for national security, had worked to make the country great, creating a history whose example to the present could hardly be exaggerated, in the account presented in these serials (see below). India had always had "pro-development" rulers, it appeared.

Three factors in particular influenced the institutional context of the decision to broadcast prime time religion: the difficulty of maintaining private–public divisions on the scale required in the context of electronic media; the institutional insulation of broadcasting from political pressures; and the Nehruvian legacy of secularism. Given the volume and velocity of image flows set in motion with electronic capitalism and the new conjuncture represented by liberalization, it is unlikely that the *cordon sanitaire* between "community" and "secular" life could have been maintained for long, even if the precise way in which it was breached made all the difference. Within the commerce of images itself, we observe the tendency of the rate of return to fall, and the imperative to seek new sources of value. Resorting to religious and community culture draws not only from those spheres' own considerable affective power, but their status of semi-exclusion from the public realm affords a surplus charge, as a quasi-forbidden pleasure. Regarding the political institution of broadcasting, state institutions perforce relied on expediency, in ad hoc responses to the complex combinations of pre-capitalist and capitalist cultures they had to engage with. Under such circumstances, existing political authority could interfuse independent institutions and bend them to its will. It was perhaps a matter of time before the Nehruvian etiquette of an earlier generation of bureaucrats and politicians gave way to the resort to more particularist forms of communication, although just how these would manifest was not foreseeable. This brings us to the Nehruvian legacy itself, and the desire to preserve a minimally neutral ground in a society with plural castes and creeds, going around rather than through the complex differences of the different communities, and establishing a political meeting ground removed from these; this was in fact the *modus vivendi* of Nehruvian secularism.[36]

The secular Nehruvian demand to exclude religion from programming assumed, of course, the possibility of separating and compartmentalizing it from the rest of existing art and culture. A former Director-General of All India Radio noted that while this was possible with, say, Bombay film music, most older works could not be easily

classified in this way. Thus he noted the difficulty of finding songs that
could be divorced from the creed that inspired them.[37] A series of
makeshift rules evolved to deal with the problem. The public celebrations of festivals of all communities were covered; and on important
religious occasions, special programs of religious music were broadcast.
Until 1942, weekly religious broadcasts on particular days were maintained at various radio stations. In Delhi, for instance, there were
Islamic programs every Friday and Hindu programs every Tuesday,
and so on. The official policy however, was that religious programs
should be avoided as far as possible, formalized in a 1942 Station
Directors' Conference. This meant that religious broadcasts on fixed
days of the week were thereafter ruled out.[38] However, beginning in
the mid-1950s, the first transmission in the morning began to be devoted to a half hour of devotional music, intended to represent all
religious communities; in practice, it was music in praise of particular
Hindu deities that dominated. A seminar organized by All India Radio
in the mid-1960s on the issue of communalism recommended canceling the prayer in its prevailing form. The National Integration Council,
asked to consider this recommendation, chose not to make a judgment
on the matter.[39] The daily recital of Tulsidas's *Ram Charitmanas* from all
stations in the Hindi belt was a practice that began during the Emergency in 1975. The I&B Ministry, headed at the time by V. C. Shukla,
defended the practice saying that the *Ram Charitmanas* was "folk culture" rather than religion. When the Janata Party came to power after
the Emergency, the new I&B Minister, L. K. Advani, had no objection
to the *Manas* broadcasts. The feature therefore remained.[40] The political character of programming was in this sense explicit: a program was
seldom incidentally Hindu or Muslim but rather intended as such.

If an awkward, serial emphasis on religious identity was a way to
plead impartiality before a diverse audience, the language policy revealed a clearer bias. This was one in favor of the Sanskritization of
Hindi, which was envisioned as becoming the sole national language
over time; this meant moving away from the spoken Hindustani and the
Urdu script, which derived more from Persian and Arabic, and shifting
to the Devanagari script. That the move would be most sharply registered amongst Muslims was not lost on the nationalists in favor of
Sanskritization.[41] To Sanskritize the language of state, in its legislative
acts and pronouncements, its press releases and school textbooks was
one thing; to ensure intelligibility with a wider public was another.
There emerged what has been called Hindi diglossia, with a more

complex "high" form superposed over the primary dialect of the language.[42] The high form derives its words from Sanskrit while syntactic and semantic structures are often from the English language. In contrast, colloquial Hindi may borrow words from English, while other aspects of language use are themselves closer to pre-existing forms. What results is a structural and functional compartmentalization, reproducing the contradiction of what I have called a split public (see chapter four), with colloquial Hindi dominating in spheres of informal use.

Early on, experiments in "pure," i.e. Sanskritized, Hindi drama by Bhartendu Harishchandra and others had proven unable to attract audiences, even if the plays themselves were deemed artistically meritorious, because in fact the spoken language of most northern Indians was closer to Urdu.[43] In-house AIR and Doordarshan programming tended to use Sanskritized language as well, and its Hindi was criticized for its distance from spoken language, and its resulting unintelligibility.[44] The lack of popular understanding, however, proved no deterrent.[45] Indeed popularity could be seen as threatening. Thus in 1952 the broadcast of film music was banned on All India Radio, as the Minister of Information and Broadcasting, B. V. Keskar, who held office between 1952 and 1960, regarded it as vulgar and dominated by Muslim rather than Hindu culture. It was decided to popularize classical music instead. The principal result was to shift audiences from AIR to Radio Ceylon and Radio Pakistan, where programs of film music were made available. Finally in 1957, film music was re-introduced, in an all-India variety program, *Vividh Bharati*, resulting in audiences gradually returning to AIR, while the program itself lengthened to span most of the daytime period.[46]

This is the context in which the decision to air serialized mythological epics must be situated. The decision represented an important departure from previous practice in three respects. At a fixed time every week, there would be a program marked by the symbols of a particular community. The broadcast was to a nationwide audience, not to a local or regional one. And, by rendering it in a format meant for a general audience, Hindu programming was now being offered not as part of some quota system, but identified with culture in general, not limited to particular festival days, stations, or communities.[47]

The Ramayan was the show that definitively established the Delhi-centered, Hindi language medium across the country's diverse population: a serialized version of one of the world's oldest epics, featuring prominent gods and goddesses of the Hindu pantheon. It drew huge crowds every week. Audience research estimates compiled by market research companies climbed from 40 million to 80 million viewers per week over a few months. City streets and marketplaces were empty on Sunday mornings. Events advertised for Sundays were careful to mention: "To be held after Ramayan." Crowds gathered around every wayside television set, though few could have seen much on the small black and white sets with so many present. Engine drivers were reported to depart from their schedules, stopping their trains at stations en route if necessary, in order to watch. All of this represented something more than a merely popular TV show. The Rama story belonged to the public domain, it seemed: the constraints of the workplace and the imperatives of commerce, usually pre-eminent, gave way to the authority of the weekly broadcast. At the same time, the sponsorship of the serial was clearly a profit-making enterprise; the show itself had twenty-minute periods of commercials before and after it.

For Doordarshan, the serial represented a breakthrough in a number of ways. It succeeded in achieving high viewership across linguistically diverse regions and extended the audience beyond anything previously achieved.[48] The show made Sunday mornings, previously a "soft" spot on the television schedule, into advertising prime time, earning nearly $40 million in revenue for Doordarshan every week, a record at the time. At the same time, the new medium acquired a legitimacy that had never been envisaged, as a potential source of "moral entertainment." The serial's success came after the genre of mythological films, which used to dominate the Hindi film industry's output, had virtually disappeared, and its decline was accepted as final by Bombay film makers, although regional language channels continued to screen them. Explanations about the perennial popularity of mythologicals were therefore incomplete. Vijay Bhatt's *Ram Rajya* (1943) and Babubhai Mistry's 1961 *Sampoorna Ramayan* were films that succeeded as musical dramas; this time around, the story was being told rather differently, in a more devotional vein.[49]

Retroactively, after the screening of the Ramayan, Hindu myths and rituals began to be declared as legitimately belonging to the public arena, inviting the participation of one and all in their commemoration and re-enactment. The popularity of the serial was seen, after the fact, as sufficient to silence any criticism of the state's involvement in defining public culture. One prominent civil servant, however, supported the Ramayan serial explicitly, in a significant intervention in the issue. In a 1988 op. ed. piece, S. S. Gill, who had recently retired as Secretary to the Ministry of Information and Broadcasting, explained his reasons for commissioning the tele-epic. Writing as the main body of the serial was soon to conclude, he defended the broadcast, squarely identifying the Ramayan with the national-popular. The serial's success with viewers was thus presented as a challenge to any attempt that would maintain the secular as a kind of rarefied zone:

Ramayan is basically a secular epic which portrays a bewildering range of human relationships and socio-political situations. Its enduring appeal lies in the strength of its story-line and the delineation of its epic characters . . . It is this unique combination of a gripping plot of cosmic dimensions teeming with hordes of sharply delineated characters, and its ingenious use as a vehicle for articulating the major individual and societal issues of abiding concern from an essentially humanistic and ethical standpoint that explains the hold of Ramayan on the Hindu psyche . . .

In his search for an expressive metaphor to symbolise a welfare state of his dreams, Gandhiji could do no better than think of Ram Raj. You go to the countryside and see how frequently Ramayan is quoted in the commerce of daily life. You take away Ramayan from the consciousness of the Hindus and you leave them socially and morally maimed. And despite Ramayan having permeated every pore and fibre of our culture and served as bulwark of our social morality, our intellectuals cry wolf when this epic is televised as a serial by Doordarshan and describe it as an attempt to pander to the majority communalism . . . It is interesting to note that liberal Hindus feel quite embarrassed and guilty about the preponderance of their community in the Indian population . . . But the fact of the matter is that the Hindus do constitute 83 percent of the country's population . . . [B]y and large Indian ethos is predominantly Hindu and Ramayan is its centre-piece.[50]

Beginning with the argument that the Ramayan is universalist and humanist, Gill proceeded to describe it as essentially Hindu, and then to say that India itself is essentially Hindu. He attributed the Ramayan's power successively to its plot and characters, its values, and its omnipresence; Gandhi's ideal of Ram Raj, here defined as a "welfare state," was held to confirm this importance. Disagreement could only spring from liberal guilt, or from minorities, who were in any case outnumbered, he suggested, in an argument that resisted falsification. Political uses of the serial were not to be blamed on Doordarshan, he asserted. The reference was to the star of the show, Arun Govil, campaigning as Ram during the previous year, and promising Ram Rajya on behalf of the Congress Party.[51] Gill was critical of the producer-director Ramanand Sagar's serialization; he condemned its promotion of superstition and obscurantism as "contrary to the original guidelines." "There was really no need to seek the support of cheap devices to enhance its popularity," he wrote. The popularity of the serial appeared as the last word in the argument, used not to condemn the uneducated majority, as it would have done for B. V. Keskar (see above) but as conclusive proof of the serial's worth.[52]

Gill's strategic use of the idea of popularity trumped any criticisms pertaining to the political sphere. His argument sharply poses the problem of how to understand a narrative tradition such as the Ramayan, time-honored and ubiquitous as it is, while retaining the ability to make critical judgments regarding its selection and staging. Received understandings of the tradition may bear little relation to its actual uses; considering how its component parts are brought together helps clarify questions of the tradition's meaning and influence. Inquiring into questions of genre and issues of narrative structuring, I suggest, can help us begin to comprehend the situated practices whereby the Ramayan's popularity was acquired.

SITUATING CONTEMPORARY USES OF AN EPIC TRADITION

Scholarly approaches to the study of the Ramayana may be broadly divided into three categories – textual, historicist, and culturalist. These approaches understand the epic, respectively, in terms of its narrative characteristics, in terms of the historical context of its composition, and in terms of the culture in which it is located. There is a fourth approach of somewhat more recent provenance, which, foregrounding the diversity of the Ramayana tradition, examines one or more of its constituent parts, and its subcultural meanings and uses. There is no single approach or method to be distilled from this breadth of scholarship; my interest is rather in crafting an access route to analyzing the Ramayan television serial.

Works cannot be understood exclusively in terms of the historical conditions in which they are produced; this is particularly true of works of exceptional power. The Ramayana, for instance, has been thought to describe the contrast between a hunter-gatherer and a settled pastoral society, and to be in effect a tract announcing the emergent institution of kingship. These may be important factors in the formation of the work, as for instance Romila Thapar has suggested.[53] But if these features entirely determined it, the work would have mainly archival interest to those in subsequent ages. Sometimes, works may lift themselves out of the specific historical domain within which they were conceived, or may gain in importance over time as new meanings accrete, adding not only to its understanding but as well to the aura of the work. The Ramayana plainly belongs in this group, living in what Bakhtin has called *great time*.[54] Great time transcends the moment of its origin, but is not for that reason beyond history. Rather, its significance lies precisely in the centuries it accumulates and in the meanings and resonances it captures through this passage of time.

The difficulty in discussing the Ramayana is that we are not referring to a single literary work, whose semantic depths are progressively explored, unveiling strata of meaning previous eras were blind to.[55] Rather, it refers to an extraordinarily broad range of texts and performative traditions, from devotional Vaishnavite re-tellings, to Buddhist and Jaina variations, to political propaganda, to folkloric domestications of a high classical form, and beyond. Even if it is Valmiki's text that is placed at the origin of the tradition, as scholars have tended to do until recently, the textual details of this version are less well known than the basic story line. If we wish to argue for Valmiki's formative influence, we may still be compelled to depart from a notion of the text as a defined corpus. What we have rather is a narrative skeleton and a moral ethos, and it is these if anything that get reproduced, criticized, amended, and sometimes inverted by successive authors and in various art forms.[56] The procedure of locating a founding author and an *ur*-text in literary explication is in any case only *one*, albeit influential, philological tradition, imbued with historically specific understandings of the nature of texts, audiences, and the institution of authorship. In the case of the Mahabharata, "the other" Indian epic, the frustration experienced by scholars in their life-long attempts to separate the "core" text from what one or another of them considered interpolations was noted with amusement by the philosopher Matilal; "[P]eeling off onion skins does not lead to any core, as we all know," he observed.[57] If we regret that a comparable degree of difficulty did not attend the work of Ramayana scholars, we should note that in both cases, a fixation on the idea of an epic nucleus has tended to detract from the significance and uses of its embodied manifestations. At least some of the mystery surrounding the centuries of popular fascination with the story can therefore be attributed to scholars' own mystification of the story as a singular, luminous source, and the resultant failure to notice the many different forms it actually took.

The power that has been attributed to the Ramayana is extraordinary – to know the Ramayana is to know India, it has been said.

Generation after generation has been said to confirm the remorseless power of the epic, as people seek guidance in its counsel and enact it obediently.[58] A superficial survey might appear to confirm the claims made for the epic's influence, given the plethora of re-tellings in virtually every South Asian language and dialect, and the ubiquity of the names and images of its central characters in everyday life. But it is questionable to assume that an underlying essential message has been imprinted on every variation of the Rama story or on every image or symbol derived from it. Indeed, if this were so, we might ask why we should restrict the scope of this assumption to the arbitrary political boundaries of the Indian republic. Burma, Thailand, Laos, Malaysia, and Indonesia all have a tradition of the Ramayana as well. If influence is claimed, its basis and limits need specification. The argument under view could perhaps be expressed in motto form, *one text, one genre, one nation*, with the order of importance inverted: it is the text that appears at the top of this hierarchy. If the litany has an unpleasant ring to it and the priorities seem skewed, a preliminary glance at the variety of genres comprising the Ramayana tradition immediately complicates this view.[59]

Thus in women's song versions of the Ramayana, there are accounts of Kausalya's labor pains and a description of the actual birth of Rama, offering a backroom view of epic events as it were, contemporizing the story and creating an immediate identification with its characters. When Rama banishes Sita to the forest on suspicion of infidelity, there is little attempt to justify his action; on the contrary, all sympathies are with Sita.[60] Low-caste appropriations of the story may reject verses mentioning brahmins, or those in praise of ritualistic worship, or of other deities in the text they use, physically striking out objectionable passages even while revering other portions, as with the Ramnami sect of Chhattisgarh.[61] Michael Madhusudhan Dutt (1824–1873), in his *Meghanadavada Kavya*, excerpted and retold in Bengali the story of Ravan's son Meghnath's battle and eventual death at the hands of Lakshman, Ram's brother. Using similies that likened Meghnath to Krishna, Dutt transformed the typical showdown of good versus evil into a Homeric clash of well-matched heroes. Ending the story with Ravan performing Meghnath's death rites, the demon king was made to acquire a majesty and solemnity that rendered readers unable to simply reproduce the epic's traditional moral wisdom. In Dutt's opinion, Ravan was "a grand fellow," with full-blooded, manly virtues similar to the energetic virtues of the English, and so more fitting for emulation by his countrymen than those of "Rama and his rabble."[62]

Such variations clearly render a text-as-demiurge approach im-plausible. These examples belong to different genres: a folkloric version, a selective and willful response (which we may identify as a sort of speech genre, after Bakhtin), and a kind of counter-epic respectively.[63] They offer instances of the diverse kinds of imprints made and responses evoked by characters and story-elements from the Ramayana. If we group them together we combine irreconcilable narrative tensions, so that no coherent textual influence can be claimed. What we have in common are certain names, characters, and plot-elements, in a sym-bolic repertoire of sorts that diverse texts and social practices have drawn from in widely varying combinations. To infer a unity across all these combinations and all the forms they manifest is to conflate the distinctions between text, genre, and society. Any singular definition of such a diverse array of phenomena is unavoidably marked by the particular uses and interests for which it is framed; we are obliged, then, to explore how the story is used in specific forms and circumstances, rather than make sweeping claims for any individual definition. A discussion of the category of genre is helpful in this context.

Genres represent the space in which given groups of texts function, and thus demarcate classes of texts from each other, epics from ro-mances, and sermons from folklore. At the same time they enunciate the flexible, often overlapping, but nevertheless distinguishable set of rules operating internally within a group of texts. Genres emerge and are validated in social discourse, as particular groups of texts are declared to belong together, and are perceived to share certain themes and certain rules of composition. Thus genres evoke certain characteristic expecta-tions from audiences, internally with respect to elements such as narra-tive cadence, story progression, manner of closure, and externally with respect to their relation to the world, i.e. to their forms of textuality. This understanding of genre as a mode of textualizing the world, as a set of rules for transcribing a given historical time within the space of a text, which I draw from Bakhtin, allows us to go beyond merely formal analysis and pose questions of the relationship of a given genre to historical change.[64]

Bakhtin's definition of the epic summarizes an influential description of the genre, and is thus a useful point of departure. The epic genre describes a golden but distant and inaccessible past, in his view. Its tone is reverent, but it views its subject at a remove rather than intimately. Distance and reverence are related, for greatness appears to posterity, not to contemporaries. High genres until relatively recently considered the contemporary as belonging to a lower order, and confined their attention to past events. In this sense, to remove the boundary between the epic's time and that of the present, Bakhtin argues, is to change the genre: it would no longer be epic. Genres that focus on the contemporary as such, the here and now, capture a sense of the flow of time without memorializing the past or entombing the present for the future. These have historically been the "low," folk genres, wherein living reality is appraised and laughed at, and high genres criticized and parodied.[65] By contrast, the epic belongs to the absolute past. The knowledge it refers to is a closed system; thus, Bakhtin insists that the epic is a dead genre, with the beginning of its end brought by the birth of polyglossia and the inter-illumination of languages.

The relationship assumed here between genre and historical time needs qualification. If Orientalists held that genre expressed historical time (so that the epic depicted the ancient past) while entombing it (so that the Ramayana condemned India to eternally repeating its immortal lessons), Bakhtin's discussion of the epic implies a mere reversal of this relationship: a change in historical time renders a particular genre obsolete and irrelevant. How then do we describe a two-voiced work, one that describes the epic past with one voice, but in its other calls attention to another time or place? In Sanskrit *kavya* literature, for instance, *dvisandhana* or a two-in-one style of writing was a well-developed form in itself. Bakhtin does not consider such variations, because the epic belongs in a monoglot world, in his view, and language does not carry multiple voices in a condition of monoglossia. This is symptomatic of mythological thought, which for him is the absolute bonding of ideological meaning to language, and the absolute fusion of word with concrete ideological meaning.[66] The bulk of extant versions of the Rama story cannot in this strict sense be described as mythological. If the first versions of the Rama story were composed in Sanskrit, it is in its regional versions that the great majority are familiar with its tales, and these vernacular tellings are invariably composed with knowledge of their Sanskrit predecessors. The Sanskrit versions themselves are often highly stylized and self-conscious literary works. Thus an influential sixth- or seventh-century composition, the *Bhattikavya*, also known as the *Ravanavadha* ("The Killing of Ravana"), tells the bulk of the well-known tale, while simultaneously outlining in proper sequence the rules of Sanskrit grammar and poetics.[67] Devices such as *slesha*, or *double entendre*, and *sandhi*, the practice of running phrases together, allowed writers to deploy the highly metaphorical character of the language to offer diverse interpretations all at once; it was left to readers to decide how to parse the phrases and construct a reading.

We cannot identify a particular historical time indissolubly with a given genre, or present history simply as a linear sequence of different forms of historicity, each succeeding and replacing the previous one. In his discussion of the novel, however, Bakhtin offers a more complex view of genre. He understands the novel as a genre-in-the-making that captures modernity's spirit of openness to the present, encapsulating within a single time-frame multiple viewpoints and voices without privileging received wisdom. As such, the novel is always incomplete, and forever struggling to actualize itself, and as only partially embodied and actualized in any existing works. Genres that inhibit the depiction of the contemporary, and so effect closure to the text, fail to express the historical possibilities of the modern era and are thus found wanting, in this view. This notion of a struggle among genres, and the emergence of a genre expressing the most progressive possibilities of a given historical time, offers a powerful heuristic. It offers an important means of relating the study of cultural form to social power, and of discriminating between the social function of competing genres. But the relation between historical time and its mode of representation clearly becomes far more complex in the modern era.

We are now confronted with multiple genres, and multiple possible ways of knowing the world, so that the distinctions Bakhtin makes between pastness and presentness and the political implications that flow from particular genres are too unilateral. A politics would have to be judged not merely by its openness to the present in all its diversity, but as well by the presence of the past, the mode of whose appropriation is not given in advance.[68] We are obliged to admit, given the co-existence of diverse genres such as the epic and the novel, the possibility of *the reflexive appropriation of a historical sensibility*, something that becomes possible when one's own historical era is experienced as self-conscious, amid a disenchanted world. Thus the epic can be read for the sense of "pastness" it conveys, and the novel for its sense of "presentness." As modes of figuring the world for any combination of purposes, including enjoyment and social transformation both, they can thus be rendered contiguous; to argue that one use excludes the other appeals to a linear view of history. Different genres can be seen to capture different aspects of historical experience, of arrested development and backward formations alongside more dynamic and up-to-date systems of production, of relative stasis amid a tremendous churning and social turbulence.

The medium of television itself exemplifies this more open mode of engagement, bringing diverse worlds together on one screen, widening the sense of history but at the same time attenuating the perception of its depth and texture, and thus thinning the experience of time for the viewer. This is reinforced by the context of viewing, which is domestic, and interwoven with the flows of daily life. It is this very feature, of course, that lends the medium itself more utility, as a diversely received event may nevertheless be yoked to agenda defined by far narrower readings of the text. The Ramayan serial illustrates this well.

In the case of the Ramanand Sagar Ramayan, we clearly have a hybrid genre whose significance requires clarification.[69] Commentators described it variously as a mythological soap opera and an epic soap opera. Given the genre confusion regarding the Ramayana's manifestations, we can begin by acknowledging that the television serial represents a hybrid form of soap opera.[70] The "soap opera" is usually defined in terms of its open-ended narrative, one that can potentially be stretched on forever, its mundane, often domestic concerns, and its mainly female audience.[71] None of these features applied to the Sagar Ramayan, strictly speaking. The Ramayana was a story with a definite ending, although which one Sagar would choose was not certain; it had an epic rather than a mundane subject, and its audience was evenly divided, although there was a larger number of "serious" female viewers.[72] This suggests that we need to clarify the definition. The soap opera is made and presented *as if* it had no definite ending and *as if* its subject were mundane. That is, the genre is defined by formal characteristics, by certain styles of treatment and rules of production relatively independent of the content of the show or the composition of the audience. It is also defined in relation to other genres, as an accessible, popular form rather than an erudite or specialized form catering to limited audiences.

In the Hindi press, the Ramayan was described as a *dharmic serial*. The ambivalent connotation of the English language description, with a soap opera as a low or degraded product, is entirely absent in this term. "Dharmic" in this context refers to matters religious or spiritual, and "serial" is of course a neologism, referring to a periodical issue, in this case of a weekly television program lasting anywhere from thirteen weeks (the typical length of a Doordarshan serial) to two years or more. As a *dharmic* form, the Ramayan serial drew from and appealed to long-standing traditions of attendance at religious story-tellings, *kathas*, which could draw daily audiences running into the thousands for months together. This aura of spiritual sanctity is important in understanding the size of the audiences drawn by the Ramayan serial as well as by its successor, the Mahabharat serial produced by B. R. Chopra. Large crowds would congregate around television sets during each broadcast, at available public sets, or in homes where sets were accessible. On occasion I observed passers-by gathered on the sidewalk watching a television set placed in a store, during the serial one Sunday morning. The set was a black and white one, and in the glare of daylight it was not easy to pick out details on screen. "We had heard about it before. Now we can see it," was a remark many viewers made. "Many people watched it out of devotion. They felt that God was giving them *darshan*," said one viewer, Ashok Kumar Gupta, a mechanic.

Darshan, literally sight, is what one partakes of when one sees a deity, or someone of exalted status. The word connotes a more physical sense of space than its English language equivalent; the deity gives *darshan*, and the devotee takes *darshan*; one is "touched" by *darshan*, and seeks it as a form of contact with the deity.[73] The relationship it establishes is tactile as much as it is visual, rendering the televisual image into a material presence, at least for the duration of the dharmic serial. The sacred image sanctified the space of its presence, and to share that space was to partake of the *darshan*. Thus the Ramayan serial was a congregational experience, among other things, as people acknowledged the importance of watching even if they could not see the show.

In this sense, the Ramayan serial was able to create a collectively observed weekly ritual, one that was extraordinary to witness. Normally thronging bazaars were silent during the Sunday morning time of its airing, and city buses ran close to empty. A film director intending to shoot a scene on the busy Manikarnik Ghats of Benares, usually filled with priests, lay devotees and sundry bathers in the Ganges, had asked authorities if space could be made for his crew. He was told to do his filming during the Sunday morning hour of the Ramayan, and sure enough the place was empty then. He repeated this story to me with an air of disbelief; it was as though the most crowded urban intersections, such as Victoria Terminus in Bombay or Connaught Place in Delhi, had suddenly been vacated. A team of policemen was assigned to the film unit for security, but its members too left to see the show.[74] Traveling in a rickshaw just before the show one Sunday in Delhi, I proposed to the driver, whom I had no prior acquaintance with, that we stop at a randomly selected house to view the morning's serial. There was no hesitation in his agreement. We presented ourselves at a street-side apartment and asked if we could watch the Ramayan with them. It turned out we were not the first ones with that idea; we joined the group of five or six already assembled there. Not only was our request unobjectionable, there was a mutual acknowledgment of the occasion, and a wordless readiness to share it, although we were otherwise unrelated.

There were stories in the newspapers of viewers who bathed before the show, who distributed sweets after it, who decorated the TV set with flowers and incense sticks as it began, and so on (see chapter 3). If these standard devotional practices were modes of fetishizing the medium, they acknowledged the time-bound nature of fetish-power, with decorations emerging only around the hour of the broadcast. They were also a sign of the novelty of the event. As mythological serials became a staple on television, at any rate, the practice, if it continued, ceased to attract attention.

The ninety-four-episode Mahabharat serial, which followed the Ramayan and overlapped with it in its last weeks, was also received as a *dharmic serial*. Scripted by the noted Urdu writer Rahi Masoom Raza and directed by B. R. Chopra, it largely avoided the devotional motif of its predecessor, relying instead on a more realist-historical presentation of the epic's stories. But the Mahabharat played to even larger crowds. Although the viewership was a fraction of the total population (the number of television sets was at the time all of fourteen million, in a population of nearly 900 million), a swift syllogism claimed 80 percent of the subcontinent for the serial's audience, in Hindu nationalist arguments. The ambiguous character of this collective formation is noteworthy. It arose and was rendered proof against criticism by the perception of its seclusion within the home. It accumulated a political force as a result of this protection, but any minority claims were pre-empted by its putative location in the private realm, and appeared to add to the symbolic repertoire available to commemorate Hindu glory. One columnist wrote, in September 1989:

Critics should take note of the healthy national addiction – the telecast of Mahabharata every Sunday morning. It is a great pleasure to find a whole subcontinent in front of their television sets reliving the drama of bygone years, and finding their echo in today's world. It is reassuring to know that at least 80 percent of this nation in "bondable," and that the binding thread is the charisma of an epic rather than the bogey of an impending war or the rhetoric of a charlatan leader.

As an Indian Hindu I am relieved finally at sharing a common identity with millions within the privacy of my own home, and without having to extend an

apology to the likes of Syed Shahabuddin.[75] For many of us Hindus, these
telecasts provide an opportunity to shed our self-consciousness and come out of
the closet and relish our heritage.[76]

Viewers consume not only the product but the act of consumption itself,
when they re-stage it in imagination, and perceive themselves as part of
a grander design, proof of a larger intelligence at work than merely their
own. How the character of that intelligence is perceived, of course,
varies. This writer clearly sees the show's appeal as an affirmation of a
Hindu collective consciousness.

   The above quote emphasizes the importance of both the medium and
the context of reception, and warns of the limits of a purely text-
centered understanding of genre. Invariably referred to in one breath,
as Ramayan–Mahabharat, and in that order, it became a touchstone of
what was good about Hindu culture and a lesson for the times, or for the
secular minority, a portent of the rightward drift of Indian society. The
mythological, or the dharmic serial, became a staple not only on
Doordarshan but on the independent channels that emerged subsequently as well, with Sagar himself receiving the coveted Sunday morning slot for another popular mythological, *Shri Krishna*.[77] Costume
dramas similar in appearance, with special effects and based on historical or fictional themes (e.g., *Bharat ek Khoj* [based on Nehru's *Discovery of
India*], *Chanakya*, and *Chandrakanta*, the latter surpassing the revenues
earned by the *Mahabharat*, and other such serials) came to be among the
more prominent of Doordarshan's shows. It should be noted that the
mythological genre tended to be denied to shows based on Muslim
subjects, which were labeled "historical" instead (e.g., *Akbar the Great* and
Alif Laila), or "quasi-historical" (e.g., *Akbar Birbal*),[78] with one arguably
historical serial, *Tipu Sultan*, actually labeled "fictional" because of
protests by Hindu conservatives. Even when Doordarshan allowed
non-Hindu aspects of Indian culture to be commemorated on television,
Hindu conservatives zealously preserved truth claims as the right of the
majority community alone, and the bureaucracy bowed obediently to
their will. If Hindus possessed the force of numbers, there was nevertheless a convergence of activity at many levels through which a new kind
of audience came to be defined as representing the country as a whole.
Interestingly, as Doordarshan competed with independent stations for
commercial revenue,[79] mythological and historical serials became something of an imprimatur for the state television system: such programming was used to distinguish it as the unique repository and expression
of a national-popular culture. Thus one advertisement promoting

Doordarshan as "the Real Value Network for Advertisers," with a half page of stills from two costume dramas, *Chandrakanta* and *Upasana*, concluded: "Nobody Reaches India Like We Do."[80]

The Sagar Ramayan offers narratives of the ethical life and its trials, tribulations and rewards, told in alternately melodramatic and devotional modes. At times, Sagar attempts to re-craft these into narratives of improvement, education, development, and success. Thus Sagar introduces interpolations, on the princes playing together as infants, and being educated as brahmacharyas at Guru Vasisht's school. As Ram and his cohort travel through the forest, they encounter a succession of sages who offer their wisdom for Ram's benefit. At the same time, the characters are stereotypes who steadfastly reflect their invariant qualities on the pageant of events as they unfold, doing in each case precisely as is expected of them. Thus Ram is always calm and composed, and slow and sedate in his movements, ceremonially offering his front view to the camera. Presenting a slight but constant smile on his lips, he is the picture of self-adequacy and virtue, poised to grant audience to devotees for worship. This is a histrionic convention originating in the mythologicals of the playwright Radheshyam Kathavachak.[81] Sita acts similarly, except that she has little dialogue and is cast in a role that is passive, and submissive to Ram. Lakshman acts as counterpoint, quickly aroused and ready to fight, yet devoted to the service of Ram and Sita, his ardor and impatience reinforcing the impression of their composure. Lakshman thus serves as the dramatic lynchpin of the trio, providing emotional tension as respite from the devotional scenes. Broadly, there are two genres co-existing in this representation, at first sight incongruous but in fact compatible. One is that of melodrama, which is at the heart of the soap opera form, and the other, that of the mythological. Both genres are moralizing in intent and emotional in tone, and although the former is mundane and the latter other-worldly, they come together in a curious conjunction.

Although there is a tradition of Christian mythologicals emanating from Kerala, the mythological genre in India is largely Hindu in content, presenting religious fables and legends based on scriptural and demotic sources. It is arguably the first genre of films to be made in India, beginning with Dadasaheb Phalke's *Raja Harishchandra* (1914), *Shri Krishna Janma* and *Lanka Dahan* (1919). Phalke, who was inspired by a screening of *The Life of Christ* (1910), saw his work as contributing to an indigenous national culture, wherein ordinary people would be able to draw inspiration from their own epic traditions. The genre has its beginnings in the mythological paintings of Raja Ravi Varma, which began to be mass-produced in 1894. Varma's oleographed paintings of gods and goddesses, made in an enormously popular naturalist, "realist" style, were promoted by the royal house of Travancore to create a brahminical cultural lineage rivaling that of the British. Simultaneously, this attempted to deflect insistent demands for social reform from below by illustrating an idealized myth-history of a golden age whose rulers practiced a steadfast benevolence, culminating in the present.[82] Phalke's *Swadeshi* politics deflected this quasi-feudal impulse in a nationalist direction, although retaining an ambivalent legacy of elements. A third formative influence on the mythological genre was the above-mentioned playwright who worked in the Parsi theatre, Radheshyam Kathavachak. Kathavachak drew on his family's roots in the popular Northern and Central Indian traditions of enacting the *Raslila* and *Ramlila*, and helped shape the adaptation of this tradition for the Hindi cinema. Mythologicals have been used variously to promote nationalist patriotism, as in the films of Vijay Bhatt, who made an influential version of *Ram Rajya* (1943), to boost regional chauvinism as in Raj Kumar's Kannada films, to foster the revival of a Brahmin orthodoxy as in G. V. Iyer's recent films, or as propaganda for cults around deities ranging from *Jai Santoshi Ma* to films on the Guruvayoor and Sabarimala temples.[83] As a flexible set of textual rules, the mythological genre easily accommodates itself to grafts in the form of historicals or of melodrama.

Melodrama works by the infusion of excitement into the narrative depiction of daily life. It is realist in its delineation of characters and *mise-en-scène*, while relying on a surplus of emotional display for its effect. The etymology of the word refers to the use of music as narrative accompaniment, highlighting moments of suspense, terror, or pleasure through the crescendo of violins, the clash of cymbals, or the lilt of a flute. Across the many forms it has taken, melodrama can most simply be characterized as a style that heightens dramatic contrasts and adds story emphases, conveying social change into the turbulence and uncertainty of individual experience.[84] Great events and historical developments, if they figure at all, usually appear as backdrops. Nature and natural surroundings are used to reflect dramatic mood in a direct way, with stormy emotions reflected in thunderstorms, for instance, or happiness in fine weather. The repetition across *mise-en-scène*, plot, and soundtrack of the same intended effect undeniably lends an air of simplicity to the melodrama. As such, it has been used for pedagogical purposes, in forceful arguments for social reform and for a humanitarian approach to progress. In nineteenth-century Europe in the novels of Dickens and Hugo, and more recently in India in the films of Raj Kapoor and Guru Dutt, realist portrayals of urban misery and the moral degradation bred by industrial work-life made for dramatically heightened contrast and shock effect. But as the example of the Ramayan serial suggests, the range of its uses is much greater.

The reliance of melodrama on emotional effect achieved through elementary devices has often led to the genre's identification as a low one. But arguments about it have tended to be dismissive as well, placing it in a functional relationship to historical context, e.g., as dramatizing everyday life for those needing compensation for the loss of religion and tradition.[85] For instance, it has been argued that the Hindi film melodrama attempts to culturally mediate the transition from feudalism to capitalism.[86] There are a number of objections to such an argument. Firstly, popular cultural texts offer an important source material to question and complicate a simple teleology established by the master narrative of the modes of production. Thus although gift exchange and commodity circulation are typically considered to represent archaic and modern economies, I have argued that they in fact represent narratives, mutually dependent rather than sequential, and are recognizably contemporary in their prevalence (see introduction and chapter three). The self-description of the capitalist economic system, however, tends to disguise or deny its cultural hybridity and its dependence on other modes of production. Secondly, if we take seriously the machinery of film or television and the political economy within which they function, these are far removed from a feudal setup. It is not sequential but combined and uneven development that is at issue here, and much remains to be learned about the hybrid cultural patterning of social formations if we can avoid the constraints of a deductive typology. Finally, to emphasize the cultural transmission of historical change risks treating the technology of the medium as transparent, as a passive intermediary. Studying the technical and discursive practices shaping cultural texts on the other hand allows us to detail how the medium may be used to articulate specific political effects, and thus elaborate on the inter-animations between politics and the media.[87]

We can acknowledge then that the melodramatic form cannot be reduced to questions of socio-historical function. It does, it is true, have clearly delineated tropes of good and evil, of heroes and villains, and effects decisive closure to its narrative. But this has to be taken together with another crucial, even defining feature, in a narrative form, after all, whose movement is spiral rather than linear, and whose chief distinction is as much its punctuations as its progressions, its hyphens, ellipses, and exclamation points, which serve as detour from the onward rush of the story. Taken together, they signal a complexity of movement that should at least qualify its identification as a narrative of development. Melodrama conjoins expression of uncertainty and reassurance regarding social change, through its emphasis on emotional communion in a "pure" mood whose experience stands apart from the confusion of daily life. Its narrative is full of reversals and suspense but is ultimately conventional, with its ending meant to flatter prejudice and reinforce "commonsense." For obvious reasons, then, it has served as a flexible genre expressing a range of political sentiments from conservative to reformist, though it has veered to the former.

The judgment of melodrama as a transitional form takes its teleological sense when made from hindsight. In societies characterized by late development, the onset of capitalist relations has typically been compressed within a far briefer period. We cak speak of "transition" here, but in a different and more uncertain sense. Here the presence of the past may be felt in a variety of ways: in non-Weberian relations within bureaucracies and corporations, between political leaders and their constituencies, and in caste, kin, and other patronage networks buffering the uncertainty of market dynamics and promising (but not always delivering) insurance against its perils. Overarching all of these is the attraction in idealizing feudal relations against a cash nexus that may be perceived as an encroachment rather than as a development in its own right, as a degradation of time-honored rules sanctified by custom rather than as a promise of new freedoms in a world being born. Given the historic compromise between emergent bourgeois and residual yet tenacious and adaptive elites, on the one hand, and orthodox opinion on the other, in countries such as India, capitalist development in its late forms may seek cultural registers significantly different from those of its earlier ones. The Ramayan serial's success illustrates this difference, I suggest.

TELEVISING A LOST UTOPIA: ANCIENT SCIENCE, BENIGN OPPRESSION, AND A PROTO-MODERN STATE

The main inspiration for Sagar's serial appears to have been Tulsidas's *Ramcharitmanas*, which rewrites Valmiki's *Ramayana* from the perspective of the bhakti tradition.[88] Acknowledging this, Sagar claimed, in addition, to have read "all Ramayanas available in Indian languages [*sic*]," including versions in Telugu, Marathi, Bengali, Kannada, and Hindi.[89] If he covered his regional bases carefully, Sagar was no less adept at aiming at the box office register. In his own view a "romanticist,"[90] he rendered the story in sentimentalized fashion, with a glacially paced script, and copious use of deep close-ups. He introduced the conventions of the Hollywood soap opera to an epic tradition, with shot-reverse shot sequences and alternating close-ups following every master shot. This replaced the embodied narrator of poetic convention, of a Valmiki or Tulsi rendering a highly personalized story and making his direct address to audiences a thread parallel to and interwoven along the entire length of the epic.[91] Sagar's production positioned a disembodied, omniscient spectator akin to that of conventional cinema. This paralleled a certain voyeuristic emphasis in presentation. Emphasizing the idealized behavior of the story's protagonists, Sagar used the small screen to advantage: the deep and prolonged close-ups suggested the visual capture of emotions, and the extraordinary *bhava*, the feeling, of each act. The repeated reaction shots served to reinforce the sense of a tightly homogeneous moral community with the entire cast unfailingly responding in like fashion.[92]

The highly romanticized relationships depicted an idealized inter-subjectivity in which the protagonists made unearthly sacrifices for each other casually; and that is indeed the ethos of both the Tulsi and Valmiki Ramayans, from which Sagar claimed chiefly to have drawn his material. As figures in a distant past, the characters engaged in secure, selfless relationships that showed no hint of the uncertainty customary in real life. Viewing therefore had an important vicarious aspect, with the serial seen as endorsing much-desired possibilities unrealized in present-day society. The abstraction employed in Sagar's Hollywood-influenced positioning of the all-seeing absent viewer is a crucial technical determinant of this vicarious reception.

The introductory section in the Ramayan serial contains in condensed form the main themes conveyed in the serial.[93] The video begins with a shot of a saffron-clad man writing, sitting cross-legged in front of a temple. There is a choral voice-over:

What Shiva, Brahma, Goddess Saraswati, the Vedas and scriptures, affirm, denying all others, Thou art That [which] all deities sing of in eternal worship.[94]

Voice-over of film star Ashok Kumar:

When Goswami Tulsidas-ji wrote in his regional Avadhi, it set off a controversy.

Close-up to saffron clad man.

But the Goswami did not change his mind, because he believed the story of Ramayana had to reach the common man.

Cut to a close-up of Ashok Kumar, wearing dark glasses and a shawl.

The *ideals of human behaviour* had to reach the common man and guide his life to show him the true path.

After invoking deities and scriptures, the introduction switches to a secular note, presenting Tulsidas as a variation on a humanist educator. At this point the camera draws back to reveal a library as the setting, confirming this impression. Ashok Kumar proceeds:

Ramayan is not only a scripture, but *a cultural document*. It transcends barriers of race, color, faith, and nation . . . Ramayan has influenced the common man so deeply that it teaches him to live daily life better. That is why it has been translated into practically all world languages.

He is concerned to deny the obvious but here ineffable charge of promoting Hinduism. Culture emerges as the category transcending all divisions, hence the invocation of daily life and the common man; the aim moreover seems to be improvement, rather than worship as suggested in the opening stanza.

Ashok Kumar continues:

Germany, France, England, Russia, China, Iran, Thailand, Indonesia and other countries have honoured it as much as India.

Cut to statue of the Buddha.

The reason for this is India never sent out armies to capture foreign lands. India always sent forth only apostles of love and peace.

Cut to a painting, focusing on a pair of sandaled feet. Slow pan upwards to reveal Gandhi's portrait.

Messengers of peace and love. Apostles who conquered hearts, not lands.

This echoes a familiar nationalist reformulation of history. If foreign armies had humbled the country, that was because its true strength lay elsewhere. What is asserted in place of conquering lands is conquering hearts. If the emphasis is meant to be on hearts, the metaphor of conquest persists, pointing silently to the memory underlying it.[95]

Cut to saffron garbed sage, writing with a peacock feather.

Sage Valmiki first wrote the Ramayan in Sanskrit.

Voiceover Valmiki verse:

As long as the mountains stand firm, as long as the rivers flow,
So shall the story of Ramayan be heard and loved by the people.[96]

Cut to Ashok Kumar, who then introduces, one by one, different regional poets, shown composing their respective Ramayans. In each case, the poet is attired in supposedly characteristic regional garb, with iconically "regional" architecture as background. The serial claims to have been drawn from all the major Ramayans. The credits scrupulously list Ramayans in Telugu (Ranganatha Ramayan), Tamil (Kampa Ramayanam), Malayalam (of Atuvakshan), Kannada (of Nagachandra), Bengali (of Kruttibas), Marathi (of Eknath), and, significantly, one in Urdu (of Chakbast), in addition to Valmiki and Tulsidas. This strains credulity: no version of a story can simultaneously manifest all its variations. For instance, in the Valmiki version, Ram ultimately drowns himself; in Kruttibas's Bengali telling, Ram is slain by his sons; Tulsidas, whose Avadhi version was the main inspiration for the television version, himself ends his story with Ram's coronation. Whether genuine or not, Sagar's claim helps forestall criticism from regional groups, while legitimizing the serial as part of one living, continuous tradition. Diversity is here acknowledged and affirmed while different regions are reduced to stereotypes, linked by a common tradition to comprise the Ramayan.

Cut to Ashok Kumar again.

The story of Ramayan strengthens in man this belief, this trust, this faith, that when the forces of oppression – that is, "autocratic powers" [*sic*] attempt to crush humanity underfoot, then divine power manifests itself in human form. And challenges the forces of oppression using only truth, love and self-confidence.

The camera zooms in a little closer.

The tradition of Ramayan is based on this – when oppressive evil grew rampant in the form of Ravan – a tyrant who crushed the very earth in his arrogance, then Mother Earth, rishis, munis, and the devatas . . . sought Lord Vishnu's help . . .

"Autocratic" and "divine" powers vie for supremacy. History, no longer simply the enactment of divine will, is now a struggle for power. Ravan is in most accounts a demon with God-given powers whose followers attack holy men performing Vedic sacrifices. Here he is represented in terms of "autocratic power," implying a political understanding of demonic abuses. The rhetoric is similar to Enlightenment critiques of arbitrary rule and despotism, but India's greatness prepares it for a different destiny. To deliver humanity from oppression, divine power comes to the rescue, using "truth and love and self-confidence," human qualities all, again secularizing the battle: no mention of the various supernatural weapons finally instrumental in the victory.

Here we have an ancient epic tradition thoroughly scrambled with a national origin-myth of more recent vintage. In asserting the compatibility, indeed the mutual dependence of faith and reason, Ashok Kumar, and in the remainder of the serial Ramanand Sagar, offers an improbable couplet. In conventional understanding, faith requires the suspension of reason, and reason dissolves the certitudes of faith. They may of course co-exist, but the persistent assertion that they are united or continuous with each other requires clarification, at the very least. But over and over, it is offered as a self-evident truth, presenting the nation's past as already scientific and progressive, yet steeped in a devotional, spiritual culture. In a state-sponsored serialization of an epic, the apparent endorsement not only of one particular religion but also of the deeply anachronistic values of an ancient work understandably requires tact and negotiation. The Ramayan is a story in which the characters may each rise to heaven but belong to emphatically different groups on earth, whether female, low caste, tribal, monkey, or demon, requiring different codes of conduct and summoning different forms of behavior from their superiors and inferiors. The translation of this deeply hierarchical conception into the universalized category of "humanity," with democratic aspirations and scientific capabilities, is to extend the devotional bhakti philosophy of Tulsidas into new and awkward territory. If these are the kind of values that government-sponsored media are supposed to promote, they are nevertheless not values contained in the Ramayan texts cited by Sagar. To selectively contemporize the story is a choice, one that becomes feasible within a definite context. If Sagar chose not to dramatize the story in a more historically distanced form, it was in order not to detract from the sanctity of the epic, and to present an unambivalently positive message in the Ramayan. Ancient society is shown as having successfully dealt with the problem of order, at any rate once the demons were dispatched. If in its means it was simple, in ethos, mores, and social organization it was without fault, it is implied. As such, it implicitly offers rebuke to present-day society, whose glaring failure in all these matters reverberates as a steady *obbligato* throughout the serial.

While Ram Rajya, the golden age of the rule of Ram, has long been held as a utopia, and has repeatedly been utilized as a mobilizing symbol, the realist convention adopted in Sagar's dramatization and the extended serial format of the presentation gave the symbol a discursive detail and a verisimilitude it can seldom have had before. Moreover the claim of a panacea for modern society in ancient Hindu culture, offered as a nationalist message on a state medium, had clear political implications.

When Ramanand Sagar depicted ancient Hindu society as politically and socially equal to the challenge of modernity, indeed to have anticipated and surpassed it, he drew on an Orientalist-inspired current of thought that had achieved considerable circulation by the nineteenth century. His ability to stage it on national television, with the approval of government censors as well of enormous audiences, indexed its continuing political potency.

As early as episode two, Sagar signals his intention to champion native learning, after a fashion. Guru Vashisht, the preceptor of King Dasarath's court, is lecturing to his students, among them the four young princes. A patriarchal figure with flowing white hair and beard and saffron robes, Vashisht is seated on a platform under the tree, while his students sit cross-legged before him.

The body is composed of five elements, earth, water, fire, sky and air. If all the five elements are perfectly balanced, the body remains healthy. The factors that affect the human body are food, drink and the environment, his thoughts and actions. All must be simple and restrained. Besides this is the effect of the magnetic force because of which everything in the universe remains in place. All the stars in the universe, because of the force of mutual magnetic attraction stay firm in their place. From this magnetic force flow waves of electricity. Not only the sun, moon, stars and our earth but even our bodies are affected by these waves.

The sky darkens, and colored graphics of spiraling lights and bright spinning discs appear.

Look, I'll demonstrate it in my body . . . Remember, the human body has magnetic nodes. These waves move in circular motion around the nodes. They are invisible but have a deep effect on our bodies. They are essential for our physical and mental health. That's why you should sleep in a direction that will enable the earth's waves to act in your body.

In an interview, Sagar boasted about this sequence as an improvement he had made over existing Ramayans.[97] A little later, Vashisht goes on to mention the *kundalini* (a "magnetic node," in Sagar's formulation). It seems to be part of Sagar's attempt to modernize ancient education, or our understanding of it. Sagar here draws conclusions for human conduct from scientific descriptions of the universe, creating a kind of updated, unified system of knowledge on behalf of the Vedic age, as it were.

Most of the other signs of ancient science, however, are pronouncedly military in character. The Marich-Subahu incident, in episode four, is the first disclosure of the largely "defense" oriented understanding Sagar offers of ancient Indian learning. The incident also provides the first encounter in the story with an "Other," namely the rakshasas (demons).[98] Vishwamitra the great sage, in the course of his sacrifices, is disturbed by the rakshasas, and as they violate the sanctity of the rituals, he is forced to abandon them. This eventually leads him to ask King Dasharath for the loan of his sons Ram and Lakshman, for help in putting an end to the rakshasas' interference.

The scene:

A number of grey-bearded *rishis* (saints) are seated around a fire, chanting prayers as they perform a ritual. At their center is Vishwamitra. The camera pans upward to the sky, where, with a whizzing, aeroplane-like sound, two large, swarthy figures arrive. They wear crude necklaces with irregular wooden beads, fierce mustaches, and large earrings.

The following exchange ensues:

First Rakshasa: Subahu, it seems Vishwamitra is performing a new sacrifice.
Subahu: It seems so, Marich.
Marich: Before they complete it and gain spiritual powers, we must desecrate the sacrifice. This is what our lord King Ravan ordered. He says the poet-sages are the greatest power of the Aryans. In their sacrifices, great scientific experiments take place. Through this the Aryans gain new powers. With the aid of this spiritual power, they combat our powers of illusion.
Subahu: So our magical tricks fail against their spiritual power.
Marich: Right. Let's destroy this sacrifice. But don't go too near. He has great mystic powers. He can destroy you.

There are a number of interesting reformulations in this segment. Though Marich and Subahu are rakshasas, demonic in character, and habitually evil in their designs, Sagar's version is more equivocal. The discourse here suggests a rivalry more akin to rival nations. The Manichaean conflict between good and evil is softened and secularized: the rakshasas' malevolence becomes, in Sagar's screenplay, the uncomprehending hostility of a less civilized people towards a superior culture.

Shifting the terrain of conflict from an elemental moral one to a clash of knowledge-systems is an intriguing move. The adoption of the language of modern science to describe the Vedic rituals of the rishis is interesting in this context. The repetition of the word "new" signals the intention to portray traditional knowledge as dynamic and changing, inverting the tendency for tradition to claim the authority of a timeless past. Against this scientific-cum-spiritual power are the predictably unsuccessful tricks of illusion and magic the rakshasas perform. In this way, the archaic contest of good versus evil is reformulated as a teleological encounter of primitive versus proto-modern. The narrative thus leads implicitly to present-day society, with its emphasis on scientific experimentation as a means of gaining "new powers." The association of science with powers of combat exercised by "the Aryans" as a race/nation is also striking. This extension into the past of the national security state, undertaking scientific research to battle its enemies, figures repeatedly in the serial.

The foregoing does not exhaust the meaning of this scene. Against this reformulation is the culturally prevalent notion of the rakshasas as evil, against the pure goodness of the rishis. This popular understanding is conveyed in their appearance and actions. The rakshasas are pronouncedly darker than other characters, with fierce mustaches and wild hair. As they desecrate the rishis' sacrifice, dropping sides of meat and pouring pots of blood on the sacrificial fire, they laugh uproariously at the rishis' dismay. When *en masse*, however, they are pronouncedly darker than the other characters, with fang-like teeth, wild hair, and reddened lips, and their speech is punctuated with villainous laughter. The representation of the rakshasas, then suggests a compromise between textual tradition and its putative historical referent. The portrayal of Ravan represents the furthest move in this direction. Ravan, the demon king, is portrayed as a devout worshiper of Shiva and a connoisseur of the arts: our introduction to the court of Lanka is with a lengthy performance of classical bharatanatyam dance. The encounter with Marich and Subahu is used to dramatize a number of themes: the rendition of "Aryan" sages as the repository of ancient Indian wisdom who, it appears, anticipated Western science, and fought indigenous tribal people to preserve and enhance this knowledge. While it was scientific knowledge, it was spiritual too, as the product simultaneously of mysticism and experimentation. It is difficult to say which term has more power here, but certainly Sagar's qualification of the activity as "science" gives the otherwise somewhat nebulous Vedic goings-on a startling sense of contemporaneity. The spiritual aspect resonates with the assertion that the experiment was for the benefit of humankind. The scope and power of this benevolent knowledge is suggested, paradoxically, by its destructive capacity. We are assured, however, that it is unleashed only against its enemies, such as primitive people, who in their ignorance are threatened by it. The encounter is suspiciously similar to the parable of conquest by the West.

The theme of "spiritual science" and of benevolently controlled powers of destruction recurs frequently. After Vishwamitra has brought Ram and Lakshman with him, and Ram succeeds in killing the demoness Tadaka, Vishwamitra rewards him with special weapons that he has obtained after years of prayer and austerities. In this scene, Vishwamitra and Ram are seated facing each other, seen in silhouette, with a dim, mysterious light illuminating them from behind.

I'm going to give you weapons which in all three worlds only I possess . . . Through worldly, heavenly and scientific research and spiritual power I possess weapons . . . For aeons I have sought a man worthy of receiving them. One who will use my powers for the good of the world. I can see that, in the future, Aryan lands must be saved from demonic evil. And the task will be yours . . . As *guru dakshina* [gift-payment to the teacher] I shall claim only this – that you shall not misuse them on any innocent being. But where you see sin, injustice and oppression . . . use the weapons to kill the sinners and oppressors . . . Son, weapons have many energies and powers. Some powers are born of harnessing science. Some are wrought from the heavens by spiritual penance. They are energized by the power of atoms . . . And there are some weapons whose tips embody great divine powers like Shiva's awesome *Trishul* [trident].[99]

Drums and martial music are heard, as a large trident appears. Vishwamitra smiles with satisfaction as Tadaka writhes with arrows in her belly. The scene has all the aura of a religious initiation ceremony. The awesome power of the weapons is conveyed; the moral ambivalence in possessing them, and the insistence that they be used for "the good of the world," by "a man worthy of . . . them" echoes the contemporary moral dilemma with nuclear weapons. The disclosure that "they are energized by the power of atoms" makes the parallel with nuclear weapons explicit. There is a convention of taking the mention of these weapons seriously. In the *Ramcharitmanas*, there is a lengthy footnote at the beginning of Book Three:

Our scriptures mention a number of missiles each presided over by a particular deity and varying in its potency according to the god by whom it is presided over and which can be invoked on any earthly weapon by means of spells. For instance we hear of an Agni Astra presided over by the fire-god, Pasupatastra,

presided over by Lord Shiva [Pasupati] . . . and so on. The Agni Astra, when
discharged, rains volleys of fire; the Vayuvastra lets loose strong winds; the
Parjanyastra releases clouds with showers, and so on. It is unfortunate that the
knowledge of this science, which was evidenced till the end of Dwapara Yuga
[the second great epoch in Hindu cosmology] has become extinct now.

The notion of righteous destruction as a fit means to deal with "sin,
injustice and oppression" is categorically affirmed: "[U]se the weapons
to kill the sinner and oppressor." There is the suggestion of the necessity
of national/racial defense ("In the future, Aryan lands must be saved")
though the source of danger is left obscure. The repeated sanctification
of weaponry is noteworthy. "Research" in the serial is always in connection with instruments of war, although such research is only performed
by spiritual men. They are the very image of benevolent patriarchs,
seated cross-legged in a pose of worship. While scientific research is
mentioned, their spiritual energy as well is understood to be responsible
for their accumulation of destructive powers.

The Rama story, in being retold, communicates not only the story
itself, but also responds to, sets itself alongside, and against a context. It
acts as a commentary of sorts, situating itself in the time of its composition. Thus Tulsi's composition is imbued with the language of the bhakti
movement, and, written in a Muslim-ruled kingdom, seeks inner spiritual transcendence rather than a this-worldly association of spiritual and
political power. Another telling of the story, Sandhyakaranandin's
Ramacaritam, composed in the twelfth century, makes ingenious use of
the Sanskrit device of *ślesha*, or *double entendre*. Sandhyakaranandin's epic
poem, taken in one sense, tells the well-known Rama story; taken in
another sense, it tells the chronicles of his king, Ramapala of Bihar. The
English translation, accordingly, interprets each verse twice: version
"A" giving the Rama story, and version "B," Ramapala's exploits.[100]
Ramanand Sagar's serial too could be said to have two parallel translations, with one version giving the Rama story, and the other, an account
of the modern Indian state, conducting weapons research and missile
warfare, while expressing the rhetoric of an enlightened patriarchal
society, sanctified by the spiritual and virtuous conduct of its rulers. The
patriarchs, their power to destroy and their power to protect and love,
the respect they command and the impartial justice they bestow in
return, can be seen as signifiers of the authority of the modern national
security state. Thus the marriage of Ram and Sita "will unite two great
Aryan powers," Ayodhya and Mithila, we are told. A tribal king loyal to
Ram is asked to guard the kingdom's borders until his brother Bharat

has secured his rule, as though Kosala, Ram's kingdom, were a terri-torial nation-state.[101] Dasaratha lectures Ram on the need to be able to sacrifice all for his people, as a king.[102] Social mores are updated as well. The lower status of the bride's father vis-à-vis the bridegroom's father is invoked and rejected, with Dasaratha expressing magnanimity, and Janaka, Sita's father, ostentatious humility.[103] The tribal king Nishad is seated beside Ram with a reminder that after all he is a Harijan, and beloved by god.[104] Unlike the characters of Valmiki's composition, or those of most other Ramayan poets including Tulsi, none of the figures in Sagar's serial utters any derogatory remarks about any group of people, whether they be women, lower castes or rakshasas. In their place are genial and patronizing sentiments, affirming the same distinctions in a self-congratulatory way.

Sagar also interpolates themes that seem directly inspired by the then nascent Ram Janmabhumi campaign. When Ram arrives in Chitrakoot and sets up house, he places a clod of earth wrapped in saffron cloth on a mantelpiece. He has apparently been carrying this parcel in his waistband through the forest. Placing it next to a lamp, he prays to it:

> *He meri janmabhumi ka pavan mati*
> *Aaj teri charan raj se meri parn kuti pavitra ho gayi.*
> O sacred earth of my birthplace
> My abode has become pure in your auspicious presence.[105]

The worship, which fixates on a portable piece of his birthplace, is a sequence unconnected to the rest of the episode, and appears to be on a different narrative arc. Rituals of prayer and worship typically involve an interaction between two or more people in the serial; in this scene, Lakshman and Sita are absent, as Ram communes with his birthplace alone, in a purely solitary gesture, echoing campaign rhetoric of the VHP. The incantation of Sanskrit verse, by none other than Ram himself, sanctifies the sequence, and highlights the traditionalist medi-ation through which the serial seeks to win the identification of individ-ual viewers with novel ritual practices.

The predominant mood of the serial cannot be conveyed by a discussion of its component parts. Much of the message is wordless, felt rather than heard, and communicated in the expressions and gestures of the actors, in the camera angles and the cutting and zooming, in the timely coordination of pictures and music. A key component of the mood is one of reverence and devotion. This alternates and intermingles with the engagement induced by the narrative itself. It is a powerful means of winning the viewer to go along with the story.

In the following piece, I will try to convey some sense of the mood evoked. This is the story of Shabari, from episode thirty-four of the serial. A short episode in the Forest Book of Valmiki's Ramayan, the story of Shabari has gained popularity in folk retellings. By the time Tulsi tells the story, it has changed considerably. From being merely an aged ascetic who meets Ram, Shabari is turned into an old tribal woman atoning for her sins in an ashram, who has been told by her guru to await the arrival of Ram and seek his blessings. The story is meant to illustrate the magnanimity of Ram in embracing all those who worship him, however lowborn and wretched they may be in the eyes of society. Sagar provides a lengthy, embellished version of Tulsi's story in the serial.

The first scene shows Shabari, a bent old woman in widow's garb; her white hair is untidy and her appearance in general suggests the simplicity of constraint rather than choice. Unsteadily, she is strewing flowers on the path leading to her hut; with each step she calls out in a quavering voice,

Mere Ram!

The whole path, about six feet wide, is covered with flowers. Three sadhus are passing by. They pause near Shabari. The youngest of them says:

You mad woman! How many years will you spend like this, waiting for your Ram? Has your Ram come yet?
Shabari [crouched on the ground, in a tearful voice]: No, but he'll come. He will definitely come.

The sadhu laughs.

Shabari: My guru-dev Matanga's word cannot be wrong. So every day, every moment, I prepare for his visit . . . Please do not step on these flowers . . .

She cries a little, and resumes her labor of love, calling out Ram's name. The sadhus walk on along another path. The young sadhu says: "Sometimes it seems to me that the old woman is mad." The oldest of the three replies: "It's possible. But don't forget that bhakti and madness are not so different. If you look at it in a worldly perspective, the *bhakt* is just like a mad person. Shabari is a great worshipper, and displays no trace of vanity. This is the sign of a true *bhakt*."

Cut to Shabari, who continues to strew flowers and call out Ram's name. Ram and Lakshman appear.

Shabari: Who are you?
Ram: We want to go to Mata Shabari's ashram. Could you take us there?
Shabari [with great emotion]: To Mata Shabari? But who are you?
Ram: I am Ram, and this is my little brother Lakshman.

A sitar begins to play. Camera cuts to Shabari, zooms into a close-up. Cut and zoom in again, twice.

Cut to a smiling Ram (close-up).
Cut to Shabari, zoom in to extreme close-up (extremely close-up).
She is tearful, and breathing heavily.
Cut to Ram, smiling at her.
Cut to Lakshman.
Cut to Shabari (e.c.u.).
Cut to Ram, smiling.
Cut to Shabari.
Cut to Ram.
Cut to Shabari.
Cut and zoom in again to Shabari.
Shabari: Raaam! Lakkkshmmann! [Drawing the names out.] You have come, my lord! You have come to Shabari's hut! I did not recognize you. [She falls at his feet. Her voice rising:] Forgive me!
Cut to Ram, smiling.
Cut to close-up of Ram's feet, Shabari's head above it. Tear drops fall on his feet.

Shabari puts more flowers on the already flower-strewn path, and leads them into her hut.

Shabari: Today my hut has become pure.

She seats them on a straw mat, and attends to them.

Shabari: My lord, you must be hungry?
Ram: Yes.
Shabari: I'll get fruits. I'll get fruits. Everyday I bring sweet plums for you from the forest, my lord.

She places a straw tray of fruit before them. The camera closes in to reveal each fruit has been bitten into, as Shabari in her naïveté wished to ensure the fruits were sweet.[106] Ram looks at her with great feeling. His look is searching and intense, far from the merely gracious look that might be expected of a lord receiving his due. His expression is one of deep emotion, of both amazement and recognition, and a sense of a longing finally satisfied. The lord has encountered a true *bhakt*.

Cut to close-up (c.u.) of fruits.
Cut to c.u. of Ram.
Cut to c.u. of Shabari.
Cut to c.u. of Ram.
Cut to Shabari.
Shabari: Please eat, my lord. They are very sweet. I have tasted and picked them.
Cut to c.u. of Ram. He smiles.
Cut to c.u. of tray. Ram picks one and eats it slowly.
The sitar plays on.
Cut to Shabari.
Shabari [in a tearful voice]: Eat, my lord. Take another one. Take another one.
Cut to Lakshman, who wrinkles his face in characteristic counterpoint, as the already-bitten fruit offends him.
Ram: Eat, Lakshman.
Cut to Ram.
Ram: Vah!
Cut to c.u. of Shabari.
Shabari: It's good? It's sweet?
Ram: I don't have the words to praise this.
Cut to c.u. of Shabari. She shakes her head in disbelief and gasps.
Ram: After so many years, it feels as if Mata Kausalya is feeding me with her own hands.
Cut to c.u. of Shabari, who shakes her head in disbelief.
Ram: Lakshman, only the gods in heaven eat such sweet fruit.
Shabari: My service to my guru has given me the reward of your *darshan*.
Ram: In seeing you, the merit of this life and all my previous lives has borne fruit.

This episode is important, and emblematic of the serial in both formal and thematic elements. As an extended depiction of the feeling of bhakti, and of Ram's compassion for his devotee, it offers us a concentrated sense of the power the serial had for its viewers. The copious cutting and zooming and use of close-ups and extreme close-ups would be redundant in a linear, narrative account of the story. But Sagar is using the small screen to advantage, to suggest the visual capture of emotions by deep and prolonged close-ups, allowing viewers to project their own feelings onto the actors.

As an idealized account of the self-realization/self-effacement in submission and surrender to a deity, the sense of the numinous, which the episode hints at, cannot be reduced to any ideological analysis. But the intimations of unrealized worlds, however potent, are a subjective, private affair. When they escape those bounds and manifest themselves as action, that is, as the story continues, they become subject to all the inescapable constraints of social action. The power of the numinous may then be put to all-too-worldly uses, as in fact it usually has. The Shabari episode, while a moving portrait of the mutual recognition between lord and devotee, is also a story of the magnanimity of Ram in accepting the tribute of a low-caste woman. Her name is a marker of her ethnic status. The Gita Press edition of the *Manas* offers this footnote as explanation:

Sabari was known by the name of the wild tribe (Sabaras) to which she belonged. Though low-born, she had already acquired some celebrity for her piety and devotion; hence the poet has chosen to call her abode a hermitage (a name generally applied to the abode of sages and hermits). This can easily serve as an illustration of the catholicity of the great Hindu religion, which, though rigid in social matters, does not fail to give proper recognition to individual merit and virtue. The whole of this episode is an eye-opener in this respect. (Footnote to 3.33.3)

Tulsi himself is good enough to specify prevailing etiquette, in lines Ram speaks immediately before encountering Shabari, absent in Sagar's screenplay: "A brahman, even though he curse you, beat you or speak harsh words to you, is still worthy of adoration: so declare the saints. A brahman must be respected, though lacking in amiability and virtue; not so a Sudra, though possessing a host of virtues and rich in knowledge" (3.33.1–2). The Shabari story emphasizes that the lowest of the low can be saved – if they have enough bhakti. The elevated sentiments are moving, but what is left implied gives pause: in a kind of meritocracy of bhakts, few among the lowborn can hope to be saved.

The devotional appeal of the serial was interleaved with a melodramatic drawing out of well-known parts of the epic, such as the *agni pariksha* or fire ordeal, creating a narrational counterpoint that filled out the viewing experience. Sagar's fire ordeal reveals some of the serial's deeply patriarchal assumptions, while showing awareness of some of the more modern interlocutors the event would summon. At the same time, the material means by which the story is stretched out while sustaining its discursive tension are clearly visible here.

In Valmiki's account of the fire ordeal, as in some others, Ram rejects Sita after she is won back: his honor is satisfied, but now he cannot accept a woman who has lived in another man's house. Stung by the imputation, Sita resolves to submit herself to a trial by fire. If she has swerved from her devotion to Ram for an instant, she declares, the fire should burn her up. She enters the fire and is untouched. Ram's suspicions are put to rest. Perhaps more importantly, Sita makes a spectacular public display of her virtue. Tulsi, anxious to keep Ram's conduct blemishless, as well as to banish all suspicion about Sita, introduces a new element into the story, taken from the *Adhyatma Ramayan*. Ram asks the "real" Sita to "abide in the fire" until he completes the destruction of the demons (3.23). Sita then enters the fire by herself. Only a *maya*, or shadow Sita, is left behind, who is however indistinguishable from the original in all respects.

In Deorala, Rajasthan, in 1987, a young widow was made to burn herself on her husband's funeral pyre. Local politicians and political aspirants celebrated the sati, as feminist groups protested the murder, and the government reluctantly followed with a ban on glorifying widow-burning. Nevertheless, a temple was built on the site of the burning, and thousands marched in support of the sati. This too formed part of the backdrop to this episode. As the agni pariksha episode drew nigh, there was speculation as to how Sagar would handle it. Sagar's portrayal, eventually, turned out to be an ingenious exercise in equivocation. In the Valmiki account, the drama of the episode derived from its unexpectedness, coming as it did right after the battle to win Sita back. Far from showing delight at seeing Sita again, Ram actually rejects her. Following a scornful, yet stirring declaration of faith, Sita enters a fire to prove the indestructibility of her virtue. The extraordinary importance of virtue, to the extent that a woman's life depended on it, gives the scene a terrifying urgency. With Tulsi's device of the maya Sita, the whole purpose of the fire changes from an "ordeal" to a mere retrieval (6.108). In Sagar, the equivocation goes much further. He omits the preliminary creation of the maya Sita, suggesting thereby that Valmiki's precedent would be followed.

Sagar's narrative strategy of sequential climaxes that repeat the same point is one he uses throughout the serial. At first, Ram sternly orders Lakshman to prepare a fire, saying that Sita would have to be tested. Lakshman launches into a furious protest at this mistreatment of a woman who sacrificed everything to accompany her husband. Ram lets him finish, and then reveals that he had actually entrusted Sita to the Fire God, and now had to retrieve her. The mention of a test is thus proved to be misleading. There follows an extended flashback of the transaction. Then for a third time, when Sita arrives, and Ram sternly orders a fire to be prepared, we are led through the same elements, although with a different set of characters. The sequence is an elaboration of patriarchal ideas that, by the similitude of response in one frame after another, appears like the savoring of a profound yet undeniable truth.

In Tulsidas, Sita asks Lakshman to prepare a fire at this time, for her trial by fire, to satisfy Ram's suspicion. Sagar chooses to make the fire appear from Lakshman's magic rather than show him prepare a fire in the usual mundane way, as both Valmiki and Tulsi chose to do. The remarkably repetitive way in which the narrative progresses and the prodigious wealth of detail deserves a brief glimpse, to appreciate an essential aspect of the serial's importance, namely the technical mastery of the facts that this conveyed to viewers.[107]

Long shot of Ram and Lakshman from behind Sita. Camera zooms in on Ram and Lakshman. Lakshman shakes his head in great sadness. Cut to shot of Ram and Lakshman, from the back. Lakshman turns to Ram, his face contorted in tears.
Cut to front view of Ram. Camera zooms into tight close-up. He appears stern.
Cut to close-up of Lakshman, who folds his hands in prayer.
Cut to tight close-up of Ram. He nods to Lakshman, to go ahead.
Cut to shot of Ram and Lakshman, from the back. Lakshman bows to Ram and moves ahead.
Cut to front view of Ram.
Cut to Lakshman, looking back at Ram reproachfully.
Cut to long shot of assembly. Lakshman walking towards Sita mid-stage, Ram with his back turned, in foreground.
Cut to close-up of Ram, front view.
Cut to long shot of Lakshman and Sita, with the *vanars* arrayed on either side. Lakshman makes a conjurer's gesture with his hands and a fire appears before them.
Cut to Ram.
Cut to previous shot. Zoom in on Sita.
Cut to long shot. Zoom in on fire.
Cut to long shot. Zoom in on Hanuman.
Cut to close-up of Sugriv.
Cut to long shot. Zoom in on Sita.
Cut to long shot. Zoom in on Ram.
Cut to long shot. Zoom in on Sita.
Cut to long shot. Zoom in on Ram.
Cut to long shot. Zoom in on Sita.
Cut to long shot. Zoom in on Ram.
Cut to close-up of Ram, looking stern.
Cut to close-up of Sita, pensive, eyes lowered.
Cut to long shot, with Lakshman on left, fire in foreground, and Sita behind the fire.

Crowd all around.

Cut to close-up of Sita. Slow zoom backward. She folds her palms and bows to the fire.

The Shree Geeta Press edition of Manas translates her words on this occasion as follows:

"If in thought, word and deed I have never set my heart on anyone other than the Hero of Raghu, may this fire, which knows the working of all minds, become cool as sandal-paste to me" (6.108.4).

She points to Ram, shakes her head, as if to deny any infidelity to him.

The *bhajan* continues.

Cut to long shot of Sita praying to fire.

Cut to close-up of Sita, praying.

Cut to long shot. Sita walks into the fire.

Cut to reverse long shot. Ram, back turned, watches Sita.

Cut to close-up of Sita, smiling, hands folded, engulfed in flames.

Cut and zoom in on Ram. He looks stern.

Cut to Hanuman.

Cut to Sita, smiling amidst the flames.

Cut to tight close-up of Ram, looking stern.

Cut to several gods in the sky, looking down at the scene, hands folded.

Cut to smiling Sita.

Cut to tight close-up of Ram.

Cut to several gods (a different group this time), looking down from the sky, hands folded.

Cut to smiling Sita.

. . .

Bhajan begins.

Even though there is suspense about precisely how the story will turn out, it is still so well known that Sagar can afford to bypass all dialogue. The characters simply mime their responses, and choral singing provides the audio background. Dialogue may be superfluous, but facial expression is everything: it is the central selling point of Sagar's production. Even unnamed secondary characters are not passed over. For every incremental progression of the plot, the pleasure, surprise, disbelief, or shock of each person is serially recorded; several movements have as many as thirteen reaction shots, of which five could be of one person alone. One critic described it as "reaction mania."[108] The seamless editing technique of Hollywood soap operas is adopted, master shot followed by shot–reverse shot sequences and alternating close-ups. This leads to the viewer unobtrusively occupying a privileged vantage-point, from which "everything" about the characters can be known. But the reaction shots are redundant from the point of view of moving the story onward, since in a moral community as tight as that in the Ramayan, responses are unfailingly unanimous. The point, as Robert Allen suggests about soap operas, is to confirm the strength and the extent of the moral community itself.[109] For those interested in this community, it is a matter of obtaining complete knowledge. Numerous viewers, during my fieldwork, asserted that Sagar had shown *everything* in his version; previously people had only heard or read about it. This sense of omniscience obviously lends a powerful verisimilitude to the version of events Sagar constructs. If there is an exhaustive detailing of all that went on, surely it must all be true.

OLD SYMBOLS IN A NEW LANGUAGE OF POLITICS

I argued in chapter one that the conjuncture of liberalization can be seen as the latest phase of a passive revolution, whereby the leading class coalition forges its internal compromises, and advances on a political terrain that does not allow for outright domination. What it attempts therefore is to win the consent of the majority to prevailing circumstances and modes of governance, in a series of provisional reforms and maneuvers that are not assured in their outcome, and require constant revision and renewal. Television, as a centralized means of communication, is clearly significant in this process, because it affords a means of assembling and gauging popular opinion. But as I have argued here, it was difficult for a government bureaucracy to descend from its sovereign heights and be responsive to the fluid and uncertain allegiance of audiences. There was thus a fundamental incompatibility between the mode of governance and the form of communication that needed to be resolved.

There is no sense in which an inevitable train of events was initiated by liberalization or for that matter by the Ramayan broadcast in particular. A given economic condition does not by itself define historical events; rather it creates circumstances where particular kinds of ideas and modes of thinking are perceived more favorably, leading to ways of understanding and resolving problems, sometimes in lastingly influential ways.[110] It was clearly impossible to have foreseen the popular response the Ramayan telecast generated. Even if the Congress party had correctly calculated the serial's popularity, the kinds of uses it attempted suggested too automatic a conception of propaganda for much to have been achieved, e.g., the use of the actor, Arun Govil, who played Lord Ram to rouse crowds in a Congress by-election campaign, or Rajiv Gandhi's offer to provide Ram Rajya in exchange for an electoral victory.[111] It was finally the Hindu nationalists, with their supple combination of parliamentary and non-parliamentary wings, and the privileges peculiar to an opposition movement, who were able to steal the advantage intended for the ruling party itself.

As institutional sponsor of a religious epic, Doordarshan was in conflict with its other role, as a secular state apparatus meant to be impartial in matters of religion, promoting "education" or "education-al" values rather than devotional programming. In the event, the contradiction was breezily dismissed by bureaucrats and politicians, the serial's ratings and revenues being held as eloquent confirmation of its pro-social values. The commonplace status accorded to television in this understanding accrued to the broadcast's ideological force. The fact that people across the nation laid aside their other duties and came together quietly, weekly celebrating their common heritage, was unex-ceptionable in this view, and beyond all narrow political interests. Besides, Muslims watched it as well, it was often said, in what was intended as crowning proof of the telecast's non-partisan nature. Coming at the height of anti-Muslim riots and Hindu zealotry, the claim was difficult to take at face value, assuming as it did that Muslims were a discrete cultural entity, whose conquest by Hindus only required confir-mation. Such a view made little distinction between the defensive tactics of a fearful minority and free participation in a pluralist culture. Instead, the uncoerced viewing appeared only to confirm the free character of individual acts of consumption. The collective "recognition" of the nation's bygone past thus served as backdrop against which assurances could be made for a reformulated nationalism, in Ramanand Sagar's judicious rendition of the story.

Sagar's telling of the Ramayan portrayed a sanitized version of ancient society, where olden wisdom was made into a dynamic and changing military science, albeit one practiced by venerable sages. Women's and caste oppression were rewritten as benevolent protection. What stayed constant was a patriarchal ordering of society, in somewhat more casual guise. Explicit glorification of Hindu identity per se was occasional; viewed with the right lens, however, it could seem like "the sky, the horizon, an authority that at once determines and limits a condition."[112]

The Sagar Ramayan brought different conceptions of society and politics together in one of the country's most recognizable narratives. Audiences could read the serial as offering a benign tale of a bygone age, or as one with an urgent message for the present. Viewers could understand the Ramayan as offering a way of talking not just about faith and the epic past, but about what kind of leadership a society required, and the mode of public engagement appropriate for its members. But if English-educated elites saw in the serial's popularity mainly the excess of tradition in a society that had moved ahead, rather than the prevalence of a still-relevant system of ideas, this was an indication of a split in the televisual public.[113] What could, for the majority of viewers, be an acceptable way of thinking about politics might appear to elites as a pre-political or a para-political fact. The Ramayan's popularity brought this division to the surface in a sense, making elites aware of their cultural marginality, while emboldening the most articulate sections of orthodoxy with a sudden sense of their contemporaneity and relevance. Both these sections of society, ordinarily so far apart in terms of social distance, were brought closer whether they wished it or not, with the weekly broadcasts that became a fixture on national television. The currency given to the tele-epics soon bestowed on them the status of a Durkheimian social fact, subject to a range of interpretations to be sure, but present as an undeniable reservoir of popular significance.

My interest in this chapter has been in bringing assumptions from the text to the surface to show the influence of the contemporary in this tele-epic. Rather than treat the Ramayan serial as either an aspect of unchanging tradition, or as an interesting but epiphenomenal event, I prefer to see it as a useful commentary on the present. As the pressures of market liberalization abroad were putting an inefficient developmentalist state on the defensive, and the fractures and dissonances within the society made it difficult to win consent for major departures from existing policy, the onset of television presented both a problem and an opportunity to the Indian state. On the one hand, far-reaching communication was suddenly possible using intimate forms of address, in a society beset by deep economic and cultural cleavages. On the other hand, the results of this communication were now visible as never before, as audience ratings, "popularity" and profits, so that the gap between state pronouncements and public sentiments acquired an unprecedented salience. As the era of economic reforms approached, Hindu nationalism saw its opportunity to act as a hinge or point of transfer between old and new dispensations, providing assurance of a symbolic continuity between them, with the Ramayan available as part of its armory. That the hitherto secular Congress Party itself introduced

Hindu epics on television, only to be overtaken in its initiative by a more adroit opposition, perhaps only confirms the overdetermined nature of the shift in public culture. What immediate responses did the Ramayan serial provoke among viewers, and how can we make sense of the sangh parivar's claims of a resurgent Hindu public in the wake of the broadcast's success?

The next chapter explores these questions, examining perceptions of television as a communicating medium and as an aspect of material culture, and asks how pre-existing languages of politics could accommodate and vernacularize state-sponsored programming. In doing so, we can extend the insights of this chapter, to see more clearly the transactions between politics and other realms of society that were in some ways insulated, gradually being brought into a single circuit of exchange, and increasingly yielding a new mode of power and a reformulated linguistic universe.[114] It is in this sense perhaps that we can best understand the changes in political culture, as not simply a one-way deterioration of politics into an emphasis on identity. Rather it allows us to imagine the possibility of transactions between different realms of politics in a more productive manner. More efficient means of communication challenge and undercut the top-down character of state control; at the same time they enable state power to mimic the new media, being more intimate and familiar in its language, and more solicitous of the individual lives of citizen-consumers.[115] To what extent these professions can be fulfilled is of course uncertain; indeed, the new rhetoric to some extent compensates for the now diminished capacity of the state, as the discipline of international trade and lending agencies and of world markets hems in the possibility of effective autarkic intervention. Nevertheless, a more Hinduized set of symbols, once made publicly available and endorsed with the imprimatur of state broadcasting authority, produces effects that have their own force, and entail their own consequences. The third chapter considers the kinds of shape the resulting politics might take, through the imbrication of languages of community and of democratic politics, as we trace the contradictory workings of the televisual form.

CHAPTER 3

The communicating thing and its public

I remember when we first bought a television set in my parents' home in Madras. The year was 1980, about five years after television had come to town. For years we had seen our Marwari neighbor pack his terrace with thirty to fifty people, mostly children paying half a rupee per head, when feature films were shown on weekend nights. We had no entrepreneurial ambitions ourselves, but we were weekly reminded of the draw of the medium by the scene across the road, if by nothing else. There was an air of excitement and adventure about the purchase. We had been trooping to neighbors' homes to watch programs, and there was an unspoken sense that it could not go on, so there was no one arguing against the idea. The amount was not a small one, over 3,000 rupees (then US $375) to buy a nineteen-inch black and white set. A college-mate who had some influence with television dealers told me whom to contact. No discount would be available on the set, the dealer informed us. But we could save money on the accessories we would need – on the blue add-on screen to absorb "glare," and on the rooftop antenna, to ensure clear reception. (The sign of a good picture was when the eyelashes of the newsreader were visible, according to an ad for Solidaire TV – "that seldom fails.") As we later learned, neither purchase was necessary. The blue screen dimmed the picture, and an antenna was not needed when we lived five miles away from the broadcasting station. But the idea of requiring supplementary paraphernalia for such an important purchase was intuitively acceptable. As much as we perceived television itself, what we saw was its aura of novelty, and the accoutrements needed to contain and to enhance its magic.

What is the effect of television when it arrives as a new commodity? Admittedly, my reception study was performed in 1988–89, and television had existed since the mid-1960s in New Delhi, one of the sites of my reception study. But the viewing population remained infinitesimal until the late 1980s; the experience of regular interaction with the medium was still relatively new for most people. There existed a state monopoly over broadcasting during the period of this study: television was synonymous with Doordarshan at this time.

One newspaper columnist wrote about the excitement in the wake of television's arrival, as a social presence requiring attention, and thus also a new currency available for truck and barter:

In many localities, the "Haves" oblige "Havenots" by throwing their door open and the latter reciprocate in many ways. They would fetch milk from the booth, bring home-made dishes on occasions and be always available for petty jobs at short notice. However there are instances where strained relations develop because of TV . . . Visitors during the "show" are devoid of common hospitality. It is also a very common experience that a discussion or even a chat is cut short as soon as the favourite programme appears on the screen . . . I have great regard for "Chitrahaar" and the "film days" for the simple reason that I find these days very convenient to make social visits. It ensures my meeting the person for sure. I also utilise these days as my laundry days as the sick tap on the top floor becomes very generous especially for those three hours. Then again, this is the best time to travel in a DTC [Delhi Transport Corporation] bus and also to do a little shopping in the otherwise busy markets . . . This is also the most convenient time to steal roses, radish and papaya from the neighbour's garden.[1]

Nearly always black-and-white rather than color, the television set was an important object in whatever room it was placed, in the houses I visited – there was never a chance of missing it at first glance. Through a strange heliotropism, furniture tended to arrange itself around or facing the set, as if acknowledging its power to realign people and things. The top of the television was often adorned, if nothing else with a piece of colored cloth, embroidery, or matting, and sometimes with plastic flowers or other decorative objects. Sometimes the television itself was sheathed in a cotton or plastic vestment, so that when evening came, a preliminary ritual of unveiling inaugurated the viewing.

Television makes its arrival as an enigmatic thing, welcomed but ill understood. When inquiring how audiences respond, there is then a difficulty in giving voice to what is not only experientially new, but also perhaps inexpressible. There is an element of enchantment in it, as an object distinct from any before it. There is both pleasure and danger, in the quiet flattery of having the world served up to you, on the one hand, and the perils of the unknown that the home is meant to guard against, on the other. This is a medium that appears as a freestanding object. Yet a vast infrastructure is required to make it work, requiring little of the viewers who in spontaneous but synchronized movements, recline and watch at leisure.

Television, as a communicating thing, signifies important aspects of modernity – a new mode of communication, and a certain kind of thingness, a desirable commodity pointing to other desirable commodities. I can remember when we first bought a refrigerator, on a bank loan my father obtained for the purpose. I was nineteen, but I knew I could have been five, as I stroked its shining white surface and put my arms around it. I joked to my brother that we should put it on a revolving table in the hall, so that every guest could admire it. Its function played little part in this celebration. To an unbiased spectator, its physical beauty too could not have been great, as a large, unbudgeable white cuboid of metal. It was something else, something hard to express, pointing to things and worlds beyond us, things we desired as well, that this thing reassured us we might after all attain. Indeed it was not so much the having of the thing as the state of being thereby reached, or being reached out to.

TELEVISION AND THE RESTRUCTURING OF POPULAR AND DOMESTIC SPACE

"Why is such a beautiful thing called *TB*," one viewer, an old woman in a resettlement colony in New Delhi, wanted to know, pronouncing "v" as "b," like many native speakers, and so making it into the abbreviation for tuberculosis. If television's "beauty" as a signpost of modernity was evident, its totemic power perhaps made it harder to understand. There were those, of course, who rejected television entirely, even for an auspicious purpose such as viewing the Ramayan. "*Bakvaas hai* [it's nonsense]," responded an old farmer, pausing at his hookah, when asked what he thought of the serial. "The Ramayan is a matter of the heart, not something to be watched." Sure enough, there was nothing that he watched, whether it was the Ramayan or anything else.

Television quickly became pre-eminent among consumer durables for working and lower middle classes in India, displacing the refrigerator, and becoming a fixture in marriage transactions where dowry was given. In Kanpur, electronics goods dealers reported a ten-fold rise in sales during the marriage season.[2] Increasing competition among TV manufacturers led to a range of loan and installment schemes, so that the lowest level of salaried workers, including sweepers, were purchasing TV sets. "What is the point of a 'fridge in a dowry?" asked Murti, a part-time domestic manservant. "You have to keep eating stale food. With a television you don't have to stand in long cinema lines."[3] Indeed the increasing demand for this and other durable goods elevated quarrels over dowry to an unprecedented level of ferocity, as middle classes began to draw lists of the kinds of commodities indispensable to any respectable household.[4] Although television represented a major shift in the mode of social representation, it appeared first and foremost as a tool, a bargaining chip or a status symbol people could wield in their lives. Thus television appeared to reflect the world around it not only in its work of mediation, but also as a thing, merging into the backdrop even while transfiguring it.

Valentine Daniel offers an extraordinary story illustrating the power of commodities, and the difficulty of understanding the emotional investment they induce. He recounts meeting a Sinhala man in his twenties whom he knew to have taken part in the mob lynching of a Tamil boy who worked in a Hindu temple. Daniel had known the Sinhala man (whom he calls Piyadasa) since the latter was a young boy. Piyadasa recounts the story of the crowd gathering around the boy, and going round and round him, while the boy urinated in terror. Someone took a stab at the boy, and then they all fell upon him with knives and sticks, and then doused him with petrol and burned him. Daniel could perhaps only have followed with a *non sequitur*. Having just begun to encounter confessions of violence in his fieldwork, and not yet knowing what a suitable response might be, he proceeded to ask what he felt was an irrelevant question: "What is your goal in life?" The reply came unhesitatingly: "I want a video [a VCR]."[5]

Neil Postman has offered this felicitous way of thinking about media: we should inquire not just how *we* use it, but how *it* uses us. In addition to what television *communicates* then, is the question of how *it* communicates, over and beyond the programming itself. This is an analytic separation to be sure, of content and form. When talking to people about television, these questions appeared scrambled: it was sometimes as a reality function, as a window on modernity, offering lessons on how to eat, sit, walk, and dress without betraying one's origins, to aspiring members of the middle classes. It often worked as a machine dispensing private space, offering a refuge from the distractions of family and neighborhood. In crowded urban locales, the blessings of such a function overrode the limitations of any particular program offering. Television could be used by parents to lure children indoors and control their errant movements; the same force could be used to challenge authority, not only by children, but also by women in the home.

The flaws in Doordarshan programming were legion, and indeed, writings on TV in the press were largely lists of the latest gaffes and confusions. For example, censorship could reach an extent that was ludicrous, negating itself by making the fact of censorship evident:

An assassination attempt on Prime Minister Rajiv Gandhi on October 2, 1986 at Rajghat in New Delhi brought television crews from all the world's capitals, but Doordarshan viewers received no word of this event. The truth is that the servitude of the government media is so great that its officials cannot even drink a glass of water without permission from above.[6]

The ramshackle character of Doordarshan's operation meant that the broadcasts often reflected their often less than expert input. Producers in Doordarshan often pronounced it "a miracle" that anything went on the air at all.[7] Weekly columns could be scathing on the subject:

The number of pauses and the periods when viewers are faced with a blank screen, programmes summarily interrupted with advertisements, or with news bulletins, sports matches cropped in their presentation, wayward cameramen who focus on interviewees when they are picking their nose rather than when they are answering questions . . .[8]

Viewers themselves were seldom critical of the government's monopoly or of the manner of its exercise. Although cynicism with respect to politics was well nigh ubiquitous, it appeared to leave the televisual medium largely untouched. There were of course complaints about the timing of programs that interfered with children's study hours, enticed viewers away from a good night's sleep with feature films, or, indeed, kept them up wondering what would air next since the programs were not always detailed in advance.[9] Sometimes disapproval of the schedule could include incisive critique about the limitations in its conception. Thus one newspaper article reported the complaints of a housewife, Kamal Verma, on the limited nature of afternoon programming, focusing as it did on cooking and household tips:

In any case, non-working women are adept at *achar-murabba* [pickles and preserves] activity – why don't [they] show us more political news . . .? We get only one Hindi paper, which my husband takes to the shop. In the mornings I'm too busy cooking and sending the children to school and the same thing happens in the evening. So I never get a chance to know about political news.[10]

But most viewers appeared to attach little importance to the (seemingly more important) matter of propaganda. "It's their house. It's their family. Whoever is biggest in the house will promote themselves," said an airport maintenance worker, Pyarelal, in an oft-repeated view.[11] Congress supporters would sometimes defend such promotion: "If I'm

ruling my family, and people see that I'm doing my job properly,"
another airport worker, Omprakash, said, "my kids are eating and
living well, won't the neighbors say – he's looking after his family well?
. . . So if the Congress is doing its job properly, and they show it, what's
the mistake in that?"

Such views resonated with a traditional view of power, one that did
not question its distribution per se, and asked mainly that it be used
appropriately. Thus those who were critical denounced the government
fiercely. "Neither the Janata [Party] nor the Congress does any good for
the people," declared Shyamlal, a factory worker. "They're all crooks."
Some viewers in fact saw the motive for communication in purely
material terms: TV sets were sold, and money made. "The government
surely benefits from the tax on sets," surmised Gopichand, a shop-
keeper. "I'm sure it gets at least 300 rupees for every set sold." The
possibility of interested and thus systematically distorted communication, if perceived, provoked little concern. "Forget what the government
is saying. It's a straightforward matter. TV for us is just entertainment,"
Rai Singh, a telephone lineman, commented. "It lightens the burden of
the heart. It's a form of play. Why talk to anyone? We go to the TV and
'open' it [*sic*]. It lightens our mental load."

These and other viewers saw the people in power as partisan one way
or other, either taking care of "their own family" or failing in this duty;
that is, they did not conceive of a democratic system of power as such.
Their understanding of communication, however, held it to be entirely
unmarked by its sponsors' intentions, as something free and pure. Many
of them otherwise expressed a profound sense of marginality, or, if asked
about the government's management of its institutions, made fierce
denunciations of corruption and abuse of power. When they spoke
about television though, such criticisms had no place.[12] Bhanwarlal, a
worker at the New Delhi international airport, who was scathing about
self-seeking politicians and their pretenses during election time, said:

TV is there to provide knowledge, information. Many people don't know how
to read, but by listening to the news they can get to know what's going on in the
world. Just sitting at home, you can find out how to walk, talk, eat, live –
everything . . . The educated people already knew how, but the ones who do
not – it helps them. Television is like a guru, from whom you get learning. It has
everything . . . It is very helpful.

Amar Singh, also a worker at the airport, insisted that all the programs
on television were good, none bad: "Like for the village people. I used to

live in the village. I learnt how to eat properly. People are influenced on how to dress, how to behave, how to live, from TV. We also get an idea of how much the country has developed." He explained: "In the villages, they live in quite a backward way. We would eat *rotis* on the floor, or on the *charpoy*. But TV tells us what to do and when."

The class dimensions of this understanding are striking. Having described television communication in terms of gift exchange, we can tentatively elaborate on this model. Dominant and subordinate classes exchange with each other in the process of mass mediated communication. Subordinate classes see themselves, or are invited to see themselves, in the forms of communication put out in the mass media. The dominant groups provide class-based knowledge previously held more exclusively, available only to the literate and the schooled, and to members of designated status groups. They proffer the symbolics of class membership, in other words. "[Y]ou can find out how to walk, talk, eat, live – everything." That is to say, all persons can engage and if they choose, identify with the symbols offered, there being no limits on who may do so (save language). This is the cultural experience of democracy, without its complement in economic terms, of genuinely equal life opportunities (through material and not merely symbolic redistribution). In return the subordinate classes offer provisional consent to the terms of class membership. Marcel Mauss has written: "Society always pays itself in the counterfeit coin of its dream."[13] What is that dream today if not that of communication itself? The dream that everything can now be known and spoken because the means to do so are abundantly available and in use.

If we follow the logic of gift exchange, what the subordinate classes seek is membership, and what they win is subordination, but they do not necessarily know or accept this fact. It is in this indeterminacy that the notion of communication is made possible. Television appears to create a sense of perfect communication irrespective of its content. There is an enjoyment of the experience as mediated by an object rather than a person ("Why talk to anyone?"), and thus pure and unsullied, welcoming individuals regardless of their status or disposition. It is one way communication, but few viewers reported any sense of being imposed upon. It is the *idea* of communication that triumphs, even if the *fact* of non-communication and misunderstanding is essential to its maintenance.

Thus for instance, an unemployed worker in Kaynagar, Anil Kumar, told a story of how on a children's program on television, schoolchildren had sung a song calling the then Prime Minister a thief. (The incident actually occurred at the All India Radio station in Patna in 1988.)

> *Gali gali mein shor hein*
> *Rajiv Gandhi chor hein.*
> (The cry in the street and in every nook,
> Is, Rajiv Gandhi is a crook!)

It was this event, Anil Kumar said, that initiated screening of all programs for criticism of the government. He presented a fable that rendered censorship into expressing, not reasons of state, but a human response of indignation to a child's prank. The unilateral exercise of authority was thus transformed into part of an ongoing, animated interaction between the government and its subjects. While dramatizing the arrival of television and the authority it exercised, such an account also indicated how it could be rendered commonplace and familiar, so that its novelty did not challenge the imagination.

Television is a means of communication and also an object entering the life-world, taking its place amongst other things.[14] In various ways, the novelty of the object tends to get subdued and normalized, as it is folded into prevailing modes of understanding. Examining the forms of perception through which television is domesticated and incorporated into daily life can illuminate the character of its influence, and provides an important complement to the textual readings performed by different sections of viewers. In this chapter I point to two broad, overlapping conceptions of television, as an object dispensing unqualified good, and as a more ambivalent force, capable of good and ill both.

Two kinds of problems require negotiation in reception studies. The medium's influence can easily dissipate in the diversity of audience readings, which are then understood either as "resistance" or as "no effect." Secondly, the wider context tends to be invoked rather than investigated, so that even when influence is attributed to the medium, it is assumed rather than argued. A media-centrist approach is at the heart of both problems. What requires study is how social and media events unfold and interact in historical time, in diverse and unforeseeable networks of action. No amount of attention to the medium or its audience can elicit these contingent political processes. To trace the complex interactive process through which the media becomes influential requires attention to historical process, institutional context and cultural meaning, and the ways these are related.[15] To reiterate, the media do not form the center of a critical theory of the media.[16]

Nonetheless, even an approach that considers the mutual influence of media and historical events needs to account for the distinctiveness of electronic media. Print-based conceptions that conceive of the media in spatial terms, as a set of texts occupying linear, one-dimensional time, dominate existing arguments. Television, however, is not simply a locus of texts but a mechanism that processes time: the viewing time of audiences, subjectively experienced in different ways, is yoked in tandem with the time of the image in one multi-layered flow.[17] This highlights the decentered, displaced character of television's power. Sponsors pay for audience attention although unaware of the precise character of viewers' responses; viewers for their part act as if reception is a sphere of autonomy, rather than an economic transaction in which they are the commodity.[18] Disjunction is inherent to television's influence: the medium is perceived as unthreatening because its power accrues elsewhere, in a mediated fashion as it were. The time lag between the moment when viewers pay attention and when they consume goods, or pay ideological allegiance is significant here. Collapsing this interval to render viewing as a straightforward act of exchange distorts its structure, and ignores the subjective truth that contributes to the distinctive character of television reception. The objective knowledge of the interested nature of programming sponsorship may be overlooked, to constitute the "free time" of viewing as indeed autonomous. The experience of television programming as "free gift" is reinforced by the prevailing software content, which leans toward entertainment and the inculcation of private fantasy.[19] The question of television's influence unavoidably points us, then, to the larger social field, and calls for understanding the forms of popular participation without the usual filtering mechanisms of institutional representation, of class and party politics.

The space of the popular that viewers occupy is a fluid space of diverse desires, with no necessary or inherent logic linking them together. The language of class analysis is built around a more deterministic set of conceptions, of the interaction of definite forces and relations, and their development within specified modes of production. The terms this offers however, are insufficient for grasping the more mass-based character of popular phenomena. In the case of the latter, contingency rather than necessity is the motor of action, and it is through a provisional series of strategies and tactics that political formations and alliances are made.[20]

The establishment of national television signals the emergence of a key institution providing an anchor for conceptions of the popular. The simultaneous transmission of images to large audiences creates the sense of a shared ground, which in actuality encloses a profusion of different understandings and views. Televisual popularity may then help sanction initiatives in the name of "the people." Disparate sentiments, emancipatory and reactionary both, can be found in popular understandings of the Ramayan serial. What emerges in political practice is hence contingent on the kinds of mobilization carried out. Discussion of audience responses to a religious serial can thus help to question the cultivated incomprehension the secular imagination evinces of "communalism," as inaccessible to rational inquiry. In the rest of this chapter I elaborate on the significance of the Ramayan serial's broadcast for viewers, and explore how television enters the popular realm, in its distinctive fashion converting hitherto hidden energies into demonstrable public facts, thereby changing the context of politics.[21]

Many viewers were relatively blasé about the medium; it was an instrument of leisure to them. As such, it was a bonus. It saved money on movie tickets, and spared them the bother of finding ways to divert themselves. They expressed little interest in educational programming. Entertainment was the dominant motive for watching television. It was an explanation offered from diverse class positions. Entertainment was beyond politics; it was a form of relaxation and enjoyment, tempering the medium's novelty with familiar idioms. Several viewers perceived however that as a gravitational center within the home, television re-aligned domestic relations. It offered men a reason to stay indoors upon returning from work. Women arranged their housework around it. And children could not stay away from it, it seemed.

Ashok Kumar Gupta, a bus mechanic, offers a picture of a household on which television's influence is felt:

> I come back from work around 6:30 p.m. and switch on the TV. I don't like going out, so it's the best way to pass the time . . . I think TV is very good. If they increased the serials, and started at 4:30 or 5 it would be even better. Earlier women used to get together in meetings, in the afternoon or evening. Now they do it less because of TV. It's good. Earlier, when they got together, they used to fight. Now the fights have lessened. Also, their knowledge has increased a lot after watching TV.

The difficulties of negotiating personal relations could thus be bypassed altogether, with television serving as a kind of time-sink, absorbing the unruly energy of social intercourse. Television creates private space, as a kind of refuge from unwanted sociality. We cannot ignore the positive character of this activity: where dwellings are small and neighborhoods crowded, making available such a space asserts the propriety of such a need. As each person faces the screen, they can simultaneously "screen off" others, and resist demands whose prerogative might otherwise be overriding. It says much for the medium's authority that, whatever is on, adults can watch without excuses. (Children have a harder time of it, as I explain below.)

However, if television privatizes social space, in the process it can effectively usurp it too. Some people observed this, and were critical. Satyabhama Devi, housewife, and member of the Communist Party of India (Women's Wing) observed:

There are great changes in social habits. Even if visitors come during a program, the kids won't get up to bring a glass of water because the main thing is the program . . . Everyone is so fascinated by it that guests are treated as a nuisance . . .

Prakash, a worker in the airport, was vehement:

Social life has reduced drastically. Before, people would sit together and talk . . . smoke a hookah and discuss things. They would speak their minds, and each would learn from others. Even enemies would sit together and smoke on the same hookah . . . Now, after TV has come, each person stays in his own house. So people meet less, talk less. Each one is just sitting in his house, watching TV. TV should be stopped! It only causes damage . . .[22]

Most people, as I have said, thought of television as having a positive effect overall; one criticism, though, was nearly universal. This was against love scenes and romance. Shafiq, a worker, expressed anger: "If there are girls in the house, you should never buy a TV. They show . . . how people fall in love and then get married. They show everything. We don't have TV in our home . . . and if my wife finds out that the kids have been watching, she beats them soundly."

Children, especially girls, are considered most vulnerable to the love scenes. The scenes offend traditional sensibilities, which dictate that intimate relations are to be strictly private. Most of the objections I heard were to the scandal of having to watch them in the company of one's children, however. Bashir Ahmed, a postal worker in Kaynagar, confessed: "My children ask me, Papa, what is this? And we don't know what to say." Obviously, the awkwardness arises in the implications: Mama and Papa are assumed to behave in a similar fashion. While marriage is the sphere of legitimate romance, its legitimacy, in this culture, depends on discretion and secrecy. But it goes beyond this. To

depict physical intimacy, even in the relatively limited ways Doordarshan did, was to deeply compromise the authority of elders altogether,
in the opinion of many viewers. A Kaynagar businessman, Ishaq Bhai,
was emphatic about this: "In a sense, the modesty and dignity of our
social norms is violated. The prestige of the father-in-law in front of his
grandchildren and daughters-in-law is destroyed."

Joshua Meyrowitz's arguments, which extend Goffman's dramaturgical observations on social interaction, can be recalled here. To summarize briefly, television equalizes status by robbing power of its mystification. "Backstage" activity has traditionally been private, helping to
bond those in power by serving as a shared secret. Due to the all-seeing
eye of television, it is now blurred with "frontstage" activity.[23] With the
decline of shared secrets, the distinct characteristics of any in-group
bleed away. Meyrowitz's argument exaggerates the medium's effect and
ignores its institutional force, but it powerfully elucidates the domestic
transformation wrought by television. Ramesh Saxena, a small businessman in Kaynagar, explained:

> Small children are able to see how love is made between two people. If they ask
> their parents, their parents cannot reply. Sometimes there is such conversation
> on TV and we lower the volume. The kids ask, Why are you [doing that]? And
> what can we say?

Parents thus respond variously to the threat. Some simply cede the floor
to television, like Mohanlal; some turn down the sound but keep the
picture going, apparently; and some beat their children for watching.
Most of those I spoke to chiefly expressed discomfort, and while they
thought such scenes should not be broadcast, there was little sign of their
doing much about it – nor could they do much. Stories of love and sex
abound outside the home as well. Sequestering information about
backstage behavior is difficult, then. What is threatening is acknowledging the information, however tacitly, in their children's presence. This
can be uncomfortable to the highly structured and somewhat formal
relationships between parents and children. Dhara Bai, a worker in a
government ministry, and an activist with the Communist Party of
India, put it thus: "[T]here are things that are private, not fit to be
openly discussed. There are curtains in every house and some things
happen behind the curtain. To exhibit everything is bad." On the other
hand, some viewers saw such scenes as relieving them of the greater
embarrassment of imparting advice on intimate matters. Ashok Kumar
Gupta remarked: "TV increases knowledge . . . about sex and other

things. Things which we cannot tell our children, they learn from TV so that they don't go and make any mistakes in the future." The effects are uncertain, so we cannot assume, as Meyrowitz does, that all roles will be blurred, and all power compromised. "Whatever the government does," Dhara Bai said, expressing the view of many, "we have to put up with it – even if it is bad." Some parents, like Ashok Kumar Gupta, define it as an issue of information rather than of morals, and are relatively unperturbed by it.

Television impinges on domestic relationships in many ways that ethnography has just begun to address in detail.[24] In my interviews, I received some hints of the kind of changes occurring. A laborer in Kaynagar, Lakhan, said: "[Television] has a disadvantage, regarding the women of the family. Your mother, or sister, or daughter will say, Let's watch the film first. We'll do the cooking later on." Lakhan did not have a set of his own, but he had observed this in the homes of acquaintances. Murarilal, a sari merchant in Kaynagar, went so far as to relate changes to the decline of morals in modern times:

Things have become so bad these days that if you call your children, they will not respond because they are sitting in front of the TV – even the women don't finish the cooking in time – until the program is over they won't get up from the TV. If we are sitting and waiting, we simply have to continue waiting until they've seen what they want to.

The time-bound nature of the programs – an eight o'clock show could only be seen at eight o'clock – reinforced television's authority to re-order duties and pre-empt attention. Its quiet, unthreatening presence made it difficult to object. The women were not asking to go out of the house, after all, nor was any stranger entering within. And the men too could watch, if they liked. A related issue was control over children, expressed as a disruption of study habits. Parents had to pull children towards their schoolbooks at times, and they were not always able to wean them from the set. Children were distracted from their studies, as almost anything they found on television was more attractive than their texts. In some homes, then, television gave rise to new rules: study curfew after seven o'clock, no more than four hours of television on Sundays, and so on.

However, many parents said they had bought their sets largely for their children. "I don't watch TV – it's just for these kids. Ask them, they watch everything," said Kishen Chandra, a worker at the airport. "They were going over to the neighbors' all the time, so finally I decided to buy one." "Sincerely speaking, I had no interest in it," admitted P. K. Kothari, a bank clerk:

> But the minute the kids grew up and learnt about it, they wanted a set. I'm not in favor of TV myself. But that's my personal feeling. Even my wife was after me to buy the TV set – the kids had grown up . . . You see, all the neighbors have TV sets and their kids go to their homes to watch it. I didn't have a set. The kids would aimlessly wander outside the house. So, rather than have them go astray, it's better to have them at home watching TV. It's been four or five years since we bought a set. It has had a good impact on the kids too. The quiz program was very good for them. [But] perhaps they have also picked up bad habits from TV.

Kothari seems unsure whether television has had a good influence on his children. But its influence is mediated through the safety of his own home. Television undermines parents' authority, rendering their injunctions powerless against its own appeal. At the same time, this appeal itself is used as a form of social control of last resort.

Those with a television set had a better chance of patrolling the space of their homes, then, and in regulating the ways in which members of the household spent their time. But as a mechanism for processing time, television's uses were many, and among them was the expression of sheer excess. Thus, one frequently mentioned use of television was "time pass" [*sic*], offered as both cause and effect of watching television. For instance, I asked Naresh Kumar, a messenger at a bank, what he watched. "Well . . . we just see whatever they show on TV," he said. "We just switch on TV for 'time-pass.' For entertainment." When I pressed him to say more, he did not have much to add: "We just watch it for entertainment. We have to pass time, so we watch it."

The term "time-pass" has gained currency in recent times, indicating in the retention of its English form a new kind of activity or meaning. On train journeys, I have noticed hawkers selling peanuts crying, "Time-pass, time-pass!" instead of calling out the name of their wares. There is here not the idea of peanuts as food or snack, but rather one lacking content as such, referring instead to the duration of its value. A language of abstraction unrelated to any concrete purpose may now define socially legitimate activity. As justification, it is disarming; it makes no pretense at any function or utility. Rather than conceive of it as a scarce productive resource, we have here a notion of time as surplus, but capable only of being wasted.

Television is implicated in the process of extending industrial "clock time" beyond the workplace. Paddy Scannell has observed that this may be one of the most crucial functions of broadcasting: regulating the rhythms of domestic life for modern urban workers.[25] E. P. Thompson has discussed the change from a task-oriented sense of time in pre-capitalist society, e.g., "a rice-cooking" (about half an hour), or "the frying of a locust" (a moment), into a sense of an irreplaceable resource in industrial capitalism, associated with thrift ("time is money"); those who wasted it were not just prodigal but immoral.[26] Unpaid, "free time" comes to have a similar character to work time in its sense of an abstract duration independent of content.[27] With "time pass," consumers hand over their money for the privilege of spending time, perhaps ranking the variety of ways in which they may do so in a hierarchy of consumption habits. But as the language itself suggests, "time-pass" is a refuge from and a measure of boredom, both a defense against vacancy and a proof and example of it. The term suggests both an expression of will and a resignation to circumstance, hesitating between enjoyment and drudgery. As such it may signal a truth about what follows in the wake of television. In audiences' relatively eventless experience of duration, often devoid of personal social significance, I suggest, we can find expressions of an emergent and ambivalent consciousness about the new civic responsibility of processing time (while television itself permits, and symbolizes, its accumulation elsewhere).

TELEVISION AND THE TRANSFORMATION OF THE CONTEXT OF POLITICS

Television's curious position as a domesticated symbol of modernity gives it authority without being threatening; if it leads, it does not command. When people attribute power to the medium, it is primarily in matters of morality and education. The familiarity of television's "positive" values, as people describe them, helps banalize the novel character of the medium. A fundamental assumption here is that power is not exercised over people without their knowledge. But even in the familiar ideas or values offered in the medium, power is exercised in the mediation. In this obscuration of its social power lies television's strength. Each viewer participates in a symbolic event, such as the Ramayan serial, out of his or her own volition. No shadow of coercion mars the event. What might be seen as the orchestration of millions of identical acts of volition appears to viewers as part of the broadcasting calendar, a taken-for-granted backdrop against which individuals structure their actions. During the Ramayan broadcasts, for the first time there existed one stage around which daily gathered a national audience that, by virtue of its size and regional spread, could serve as surrogate for the nation. It should not be surprising, then, that this inaugurates a new era of symbolic politics.

Self-evident as the legitimacy of the popular seems in a democracy, cultural filters nevertheless color the ways it is perceived, and accord or deny it a certain sanction. This was evident in critical responses to the serialization of the Ramayana. Sections of the English-language press had difficulty in writing about the Ramayan serial's success. If the epic was understood as high culture, the preferred mode of presenting it would have been as a self-conscious historical work, in a taste suitable to such an *œuvre*. Here was a production that seemed to cater to the lowest common denominator of taste, with no apparent aesthetic or historical distance. That a TV serial should draw record audiences and earn unprecedented profits was undoubtedly an event for celebration, and this fact was duly greeted in the newspaper and magazine columns. The fare itself, however, was low-grade kitsch; this was hardly a suitable manner in which a modern nation should take its bows on the global electronic stage. The slow pace of the serial, and the frequent pauses for devotional reverie; the seeming suppression of spontaneity and individuality at every turn, in favor of a cheerful and unquestioning obedience to orthodoxy: these were the features that I myself registered initially. Explanations of the Ramayan's popularity ranged from dismissal to apprehension, evoking the show's gimmickry, its melodramatic rendition,[28] and its exploitation of blind faith in religious myth.[29]

The serial's religiosity was in fact an often-cited explanation of its popularity, raising questions of the political import of the broadcast. Airing a religious serial on state-controlled television raised questions about the government's commitment to secularism. The audience's enthusiasm raised apprehensions amongst the intelligentsia and minorities about a wave of state-sponsored Hindu chauvinism, and their possible repercussions on minorities. In this way, two streams of thought came to converge: those that viewed the inclusion of religion or traditional culture in a state-sponsored program as violating the principle of a secular, modern society, and those that resisted such inclusion on more pragmatic, political considerations. But where did the popular fit into this picture? The following news item, and a prominent public figure's comments on events of a similar nature, point to the uneasy conscience of old-style secularism in this contest:

IRATE FANS STONE POWER HOUSE.

JAMMU: July 31 1988 (United News of India dispatch):

Power failure during the popular television serial, "Ramayan" this morning upset the people of the Jewal Chowk area of the city, who damaged a state government bus and stoned the power station. A spokesman for the electricity department said that power supply to some parts of the city was affected due to short circuiting in a portion of the canal power house.

Interviewed about the impact of the Ramayan, a prominent lawyer had this to say:

[W]e profess to be a secular country but we don't behave like one. How can you justify people throwing stones at power stations or setting them on fire just because of the electricity failure? Had this sort of reaction come from the same group of people for any other serial when the lights go off . . . India has always been a secular country and we should learn to be tolerant.[30]

Secularism seems here to be identified with peaceful and law-abiding behavior, implying that the violence instanced above is fanaticism motivated by religion. There is some confusion here as to whether secularism in India is an "is" or an "ought," between what "India has always been" and what "we profess." Between secularism as fact and as imperative lay the indeterminate reality of the society, obdurate to reformist efforts. The character of the "secularism" so derived is therefore a constant source of anxiety, and the difficulties created for a modern self-image acute. But viewers themselves tended not to approach the serial with polar categories of religious or secular, as evidenced on the following pages.

Responses to the Ramayan were wide-ranging, and included observations on religion, culture, morals, science, government, and nationalism. A few quotes from letters will illustrate some characteristic preliminary responses. The praise was often fulsome:

My spontaneous reaction is that the LANGUAGE of the dialogues is most scientific, most expressive, most soothing, most natural, and has achieved the task of directly entering the heart.[31]

To the best of my knowledge and belief, the vivid description of Maharishi Valmiki's work has left an indelible mark on the national and international scene. Those who watched the epic on video . . . deeply admired the serial. Non-Indians, although a few, also eulogised the serial and its content . . . Not only the Hindus but the member of other religious communities were equally impressed . . .[32]

The immortal nectar-filled story of Ramcharitmanas whose stream you have made flow into the desert-like hearts of people . . . for this work, I offer you a thousand thanks.[33]

SALUTATIONS TO YOU! INNUMERABLE SALUTATIONS TO YOU! . . . YOUR NAME WILL
BE REMEMBERED AND YOU HAVE THUS BECOME IMMORTAL! SALUTATIONS TO YOU![34]

Some respondents chose to reflect on the signs of popularity:

Nowadays if you ask second and third class students who wrote Ramayan, the
prompt reply is – Ramanand Sagar [the director of the Ramayan serial]. You
can see its popularity from this. In my house, my grandmother would not eat
before she watched it, just as she would not eat before doing her daily worship.
And granny would take her slippers off and bow to Ram-ji before watching it
with great absorption.[35]

The family next door used to perform their ablutions and bathe before they
watched the serial.[36]

While viewers' accounts suggested that they might have responded
emotionally, they discounted the possibility of the viewing experience
carrying over into daily life. One letter from a viewer stated: "Everything in the serial is simply too good. We become so emotional while
watching the relationships between Ram and Lakshman and between
Ram and his mother." "Often tears come to my eyes," said an ex-
Parliamentarian in an interview. "Then I think life should be like this,
on the basis of ideals." But many viewers were scornful about the idea
that the serial would affect people: "The way Ram gave up a kingdom
and went to the forest to save his father's honor . . . Who would do that
nowadays?" wondered one worker. "Today a son would say, *you* go to
the forest, I'll stay here." Another viewer, a small businessman, expanded on this theme: "People take the Ramayan as entertainment."
"Rarely you will find in families today that members fulfill their duties.
Today we don't want to sacrifice. Today we want that Bhagat Singh
should be reborn, not in my family but in the neighbor's . . . Today's
mentality is that *he* suffers, *I* enjoy the fruits."[37]

Viewers are usually quick to discount any question of effect on
themselves. What these answers suggest rather is that the Ramayan
serial made images of sacrificial relationships, via personable Hindu
icons, seem painless and even desirable. Projected onto a distant past,
both the plausibility and the implausibility of the story could be accommodated together in a dynamic contradiction, becoming part of the
tragedy of the nation, which had once attained greatness and today was
in so dire a condition. Critics faulted the Ramayan serial for presenting
relationships in a syrupy, sentimentalized fashion, that seemed to idealize submissive and self-effacing behavior. Most viewers appeared to like
just those aspects of the serial: an idealized inter-subjectivity, with a

fantastic spirit of self-sacrifice pervading society, surfaced repeatedly as themes in viewer accounts. Every hierarchy in the world of Ram Rajya was in principle reversible, elevating relationships to such a moral height that criticism was unseemly. The one-sided portrayal of relationships in the serial depicted a painless effacement of ego-boundaries, a fearless giving and taking of love and respect. This represents the fantasy of a self-abnegating altruism, where giver and taker meld into each other, and one achieves the best of both worlds. Altruism is the social cement of this idealized community, and the solvent of all social problems, with its claim of dissolving power hierarchies. If in reality the costs of such sacrifice and devotion are acutely felt, this is nowhere depicted, allowing identification with the relationships portrayed while avoiding the shock of recognition. It was this sense of painless affirmation that appeared to underwrite the desirability of the society portrayed.

The theme of loss, alluded to but never directly addressed, underlay the entire serial. In interviews, it was explained that the culture and values of olden times had been lost, that people required reminding of them.[38] Viewed in the privacy of the home, the notion of a great Hindu culture as a libidinal collective came to exist in the intimate spaces of people's lives, and over the lengthy period of broadcast, these images became familiar and comfortable. This was arguably a key symbolic backdrop against which the Ram Janmabhumi movement can be seen to have "taken off."

In my interviews, which were mostly done in the spring and summer of 1989, few of the people I spoke to mentioned the "Hindu" community, or the need for its political assertion, in Delhi or in "Kaynagar." What viewers remarked on, incessantly and ubiquitously, was rather the absence of community. What was paradoxical – and here lay the political opportunity of the Ramayan serial – was that it was a collectively recognized, collectively lamented absence.

Prempal was a daily wage worker living in one of the dense resettlement colonies in New Delhi built in 1975–77, during the Emergency; his wife was a temporary worker in Doordarshan, the government television center. Their family had come to a relative's in Delhi in search of work several years before, from eastern U.P. From frequenting the television center, I met his wife and so was introduced to Prempal. When asked what he liked about the Ramayan, Prempal did not talk about the plot or the characters, how they acted, or the quality of the production. His immediate reference was to the past, as with many other people.

There is a great difference between the days of the Ramayan and these days. These days, fights happen in the family, and at that time, it was between kingdoms. Nowadays, brothers fight with each other. Those days the fighting was for land and for kingdoms – nowadays, it is out of greed. Nowadays, people fight for any little thing.

He did not idealize the past completely – there were fights then, but for more legitimate causes, in his opinion. Within families, there was selflessness and unity. In contrast, his picture of today seems Hobbesian:

Today, it is better to be separate! Before, people were better – they had cool heads – they didn't get carried away by anger. People used to calmly discuss things – nowadays people get heated up for any small thing. Before lighting the fire in the stove the water starts boiling! This is the way men think nowadays.

When he tried to elaborate on the changes, his indictment became all-encompassing:

Times are changing – society is changing. When the wind moves the leaves tremble. The leaves can't move on their own, without wind. And even with a slight gust of wind the leaves will move. That's how it is. Before, the people would wear simple cotton clothes but would be fed well. Now it is all fashion – they go hungry but still they want to wear tericot![39] Real country ghee – who eats it nowadays? Where can you get it? All adulterated. Even when you pay such exorbitant prices.

Inflation, changing fashions, changing diet – everything becomes one more manifestation of the descent from the past – from honesty and simplicity to vanity and corruption. It's not inherent in human nature to be bad, he implies – it is the wind, the climate.
     But when did the changes begin?

Looking at the state of things today, and from the stories I have heard, those were the good days, when the English were here. In fact we should call the English back – yes, that's what we should do. But on the other hand they may not want to come back, seeing the state of India today. In each age of the world Krishna or Ram came to earth. And who has come in this age? No one seems to have arrived yet! Well, we have to do what we can – that seems to be the essence of this age.

Prempal's response is of a person seeing rapid social change, and his condemnation is sweeping. His idealization of the British Raj is start-ling, and goes against the evidence. But clearly, it signals a depth of disillusionment and despair about politics that it is hard to imagine shifting. Whether this is the press of "rising expectations" or the pull of the chronically deprived, the sense of outright rejection of available worldly, secular institutions is hard to mistake. He calls rather for an end to politics: without divine intervention, he suggests, the world cannot keep its course.[40]

Vinod Anand Jha was a cycle-rickshaw puller in Kaynagar, and occasionally worked for a Kaynagar-based acquaintance who served as my entry point into the town. A medical doctor who was a Communist Party member, the latter introduced me to Jha, as well as to several others in Kaynagar. Jha decided to befriend me. He was careful to pronounce his entire name, making sure the Brahmin surname registered. He hinted that he could have been doing better things – it was his free spirit and indifference to material things that led him to his occupation. Clearly déclassé, Jha was lively and talkative, and eager to be interviewed.

At the time of the Ramayan people used to say that everything is truth. Now there is truth in nothing. All "departments" [*sic*] are corrupt. It wasn't like this before – and this is the difference. Of course, even then there was poverty, but even the poor were knowledgeable and honest. Today, the wealthy and educated men are the most corrupt.

Jha's comments are pointed. Everybody is not equally bad. It is the wealthy and educated – they have betrayed their responsibilities.

Why is this? Because that is the way today, to blow with the wind, to run wherever there is a crowd. Even the *sadhus* today are fakes. The people have been spoiled by greed, lust, bad atmosphere, ignorance. Before, people would not look outside their caste for a wife or employment. Now people get married to upper or lower castes as they feel like – and the bloodlines get ruined – as is the seed, so is the tree. The main thing is – there is no "discipline" [*sic*]. So if there is no "discipline," there is no obedience, and no wisdom – then what is left?

His criticisms are hurled pell mell: greed, lust, bad atmosphere, ignorance, absence of discipline. Everything seems wrong about the world, just as everything was right back then. His caste consciousness as a déclassé Brahmin stands in sharp relief. Today, frauds abound, pretending to be what they are not. The restraints of the old order have been lifted. Destruction and anarchy result. There is a popular theme here. The fate of the family, i.e., of patriarchal authority, in ensuring discipline, is linked closely to the fate of society at large. The solution however, may lie at the societal rather than the familial level: political authority must become responsible.

Today, only violence and corruption work . . . Society will improve when people are conscious of their status, their responsibilities, their duties . . . Three levels are there, and they have all become rotten: PM, CM, and DM.

Jha referred here to leadership at three levels, i.e., Prime Minister (at the national level), Chief Minister (at the state level), and District Magistrate (the judicial officer at the local level), somewhat reminiscent of the trinity of *sarkar–sahukar–zamindar* in Guha's *Elementary Aspects*, who constituted the figures of absolute authority for Indian peasants under colonialism.[41]

When these three – PM, CM, DM, are good, things will improve. That is why conditions are bad. As long as the PM, CM, DM don't change, society will be rotten.

His constant repetition had an incantatory quality. His comment is sharp and witty, a sort of symbolic mastery of the political structure in a telling rhyme. The understanding it expressed was also characteristic. Betrayal of trust by political leaders was at the root of problems. The leaders must change. The source of the problem must also be the source of the solution.

   Ramnath, 44, was a well-to-do plastics factory owner in Delhi who watched the serial devoutly. Ramnath talked about the Ramayan:[42]

The impact on the public – the total impact – rightful thinking, devotion, and affection – these were the things. Moral values which probably day by day we are losing and should try and recapture . . . People are, to my mind, seeing Ramayan at least for a couple of hours after that. They are cool, they don't quarrel . . . So that is the impact . . . For the villagers, those who have come to city life, they're inculcating the city habits. And they forget the old ones. And these days, you know – hoodwinking, dodging. This type of thing . . . Straight people hardly make money these days. More and more we are approaching the Western type of life. And in fact, I shouldn't say it's bad. It's good. But your basic concepts of Indian society and all that, you *must retain*, and inculcate the best out of the West. We should have a combination of all the best.

He began by lamenting the loss of moral values. He associated this with the old, with village rather than city life, with the move towards the West. This is a familiar narrative of tradition, vitiation, and corruption. But he abruptly departs from this. "Basic Indian" values have to be retained, he says, implying much is peripheral. Meanwhile Western influence is good, not bad. His exhortation to get "all the best" assumes a fluent transmission of cultures in both directions. He is comfortable with each, and the need for a sensible accommodation is obvious to him. What would govern the choice from each culture is not specified.

Presumably, the needs of the moment would issue clear summons. What was the society of the Ramayan like?, I asked him.

People were innocent. They were not material. Love and affection were in much more value than the money part of it . . . We are much more selfish. But that notion of sharing or utilizing – you know – the richness . . . the whole *concept* has changed. Now your riches are for *yourself*. Not for the good of others . . . Probably we're going on the wrong path and a time will come when somebody else like Ram or Krishna or some other avatar will come . . . Let's hope.

Now he returns to his earlier theme of corruption and decline. He seems to shift between treating the Ramayan as comfort and as accusation, something that reassures, but on examination, disturbs, even subverts that sense. Distancing it was perhaps a way of managing its power. But he had said moving towards the West was good. Could he explain?

I have an example for that. There's plenty of things to learn from Japan [*sic*]. National spirit. Discipline. Being on time. And when you are on duty you have to work for that time, not while it away as we do. That's what I say. Good things must be welcome.

The meaning of the Ramayan is real for him, but it seems unmanageable in the language of work-life. On the one side is a welcoming community life of love and affection. On the other side is the present, less well defined, but more real. Society may change, but "work" must go on. "Work" becomes a bridge between past and present, with its imperatives as buttressing values: discipline, duty, punctuality, national spirit, qualities of "the West" realized in Japan. Ramnath expresses a muted critique of materialism but reformulates it as a potentially transferable set of values. A benevolent patriarchy can re-emerge as capitalism, Japanese style. As symbol, then, the Ramayan could be used to inspire the community to overcome differences, and to coexist selflessly.

Murarilal, Kaynagar sari trader and member of the VHP, spoke with passion about the values in the story, and went onto extrapolate them into expressly political views:

In those times, people were more concerned with spiritual matters. Material benefits would emerge from virtue – they were not primarily concerned with material goods. These things would come from their spiritual activities – their meditations and sacrifice. Today no one does these things nor do they get the fruits of these actions. Before people would do it openly. Today they will be mocked and despised if they do it.

Murarilal echoes understandings of traditional Hindu cosmology here, according to which the present is a time when good is despised and evil celebrated. The piety, worship, and altruism of the ancients were what kept them going. None of that obtains today. The situation can be rectified only through sacrifice. Even for the ills of society, the solution is personal virtue, he says.

Altruism has its complement, however, in the political sphere:

Today there is discontent because we have a democracy. In the days of kings there was no such discontent. Nowadays there is no fear of punishment. Thieves and murderers get off with a bit of bribery here and there. So why should people be contented? They would rather steal. We will never get a good ruler the way things are now. What is wrong with a dictatorship? It has strength. It can put down unrest. With democracy, there can never be a disciplined government.

Many people saw the descent of an avatar as the precursor to any real change, but doubted if the present age would see one. In Murarilal's view, a solution is at hand, if people are willing to surrender the power they so abuse. If virtue does not come from within, it can be imposed from without, by the discipline of a strongman. In his insistence on "discipline," Murarilal echoes a theme expressed by a variety of people, including some of the poorest. Rules need to be obeyed, people must cease giving in to their base instincts. Most people, however, fasten their faith on good leaders. Calling for a change in political systems immediately distinguished Murarilal's response from that of many people. As a member of the VHP, his confidence had a firm institutional anchor.

Keshavram Chaturvedi, 38, was a City Council member, and head of the Bajrang Dal in Kaynagar. The Bajrang Dal, named after Ram's invincible warrior-servant, is a militant association formed in the mid 80s to "protect" Hindus; it is comprised mainly of young men. Chaturvedi expresses little concern about a long-term decline in values, or about the need for a general moral re-armament. He is skeptical about the idealization of the past. He has no use for that history. The only one that concerns him is the one that places Hinduism at the source of all Indian culture. This, for him, redefines the relationship between religion and nationality. Most of the Muslims and Christians in India were converts from Hinduism, he explained, switching out of greed or fear. Some generations ago, their ancestors were Hindu. "The way of worship may change but the essential culture remains the same," he explained. "At heart they have remained Hindu."

In countries with a Muslim majority, the Muslims were doing whatever they liked. Hinduism, on the other hand, was a completely liberal religion. But Muslims and Christians were rigid in their beliefs, and tolerated no differences. Why should Hindus not assert their majority, like the Muslims did elsewhere? In any case, it could only be beneficial, since the religion was so liberal. What was essential was that all Indians should have allegiance only to India, and this could only be done by emphasizing their Hindu cultural identity.

Until Muslims and Christians have this allegiance there will be problems with Hindus. Such as when the Muslim League wants to fly the green flag over the Red Fort.[43] Even when there are cricket matches, the Muslims all want the Pakistan team to win. They have no loyalty to the soil of this country.

For Chaturvedi, to be Indian was to be, in essence, a Hindu: after that acceptance of the faith, everything else was irrelevant. What matter that Christians had been in India since the first century A.D.? They were Hindus before that. Or that lower castes for centuries converted to less hierarchical systems of faith? Wayward Hindus, to be forgiven their greed for the proselytizers' gold, or their fear of the sword. And if they declined to be forgiven, and persisted in their ways? Here, for Chaturvedi, lay the danger. A refusal to acknowledge error could stem from pride – or worse. Since religion and state are inseparable – and this was the axiom shaping all his understanding – lasting impenitence could only signify disloyalty to India and allegiance to foreign powers. Today, they cheered enemy teams on the cricket field. What might happen next? Others saw a crisis of values in society – a surfeit of materialism, a lack of spiritualism, disrespect, competitiveness, corruption. Chaturvedi mentioned these in passing. For him, there was one over-riding problem, the enemy within.

Unsurprisingly, people express a diversity of responses to the Ramayan. Clearly, the individuals I spoke to did not all hold on to the same notion of an idealized community (as a "lost utopia"). People variously demystified it (Keshavram Chaturvedi), found it threatening and reformulated it (Ramnath), idealized it out of devotion, despaired of realizing it (Prempal, Vinod Anand Jha), or derived political strategies from it (Murarilal). In the event, the last category became consequential for the others. A range of effects provoked by the medium was thus harnessed, allowing the impression of unanimity or consensus for a single political project.

To investigate audiences in some fixed sense presupposes that the realm of the popular is stable and measurable, whereas in fact it is fluid

and changing. Popular responses are deflected, re-focused and amplified, as different political forces vie to claim them for their own purposes.
Varied, complex, and often oppositional ideas and feelings are routinely
accommodated, re-defined, and organized into powerful political lobbies that may have as little to do with their constituents as an army's
strategies with its soldiers' sentiments. In characterizing the popular,
then, it is misleading to extrapolate directly from ideas expressed by
individuals to themes espoused by organizations or parties.[44]

It should be clear that I am not arguing for a mechanistic causal link
from the medium to social and political phenomena. What this reception study shows is how the effects of a widely watched broadcast can
take on an entirely naturalized presence, articulating with existing
concerns and familiar symbols. The basis for a widespread concordance
of concern is rendered ordinary and given the status of something
already known, in most people's accounts. Thus the Ramayan telecast
received little attention as an unprecedented event enabled by a new
technology. Of course any political consequences depend on contingent
events around the broadcast. In this case the perceptual field generated
by television had a decidedly unfinished character, given an environment where only a minority had receivers, and where watchable
programs were relatively scarce. Thus the fissures and cleavages in
this new visual regime were quickly revealed, but through the more
market-sensitive medium of print rather than through state-controlled
electronic media, as English and Hindi language presses absorbed,
digested, and transmitted their perceptions (see chapter four), and as
these interacted with the efforts of the sangh parivar in rallying Hindus
behind the mosque demolition effort. The movement from the text and
its technical medium to the wider context was thus hardly a simple or
straightforward one. It was mediated through a series of different,
interacting forms, of the language presses, as well as of the political
rhetoric and the performance of the movement, and was thus unpredictable in its precise outcomes.

Granted that a series of fortuitous events joined to shape the Ram
Janmabhumi movement, what were the contours and the character of
politicization engendered by television in a postcolonial society like
India's, where narratives of religion and community retain wide-
ranging influence both in private life and as plausible charters for
social action? Hindu nationalism organized citizenry against the reign-
ing forms of political expression and the institutions that embodied
them. Whereas the existing institutions of civil society, shaped through

the Nehruvian era, sought a secular public role in a multi-religious society, Hindu nationalism attacked these institutions on multiple fronts, its criticisms centering on the exclusion of the majority Hindu culture from an allegedly democratic and representative system. Thus Hindutva derived its legitimacy from its status of exclusion from the dominant public, and formed its critique around the purported effects of this exclusion. Arguing that post-independence government was in many ways a continuation of a colonial legacy of suppressing indigenous culture, Hindu nationalists identified Hindu rule with the achievement of genuine independence. Paradoxical as it was, what was sought was the creation of a Hindu public, one that claimed a rigid and exclusive set of rules for participation while expanding its ostensible scope and access to hitherto marginal sections of the population.

NARRATIVES OF COMMUNITY: THE EFFECTS OF GOING PUBLIC

In an influential argument we can use to situate the Hindutva critique, Oskar Negt and Alexander Kluge have criticized the abstraction of the concept of the bourgeois public sphere for its correspondence to the character of market exchange: the public sphere is in fact modeled on the assumption of autonomous individuals engaging in free market behavior. In their reading, the systematic exclusion of lived experience is akin to the subjugation of potential resistance and helps ensure the dominance of unequal social relations.[45] Negt and Kluge offer the notion of a counterpublic sphere, posing the immediacy of excluded experience against the idea of the bourgeois public sphere.[46] They suggest that coming to terms with these excluded experiences (within counterpublic spheres) can help individuals make coherent sense of their lives, and thereby effect social transformation.[47]

This argument risks confusing the the restraints imposed by historical factors with the theoretical limits of the category of the public sphere itself. It is as an ideal type that Habermas conceptualizes the term; the moment the public sphere claims to include or represent lived experience, it becomes particularistic and exclusionary. The notion of a counterpublic sphere suggests a semi-autonomous, subterranean domain, unbeknownst to or beneath the gaze of dominant powers, and capable of generating insurrectionary energies. But since such a definition renders the counterpublic sphere beneath the realm of politics itself, it cannot properly be called a public sphere. It is more useful to think of different languages of politics, those circulating in the bourgeois public sphere and in more marginal spheres respectively, which translate into each other only partially and imperfectly. All translation between languages is flawed and incomplete, to be sure. But there tend to be constraints that lead to systematically distorted communication, e.g., colonial legacies of subordination, institutional limits of metropolitan broadcasting systems, and technocratic approaches to social and political issues. This leads to what I have called split publics (see my Introduction and chapter four), residing across distinct language strata, media, and socio-cultural domains. The interaction or lack of interaction between these spheres is itself part of a larger historical and political process, through which relations of domination and subordination are reproduced and changed. The introduction of a new system of representation, in this case television, sets up new circuits of exchange across a split public, thereby casting the existing terms of translation, and the status of the bourgeois public sphere itself, into crisis.

Every public sphere claims universality for itself, and battles marginal groups and subcultures in its effort to maintain dominance. It is through struggles of representation and claims of representativeness that these efforts for dominance are waged. These struggles are the substance of politics proper. It is essential to mark the irreducible heterogeneity of such processes, rather than to understand them through categorial dismissal, i.e., by distinguishing between good and bad publics, correct and false representations, rational and irrational politics, and so on. Hindutva made claims to universality and tolerance, and to inclusiveness with respect to lower castes and non-Hindus, which sat alongside its more brutal and aggressive upper-caste Hindu domination. The widespread appeal of its critique of the colonial hangovers of the post-Independence state pointed to truths beyond its traditional social base of traders and small town intelligentsia, requiring understanding on its own terms.

In many ways Hindutva indeed claimed for itself the status of a counterpublic. Positioning Hindu religion and ritual as the sphere of authentic tradition, whose revival would lead to national rejuvenation, Hindu nationalists claimed to stand for the suppressed truth of Hindu identity, that public-minded citizens ought to champion. Corrupt politicians eager to cultivate minority vote banks, they asserted, suppressed this truth.[48] Thus militant Hindu leaders such as Uma Bharati, Sadhvi Rithambhra, and many others, who drew on their authority as spiritual figures and declared that Hinduism was in danger, called for a range of responses to this religio-political threat (see chapter five). Popular pamphlets such as "Angry Hindu! Yes, Why Not?" (see chapter one) illustrated a characteristic device at work, eliciting audience identification through powerful, emotive words, challenging "Hindus" to defend themselves against taunts of cowardice and shame, and offering different kinds of political participation in answer. Symbols of Ram and his birthplace, and appeals to Hindu identity could provoke responses that gave the appearance of converging mass intentions while in fact stretching across a broad social spectrum. As such, Hindu nationalists skillfully tapped the critical awareness provoked as the social distance between different language strata suddenly became conspicuous through the new visual field instituted by television.

The Ramayan serial was presented through a series of images that could be identified both with the magic of television and with the affective charge of the narrative itself. As a story tradition, the Ramayan encloses key narrative tensions, between models of obedience and devotion, and of reciprocity and mutual acknowledgment, and between images of a male-dominated, warlike culture and those of a more effeminate and gentle one. The accounts viewers offered spelled out contradictory possibilities whose enclosure within one narrative gave the story much of its power, combining authoritarianism with complete mutual recognition between rulers and subjects, and offering individual fulfillment through collective submission. Different political possibilities were in fact contained in its contemporary meanings. Television's invocation of the Rama story straddled these divides, ensuring that the aggregative power of its symbols was not lost to varying interpretations. Symbolizing as it did in its popularity an apparently incontrovertible fact, the serial was used by Hindu nationalists to refigure the way in which these strata could relate to each other. This was buttressed by popular readings of the Ramayan serial itself, but in a peculiar and disjuncted sense. The medium served as a nodal point where different temporal flows were tied together in one symbolic event, the majority of viewers looking back to an idyllic past while a minority perceived it as a resource to represent social consensus for new political initiatives. Television extended the reach of the prevailing political terrain, bringing into one orbit zones of society that seldom encountered the same ideas simultaneously. If secularism had been declared by state fiat, the power of new communications brought home the fact that secularism existed, willy-nilly, as largely the sign and the exercise of membership in a cultural elite.

As I have shown in this chapter, the Ramayan broadcast provoked a range of often far-reaching reflections on the problems of Indian society, offering viewers the illusion of an external standpoint from which they could make their judgments. The perception of an external standpoint was fostered not only by the epic subject matter, but more importantly by a technology that appeared to guarantee the existence of ongoing social dialogue irrespective of viewers' participation. In this way audience experience of television offered up society itself as an object for commentary, with the Ramayan serial serving as the medium of this commentary, provoking mutually recognizable responses across wide social distances. If the Ramayan phenomenon reinforced anything, it was not national identity so much as an immense national dis-identification, the sense of confirming what the nation was *not*, in the innumerable perceptions of millions of viewers. Together with the spectacle of en masse viewership, this introduced a political problem or opportunity, one that Hindu nationalists productively drew on, as they redefined it for their own purposes. Working through the particulars of the televisual event, of broadcast and reception both, is indispensable in clarifying the logic at work in this process.

In the first chapter, I discussed the conjuncture of liberalization that took shape in part through the media, and also formed the context in which the particular media events preceding and influencing the Janmabhumi movement occurred. Here and in chapter two, I have studied the world of those media events themselves, in terms of the institutional context, the media text itself, the diverse and multiple positions that viewers occupied with respect to the media and the Ramayan serial in particular, and some of the possibilities for political language and symbolism thus created. I next examine the larger world the media connects with, beginning with institutions of print media which coexisted alongside television, and formed the site for working out many of the contradictions in television's relationship to society as a whole.

CHAPTER 4

A "split public" in the making and unmaking of the Ram Janmabhumi movement

With the establishment of a unified visual field by nationwide television, for the first time there emerged a single platform of representation across a society, me with profound social and cultural divisions. The technology was of course seen by the Ministry of Information and Broadcasting as an instrument of national integration; the intent of the Ramayan broadcast was described more or less in these terms.[1] There can seldom have been so great a failure of imagination in any attempt at social engineering. For the first time, the bewilderingly varying parts of Indian society were simultaneously exposed to one of its most familiar narrative traditions, and represented to themselves as behaving in unison across its considerable breadth. The proof of this extraordinary claim was that everybody watched the Ramayan,[2] a claim reiterated and amplified in the press. If the Congress or the BJP understood the formation of a nationwide televisual audience as the realization of a collective consciousness, however, the dependence of this presumed consciousness on a particular apparatus was completely ignored. The Indian public was after all hardly a single entity, even if the technology for its unification, or for imagining its unity, appeared to be at hand. But the avowal that it was indeed a single entity was never before granted so much attention by so many people since the time of Independence as in the wake of the Ramayan broadcasts. Even this immense convergence of attention was not sufficient to render a deeply divided public whole. What was eventually accomplished, amidst attempts to redefine the Indian public as a unified Hindu public, was a spectacular fragmentation into its several parts, as caste assertion broke the Hindu vote apart. The specter of Hindu unity remained as a politically potent weapon, even while it came to be acknowledged as an unrealizable goal. In the process, the contours of Indian politics were permanently changed. In this chapter, I describe the first phase of this process, namely the coming to self-consciousness of a multiply fissured rather than a seamless public, and the development of one set of divisions within this public through the *print* rather than the electronic media.

I use the term split public as a heuristic in thinking about an incompletely modern polity, standing for the relationship between the configuration of political society desired by modernizing elites and its actual historical forms. Central to this split is the unfulfilled mission of secularism in a society where a compromise between Hindu orthodoxy and progressive nationalism launched an anti-colonial independence movement, one that culminated in the declaration of a secular state. The distinction between an officially maintained secular public sphere and a more heterogeneous popular culture was not likely to survive the proliferation of new electronic media, however, as the boundary-piercing character of television ensured the blurring of programming genres. Sure enough, political parties themselves began to invoke the authority of faith to reinforce their diminishing electoral credibility, while citizens drew on the narrative resources of religion to make sense of an often disorientingly unstable polity. The media's reliance on the state to set its own moral compass as it professed reportorial norms of objectivity then led to a crisis of interpretation.[3] This crisis, which was sparked, as I have argued, firstly by the institution of national television and specifically by the broadcast of tele-epics, worked out in the coverage of the Ram Janmabhumi movement, which was perceived differently in English and in Hindi language media.[4]

In this chapter, I will contrast English and Hindi language newspaper coverage of the Ram Janmabhumi movement, to argue that there were significant variations in the understandings of news as a genre, dependent on different sets of institutional practices in the print media. English language news emphasized the truth-value of news, as information serving a critical-rational public. This reflected the origins of English language news as an elite form of discourse in liberal market society. Here, any self-consciousness about the story-telling aspect of news gave way to the sense of a transparent communication that was objective and neutral.[5] For English language audiences, objectivity and neutrality worked not only to enhance the informational value of news and to guarantee its truth content, but also served as a marker of the relationship of these audiences to power. Objectivity as a news value corresponded to the history of English as a language of colonial and subsequently technocratic nationalist rule, and rendered this history invisible, thereby avoiding a confrontation with English's status as the language of a tiny minority. Hindi news audiences had a more fraught and contested relation to power, and could not assume a transparent, value-neutral approach to the news in quite the same way.[6] Even as a means of informing citizens for active political participation, then, Hindi news was written quite differently from English news. The narrative aspect of news was much more in evidence, and perhaps understandably so, as the power relations between readers and rulers required constantly to be assessed, dramatized, criticized, or ridiculed, rather than to be taken for granted.[7]

In Hindi language news, then, objectivity was one of a range of possible values in the news, and neutrality but one of a variety of possible relationships to political power. The distinction of Hindi language newspapers was typically seen only as a failure, however, in their inability to imitate the English language press. There were no doubt many respects in which the Hindi press could improve. But such criticisms also reproduced a colonial emphasis on a conception of neutrality that was never defined, while ignoring the specific cultural and political conditions of Hindi language news production. What follows here is a preliminary exploration of how the Ram Janmabhumi campaign was represented in the press, and how these representations themselves folded back into the campaign's development,

The Ram Janmabhumi movement brought a series of contradictions to the fore: claims of secular nationhood and abundant signs of religious nationalism; claims of the English language media to speak on behalf of the nation as a whole, and the ostentatious incomprehension it evinced as more people showed an affinity for popular Hindutva, state claims of religious neutrality and the indulgence it exhibited towards Hindu militants who violated the law repeatedly. There operated a split between the ideal of the public, symbolized by the modernizing elite, including members of the state itself, and the more compromised forms through which it actually manifested. In another sense, this also took shape as a split between an electronic public, which represented the closest numerical approximation to the society at large, and the several print publics existing alongside it. Thirdly, and in the specific sense considered for the most part here, there was a split between the English language and the Hindi language print public, whose sudden mutual awareness due to national television created the context against which the assertion of Hindu nationalism gained new significance.

Unlike countries in the West, in India the growth of television has been accompanied by the growth rather than the diminution of the reading public.[8] The Ram Janmabhumi movement was, among other things, an expression of the politicization resulting from this combination of quantitative increase in literacy and qualitative change in the character of the public. Arguments about a democratic public often imply that it was in the era of print capitalism that the public achieved its highest and most redeeming expression.[9] The shift to electronic capitalism is registered as vitiating this legacy, as the profit imperative overtakes more properly political impulses, and the constraints of radio and TV reduce public information into staged displays.[10] But the public sphere is an ideal type rather than an historical artifact; such an approach therefore seems dismissive of actually existing political formations. It remains possible, then, to think about what kinds of publics could be shaped in other contexts where, for instance, print and electronic audiences were both relatively small in relation to the population as a whole, and where steep entry costs and the retention of state controls ensured that print rather than electronic media remained closest to local and regional opinion.[11] A more market-sensitive newspaper industry at this time provided venues for articulating public opinion, whereas television, which at this time was government-controlled, mirrored the state largely as it wished to be seen.

We can quickly differentiate media in terms of the market conditions in which they arose, with print serving at first small, petty commodity markets, and slowly growing to circulate in regional and national markets, and television usually beginning on a national scale, straddling locality and region, and often expanding further to international markets. This difference of scale and economic viability reflects a distinction in the way in which each medium processes time. In the case of television, we have a machine that processes and joins diverse temporal flows, the time of the image flowing alongside the time of viewing, so that while viewers engage with a program, precise economic calculations can simultaneously be made as to its cost-effectiveness in gathering an audience. (This is related to the mode of viewing, where the ceaseless onward movement of programming brings disparate audiences along with it, the content of programming itself fragmented and non-sequential in its narrative logic.) Since a range of interpretations is provoked across the medium's vast reach, questions of meaning tend to yield to a concern for the medium's effects, since these effects occur as a result of varying understandings. Television thus lends itself to distribution across wide regions, and to extending the frontiers of markets with considerable speed.

The more densely material form of print commodities makes for a more limited circulation, by contrast. If television's images linger only for an instant but across far-flung borders, print extends before and beyond the duration of the present, allowing readers a more leisurely exploration of the world it describes, and a fuller engagement with the experiences conveyed to them, and thereby with their own experiences. Any attempt at conveying detailed information through print neces- sarily involves the use of languages of a greater or lesser degree of specialized knowledge. Print commodities in a given language thus usually travel within a smaller market, with readership limited by literacy, price, and reach. By the same token, then, print goods can often express in greater depth more particular views and sentiments not shared across an entire society.

But the context of electronic capitalism alters the effects of print. If the impact of newspapers may be pre-empted by radio and TV, print is itself communicated via telephone, computer, and fax, so that the gap in information velocity is narrowed. Thus the dissemination of print media may be electronic even if its form harks back to an older era. While print and electronic media each have their distinctive modes of communica- tion and reception, electronic capitalism as a context extends across these distinctions. Thus for instance, the Ramayan serial on Doordar- shan, which broke viewership records simultaneously in the North and in the South,[12] created a common background awareness against which print coverage of the Birthplace movement, fragmented by language and literacy, registered themselves. Here the pre-existing relations of language groups, e.g., of English and Hindi, to each other, came into effect, while at the same time being transformed.

The Ram Janmabhumi campaign was described by the sangh parivar, not without foundation, as the largest popular phenomenon in India since the freedom movement. Controlled and orchestrated as it was by the Hindu nationalists, and violent as it was in many of its outcomes, it undeniably harnessed popular forces and gained wide- spread support beyond the immediate ranks of Hindu militants. It spurred debate among indigenous audiences about the place of Hindu deities in relation to national culture, and the kinds of behavior appro- priate between majority and minority communities, even as it polarized Indian society through a series of murderous assaults on Muslims.[13] It dramatized the unpredictable and even dangerous possibilities inherent in the realm of the popular. This chapter considers, first, how the Ram Janmabhumi movement gained an unprecedented salience through the contradictory working-out of a split public. Subsequently, I will examine the responses of a government whose inaction was intelligible in the Hindi press as cooperation and complicity, but could not be understood in these terms in the English language press, because the province of action for the state was so firmly understood to belong to the realm of the secular. From this latter perspective, the only rational course of action for the state was to stop the movement. The failure to do so appeared as little more than the habitual failure of the state to discharge its responsibility, more a mechanical defect than a political problem, provoking complaint rather than critique. The inability of the English language press to articulate this perception in the terms available to it, i.e, to declare the complicity of a "secular" government with the aims of a "communal" movement, contributed to the movement's advancement as much as it enabled its subsequent undoing.

THE INDIAN PRESS: GOVERNMENT, LANGUAGE, AND POLITICS

Although a large number of newspapers in India were founded during the independence movement, often by small, independent organizations or trusts, a process of economic consolidation from the 1950s onwards led to a steeply stratified structure of ownership and control. A 1979 study sponsored by the Second Press Commission, the most comprehensive thus far, found eight corporations controlling slightly over 30 percent of total newspaper circulation and nearly 62 percent of the English language newspaper circulation. Less than 16 percent of the newspaper establishments in India controlled more than 72 percent of national circulation during 1979.[14] During each succeeding decade, further consolidation has occurred, though no figures are available on its precise extent.[15] A substantial portion of the Indian press, and in particular a major segment of the daily newspapers, was found to be controlled by persons having "strong links with other businesses or industries."[16] Although no more recent study is available, there is little sign of any dramatic change since the period in question.[17]

The Indian Constitution guarantees freedom of speech and expression, but not specifically freedom of the press. B. R. Ambedkar, who oversaw the Constitution's passage through the Constituent Assembly, followed traditional Common Law in arguing that individual rights should not be exceeded by those of the press, and that members of the press were after all doing no more than exercising their individual rights.[18] Maintaining public order was the dominant concern instead. This was not only influenced by the context of Constituent Assembly debates, occurring in the wake of the Partition riots, and a reformist concern for restraining the rights of the community over the individual, but as well by a well-established colonial precedent. In the view of the British rulers, the indigenous press was chiefly an irresponsible and trouble-making body requiring strict policing, lest it foment sentiment against the government or between native communities. In practice, the two concerns became one, and an ostensible interest in protecting Indians from potential harm became indistinguishable from guarding against the threat of sedition. As a result, debates about the public sphere in the colonial context, were chiefly about public order, with British interests usually masquerading as those of the public as such. This tendency was reproduced after independence, with the public sphere understood more as a zone of possible conflict than as a realm *sui generis* for enacting debate and legitimating political decisions. This was unfortunate, because as the institutions of the state became more and more subject to manipulation by private interests, and television news remained dominated by Doordarshan, it was the press that emerged as the key arena for public debate.

In the West, "the public" is held as the irreducible realm whereby modernity as a historical condition translates into democracy as a political goal, through rational–critical debate in the press. In a country like India, by contrast, where the public becomes to a considerable extent a ventriloquism of the state, the press is often perceived instead as a threat to order. Thus in the news coverage of the Ram Janmabhumi movement, the majority of the citizenry itself became a suspect element, perceived to have been inflamed by sections of the Hindi language press. While there was much truth to this perception, it often took the place of a larger understanding of the way in which the press was working.[19]

State attitudes towards the press in the post-independence period varied somewhat between the large, metropolitan press and the provincial press. The metropolitan press was to be curbed for fear of its potential political power. Controls were achieved through limits on their growth and rationing of essential supplies such as newsprint, to say nothing of the intimidation exercised through numerous complaints to the Press Council, and the threat of withdrawal of government advertising.[20] As for the small newspapers in the hinterland, the government presented itself as their champion, providing advertisements and subsidies of newsprint to encourage their growth.[21] In fact the carrot-and-stick approach of a license-permit raj operated far more bluntly with small newspapers, with provincial governments often using them in a frankly partisan fashion.[22] Various warning notes were also sounded by successive Press Commissions about the oligopolistic nature of press ownership. However, existing anti-monopoly legislation under the Monopolies and Restrictive Trade Practices Act, which could have been deployed effectively against market-dominant newspapers, was never in fact used. This suggested that although the business-owned press could at times be adversarial to the government, the degree of convergence between their views and interests was greater than any differences that separated them. The leading Hindi dailies tended to share in this consensus, since these papers tended to be "satellites" of the national English language newspapers rather than "independents," to use the distinction attributed to Rahul Sankrityayan. His distinction between satellites and independents pertains to the Hindi press, pointing to the dependent status of the former, *viz.*, Hindi papers run by the large publishing houses as ancillaries to their English language papers.[23] The usual gulf between metropolitan and provincial papers is thus heightened in the case of Hindi since the "quality" papers lack a personality of their own, and are imitative of their English language partners.

If the English language press had arrogated to itself the right to define the nation, as, e.g., secular in intention if not in fact, not the least of its difficulties was that secularism was uneven in application. Secularism was understood variously: if for the purposes of elections, secularism forbade appeals based on religion, in the courts it was used to protect religious sensibilities from injury; meanwhile public institutions it was interpreted to mean equality of religious groups. The BJP itself insisted that secularism required stewardship by "the majority community," *viz.*, the Hindus.[24] The English language press could not solve this conundrum, to be sure, and was therefore presented with a dilemma. As far as the Hindi language media were concerned, however, the resulting incomprehension on the part of the English language press reflected the "pseudo-secular" obstinacy of a deracinated elite, that prevented Hindu culture from occupying its rightful place in society. For each, the crucial action or inaction was in the other half. For each, there was the sense of a society demonstrably not at one with itself, of a sundered half to be returned to the body social. This mutual misrecognition was generated and played itself out so that the split became stereotyped and hardened, and the friction between parts was magnified through a media-sensitive Hindu right that utilized the division to the utmost effect.

Deep cultural divisions in a hierarchically organized, multilingual society became politically salient through the media. The English and the Hindi press behaved as though they were in different societies, and it was hard to believe they belonged to the same world, the BJP public relations coordinator Amitabh Sinha observed. Language and culture did not seamlessly map onto each other; there were exceptions that disturb a smooth division of qualities in this way.[25] The division nevertheless offers a powerful heuristic.

The English language audience was a relatively coherent, well-networked national elite, with a sense of being bearers of the agenda of modernization.[26] Although their relative importance was changing, it represented the leading segment of the market, in terms of production and consumption decisions. Thus proportionately, business influence was greater in the English language than in the indigenous language press.[27] More than merely British inheritance was at work; indeed it can be argued that after independence, the status and power of English have grown in importance relative to the vernacular languages. Its history as a language of command left it remarkably free of any colonial taint, as new middle and ruling classes stepped into the role of nationalist technocrats in the task of state-led development. In retrospect it might be said that English served to make up for the absence of a cultural policy, a high wire strung above the particularist thickets of caste, religion, and region. The use of English could serve as a disclaimer against the biases that dialect, style and intonation would have made all too plain if an indigenous tongue were used. The linguistic appearance of neutrality cemented the functional utility of English for elite and majority alike. At the same time, there were tactical advantages in raiding a foreign vocabulary to utter words and phrases suddenly became awkward, delicate, or strange, as customs and mores lagged behind rapid changes. The borrowed words have a referential meaning, but are devoid of the streams of association that swirl in the wake of indigenous terms; thus for instance, the elaborate codes of vernacular etiquette, of giving and receiving respect, and the linguistic layering of formalities, invariably marked by caste, may be put aside without explicit rejection by using English instead. The gentle, almost "passive" character of this negotiation may thus be embraced by progressive and orthodox alike. The functional appearance of neutrality is of course undergirded by the real power inhering with speakers of English.[28]

In contrast, the Hindi language audience is "regional" in at least a double sense, representing only a part of the nation, the "Hindi belt," and forming within this apportioning, various overlapping cultural and political sectors.[29] Hindi language newspapers therefore tend to be more numerous and to have a greater number of editions corresponding to the dispersed character of their audience. It is in the Hindi language medium that, arguably, a "Hindu" consciousness was re-asserted so forcefully over the last several years,[30] with extensive organizational groundwork by the Hindu right serving to link different regions one to the other to form a relatively cohesive and self-conscious political force.[31]

The cultural isolation between English and Hindi print media worked to the political advantage of the Hindu right, as forms of expression, principally religious in character, that were excluded from the English language media flourished in the Hindi media, and aided in the organization of Hindu nationalist opinion. If the English media treated issues of religion as for one reason or another peripheral to their concerns, and the Hindi media treated it as a relatively familiar, living presence and as a sociological fact within their purview, the latter could become an organizing ground for the Hindu right. Not only the susceptibility of the latter to religious forms of expression, but the lack of engagement of the former were operative in this process. If the Hindi press's intimacy with the themes and the sentiments of the temple movement created sympathy, the English language press's blinders prevented it from questioning the Hindu right's compartmentalization of itself into "cultural" and "political" wings that at times appeared unrelated to each other. The resulting unintelligibility conferred on the demands made the Hindu right's militancy greater, and rendered it more of an alien force.

Centered in Uttar Pradesh (which for part of the movement's duration was under a BJP-led government) as well as in the other Hindi belt states, the Birthplace campaign lasted, in its most intense phase, for a little over three years, culminating in December 1992 with the mosque's demolition. In the post-independence period, the campaign can be said to have been inaugurated when Rajiv Gandhi's government acceded to the demand made by some VHP leaders to re-open the Babri masjid in Ayodhya (see Appendix for more details). The mosque had lain shut by court order since December 1949. At that time, Hindu militants had forcibly installed a deity of Lord Ram in the mosque, triggering unrest in Faizabad. In effect, the re-opening of the mosque sanctified Hindu violation of Muslim property rights, and granted Hindus the right to maintain worship of the idol installed there. If the

Congress Party had hoped to gain political mileage by this move, it was the sangh and its allies that seized the decisive advantage, beginning in the fall of 1989, through a series of campaigns that succeeded in mobilizing not only the traditional Hindu nationalist base of middle classes from small towns, but also professionals and the intelligentsia, on the one hand, and large numbers of backward caste youth on the other. The timing was fortuitous, and the mobilization was aided by many factors, principally the proposal to implement the Mandal Commission recommendations that backward classes be awarded reserved seats in educational institutions and central government sector jobs. Prime Minister V. P. Singh's decision in 1990 to re-activate the decade-old recommendations provoked a furious response from upper castes all across northern India. The Hindu nationalist struggle was played out on many fronts, then, ranging from Parliamentary speeches and court battles demanding restitution of "Hindu property," to artfully designed mobilizations, civil disobedience, anti-lower caste and anti-Muslim riots, all combining to advance the cause of the temple's construction.

The slogan that endured throughout the VHP campaign, painted on walls and on banners, shouted in marches, sung in songs that blared from a thousand loudspeakers in Ayodhya and other sites of VHP activity, was: mandir *wahin* banayenge – the temple will be built *right there*.[32] The overt emphasis of the slogan was on construction, but at the site of the *mosque*. The prior act of destruction was thus indispensable to the project. The implication was unavoidable, and available on asking the first question impelled by the utterance, *where?* Yet the press, English and Hindi both, maintained a tactful silence on the subject, reproducing the Centre's own alliance in the BJP's fictions of "construction" and "renovation." The Hindu nationalists themselves seemed to deftly engage in a wide variety of debates, unhindered by the awkwardness of making disparate claims in different places. RSS and BJP members entertained arguments about the legal and juridical basis of the birthplace claims; Bajrang Dal "Hanuman's Army" and VHP members scoffed at the idea that mere evidence would deter them from their goals. RSS and VHP intellectuals adduced archaeological and textual evidence to build a historical argument, while at the same time other RSS and VHP members declared that faith, and the masses of the faithful, would formulate the verdict. Against the moving target represented by this orchestrated medley, setting the factual record straight seemed to make little headway, and appeared at times like a shout in a storm.

The movement was ostensibly led by the VHP, and day-to-day

organization and mobilization were arranged through this network of Hindu right activists. Overseeing the VHP itself, as well as the BJP, was the grey eminence of the RSS. The BJP used the multiple fronts of the RSS to assert its connection to the movement when it chose to, and to withdraw when inconvenient. Thus the foundation stone ceremony, the *shilanyas*, was declared to be a VHP, not a BJP affair. Vijayaraje Scindia and other BJP members were present, but the press reported that they were present in their capacity as VHP office-bearers. Meanwhile the BJP leaders gave assurances to the center regarding the conduct of kar seva and the preservation of the mosque. As for the responsibility for the violence that accompanied the mobilization's progress, the few who raised the question found it swiftly deflected. When the mosque was finally demolished, both the BJP and the VHP pointed to crowds run riot as the culprit: no mass movement could maintain complete discipline, after all, and the passions of karsevaks could only be restrained for so long. For the naive inquirer, the Hindu nationalists presented a hall of mirrors, where any attempt to attach image to voice and so locate responsibility was futile. If one took their statements on trust, the blame always lay elsewhere. The BJP's Parliamentary leaders, such as Advani and Vajpayee, were in general more moderate in their public statements, but the orators and organizers such as Uma Bharati, Vinay Katiyar, and Swami Chinmayanand, all BJP MPs prominent in the VHP, invariably struck militant postures.[33]

For the English language press, the Ram temple movement was something "out there," beyond the province of activities intelligible to its own readers. Whether it was understood as a matter of religious faith or of communal politics, it was something alluded to rather than engaged with directly, explained in abstract concepts rather than with reference to beliefs or practices familiar to their audience. Although it was nowhere stated as such, there was unquestionably the sense that the vernacular was the more muddy, compromised realm whose modernity was uncertain, whereas the domain of English was that of secular modernity proper. The English press's apparent distance from the argumentative reach of the VHP and their allies was akin to a brahminical posture, with its language functioning as a master language, and at the same time, as a kind of overarching juridical-legal apparatus within which the effects of regional discourses could be plotted and assessed.[34] English was in this sense the latter-day equivalent of Sanskrit, a language of modern technocracy that guaranteed the disinterested expertise of those who wielded it. Its inability to access the values and beliefs of the vernacular realm was then a form of sanctioned ignorance, a sign of privilege rather than a handicap, portending none of the usual consequences of ignorance.[35]

Prabhash Joshi, editor of the Hindi daily *Jansatta*, published by the Goenkas, expressed the schism in sharp terms:

A very insulting term is used – national press. This means that [only] those newspapers published in English spread their influence across the country. By this token the papers in Indian languages are regional. But why is *Anand Bazaar Patrika* not [considered] national press? Are *Hindustan* or *Navbharat Times* not fit to represent the whole country? This is a very unsound question. In the words of Vinobha Bhave, it has split the whole country into Rahu and Ketu.[36] The few people who are in charge, know English. The principal responsibility for nationalism, for the reconstruction of the nation, has been taken by these English language literates. They are Rahu, the others are Ketu. Today even if a Shankaracharya or Tulsidas were to emerge in this country, they would be considered semi-educated if they did not know English. The grave problem resulting from this is that it is hard for those who dominate the national press to encounter the culture of the country, [to know] its roots.[37]

Underlying the relationships of English/Hindi linguistic power in news coverage of Ayodhya was a structured set of misperceptions, ensuing from and reinforcing such a bifurcated system of discourse. Beneath those misperceptions, however, lay some shared assumptions. Although there were court proceedings on the property disputes related to the mosque and to the issue of the VHP's encroachment, the VHP's claim that the birthplace of Ram was primarily a religious affair was essentially accepted by the center, and by major sections of the press. The BJP's *White Paper on Ayodhya*, published in May 1993, disclosed that P. V. Narasimha Rao, who became Prime Minister in 1991, was chairman of a group of ministers constituted by Rajiv Gandhi's government in April 1987 to work for a solution of the Ayodhya issue. In an article attributed to him, Rao discussed the matter in terms similar to those expressed by Buta Singh: "[U]nfortunately for the first time, a countrywide movement based on the deep religious devotion of millions of Hindus has been organized with an out-and-out political purpose in view, with amazing skill and astounding subtlety so as to touch the Hindu psyche deeply . . . The Hindu community . . . has been fanaticised for political ends. And once the majority community gets so fanaticised, what remains of secularism?" He goes on to say, "When communal atmosphere prevails everywhere, no political party is or can be, totally immune from it."[38]

The BJP claimed that Ram Janmabhumi was a matter of faith for the Hindu majority. To this, the Congress had no reply except silent assent. This was not surprising, since from the illicit installation of the idol, to the barring of Muslims from worshiping at the mosque and the eventual opening of the site to *Hindu* rather than Muslim worship, each significant development in the case had been overseen and steered by a Congress administration.

Narasimha Rao's essay thus indicated an acceptance of the Hindu right's construction of the basic problem. It was the religious devotion of Hindus that underlay the issue; the Hindus were the majority community; this community was now hell-bent on achieving its aim. Again, we can observe the representation of the movement as a kind of irresistible force sweeping the country, one that the Congress party could only accommodate – any other response appeared out of the question. The VHP's sadhus and sants (mendicants and saints) were legitimate discussants in the negotiations, and representatives of "Hindus," with Muslim leaders occasionally entertained on "the other" side. If the center granted the VHP its fiction for fear of its mobilizing power and as a political convenience, the media reproduced this fiction and reinforced it over time as a news routine; the impression created, as the Citizens' Tribunal on Ayodhya noted, "was one of a grand mobilisation without any dissenting voice to the 'Sangh Parivar' activities." Effectively, the media "helped in the build up," and provided "a positive impression" of the movement, the tribunal concluded.[39] Meanwhile, the entry of national political parties into the dispute made the story into a regular feature of political news, and the periodic reports on the status of "talks" approximated the norms of politics-as-usual.

Coverage in the English press was largely limited to political and legal issues, to reactions to court rulings, and developments in Ayodhya and in the capital. This had the effect of reinforcing the English press's reliance on appointed spokespersons and leaders (specifically, the political leaders in the BJP) for information on the movement, talks with Muslim leaders, petitions in court, and so on. This could be managed within the methods of political reportage. Little attempt was made to understand the meanings of the events for those concerned, or to relate the motives of actors to any larger political explanations put forth. One consequence of the reliance on political leaders' statements was that the most moderate statements of the movement tended to be emphasized and placed in the headlines, with the more extreme statements of the activist VHP leaders buried lower down in the news pyramid, or in back-page stories. This was the emphasis favored by the Congress itself, namely that "solutions" were being explored, that there was on the whole no cause for alarm, and that "all steps" would be taken to safeguard the mosque. This then became the interpretive middle ground, and contradictions between this frame and actual events were de-emphasized. But this middle ground itself could not withstand scrutiny.

For their part, critics of the movement in the English language press pointed out that the authenticity of the Ram Janmabhumi site was dubious, that Muslim rights required respect, and that Hindus were in any case not a united group. Most crucially, the blame for the movement and the political threat it represented was completely identified with the BJP and its allies. The Congress did not emerge unscathed, but its involvement was largely regarded in residual terms, as failure to deal adequately with the "communal menace." In this way, the BJP was spotlighted as a threat from without to the stability of existing order; just what this "order" was, was not questioned. But as evidence flowed in of the abundant popular support for the movement, such a view was challenged. Now the BJP appeared rather as the enemy within, releasing dormant popular energies and inciting discontent for its own purposes. Taken together, what resulted was a fundamentally incoherent understanding of the "communal threat," and of the movement as such. And this was closely tied to the conception of the existing political order, not "liberal" in the received sense of the term but assumed as such. Caste, community, and religion compromised the polity's claim to being progressive and secular, but the belief that liberal ideals were, if not prevailing then close at hand, could not be discarded easily.

With only a bipolar categorization available, of secular or communal, the English language press was hampered in exploring the numerous registers in between that characterized actual events. Avoiding the cultural aspect of the movement was a way to manage this confusion while retaining the press's class/caste distance. Thus as the first temple construction campaign following the foundation laying approached, in October 1990, *The Times of India* commented in an editorial, "The successful rath yatra ["chariot procession" led by Advani across the country to publicize the campaign in the fall of 1990] has . . . demonstrated that blind faith is too deep rooted to be wished away or beaten into submission . . . Unfortunately, such a powerful exhibition of Hindu feeling is fraught with danger."[40] What could not be seen or understood could not, of course, be defeated easily. However, the adventitious character of the exercise evoked no recognition in *The Times*.

On the rare occasions when they addressed the topic of belief in Ram, English language newspapers felt more comfortable with a historical rather than a cultural or religious approach. The following example is symptomatic of its underlying assumptions:

> Did Lord Rama ever exist? Do events of the Ramayana have any historical veracity? . . . Academicians are yet to describe Lord Rama as a historical character. The late National Professor Suniti Kumar Chatterjee explained that the Ramayana is basically a literary creation by Valmiki with, of course, later interpolations . . . Rational understanding of history suggests that the cult of Lord Rama became prevalent only with the advent of Ramananda and his disciple Tulsidas. The history of Hinduism also bears this out as there is little evidence to indicate that the deification of Lord Rama was complete before the spread of Tulsidas's verses. Nonetheless Ayodhya came to be identified as the mythical kingdom and the disputed site became a point of conflict.[41]

A rational, historical approach prevents belief in Ram, and leads to bracketing the story as mythical. The worship of Ram, e.g., by the sect of the Ramanandis, here becomes the activity of a cult spreading against all the evidence, and with it fictional notions of a kingdom and a birthplace, leading, perhaps inevitably, to conflict. A historical approach was of course a necessary part of any critical response. But the conviction that the ideas in question were wrong-headed meant, in effect, a refusal of the sociological fact of religious belief. It was thus unnecessary to engage with its actual content and dynamics. Such a narrowly conceived approach could make little headway in understanding the movement, and the only recourse could be to demand reinforced security measures. The law-and-order frame prominent in news coverage was thus an overdetermined one.

For the Hindi press, the Ram Janmabhumi movement was not only a legal and political issue, but a social and cultural one as well, whose symbols and rituals were discussed in often fluent and racy prose. Not merely the statements of leaders then, but the intuitions of journalists about the movement's popular meanings could also inform news stories. To be sure, there was a great deal of subjective and misleading reportage, including propaganda masquerading as news, and stories too implausible to count as news in the usual sense of the word. Their appearance in Hindi papers was related in part to the very different institutional environment their reporters worked in, with a structure of incentives and systems of editorial control quite different from those of most English language newspapers. But the profusion of subjective reporting signaled not merely a lack of professionalism, or the presence of communal-minded management, although these were undoubtedly important determinants.[42] In addition to these factors, such reporting indicated also the cultural proximity of journalists to the subject matter, and their access to its inner modes and meanings. Of course, the assertion of proximity is more important here than the quality of understanding involved.

Here, for instance, is a response by one journalist to a question allegedly put by American embassy officials in Lucknow inquiring as to the sudden importance of Ram, after police firing in Ayodhya in November 1990:

Twice central governments have fallen on this issue. In the past month or two, more than ten countries across the world have seen a change in government. It seems as if Sesha Nag[43] has started a disco dance. Nothing is stable, but Indians are indifferent to it. People are more agonized over the Ram temple than over *roti* [bread] . . .

There are many things to be done in Hindu society. Untouchability needs to be removed, hierarchy needs to be ended, everyone has to be linked by a common thread, *et cetera et cetera*. Ignoring all these things, the Vishwa Hindu Parishad has started working on the Ram Janmabhumi temple. There must be a reason for it. Perhaps VHP thought that with this one task, many other things would be achieved. Due to the aura of Ram, the demon of Reservation ran away. Isn't that enough? . . .

Ram is the soul of Indians. Here people are taught that he who does not have Ram and Sita in his heart should be repudiated, no matter how popular he is. This is the reason V. P. Singh and Mulayam, who until yesterday were ruling, are in the dust now . . .[44]

The idiom resists easy translation, even as it displays a cheerful hybridity, with its image of the cosmic serpent swaying to a disco beat and so sending shock waves through the world it carries on its back. The writer acknowledges the apparent material irrelevance of the VHP's temple project, but points to its political efficacy: it was able to "defeat" "Reservation," i.e., the opposition's move to divide the Hindu vote with reservations for Backward Classes, and win "BC" votes for the BJP in the 1990 Assembly elections. He does not disguise his political affiliations in his hostility to reservations, and he addresses an audience he assumes is dominated by upper-caste literates. When he writes that people care more for the temple than for *roti*, his tone is ironic rather than reverent; at any rate, he emphasizes first of all the irrationality rather than the truth of the sentiment. The answer he offers to the inquiring Americans is hardly a native secret, but could be found in any of a number of Orientalist texts. The author makes two kinds of assertions here, both implicit. First, he assumes that "communalism" enters only when the prerogative of Hinduism is challenged, such as by Muslims wishing to reclaim the mosque. In this view, for Ram to be identified as the soul of Indians is an unexceptionable statement. Second, his upper caste status, and his evident membership in the intelligentsia notwithstanding, he asserts a relationship of familiarity and power with the symbols (it chased away the demon of reservation). Proximity to religious symbols does not necessarily imply "communal" politics, although in this case they were clearly tied together.

In another column published a few days earlier, one writer had seen the symbol not in terms of ownership and its implied rights, but in terms of shared values:

The country's economic condition is miserable . . . [T]here should be popular movements on these issues . . . But nothing like this has happened. We have turned away from all other issues because the Mandir–Mandal issues have confused us badly. The temple should be built, but in an atmosphere of mutual harmony . . . I have one request to make of temple agitators. They should remember that the upholder of moral propriety, Ram, is the symbol and heritage of Indian culture. Ram is the ideal king, the ideal husband, the ideal son, the ideal friend, and the ideal enemy. While constructing a temple for such an upholder of moral propriety all values must be respected. Ram is not the god of any one community, he is the Ideal Man in the mind of Indian people as a whole . . .[45]

Not reverence for Ram but confusion and misunderstanding are at the root of problems, in this writer's argument. Naive as it is in its politics, and unwilling as it is to question the placement of Ram as a national ideal, there is here, nevertheless, qualified criticism of the temple movement, from a perspective that grants a social importance to the symbols. The sentiments at issue could then potentially become a subject for debate.

There appeared to be what we can provisionally call a sense of intimacy with the symbols in the Hindi press, borne of a cultural rather than a legalistic approach to the issue, whereas such a feeling was emphatically absent in the English language press. Hindu leaders in fact asserted ownership of the symbols, while denying the latter were property; rather, they were claimed as indispensable to life. The statements by VHP leaders were full of such declarations, which made highly quotable quotes; in pro-BJP papers, they often found their way to the headlines. Thus Uma Bharati, BJP MP, declared, in a speech in Ferozabad, U.P., on 2 December 1990: "For the sake of the temple, I will give my head, or I will take the heads of hundreds," a statement that became a headline in *Aaj*. She expressed grief that she lost the chance to sacrifice herself for the cause, and that police in the November firings did not kill her.[46] The rhetoric appears inflated: while Uma Bharati and others in the BJP may have been willing to sacrifice lives, at no point did they place their own in any danger. *Aaj* readers may well have understood the symbolic maneuvers the VHP was engaging in. A few days later, for instance, another BJP MP, Vinay Katiyar, could declare, "As long as they use Mandal, we will use *kamandal*," the title of a front page story in the same paper.[47] *Kamandal*, the Hindu mendicant's pot, was a play on the word, making explicit the tactical choice of terms in the struggle to establish Hindutva. If the ruling party would fracture the Hindu vote by offering quotas for Backward Classes, the BJP would make aggressive use of Hindu symbols in return, Katiyar was saying. Even if symbols were religious in nature, and served as objects of belief, they were at the same time part of the social vocabulary, acting as semantic currency with greater or lesser political energies at their command. The whole business of politics then was to increase, or inflate, the energy behind the symbols with which one aligned, in the battle against the competition.

In contrast, the frames of the English language press wavered between understanding the Ayodhya story in terms of normal politics, and seeing it as a movement liable to subvert the nation's foundations, thereby invoking the police and the army, which mark the limit of normal politics. In neither of these frames was a cultural understanding of the movement possible, one where the movement could be comprehended as part of the social traffic in meaning. The interplay and give and take of symbols were acknowledged, but were understood to belong exclusively at an elite level. Thus periodically there was discussion of the BJP's tinkering with its image, between weak, moderate, and strong Hindutva for instance, or between more and less openness to the entry of foreign companies. As for the masses, their faith was "blind" and "deep-rooted," presumably related to their inability to perceive these pragmatic adjustments and certainly to their incapacity for flexibility in such issues. Thus, although the perception of communal politics as a battle of images was fairly well-established in the Hindi press, the conviction that profound, even atavistic beliefs were involved never left the English language press. For all its insular presumptions of superior-ity, it was the latter who were naive and credulous regarding the issue of faith, even if it was credulity in the faith of others.

It should be noted that the breakdown of differences was not strictly along the lines I have drawn; there were exceptions on each side. *The Indian Express* was often supportive of the movement, for example, just as several Hindi language papers were critical of the sangh parivar's activities, for example the *Navbharat Times*, or *Jansatta*. Within the English language press there were columnists who wrote about Hindutva with insight and, indeed, enthusiasm, such as Swapan Dasgupta in *The Times of India* and Chandan Mitra in *The Hindustan Times*. A majority of those in the English language press were undoubtedly at least bilingual, so that the understandings circulating in the Hindi press were very likely available if not familiar to them.

What was the nature of the interaction between the electronic and the print media in these circumstances? Although television created a con-text for collective awareness, the footprint of the medium was large at this time (1987–91), with only one government-run channel available across much of the country. The speed and sensitivity with which television could respond to signals from popular audiences was severely limited for these reasons; in effect, electronic programming did not go much beyond the fare of Hindu tele-epics during this period. The print media were more regional in scope and operated on a more commercial basis, so that they worked within the footprint of Doordarshan, and could help interpret and work out the implications of a new set of social perceptions.

What then was the effect of the press's structured misperceptions on the Ram temple movement? The English language press in a sense created the movement as it would become – closed, implacable, and impervious to reason, and challenging the existing bounds of legality by embracing religious fanaticism rather than the principles of constitu-tional democracy. Yet the Ram temple movement was plainly not a monolithic entity; it enclosed a range of positions, from those critical of British colonial inheritance or desirous of more indigenous cultural influence, to the pious and devout, to those who conceived of collective revenge against Muslims as a politically liberating development. The Hindi press was able to articulate these distinctions and allow a more heterogeneous image of the movement's cultural references to emerge. This was due to both the specific history of the relationship of Hindi to English in India, as a nationalist rather than a colonial language and the more dispersed and downmarket character of the Hindi print media together with the different news values arising in Hindi media as a result of these two factors. Hindu nationalists exploited these factors successfully, so that the monolithic picture of the campaign in the English language press became the active counterpart to the more nuanced and variegated narratives in the Hindi press, which expressed a certain level of political self-consciousness.

This crucial dimension of self-consciousness was lacking in English news coverage of the movement, except in occasional discussions of leadership strategy. Such a portrayal only went to reinforce the threat represented by the BJP and its allies; indeed, those in the secular front might have frowned on granting reflexivity to Hindu nationalists for fear of humanizing those who were, after all, the enemy. Alongside the more complex accounts available in the Hindi press, supporters of the campaign could also be assured of more blatantly propagandistic coverage, replete with fabricated stories of Muslim treachery and Hindu heroism. As the BJP and its allies found their campaign being shaped in the "national," i.e., English press, in Parliament and in the courts, as a singular and unified entity dangerous to the polity, the distance of this understanding from the picture available in the Hindi language press actually helped the movement, lending it notoriety and power while masking the variety and the incoherence of its constituent parts.

A HALL OF MIRRORS: THE BJP'S PRINT MEDIA STRATEGY

For those used to a "Hindu equilibrium" in attempts to resolve long-standing issues in the subcontinent, the speed with which the Ram Janmabhumi movement developed, reached a crescendo, and fairly disappeared from public concern, taking with it the Babri Masjid itself, was extraordinary. It surely represented a failure of understanding that so few on the secular side came to grips with the extent of support the movement had won across wide sections of society, or that so few foresaw the imminence of the demolition. To what extent was this influenced by news coverage of the Ayodhya story? In the Hindi press, in the words of one commentator, a section "turned into a Hindu press, and as a result, facts and figures were distorted and events were imagined or imagination was added to the events. Headlines became exhortative and commentative and photographs were used to heighten the effect."[48] A broad section of the Hindi press was sympathetic to the movement, and its coverage was on the whole favorable. In the English press, support was more nuanced and qualified: a large number of reporters were not hostile to the BJP, especially in the capital, but different conventions of reportage and the different ways in which editorial control was exerted meant that biases were more often latent than patent.

The most important biases, I suggest, were not intentional but inhered in the language and in news values, and followed as a result of the way in which the Ayodhya story was understood. Thus criticism of the BJP did not necessarily alarm the party's media experts.[49] The biases in reportage occurred in two principal ways: by press inability/refusal to engage with the linguistic structures and frames within which actors in the news operated, symbolized by its suspicion of religion; and by isolating the BJP as the political problem to be solved. News coverage kept the spotlight on the BJP, appearing therefore to justify the party's claims to have achieved center stage in politics. If they were regarded as villains of the piece, that was of course a problem of perception. "Now all parties have to respond to us," BJP leader L. K. Advani declared more than once, "we are centre-stage."[50] The criticism that the BJP was politically dangerous lacked a cultural component: in this conception, secularism was, after all, the avoidance of religion. Precisely this lack was addressed by the BJP's emphasis on Hinduism's indispensability to the society. For all its acknowledged drawbacks, Congress secularism became the opposition's spearhead, so defining the limits of media criticism. The central government's own oscillation between admonition, occasional preventive measures, and, for the most part, inaction in the face of the Hindu right's escalation were not necessarily excused in the press. But representing as it did the leading edge of the political counter to communalism, Congress failures were the occasion for frustration rather than provocation for analysis.

In one day's paper, statements from different representatives of the Hindu right routinely ranged from conciliatory to defiant. It was a question of judgment, of course, as to which were to be emphasized, or what order of importance was to be accorded them. Following the routines of political reporting, the English language news media usually gave precedence to the statements of official spokespersons and parliamentary leaders. In doing so, they were also following the broad definition of the situation accepted by the center. While this was one way of charting a path through the maze of conflicting signals given by the sangh parivar, it had the effect of moderating apprehensions aroused by the Hindu right's militant acts.

Against this tendency, and sometimes underlying it, was a sense of simmering crisis that periodically erupted in full-blown proportion: "Nation's Zero-Hour," "A Nation Betrayed," etc.[51] The rapid rise in the BJP's share of parliamentary seats, from two to 119 in the span of just one national election, seemed ominous.[52] Constructions of extreme alarm acted as a mirror image to the BJP's own projections of the make-or-break symbolic status of its project, with the demolition supposed to usher in a new era of politics. To allow them to go ahead with their plan was one thing, but to accept the gravity they attributed to it was another. Where sympathy with their cause was absent, the BJP created fear, which proved a potent ally as well. It brought them the attention of the entire nation, and confirmed the significance of the temple issue. The alarm bells rung by the press, I suggest, helped create the storm in which the BJP hoped to sail into power, one in which terror and anticipation both had a role to play.

The BJP's attempt was to conjoin social and political power at state level, and was based on a false premise, of the unified and all-encompassing nature of Hindu society. As a project that took itself literally, it could never succeed. The sangh parivar's founder, Dr. Hedgewar, and his successor M. S. Golwalkar, had earlier quixotically attempted to negotiate this contradiction by setting out to accomplish, through daily drill, prayer, and the mesmerism of constant suggestion, the organization of the entire country into disciplined storm troopers. If it could succeed at all, it would only be by elevating the principle of suggestion to a new level, turning what had been a goal into a *fait accompli*, requiring only a small test to prove itself, such as tearing down an old building, albeit with the fanfare of making the nation anew. And then what? By then, perhaps, enough Hindu votes would have been gathered to inch past the Congress's declining total. It was hardly the most sophisticated of methods, and, given the small vote base the BJP began with, it was a long shot.

The sangh parivar had never expected the response they got from the Ram Janmabhumi movement, and the campaign itself had developed over the course of its growth, with the BJP increasing the stakes as the winnings kept coming in, as it were. "The Ram Janmabhumi movement developed slowly, according to the things that came before us," VHP Central Secretary Nanaji Bhagwat admitted. "We never expected such a big response. But the leadership was strong enough to utilize that response, not to waste its gains, and to carry the campaign forward."[53] The progress of the campaign appeared to be a result of the swelling sentiments of hitherto repressed Hindus, urged on by a committed leadership. This disclosure needs to be complemented, however, by the careful husbandry of the movement by successive governments, principally the Congress, and its representation by the media, either out of enthusiasm or of apprehension. Media coverage was a constitutive part of the movement, in both its eulogistic and critical aspects. Encouragement of course urged participants on and brought recruits and supporters. Criticism of the movement was welcomed too. "The Rath Yatra [chariot procession] will give BJP 60% political success, but if their opponents try to stop it, they will get 100% success," declared the RSS weekly, *Organiser*.[54] Media criticism confirmed the importance of the campaign's goals and preserved the appearance that more had to be achieved. The louder the criticism was, then, the greater the achievement appeared to be.[55]

The attention to image-engineering of the BJP through the media is not without precedent in Indian politics. Indira Gandhi's anti-poverty slogan, *garibi hatao* (abolish poverty), was devised and tested on sample audiences by advertising consultants against Mrs. Gandhi's own initial skepticism.[56] N. T. Rama Rao and M. G. Ramachandran, both screen idols turned political leaders in Andhra Pradesh and Tamil Nadu respectively, had both relied on carefully crafted screen personas, of a saintly or godlike presence in the case of Rama Rao, and of a populist hero in the case of Ramachandran.[57] Rajiv Gandhi's government too saw extensive reliance on photo opportunities and on copious exposure on television.[58] The BJP was not only a cadre-based party with a large number of intelligentsia who counted themselves as its supporters. As an opposition party aspiring to be the new dominant national party, it was acutely aware of an increasing turnover of party loyalists, and of the growth of what Advani called "non-committed voters," eager to bet on a winning party rather than to follow the dictates of a local big man. The BJP's claim to being a disciplined party, and a political alternative to the Congress, presumably made it attractive to those making such calculations. Image management in the BJP was at this time not simply the building of a personality cult, although some leaders such as Advani and Vajpayee clearly enjoyed favorable coverage. As I have said, there was of course a measure of outright criticism too. As the BJP public relations coordinator pointed out, criticism was helpful in circulating news about them and in provoking discussion.[59] The willingness to acknowledge criticism as a public relations strategy, although it hardly percolated to all levels of the sangh parivar,[60] marked the party's sophistication in media matters. Advani referred to image projection and political success in an interview:

I do not think election victories and defeats are a reflection of a government's performance. There is a connection, but a fragile and slight one . . . I do think that election victories and defeats have much to do with the kind of image a party projects in a state. Whether that image conforms to reality or not is not the question: the image is there and the consequences are bound to show up in the ballot box.[61]

The BJP's media strategy was part of a three-pronged plan, to improve its rapport with its support base, with the bureaucracy, and with the media.[62] These were of course intricately related: cultivating the bureaucracy improved access to the media, especially at local levels; a wider support base helped reach out to the bureaucracy and the media; and a good media image would improve prospects all around. There is evidence of slow and painstaking efforts on the part of the RSS and VHP over several years to establish good relationships with village and district level leaders, with the police and administration. Thus, for instance, a handbook for VHP activists advises cultivating friendships among the police in case of trouble.[63]

A key aspect of the BJP's media strategy was working with and using the divisions within prevailing media. Advani acknowledged that the BJP media strategy was "fragmented," given the fragmented character of the media audience.[64] There was a sense of disapproval about the fragmentation, and an intention ultimately to overcome it with a grand national schema; the media strategy was pragmatic rather than part of a finely wrought plan. Divisions between the languages were pre-eminent, but there were also divisions between regional and metropolitan media, and divisions between those accessible to certain forms of media as opposed to others, with video crossing the literacy barrier for example, and being trucked to remote places in "video vans."[65] Additionally, there were, of course, a large number of people with the sadhus (religious mendicants) who, Advani noted, were immune to anything the media might say.[66]

The methods the BJP used to influence its publicity addressed not only the product but also the process of media coverage, establishing good rapport with journalists and catering to prevailing news values with sensational quotes and eye-catching pictures.[67] Creating rapport with journalists included staging press conferences that were orchestrated as celebratory exercises, with friendly reporters primed to ask questions designed to bring out the party in its best light. Reporters from the capital were given airfare to cover quarterly party conclaves, normally considered too minor for big city journalists. Sympathetic reporters were cultivated and "rewarded" with "inside" stories, more often than not plants to further BJP publicity. This was especially effective with younger reporters hoping for a break, who would be awed by being taken into the confidence of senior leaders.[68] The BJP General Secretary Govindacharya was notable for cultivating reporters in this way. The appearance of an invitation to witness inner party planning and to peek into future strategies had the effect of bringing reporters closer in line with the party's thinking. Deliberations on whether the party was going to change its image, on whether it would "dilute" its Hindutva line, or reaffirm it, would be reported straightforwardly, as though it was natural for the party of values to be debating how much could be gained by pursuing them. In this way, audiences could adopt an insider's viewpoint, sharing in its thoughts without necessarily questioning them. Amitabh Sinha mentioned that a lot of the effort was personal, one-on-one engagement with reporters, slowly and patiently talking to them, and gradually convincing them, for instance, that the BJP bore no responsibility for the riots it was accused of fomenting, and that the places where they happened were places which had always witnessed communal riots.

Photo opportunities were carefully crafted to provide a colorful spectacle: sadhus in saffron costumes, political leaders wearing headgear out of mythological films, a profusion of marigolds, and paraphernalia such as tridents, daggers, javelins, and bows and arrows, scenes whose "newsworthy" character eluded a simple secular/communal division. The images themselves were mute, threatening to some and inviting to others, such as one of Advani with sandalwood paste and vermilion on his forehead, with a full quiver strapped on his shoulder, posing with a drawn bow and arrow. Either as an auspicious commingling of politics and faith, or as a warning to be broadcast, they were hard to resist. In the cover photograph of one English language magazine, a motley crowd of kar sevaks stood in front of the mosque, several with their mouths open in mid cry, with a saffron-clad, orange-daubed sadhu in front, wielding a club in one hand, and an empty cement pan in the other. They were posing for the photographer, obedient to the camera even if militant to the world. What looked like a wooden branch several inches long protruded from the back of the sadhu's head – his hair, rolled and congealed. He cut a striking figure, "other" in his attitudes and immune to ordinary threats, with a willing crowd behind him.[69]

The spectacle was not simply for photographers, but usually a participatory event. Coming in to Faizabad in December 1990, Advani rode an open van, with a ten foot tall garlanded picture of Ram behind him, so that his image appeared framed against that of Ram. Supporters wearing saffron caps, sashes, scarves, and armbands swarmed around the van, mingling with the crowd. Excitement was thus conveyed at different levels all at once.

Apart from the fact of Hindi's relative cultural proximity to the issues of the campaign and the upper-caste composition of the bulk of the press, three features were related to the susceptibility of the press to the campaign's propaganda: its rapid expansion in recent years; its ownership structure; and the degree of organizational development of Hindi newspapers. The period of Hindi language newspaper growth appears to have commenced with the political conscientization accompanying the Emergency. Before the Emergency, there were only a few Hindi newspapers selling more than a hundred thousand copies, such as the *Navbharat Times*, *Hindustan* and *Nai Duniya*. By 1977, there were more than ten papers selling more than this amount, including *Aaj*, *Amar Ujala*, *Aryavart*, *Jagran*, *Punjab Kesari*, *Rajasthan Patrika*, and *Swatantra Bharat*. Several dailies increased the number of pages they carried from six and eight to sixteen and twenty-four. The expansion of rural markets and the consequent growth of advertising increased this growth enormously. Subsidiary factors include the improvement of technology and communications.

It was during the Emergency that the RSS too began to realize the importance of effective contacts within the media, and thereafter made systematic attempts to influence those in leadership roles in the press, and to shape the news product from within the media.[70] In the 1970s, many newspapers were still set by hand. Transport systems to reach markets beyond the point of publication depended on road and motor transport, involving considerable durations of time. In the 1980s, electronic technology and indigenous offset presses led to the establishment of presses in smaller towns. With the master copy set in one center, electronic communication allowed it to be channeled via telephone lines, thereby wiping out delivery times of up to several hours as papers were trucked from large to satellite towns.[71] Between 1988 and 1992 alone, the audited circulation of Hindi dailies grew by 35 percent, from 2.6 million a day to more than 3.2 million a day. The number of newspapers in other languages grew also, but by the much smaller figure of 15 percent – from 137 to 157.[72]

The increased circulation of stories on Ayodhya helped fuel news-paper sales and enrich newspaper owners, and showed them the advantages of pursuing the line they did.[73] These were periods when the Mandal anti-reservation stir and the temple movement were at their height, and *Amar Ujala, Aaj* and *Dainik Jagaran* were reprimanded by the Press Council of India for grossly irresponsible reporting during October–November 1990.[74] Hindutva became economically profitable during this period: the more communal the news stories, the more the circulation and the more the ad revenue.[75] In one instance, a newspaper which carried a fictitious story in December 1990 about thirty-five people killed in Khurja, U.P. was reported to have had its modest price of one rupee reduced to fifty paise, and sold 5,000 copies on that day, with the local RSS buying up copies and distributing them free.[76] V. P. Singh's announcement of the decision on the Mandal report was cited as the single most influential political development spurring the propaganda. Newspapers also played a role in transforming upper-caste youth who were pro V. P. Singh in the anti-Congress wave of the 1989 elections into BJP supporters in the post-Mandal period.[77]

Despite rising circulation and profits, expenditure on news gathering operations did not rise proportionately, and wire services as well as reports filed by poorly paid correspondents and stringers formed the bulk of the news.[78] It is not certain, however, whether it was political or economic motives that were predominant. News was clearly perceived to be a weapon of war for many Hindi language newspapers. As such, the angle that news stories would carry was predetermined, and the malleability of facts for maximum effect was precisely the kind of advantage that should accrue from control of the press, in the agonistic view of news culture that prevailed in much of the independent language press.

This relates to the third feature, which is the relatively underdeveloped character of news organizations. Hindi newspapers at this time were for the most part dominated by owner-editors who maintained little institutional buffer between their economic interest and the day-to-day operation of the papers, and granted little security or professional autonomy to reporters. *Jansatta* editor Prabhash Joshi pinpointed the continuance of hereditary owner-editors as the most serious problem undermining the quality of newspaper journalism.[79] Reporters tended to be kept on a "hire-and-fire" basis, that is, those lucky enough to secure a regular position in the first place. By far the majority of journalists were untrained part-timers, with the multiple chores of increasing circulation, securing advertisements, and writing news stories as well. For example, in 1992 the *Jagran* group, which was among the larger newspaper groups, had fifty full-time staff correspondents and 300 "working journalists," and its total staff including part-time correspondents, district correspondents, and stringers numbered 700.[80] The Press Council of India, asked to provide accreditation for special correspondents for some newspapers, found that a majority of Hindi journalists were unable to prove that they received an income. In 1991, only 542 of the 1,662 newspaper establishments in the country had implemented the Bachawat Wage Board recommendations regarding equitable compensation for journalists. Forty-nine newspapers had partially implemented the recommendations, and 1,071 had failed to do so, according to a statement by the Labor Minister in the Rajya Sabha.[81] Paid a nominal fee and sometimes not paid at all, journalists in Hindi language papers were often required to explore all the ways in which the production of news could be used to extract money, as opposed to regular journalists who were paid by the line or by the month. One journalist described the situation thus:

[There is a] Hindi journalist in every town and he is given just a press card. What does he do? He goes to the local police station, local politicians, or even local builders . . . They are not placed in regular grades, they are not paid any remuneration. Their conveyance expenses are not reimbursed. Where would they go? They would certainly look towards the government. We compel them to work under the government, we put them under the influence of the police, we put them under those who use them and yet we expect them to file objective reports.[82]

"*Darogaji* [the police sub-inspector] is our editor. Nothing can be written without his approval," one editor remarked.[83] Along with news values, reporters were then required to have a keen sense of the channels of local power formations and know how to negotiate within them. In such a situation, reporters were liable to consult the local equivalent of the social register rather than their professional judgment in deciding how to report a story, or whether to report it at all.[84]

Ironically, two regional newspapers that resisted VHP hegemony were both independent newspapers based in Faizabad, *Jan Morcha* (People's Front), a socialist newspaper dating back to the early 1950s, and *Hum Aap* (We and You), a paper started by a freedom fighter about the same time. With a substantial circulation, *Jan Morcha* had a foothold in the surrounding districts that the VHP was unable to shake. *Hum Aap* resisted the VHP, declining offers of money as well as braving threats of violence. Its deputy editor, Sri Krishna Singh, reflected on the coercive character of the VHP's influence: "I don't drink, smoke or eat meat, I do yoga and I study Sanskrit, but I need a certificate with Ashok Singhal's stamp to say that I am a Hindu. That is the way things are here. If I said this in front of the Bajrang Dal or the RSS, I would be beaten up."[85] After the 1990 firings, *Hum Aap* gave in to threats and inflated the figures of the dead and wounded. Eventually, in 1995, when the BJP government came to power in a coalition with the lower-caste Bahujan Samaj Party (Party of the Majority), *Hum Aap* was forced to shut down.

The nature of the BJP's influence on a section of the Hindi press was simultaneously economic, social, and political. Interviews with journalists in Lucknow and Varanasi confirmed that the BJP's network of influence among the media was perhaps the core of its support base there, with reporters, editors, and newspaper proprietors taking initiative to improve coverage of Ayodhya and related events. Many reporters were rewarded individually by their management for effective publicity of the *shila yatra* (brick procession) and *rath yatra* (chariot procession) stories.[86] Small gifts and commission on ad revenue, generated through the local BJP businessmen who sponsored advertisements in the paper, helped to pad reporters' pay packets.[87] Unlike the Congress, which used money and liquor, the BJP was careful to offer assistance chiefly in kind, such as bureaucratic favors through the BJP's contacts, manpower for domestic chores, medical assistance or transport, and free meals. Reporters visiting Ayodhya often behaved like guests of honor. Remarking on the favors they demanded, Prabhash Joshi, modifying the chorus of a popular VHP song, joked that their cry was:

> *Bachcha bachcha Ram ka, kya prabandh hai shyam ka*
> [Every child of Ram [cries:], What arrangements for tonight?][88]

Nor were arrangements lacking. During one overnight stay at a Faizabad hotel, Joshi found reporters partying loudly all night long, courtesy of the VHP.[89] This was only one instance of an array of gratuities offered the press. From about 1989 onwards, free afternoon meals began to be served at the BJP's Lucknow headquarters, where journalists especially were made welcome, making it a popular den for the press.[90] The VHP and other pro-BJP organizations honored friendly reporters publicly and presented them with shawls and mementoes. Several reporters were in any case active members of the sangh parivar. One reporter named three figures in particular as stalwarts of the communal cause in Lucknow: P. K. Roy of *The Hindu*, Subhas Dare of *Amar Ujala*, and Rajnath Singh, then resident editor of *Swatantra Bharat*. The latter had been present within the mosque when it was attacked in October 1990, and had run out exulting that the structure had been torn down, joining the VHP in slogan-chanting.[91]

The paper *Aaj* normally carried four pages of city news and these came to be dominated by the temple issue. This was achieved by asking the BJP and its allies to release news locally, of happenings elsewhere, thereby bringing it under the "city news" beat. Press releases by local Hindutva leaders were often carried verbatim.[92] Shivkumar Shukla, the VHP President in Varanasi, would personally come in and hand over news briefs and would suggest where they should be placed in the layout. *Aaj* had a local reporter in Ayodhya but two additional reporters and a photographer were sent to cover the temple issue, representing an unusual concentration of resources for the paper. It was estimated that 90 percent of the Varanasi press and newspaper management were upper caste, and had swung solidly towards the BJP after the Mandal Commission's implementation was announced in August 1990. One reporter recalled that when the Ayodhya firings report came in on 2 November 1990, and he was editing it, the owner of the newspaper walked in and asked him how many deaths they were reporting. Twenty-five was the figure filed by the reporter but the owner asked him to change it to "hundreds." The owner had also on several occasions openly criticized the pro-backward caste policies of the U.P. and Bihar Chief Ministers Mulayam Singh Yadav and Laloo Prasad Yadav, saying that it was imperative to stand by "Advaniji."[93]

Newspaper editors and owners often gave clear instructions to their reporters on the line to adopt in the reports, and most reporters, including many left-liberal reporters, toed this line. The *Dainik Jagran* had an eight-column story regularly devoted to the Ayodhya episode for over a week, especially during the last week of November and the first week of December 1992, leading up to the demolition. Few other stories had such sustained and wide coverage in both print and electronic media.[94] One incident recounted by a reporter shed light on the kind of bias that existed among the press during this period. One reporter from the *Dainik Jagran* arrived at the newsroom to file his story on the mosque demolition, where it was read out aloud. When the part about the actual pulling down of the mosque came, a portion of the people in the room stood up and shouted "Jai Shri Ram," and thereupon the whole newsroom followed suit.[95] On the part of the VHP, a Varanasi leader conceded that their public relations efforts were "up to mark," but insisted that public sympathy and reporters' convictions were on their side in any case.[96] If there was a deficit in public sympathy, Hindi newspapers in the area carried little trace of it.

The most far-fetched stories were printed following 30 October–2 November firings, projecting an aura of heroism and sacrifice around the activists, and an image of historic injustice done to them by a brutal government. The following story, adjacent to the editorial and filling the rest of the page width in *Aaj*, offers an illustration. It purports to be the eyewitness account of a religious figure during the events. The author presents himself as entrusted with a secret message, to be conveyed on foot across 250 km, allegedly because communication in Ayodhya and the surrounding district of Faizabad, had been cut.

"Not only the dead, but the injured too were thrown in the Saryu [River]," by Saint Ram Sharan Das

Two blood soaked days of Ayodhya: Eyewitness account of a Saint

. . . The direct path to Ayodhya was 100 km but passing through fields, hiding from the police etc. I had to cover 250 km in five days. A person who didn't have the habit of walking 1 kilometre was crossing through rice fields filled with waist-deep water, hiding in cane fields – with bleeding and swollen feet – I kept marching ahead. I had to reach Ayodhya by 30 October to convey the message. If I did not reach in time, I would never forgive myself. By 30 Oct, I would reach either Ram Janma Bhoomi or Krishna Janma Bhoomi [i.e., jail] [*sic*]. There was no other choice. I reached Ayodhya on 30 October. On the 20th morning [Ashok] Singhalji had also arrived secretly. He was dressed as a policeman . . . Hanumanji himself appeared in the form of a Naga mahatama [snake god], then he hijacked a C.R.P.F. bus and asked kar sevaks to sit in it . . . The police were baffled. The bus stopped at the last barricade near Ram Janma Bhoomi [RJB]. Thousands of kar sevaks jumped and entered RJB . . . Then came 2 November, a historic day . . . The main aim of this day's kar seva was to reach Hanumangarhi [temple] peacefully and sing bhajans, and so maintain the continuity of kar seva . . . But, angry about the incidents of 30 October, Mulayam Singh and his officers were eager to take their revenge. They threw tear gas. Then without warning they opened fire . . . Many were killed . . . Now to proceed ahead was also a necessity because if we returned we would have been killed. Everyone agreed that it is better to be killed while approaching RJB than to be killed while returning . . .

A tear gas shell exploded at my feet . . . Kar sevaks lifted me and took me to the nearby street . . . Recovering myself I urged others . . . The entire street was filled with blood. – Red and blue [i.e., police] jeeps, picking up bodies and dumping them in the Saryu with sacks of sand, were seen dozens of times. Among them, not only dead Ram devotees but even the injured were also flung into the Saryu, so that the list of injured would not become too long. Such a cruel joke on humanity has neither been seen nor heard till today. According to my estimate the number of dead must be in the thousands. Because while organising for two days, my throat started to hurt from announcing the names of missing people.[97]

Although thousands are allegedly killed during the events retold, the narrative reads neither as history nor as tragedy. The developments essentially unfold as adventure, with the reader sharing the perils and triumphs of the protagonist/narrator.[98] For a participant's account of a political movement, there are an amazing number of chance incidents in the story, acting as crucial propellants in the narrative, and saving the day for kar sevaks. Twenty religious leaders are arrested but Ram Sharan Das alone escapes; bullets are fired at him but fail to hurt him, in one case injuring two youths instead; Hanuman appears in the form of a snake god, to bus activists past police barricades, and policemen themselves try to help the activists, unless they are Muslim. The deaths of kar sevaks (Hindu right activists) appear almost incidental to the main purpose of the narrative, which highlights the adventures of this lone fakir. If Ram Sharan Das conveyed his important message in Ayodhya, we are not told, nor do we learn, if it ultimately made any difference to events. He steels his resolve – "if I did not reach in time, I would never forgive myself" – an entirely personal meaning he gives to his mission. His leadership is acknowledged by the youths ready to die to save him. He mentions his desire to immolate himself to "heat up the movement," in an astonishing aside followed by no discussion of the content of the movement or his concern for the issue. Rather, it is a coolly conceived instrument of mobilization, offered as a further sign of the narrator's manly character. This however is frustrated apparently, by the movement's own bureaucracy, which kept his proposal as "pending," in one of the story's numerous contrasts of heroic and absurd. Despite the numerous life-threatening encounters and the terrible slaughter he refers to, the protagonist does not seem to be affected by them, nor does he have any moral to offer at the story's conclusion.

Banality rather than a sense of the collective valor and heroism of the activists dominates the narrative, serving to conceal rather than highlight the violence it refers to.[99] The oddly inconclusive ending, with its juxtaposition of tragic and trivial, gives the narrative an unthought, diaristic air, and serves to lend the political excitement of the larger events a more "personal" tone. The element of the fabulous, of course, implies this is no merely political enterprise, but one foreordained to succeed.

The most prominent sponsors of counter-propaganda, following the mosque demolition, engaged in a series of important exercises in educating the public; at the same time, the Hindu right was able to cloud their efforts over with a ferocious series of rebuttals and counter-attacks which ultimately came to dominate the publicity. It was an indication of the Hindu right's influence over the media, its relatively lengthy groundwork in shifting the terms of media discourse on issues of religion and tradition, and its influence in determining who would speak for such issues. Named for an assassinated playwright and CPI (M) (Communist Party of India [Marxist]) member, the Safdar Hashmi Memorial Trust, or "Sahmat," an independent cultural organization founded in 1989, staged a number of events culminating in a controversial exercise in the late summer of that year.[100] Beginning right after the demolition, Sahmat had distributed posters in fifty cities, to be pasted on walls and published in newspapers, saying *Ab koi nara nahin hoga, sirf desh bachana hoga* (Now there will be no slogans, our only task is to save the nation). This was followed by a "creative protest" on 11 and 12 December, with musical and dramatic performances by artists, and a photographic exhibition of the violence in Ayodhya. Subsequently, festivals were held celebrating Sufi and bhakti traditions, as representing popular spiritual protests against ideas of priestly mediation and sectarian division. Between January and April, several such cultural events were staged in cities across the country, including some cities torn by post-Ayodhya riots such as Ahmedabad, Surat, and Bombay.

The reception these events received prepared the ground for Sahmat's staging of *Mukt Naad* (Free Rhythm) on 14–15 August, in Ayodhya. The program, based on music and dance, enacted aspects of the country's composite traditions, to stress the many factors that united rather than divided its people, and to find a meeting ground in art and culture. Artists were to perform on the banks of Ayodhya's Saryu River, at Ram ki Pairi, on India's Independence day. Preceding them was an exhibition on the multi-faceted history and culture of Ayodhya and of the Ram story in particular, titled *Ham Sab Ayodhya* (We are all Ayodhya) to highlight the VHP's sectarian uses. Similar exhibitions were held simultaneously in different parts of the country. A grant from Union

Minister for Human Resources Development Arjun Singh, who gave the trust two and a half million rupees, assisted in the efforts.[101]

The BJP's response was multi-faceted, and revealing of its tactical repertoire. Violence and intimidation at the grassroots level were complemented by a systematic disinformation campaign. The resulting fear and suspicion served to advance apparently pragmatic arguments, alongside more explicitly interested ones, making the BJP's case seemingly difficult to refute. Beginning 9 August, on the anniversary of the Quit India movement, the exhibition was held in Tilak Hall in Faizabad. About twenty-five Bajrang Dal activists entered the exhibition three days after it began, while the volunteers were at lunch, and systematically tore up exhibition panels, as U.P. policemen and paramilitary officials posted at the venue looked on. Nearly a week later, BJP Member of Parliament J. P. Mathur claimed the attack was provoked by a poster depicting Ram and Sita as brother and sister. In fact, two lines in one of the eighty-three panels represented the Buddhist *Dasaratha Jataka* story, in which Ram and Sita were described as brother and sister, without any visual reference in the text. The rumor was set afloat that posters depicting Ram and Sita as siblings rather than as husband and wife were being distributed across the country, and that schools were being forced to purchase them.

Sahmat organized street theater groups from Delhi, Punjab, Tamil Nadu, and West Bengal, performing in different towns and cities from 9 August onwards, and moving towards Ayodhya, where they were to converge on 15 August. Perhaps inspired by this news, there arose the story that Sahmat volunteers would lay a foundation stone for the mosque at the disputed site, and that Muslim fanatics were forming suicide squads converging on Ayodhya, to accomplish the task. Such rumors increased the presence of security forces in Ayodhya, on the one hand, and at the same time dissuaded residents from attending the function, since they feared riots would break out again. Ultimately a crowd of about 1,500 was present at *Mukt Naad*, and although VHP demonstrators tried to disrupt the event, it was completed successfully. But on the morning of 17 August, *Dainik Jagaran* carried a front page article claiming that three Muslim shrines had been rebuilt on the site of the Babri Masjid, implying that Sahmat had indeed been a front organization for Islamic groups.

The BJP's counter-publicity succeeded to the extent that even professedly secular writers and critics denounced the exhibition, for being "insensitive" to popular feelings, for timing their demonstration during a moment of commmunal tension, and for accepting government sponsorship.[102] Even periodicals normally skeptical about the BJP chose to criticize the event, such as Calcutta's *Sunday* magazine: "As the Sahmat fiasco demonstrates, secularism is too important an issue to be left to Marxist agitators and power-hungry Congress ministers."[103] The magazine quoted Ghazamfar Ali Khan, bureau chief of Hyderabad's *Rehnuma-e-Deccan* daily: "If a common man says his sentiments are hurt, I can sympathise with and agree with him." In effect, the BJP succeeded in acting as ventriloquists of the public response to the events by a skillful combination of maneuvers. The criticism that *Mukt Naad* was to be repudiated as a Congress government-sponsored event found its mark with many critics, especially Muslims, for whom the party was hardly distinguishable from the BJP. Coming from the BJP itself, the charge was disingenuous given the systematic support it had received all along the course of its Janmabhumi mobilization.[104] But few even on the left were willing to stand by Sahmat – one by one, they issued statements that Sahmat had made mistakes in accepting state funding and in being insensitive to popular sentiments. The extent to which the BJP managed to redefine the terms of debate was impressive.

Advancement of the temple movement could not occur without Congress cooperation. The BJP was not in power, nor did it have the required votes in hand. The ideological thrust of the campaign was anti-Congress, but the BJP and its allies maintained essentially cordial relations with the Congress, threatening it with sound and fury in public, and striking deals in private. The BJP saw this as instrumental to their purpose.[105] The Congress for its part cultivated the temple campaign actively at first, hoping to gain from the Hindu vote it consolidated. Predictably, it was quickly overtaken by the BJP, which had fewer scruples in jettisoning erstwhile secular compromises. Thereafter, the Congress responded from a sense of weakness, making feeble gestures of protest in public which were nonetheless taken solemnly by a credulous press. The momentum of the movement seemed unstoppable, given the deep resonance of its symbols and themes, and the force with which they were being championed. To resist the movement would involve the use of state power, and that would surely be to the BJP's benefit by making them martyrs to the cause. This was to happen under V. P. Singh's prime ministership in 1990, when police firings gave the VHP an invaluable mobilizing tool.

THE RAM JANMABHUMI CAMPAIGN AS A MANAGED EVENT

On 1 February 1989, the VHP announced that it would conduct a foundation-laying ceremony for its proposed Ram temple, close to the site of the Babri Masjid, on 9 November of that year.[106] Subsequently, on 1 July VHP leader retired Justice Deoki Nandan Agrawal submitted a petition to the civil judge in Faizabad stating that the consent of the deity, i.e., the Ram idol placed in the mosque, was necessary before any adjustments could be made to the property. Agrawal was here improvising on a tradition in temple endowment litigation where the deity was treated as a juristic person, although the issue in this case was usurpation by the deity rather than property owned by it.[107] He also demanded that no obstacle be allowed from the part of the government or the Muslim community *in demolishing the mosque and building a temple in its place*. The VHP plan was thus stated clearly at the outset.[108] The site at which the VHP proposed to lay the foundation stone of the Ram temple was on a 2.77 acre plot by the side of the mosque and under legal dispute. Under an Allahabad High Court order, no permanent structures or permanent alterations could be made to the land. Conducting the *shila puja* (brick worship) and *shilanyas* (foundation stone ceremony) would hence be in contravention of the law. As the momentum for the shilanyas gathered, the major news frame was of government efforts to avert the Hindu right's violation of court orders. Coverage focused mainly on court judgments and statements of selected leaders, the choice depending on the paper. The underlying issue was the illegality of the proposed action, one that often tended to get buried under the details of press statements.

In what follows, I recount the main events of the campaign, and contrast the frames of news coverage against a composite picture derived from a range of available sources. From the sensationalism accompanying the campaign's growth to the mystification of the center's complicity, and the neglect of the principal actors' inconsistencies and untruths, each successive step depended, it will be clear, on a systematically differentiated set of perceptions fostered through the English and Hindi language press. The more event-centered character of this section helps to show the inter-related nature of movement and media. Specifically, what emerges is the English language press's failure to perceive the government's unwillingness to stop the demolition (something that did not alter despite mounting evidence of its imminence), although the perspective of the English press centered on the need to restore law-and-order. This failure, I have argued, arose from the epistemic and moral dilemma posed by state complicity with Hindu nationalism, since acceptance of impartial state authority undergirded the English news's own claims of transparent reportage. By recounting the sequence of developments and the news coverage presented of them, we can see how a certain space was made available for advancing the cause of Hindu nationalists despite the ostensible intentions of the English language press. By the same token, once the demolition itself had occurred, and evidence of the sangh's hostile designs finally outweighed its protestations of peaceful intent, the dismissal of BJP state governments could be presented as though the center was merely doing its duty, rather than being politically partisan.

The three key events I focus on are: the November 1989 foundation laying ceremony, or shilanyas; the rath yatra, in the context of the anti-reservation protests that stimulated it; and the July 1992 kar seva which was the period of activity penultimate to the demolition itself. I conclude with the mosque's demolition, whereafter the frames of the various newspapers' coverage themselves converge, as the destruction and rioting that followed overshadowed all other aspects of the issue. I draw from the New Delhi editions of two English newspapers, *The Times of India* and *The Indian Express*, and one Hindi newspaper, *Aaj*, headquartered in Varanasi, U.P.[109]

On 14 August 1989, the Lucknow bench of the Allahabad High Court had passed an order for the maintenance of the status quo, on the state government's application which had referred specifically to the shila puja (brick worship). Nevertheless, the VHP declared that it was going ahead with its plans, and that the site of the puja would be unchanged. On 27 October, the Supreme Court refused to restrain the VHP from shilanyas, saying that the freedom of expression of religion could not be curbed; as for the law and order problem, that was a state subject. Meanwhile the fundamental rights of citizens could not be abridged.[110] A special bench of the Allahabad High Court in Lucknow ruled on 7 November that the land which the VHP had barricaded for the purpose of shilanyas was disputed, and should not be altered. Ashok Singhal warned that stopping the ceremony would lead to "terrible, unimaginable" consequences all over the country.[111] The next day, however, the U.P. advocate general announced, on being asked for clarification by the state government, that the site was not in fact disputed. There was no elaboration on the basis of correcting the state high court, but this effectively gave the green signal to the VHP. Thus the VHP announced that it was going ahead with its plan for laying the foundation stone "at the same spot at the same time" on November. However, the Home Ministry statement to the press said the VHP had agreed to "comply with the clarificatory directions contained in the . . . [Court] orders" and that the proposed site was one hundred meters away from plot no. 586. Meanwhile Rajiv Gandhi, Home Minister Buta Singh and U.P. Chief Minister Narayan Dutt Tiwari met with Deoraha Baba, a sage in Mathura who had for years stood on one leg and so acquired fame.[112] They were advised to assist rather than obstruct the VHP program. The pay-off was announced by the VHP's Mahant Avaidyanath: "Congress-I will get the VHP support wherever there is no BJP candidate." Buta Singh went so far as to suggest that Rajiv Gandhi could come to Ayodhya to lay the foundation stone, but the VHP declined.[113]

In a further indication of the cooperative character of the enterprise, the district administration apparently specified a place for storing the consecrated bricks, identified eight routes by which the bricks could be transported to Ayodhya, and stipulated the number of persons that would be allowed to gather at the site on 9–10 November, the days of the proposed ceremony. Significantly, when veteran Congress leader Kamlapathi Tripathi arrived in Ayodhya prepared to physically stand in the way if the VHP persisted in its course, there was no sign of support from New Delhi. Eventually, Tripathi left on being reassured by the VHP that there was no cause for alarm.[114] At the same time, however, the center continued to keep up the appearance of dissuading the VHP from its confrontationist path, an appearance that each of the papers confirmed in different ways.

As the shilanyas approached, articles in *The Times* dwelt on the danger to law and order, and the imminent defiance of court orders by the VHP. Successive statements by Congress leaders, that no violation would be allowed, kept the focus on government efforts to avert a showdown and this remained the chief focus. A 26 October editorial noted the series of Hindu–Muslim riots accompanying shila processions in Bhagalpur, Darbhanga, Sitamarhi, and other places in Bihar, causing gruesome carnage to Muslims, and warned of the dangers of further violence. Unlike *The Express*, which railed against the inefficiency of district administration and the brutality of the police, making no mention of the VHP or BJP, *The Times* saw a link between the approaching general elections in November and the BJP attempt to polarize a Hindu vote.[115] Eventually the story headline on the actual event, " 'Shilanyas' peaceful," emphasized the averted threat to order. *The Times of India* editorial hailed the Home Ministry statement that the site had been shifted by one hundred meters, and complimented the VHP for its "good sense." Meanwhile on the same day, VHP leader and former U.P. Director General of Police, S. C. Dixit was exulting that they had told the government, "nothing doing."[116]

The Indian Express made no mention of any Congress warnings on the proposed violation, and thus there was little coverage of the disputed character of the event. Quoting VHP leaders exclusively, it allowed them to define the issue, reporting that the High Court order not to alter the dispute land would be obeyed, although the site would be unchanged. This was clearly a contradiction, one that was not unveiled until an 11 November editorial hailed the shilanyas as a sign that Hindus would not endure "reverse discrimination" any longer. Any suggestion that the site was *not* disputed was put out by government apologists, it was declared: in fact, it was the Hindus who had "bent the state to their will." A half-page photo spread showed sadhus and VHP members "rejoicing" as the puja was performed. The 9 November inauguration itself was covered in a headline story titled "Puja begins amid tight security." It was written not as a law and order story, but rather as a triumphant ceremony, with the crowd shouting "in ecstasy" and "some of the hundreds of policemen" joining them. It was of course the puja that was regarded as a threat, but the elaborate police arrangements raised the question as to precisely what was being protected. With *The Express*'s privileging of the ceremony rather than the violation it represented, it was easy to assume that it was the VHP saints who needed protection, against Muslims and "pseudo-secularists" who wanted perhaps to disrupt the ceremony.[117] *The Express* was perhaps the most positive of the English newspapers in regard to the Birthplace movement under the editorship of Arun Shourie, but subsequently as well. The more distanced, law-and-order approach of English newspapers was in evidence here also, except that the value placed on the ceremony was switched from negative to positive.

Aaj carried much of the shilanyas news as local stories, and at this early stage when the battle had yet to heat up, a glimpse of a many-sided debate was offered. A political science professor at Benares Hindu University presented a lecture arguing that Hindus had never worshipped bricks or stones, that the VHP temple program argued for destruction of a religious place and hence was contrary to Hinduism. An anti-communal rally was taken out by leftist students, with a substantial presence of women students and members of the Benares Hindu University. The arrival in town of Kamlapati Tripathi (a son of Benares and now a Congress veteran in Delhi) to dissuade the VHP was given extensive coverage, with photographs of crowds welcoming the garlanded politician. The shilanyas itself was greeted with religious fervor, however, in a banner headline: "Ayodhya Shri Ram Temple Foundation Progam Begins," with detailed description of the ritual ceremony, and notes on the enthusiasm of the volunteers and onlookers, and the heavy security accompanying the event. In passing, it was noted that the site of the foundation was one hundred feet away from the disputed site. Just below this story was a news item with a photograph of a smiling Rajiv Gandhi, where he claimed that credit should go to the Congress for the peaceful shilanyas.[118]

The main news frames were established by the end of the shilanyas. *The Times* took the VHP's claim seriously, that the ceremony represented a move towards a Hindu nation, and remained apprehensive about the events relating to Ayodhya. *The Express* maintained support for the temple project while cautioning against harm to the mosque. Whether out of disingenuous or simply wishful thinking, the abundant evidence of the VHP's hostile intent towards the mosque had no effect on its editorial line. Although *The Express*, unlike *The Times*, carried numerous photographs of ceremonies in Ayodhya, of kar seva and of processions such as the rath yatra, both papers, in their columns, shared an emphasis on the political as opposed to the religious or cultural aspects of the story. *Aaj*, like *The Express*, maintained that the temple should be built but without damaging the mosque. In addition to the regular political reportage, it carried news and features that candidly espoused the religio-political aims of the campaign, with none of the distance or reserve customary in the English language press. There was a profusion of photographs, not only of the successive stages of kar seva and the various processions, but also of milling crowds, as evidence of the campaign's popularity, as well as of lower level leaders whose portraits seldom appeared in the English language papers, such as Ashok Singhal, Vinay Katiyar, Uma Bharati, and Sadhvi Rithambhra. All three papers concurred that it was the Hindutva combine to whom either praise or blame was to be attributed.

In the ninth general elections immediately following the shilanyas, the Congress was defeated by a coalition led by V. P. Singh's Janata Dal (People's Front) with BJP support. Singh was able to bargain for a four-month respite in the temple campaign, following the electoral alliance, on terms that were not made public, but must have included support for the VHP's cause. For its part, the BJP required its grassroots workers to prepare for the forthcoming state-level assembly elections and had no objection to the reprieve. Debates with the Congress party over corruption charges against Rajiv Gandhi (the "Bofors scandal"), as well as factional disputes within the Janata Dal led by Devi Lal, preoccupied the new government. As Devi Lal was preparing to launch a massive rally of backward-caste supporters in a challenge to Singh's leadership, the latter announced his decision to implement the Mandal Commission report, allotting 27 percent of central government jobs and seats in educational institutions to backward castes. Although this was in fulfillment of a campaign promise, the announcement took the wind out of his opponent's sails and simultaneously revealed deep schisms in the ranks of the "Hindu" support base. Upper castes erupted in a storm of protest, and academics, university students, and the English language press, usually somewhere on the left in social issues, united in defense of the "meritocracy" they now declared was threatened.

The BJP was in a genuine quandary, as it could not afford to alienate its upper-caste core, who were overwhelmingly against Mandal and would have revolted if the party did not stand by them on the issue. Accepting the Mandal recommendations in principle, they criticized Singh for dividing the Hindu community and for adopting caste- rather than class-based reservations, and these criticisms were amplified greatly at the district and village level. It was necessary, however, to reinforce the party's appeal to scheduled and backward castes, significant sections of whom were sympathetic to the appeal of Hindutva. The protests against Mandal escalated, however, offering a seemingly readymade cover that it could take shelter behind.[119]

On 19 September, 1990, Rajiv Goswami, a student at Delhi University, set fire to himself in protest against the Mandal Commission recommendations. The action was meant to be a mock gesture of protest, with his friends pouring water over him immediately. For one reason or other, his friends did not put out the fire. Pictures of Goswami writhing in flames were in all the major newspapers and magazines in the next few days. The boy himself survived, but within the next month, more than 150 youths had followed suit, with sixty-three of them succeeding in immolating themselves. Another one hundred people were killed in police firings and riots that accompanied protests.[120] Day after day, front page photographs showed badly burned bodies of protestors, while editorials inveighed against V. P. Singh as the manifest cause of suffering.

As evidence of protest began to appear, RSS and BJP leaders decided, after discussions, that the Ram temple was still the party's best hope to cut across competing caste lobbies. On 12 September, Advani announced a rath yatra from Somnath to Ayodhya, to take the party's message to the grassroots and bolster its support.[121] It was in Somnath that Sardar Patel had commissioned the renovation of the temple destroyed by Muslim invaders, and in Ayodhya, a similar effort was necessary to restore national honor. Advani would travel in a vehicle modeled on a screen chariot, winding through nine states over thirty-six days. The image of the chariot helped convey the idea that here was a righteous mission undertaken by a spiritual figure, somewhat like the mythological epics shown over the last three and a half years in weekly television serials. Advani disclosed there had been some pressure on him to put on saffron robes, and said that as a political rather than religious figure, it was against his beliefs to do such a thing.[122] Whatever his beliefs were, the elaborate paintings of Ram and the proposed Ayodhya temple, Advani's wayside pujas which he performed wearing a crown, the slogan-shouting, saffron-bedecked volunteers swarming around the procession, and his speeches themselves left no doubt about the campaign's appeal to religious sentiment.

The press, mostly upper caste in composition, swung towards the BJP after Mandal, and coverage of the rath yatra was enthusiastic to say the least. Crowds were clearly drawn to the spectacle of a national leader speaking the language of religion, one that had not been seen in the northern region since Gandhi, and after him Vinoba Bhave. Neither of those leaders had contested elections. For the BJP, however, the systematic cultivation of a bankable "wave" was a political imperative at this point. Given the seamlessly positive coverage, it is difficult to estimate what lay behind the media hype. The BJP public relations coordinator, Amitabh Sinha, revealed that the crowds during the rath yatra were the same from start to finish, but the media coverage grew exponentially during its course, giving the impression of mounting support. As the yatra progressed, there was an insistence on the increasing size of the crowds and the political power this translated into. As the rath yatra entered Delhi, for instance, *Aaj* had this front page report:

The unprecedented crowds that welcomed BJP leader L. K. Advani in Rajasthan during his rath yatra have multiplied several times . . . If we were to accept the overflow crowds as proof of support, then there is no doubt that the BJP has

pulled off a victory. Along with this victory, the immense support obtained is
nothing short of hysteria . . . [O]ther parties and leaders are day by day being
dwarfed . . . [123]

The Indian Express carried several photographs registering the rath's
progress, the New Delhi edition carrying front page pictures as though
building up anticipation for its arrival there. Media management, overseen by the BJP's Pramod Mahajan, was well-planned and spared little
expense. A fax was sent every hour from whatever point the yatra was
at, to the party's office in New Delhi, with information that could feed
into regular press releases. One report, in the *Organiser*, went as follows:

Not an inch of space in the 1500-km route in Guajarat was without people
waiting to see the Advani juggernaut . . . It was as if in Advani's rath they saw
Ram*ji*'s chariot. For them, the decorated Toyota took the form of a temple.
Women and old men touched the tyres, took the sand below them placing it on
their forehead. As Advani customarily flung a flower into the crowd, people
vied with one another to kiss it in reverence. Women and old men stood hands
folded, young women carried pots on their head to greet the rath traditionally
. . . [A]t every place, the most common offering was traditional weaponry.
He was presented with bows and arrows, discs, maces, swords, tridents and
daggers. [124]

Not only piety but militancy as well was in harness; this was a popular
movement with teeth. Such details made for good stories, Sinha said,
and could be used by journalists to fill out what their own sources gave
them. At the end of each day, photographs would be sent to New
Delhi. [125]

   The rath yatra's success was declared proof that Hindutva had the
power to overcome caste differences and forge a unified Hindu community, which was of course tantamount to a national community in this
view. One report, for example, described the four wheels of the rath as
representing Hindu, Muslim, Sikh, and Christian, and the rath as
belonging not to the BJP but to all the people of India. [126] With sensation-
alist coverage of the anti-Mandal events, the mostly upper-caste press's
sense of moral indignation was reinforced. Not only was V. P. Singh
callous and short-sighted in the extreme, according to the majority of
newspapers at this time, Hindu unity was a necessary response to the
divisiveness causing such tragedies. Indeed, it could counteract such
divisions, several argued, and the rath yatra's success was proof of it:
"Mr. Advani's audacious Rath Yatra has shown that Hindu consolidation need not necessarily be a pipedream," Swapan Dasgupta wrote in

The Times of India, hailing the event's "spectacular success": "If national-ist forces, cutting across formal party lines, are able to build on this volatile assertion of faith, they will to a very large extent, be able to offset the devastation wreaked by Mandalisation." Ram *bhakti* could become *lok shakti,* the strength of the people, as Advani declared.[127]

The likelihood that religious feeling would once and for all transform into political strength, and that any gains achieved in the short term would endure over the longer term was far from certain. The entire rath yatra strategy had hinged on a delicate negotiation between religious and political appeals, knowing that those liable to be moved by the former might be alienated by the latter and vice versa. At one level, the emergence of a national figure championing a religious mission was meant to assure popular audiences of the sanctity of man and mission alike, as a sign that there was hope, after all, among existing leaders. Advani's repeated declarations at yatra stops that the campaign had nothing to do with any political party, and that it was all out of devotion to Ram, emphasized this fact. The strength of the campaign was in the massive display of public sentiment, and if the government did not pay heed to this it was being blind, he declared.

While Advani described the purpose of the yatra as political in interviews with the English press, this was not a construction he offered popular audiences.[128] It was one thing to invest faith in a leader and a temple. It was another, however, to transfer this faith to a political party, given that the campaign based its religious appeal precisely on prevail-ing cynicism and distrust towards politics. Those who made the leap from temple to leader to party could switch allegiances to another party, and a jump in the next poll was no assurance of its retention in the poll after that. It was clear that the V. P. Singh government would not last long, and that any government replacing it would also be a minority government at the mercy of its allies. New elections were therefore likely to be called well before the five-year term ended in 1994. This was the immediate political impetus for the strong media-based campaign, in the expectation that the party could consolidate its gains if there was a rapid pay-off. For the time being, however, the BJP basked in a media-created aura, one that the secular press itself reinforced. Deploring the "blind" and "deep-rooted" faith of the masses demonstrated by the rath yatra, *The Times of India* for instance concurred that "an upsurge of monumental proportions" had been "triggered."[129]

Amid the fiery protests of upper-caste youth against the Mandal Commission's implementation, and furious denunciations from the media, V. P. Singh commenced talks with BJP leaders. After a series of meetings, an Ordinance was released on 19 October 1990, amid protests from Muslim leaders as well as Mulayam Singh Yadav, Chief Minister of Uttar Pradesh, to hand over all the disputed land to the VHP, retaining the mosque alone under government control. The VHP was essentially being offered immunity for its violations of court orders, and it had all the signs of government capitulation. After Mulayam Singh Yadav and Muslim leaders persuaded V. P. Singh that he would alienate his own base while failing to win any political support from the Hindu camp, the Ordinance was withdrawn on 22 October. The Bihar Chief Minister was advised to arrest Advani, whose yatra was passing through the state on its way to Ayodhya. On 24 October, the BJP withdrew its support to the Janata Dal. Meanwhile, preparations for the 30 October mobilization, planned to coincide with the annual Kartik pilgrimage to Ayodhya, were carried out on both sides.

The Uttar Pradesh state government set up extraordinary security arrangements in preparation for the VHP's mobilization, sealing state borders, canceling several trains and long-distance buses, and making a number of preemptive arrests of VHP leaders. Mulayam Singh Yadav made a series of speeches in which he assured Muslims the mosque would be protected, and that the curfew would be completely effective in Ayodhya. In one speech on 16 October, he said that there were different visions of Ram Rajya at stake. He believed in Ram Rajya, he declared, but in Gandhiji's and Rammanohar Lohia's vision of it, not the kind envisioned by the sangh parivar. He claimed to be a greater devotee of Ram than Advani or Bal Thackeray. In his understanding of Ram Rajya, Mulayam Singh said, different faiths received equal respect.[130] However, the VHP was able to stir up a hate campaign against him, describing him as "Mullah Mulayam," an anti-Hindu stooge of the Muslims and the epitome of the pandering politician. This was crucial in its own efforts to publicize its kar seva, which were eventually successful beyond all expectation.

Other factors worked against the crackdown on Ayodhya. The festival of Kartik Purnima was a time when pilgrims traditionally visited Ayodhya in the hundreds of thousands. The government's restrictions thus appeared to confirm VHP propaganda about the Chief Minister's callousness towards Hindus and his steadfastness in defending the mosque. The wider public's sympathies swung in favor of the kar sevaks, and many activists were given food and shelter by villagers as they attempted to dodge checkposts and quietly enter Ayodhya. Further, the retired Director-General of the U.P. Police was also a VHP leader, S. C. Dixit. Able to obtain police security plans, he drew routes for the activists to reach the mosque. Leading the first charge on the mosque, he was able to muster sufficient authority so as to cow down the security forces, who gave way to him. After the charge was over on 30 October, and before any firing occurred, one grateful activist listed, for an inquiring video documentary team, those whom he wished to thank, namely the administration, the police, the PAC (Provincial Armed Constabulary), and the CRPF (Central Reserve Police Force), for allowing the kar sevaks ingress, and permitting them to complete their mission of attacking the mosque.[131] More than two hours later, security forces opened fire on a crowd near the site, for reasons that are not clear, killing five persons.[132]

After the firings on 30 October, *The Indian Express*'s editorial poured scorn, not on the VHP but on "secularists" for their alleged hypocrisy. Guilt was shared by all sides, so the secularists' blame on Hindu fanatics alone was "appalling," it said. V. P. Singh especially had "recklessly" thrown away the last chance he had had of defusing the "explosive situation," presumably by not handing over the property to the VHP. Meanwhile, it noted, "the dream temple cannot physically be built in a day," and what was important was that "the promise of beginning the construction on the appointed day" had been fulfilled.[133]

After the VHP's second assault on the mosque, and the subsequent deaths by police firing, the editorial was more stern: "[H]owever just the cause in one's own estimation, [leadership] should have a fine-tuned sense of direction and control of the situation," and warned that the VHP had lost the goodwill of the middle-ground opinion by its "thoughtless persistence."[134] But in fact, even as the VHP claimed that one hundred lives had been lost, more than five times the official estimate, Acharya Giriraj Kishore of the VHP was announcing that kar seva was to be intensified.[135] The temperature of the campaign was being raised, not "thoughtlessly," but as a deliberate mobilizing tactic, since the deaths could be blamed on a ruthless government all good Hindus ought to oppose. The *Express*'s persistent fiction about "construction" is noteworthy, against the kar sevaks' manifest intention of demolition. Related to this is the assumption that a peaceful solution was at hand, foiled only by reckless leaders, and that the VHP's basic program was unexceptionable.

The Times, by contrast, adopted a doomsday frame. The 30 October editorial, titled "Nation's Zero-Hour," went thus:

Developments in Ayodhya beginning today . . . will decisively determine the future of India as a united, secular and democratic republic . . . If . . . the efforts to stall the Kar Seva fail altogether, Mohammed Ali Jinnah's two-nation theory . . . will finally stand vindicated . . . If the Indian state does not uphold the law and it fails to protect the Babri Masjid, the faith of this community [i.e., Muslims] in its future well-being in India will be shattered quite beyond redemption.

The only hope against such an eventuality was the security forces deployed by the U.P. Chief Minister. If they failed, "mayhem and violence [would] grip every city, town and hamlet" where there was even a small presence of the minority community. Having raised the stakes to a maximum at the outset, the firings and the loss of life on that day provoked a front page editorial on 31 October, "Anguished India." The nation's "abject failure on several counts" had been exposed, most notably of law and order, but also in the BJP and VHP's failure to realize the destructive forces they were whipping up. On 1 November *The Times* hailed the restoration of "a semblance of normalcy," but again it was too soon; the main action was on the following day.

We have already noted the openly provocative and rumour-mongering character of a large section of the U.P. Hindi news coverage in the wake of the Ayodhya firings provoked widespread criticism. The number of dead reported, confirmed later to be wildly exaggerated, went up to the hundreds and even thousands. If, after the announcement of the Mandal Commission's implementation, large sections of the Hindi press became pro-VHP, the firings of 1990 confirmed that the battle was joined, and the attitude was one of full-fledged activism. The Press Council of India later rebuked *Aaj, Dainik Jagran, Swatantra Bharat*, and *Swatantra Chetna* for "gross irresponsibility and impropriety," observing that they had promoted mass hysteria on the basis of rumours, exaggeration, and distortion, using doctored pictures and fabricated figures, and that their intent was to provoke communal hatred.[136] Mulayam Singh Yadav commenced a set of *sadbhavna* (communal harmony) rallies in mid-September, to gather political support at the grassroots in his fight against the BJP. Hindi papers presented the massive turnout as stage-managed by the government. *Aaj* charged that pilgrims and devotees were not being allowed to chant the name of Ram, and that the police were forcing them to take the name of Mulayam instead.[137]

Several papers reported the occurrence of miracles aiding the VHP. The 30 October edition of *Swatantra Bharat* reported that Swami Nrittya

Gopal Das, a VHP leader, had vanished into thin air when the police came to arrest him. On 13 November it reported that the police officer who ordered the firing found the pupil of one of his eyes mysteriously melting away. The 27 November edition of *Aaj* reported that eggplants with seeds bearing inscriptions such as "Om" and and "Allah" were being found.[138] Sensationalism may have been influenced by the politics of the editors, but the increased sales of the papers was clearly not reducible to politics; many of the papers were reported to have launched evening editions to capitalize on the increased sales.[139]

Moderation was the immediately obvious solution to the violence, and the English language press united in recommending it to the VHP and its allies. Over and beyond the wish to stop bloodshed, however, the logic was basically mistaken. It was a fallacy to assume a moderate BJP leadership helpless in the grip of the extremist VHP. If there were different views within the sangh parivar, this represented more a diversity of posture than of politics.[140] Looking to cultivate the "moderates" and pitting them in imagination against the "extremists" was then misleading. The BJP had made a political decision to bank on Ayodhya, as a way of reaching out to the "non-committed vote," and after increasing its Parliamentary seat total from two to eighty-eight in the 1989 elections, was bound to follow up on it. Advani observed in an interview, "No party can afford to ignore the principal plank which has brought it strength."[141] Although the mosque gates were opened as early as 1986, the VHP had chosen not to start its movement until 1989, timing the foundation ceremony only weeks ahead of the general elections. The orchestration of the campaign for electoral purposes was patent. But obfuscation helped preserve their fiction. The BJP spoke of "relocating the structure with due respect," which was code for demolition. The Congress and Janata Dal positions were decidedly more equivocal: the temple should be built while allowing the mosque to stand, they maintained. But the VHP demand was for building the temple "there" (*mandir wahin banayenge*), which meant that it was plainly committed to violent rather than peaceful methods. Both the Congress and the Janata Dal seldom if ever broached the VHP's demand for demolition, at least in public, nor did the English press raise questions about it. Columns and editorials in pro-BJP papers such as *Aaj* repeatedly asserted that there was no question about demolition.

Muslim and VHP positions were irreconcilable. The Central Sunni Waqf Board owned the property and would never consent to demolition; the VHP for its part was unlikely to settle for anything less.

Negotiations were simply a matter of postponing the reckoning of forces, that is the clash of those for and against the demolition. In the final event there was no such clash, of course, and the demolition was carried out unhindered. The persistent focus on the possibility of moderates coming to the fore, or the frustration in their failure to do so, kept the news frame in the English language press as one of normal politics. In fact the thrust of the campaign was to go beyond politics as usual, carrying out a raid on a symbolic realm hitherto excluded from politics, that of religious faith, while both threatening and relying on force rather than on negotiations. Meanwhile their leaders maintained a holding operation within the political sphere proper, and hoped to ride to power on the crest of the campaign's wave.

After the BJP government came to power in U.P. following the November 1990 assembly elections, work on the mosque site accelerated. The land in front of the mosque was *nazul* land, i.e., state land administered by local bodies. Being under dispute, the High Court ordered that the state government forbear from erecting any permanent structure on it, or making any permanent alterations to it. On 7 October 1991, the U.P. government issued notification for acquiring the land, for the "public purpose of development of tourism and for providing amenities to pilgrims." In response to written petitions challenging the acquisition, the state government pleaded urgency, given the forthcoming Kartik Purnima festival when pilgrims were expected.

The High Court granted the state government's request. After taking possession of the notified land, the U.P. government started excavating and demolishing the structures on it, the Sakshi Gopal temple, Sumitra Bhavan, Abhiram Das Mandir, Gopal Bhavan, and Sankat Mochan being some of the temples demolished. This was in clear violation of the court order. Responding to questions raised about this in Parliament, Home Minister S. B. Chavan said on 25 March 1992 that members of the House could go and "see things for themselves," and requested a delegation of the National Integration Council (NIC) to visit Ayodhya. This turned out to be no more than a move to disguise the center's acceptance of the BJP government's actions. The team had no prominent Congress members – Chavan himself was the NIC Chairman but chose not to go; it was not briefed by the center, and, since a proper fact-finding visit required the compliance of the U.P state government, the delegation achieved nothing. The NIC report tersely observed that the admitted acts of the U.P. government were "not in consonance with the letter and spirit of the orders passed by the High Court."[142] The central government was advised to take "effective steps" for a negotiated settlement of the dispute, after advising the state government to desist in its actions. Meanwhile, the Home Minister told Parliament, "The [U.P.] Chief Minister has assured me that the structure will be protected."[143] News reports disclosed that many of the NIC team had offered prayers to the Ram Lalla idol on their visit, as did the Home Minister on his visit to Ayodhya on 11 July.[144] Little note was taken of the center's connivance; the NIC's visit demonstrated, not the complicity but the "inefficiency" of the center.[145] Rather, with the VHP threatening to launch a nationwide movement if the Center took any action against the U.P. government, a picture of mutual hostility was preserved.[146]

The Home Minister's bland assurance was one that had been offered again and again for years, and continued to be offered until the demolition. The English language press continued to report it with no perceptible increase in its understanding of the character and limits of the central government's politically compromised position. Thus the following diagnosis of an identical report by the Home Minister in November 1991, from one of the most critical national news magazines, is continuous with much of the English language press's perception of the entire campaign: "The centre stuck mulishly to a mute approach based on a perception of the whole problem as a law and order affair, a State subject . . ."[147] The analysis suggests that the center's actions were merely stupid, borne not of political calculation so much as of its lack, provoking exasperation rather than controversy. Taking the center's excuses literally, that it could not intervene in the affairs of a State government, was implausible, since in fact intervention was increasingly the rule than the exception in center–state relations. In any case, even if the larger dimensions of the matter were lost on the center, perceiving it as a law and order problem alone should have led to some material response. The perfidious character of its enemy served merely to explain the central government's helplessness. Thus a *Times of India* editorial during the July 1992 kar seva:

Considering that the VHP has finally thrown all restraint to the winds and begun construction of the Ram temple . . ., the Centre has clearly been left with no alternative but to intervene . . . One reason why the Centre may have hesitated to act upto now is that rarely before have the ruling party and most of the others come face to face with the kind of prevarication and subterfuge in which the BJP has indulged . . .[148]

There is a characteristic charity towards the Congress in the reasoning here. Want of knowledge, hesitation, and consequent inaction are the qualities of its behavior, suggesting naïveté and guilelessness at most. Motives may be imputed only to the villain of the piece; the political middle ground is itself neutral. What might have made the matter confusing, of course, was the appearance of the sangh parivar and the Congress as being at loggerheads, an impression that both, but especially the former, strove to maintain.

On 9 July, 1992, one day after the Home Minister had reassured Parliament based on the U.P. C.M.'s assurance that the law would be respected, the VHP had begun kar seva on the disputed site, in defiance of court orders. This may have been a dry run for the December demolition, with the sangh parivar checking to see if the temperature of the confrontation would be sufficient for the central paramilitary forces sent to Ayodhya, including the Central Reserve Police Force (CRPF) and the Indo-Tibetan Border Police, to be used against the kar sevaks. The previous few months had seen the campaign losing ground, and confrontation served to stimulate support for the VHP. VHP General Secretary Ashok Singhal declared that the land belonged to Ram Lalla and therefore building a Ram temple there could not be illegal.[149]

On 15 July, the Lucknow bench of the Allahabad High Court had rejected a plea to stay digging at the site, saying there was no fear the structure would be affected. Narasimha Rao too made it clear that he was not going to hinder the BJP. In his public statement, he said that (the then-U.P. C.M.) Kalyan Singh's failure to implement the judicial verdict banning construction would be "quite serious," but that he was sure Kalyan Singh was doing all he could to ensure law and order."[150] Eventually, Rao worked out a compromise with RSS leaders, with whom he had good relations.[151] On 27 July, he announced in Parliament an agreement halting kar seva while efforts would resume to achieve "an amicable settlement through negotiations."[152] Both parties to the discussions may have known an amicable settlement was unlikely, but to buy time was to their mutual advantage. Rao appeared to have won a victory, appeasing his vociferous critics, and by appearing reasonable the sangh parivar secured more space for itself to mobilize for the next kar seva. Eighteen days of illegal kar seva were performed, and all it drew from the center was a plea for negotiations. A repeat of this scenario could now be planned for with confidence (the demolition took only a few hours eventually). The script for the final act was in place.

The Times carried a front page editorial, "Saving the Republic," warning against the imminent subversion of the Constitution by militants pretending to uphold "faith." The Prime Minister had bent over backwards to make the VHP see reason, but to no avail, it said.[153] *Aaj* observed, in a 23 July editorial, that the question before the center only became serious upon taking a communal perspective. The mosque had not been used for worship by Muslims for the past four decades, whereas worship to the Ram idol had been carried on from even before that time at the platform outside the mosque. Ergo, it was no longer a mosque. How could there be a dispute on this matter? When the state government had given a guarantee that it would respect the court orders, why should the central government take any steps against it?[154] *The Express* regretted the NIC's "tragic failure," and found the BJP's opponents wanting for having retreated from their earlier position of consenting to kar seva. Since it was the BJP that had refused to countenance any criticism of the UP state government, and rejected the draft resolution of the committee, this was misleading. At the same time, the BJP had clearly become "a prisoner of the VHP . . . callously banking on building its fortunes on the ruins of Indian secularism and democracy." This was an incoherent interpretation, suggesting a helpless party but with diabolical intent.[155]

By November of 1992, Advani was demanding that the center allow resumption of kar seva. As the final kar seva of December 1992 approached, the Supreme Court heard arguments from the U.P. state government's counsel, K. K. Venugopal, that no construction on the disputed land would accompany kar seva. Meanwhile, the Attorney General, Milon Banerjee, informed the Supreme Court that elaborate preparations were going on for kar seva, while contempt cases for violation of court orders in July were pending. He handed over Intelligence Bureau reports to prove that the U.P. government's affidavit, promising no construction, was not credible. The Court ruled, however, that preparation was not an offense, and suggested that the state government be consulted to provide maximum security around the shrine.[156] The Court observed that in July similar arguments had been made and yet significant construction had occurred: if hundreds of thousands congregated and started construction, it would be difficult to stop them. Strangely, the Court went on to accept the state government's undertaking to refrain from violating court orders.[157] The statement was either prescient or designed as a cover of "plausible deniability" for an event the court knew to be imminent.

Subsequently, on 29 November, the Supreme Court passed its order permitting "symbolic" kar seva, consisting of singing and chanting, and provided for an observer to monitor the situation. These events received the baldest reportage in *The Times* and *Express*. At the same time, there were adjoining articles, where leading figures in the VHP were saying that kar seva meant nothing other than construction.[158] Vinay Katiyar, BJP Member of Parliament and Bajrang Dal chief, had asserted on the day of the Supreme Court ruling itself that kar seva would not just be symbolic, but would involve temple construction also. "The Supreme Court has no business deciding what is to be done in Ayodhya," he had said.[159] Between these two flatly contradictory sets of reports, there was no connection made, in the editorials and op. ed. pieces, or indeed in the comments offered by political leaders.

On 4 December, the Home Minister was quoted, however, replying in Parliament to concerns about the mosque's safety, saying: "I do not know why such doubts are being raised. Government has no reason to disbelieve the UP Chief Minister, who had said he would protect the mosque."[160] The English language press took its cue from the center: the BJP undertaking to the court of "symbolic kar seva" only was emphasized. Both *The Times of India* and *The Indian Express* carried reassuring stories and editorials as the deadline approached, and on 6 December their headlines were: "Saints defer face-off in Ayodhya" and "'Shrine won't be stormed': Saints" respectively. Somewhat at odds with its headlined story in *The Express* was the accompanying photo, captioned "Kar sevaks rehearsing to pull down a big boulder in Ayodhya on Saturday." *Aaj*, however, observed ominously, in a 2 December editorial, that everyone wanted the temple to be built; the only question was what to do with the disputed structure. An adjoining article complained bitterly of favoritism towards Muslims, and declared that if any idols were found when digging at the site, it would be necessary to destroy the mosque, because this would prove VHP claims of a pre-existing Ram temple.[161] The headline on the day kar seva was scheduled to begin, 6 December, in *Aaj* made it crystal clear that demolition was inevitable: *Vivadhit Dhanche ka ab Ram hi Rakhwala* (Only Ram Can Protect the Disputed Structure Now). The long build-up of popular feeling rendered the government powerless to protect the mosque, in *Aaj*'s representation

The Constitution, under Article 256, provided for the central government to make a non-compliant state government fulfill its responsibilities. The possibility of dismissing the government itself was always present, although it did not materialize until the demolition was over. A meeting of the National Integration Council was held on 23 November, which the BJP boycotted. The Council had offered "whole-hearted support and co-operation" to any steps the P.M. deemed essential for law and order in Ayodhya. Not to be outdone, Narasimha Rao declared that he would leave no stone unturned in upholding the Constitution and getting court orders implemented.[162] The assumption seemed to be that the Prime Minister and his cabinet required all the assistance they could get. Cartoons by R. K. Laxman, not known for his kindness to incumbent ministers, showed Rao trussed up in a chair, with Advani and, successively, others, including Jayalalitha (then Tamil Nadu C.M.), berating him for his indecision and non-cooperation. All the activity seemed to be at the BJP's end, in the view from New Delhi.

There was other news that cast the center in a different light, news that surfaced after the demolition. It was learned that the center wrote to the state government expressing concern for the medical and sanitary facilities to be provided to the incoming kar sevaks. Kar sevaks themselves had come in as honored guests of the state government, as numerous officials testified.[163] Special trains were arranged to transport them into and out of Ayodhya from A.P., Karnataka, Maharashtra, and parts of U.P.[164] This of course could only have been done with central government clearance. The then-Home Secretary, who has since published his memoirs, offers a vivid picture of the unreal atmosphere then prevailing at the center, with a bewildering succession of meetings and notes that were not followed up and led to nothing, and with the Prime Minister routinely stalling or ignoring every suggestion for intervention, while the ground situation continued to escalate. Among other things, the author mentions that a detailed contingency plan was worked out, first for July 1992 and subsequently improved for implementation in November, for taking over the mosque complex and imposing President's Rule under Article 356 of the Constitution. During the period from 15 to 19 November 1992, National Security Guard commandos were daily stationed in readiness to entrain for Faizabad disguised in civilian clothes, for possible deployment at the mosque complex. Every evening, these orders would be countermanded for want of clearance from the Prime Minister.[165]

Eventually, the demolition on 6 December provoked riots all across the country, and led to violence in neighboring countries as well. In India alone, official figures recorded that 2,026 persons were killed and 6,957 were injured in various incidents throughout the country, apart from large-scale arson and looting.[166] Tens of thousands of kar sevaks were charged with the demolition by the U.P. police. The BJP leaders were arrested, but were all released a month later. Experts said that the charges were so poorly framed that they could not sustain legal scrutiny. The Special Magistrate of Mata Tila in Lalitpur District, U.P., said that the prosecution had not been able to establish the charges. No evidence had been gathered to back up the charges. On 10 December 1992, the RSS, the VHP, and the Bajrang Dal were banned for their role in the demolition. But the ban order was not enforced; nor were attempts made to justify them through gathering any incriminating data. The majority of the 8,000-odd arrested in December were released in a week or two. It turned out that the government was unable to name even one RSS member who had participated in the demolition. Further, a senior Home Ministry official testified before the P. K. Bahri Tribunal, commissioned to inquire into the ban, in highly approving terms about the RSS. The bans on the RSS and the Bajrang Dal, which in any case were never enforced, were lifted in early June.[167]

While ineffective ban orders were placed on the sangh parivar, the BJP state governments were dismissed in U.P., M.P., Rajasthan, and Himachal Pradesh. At the same time, the ruling party did nothing to offend popular religious sentiment. December 26 was the so-called *pragat utsav*, the annual celebration commemorating the miracle of the idols' "appearance" at the mosque. Worship had been banned after 6 December. The BJP sought permission to resume it, however.[168] President's Rule had been established in Ayodhya after the demolition; nevertheless, the district administration of Faizabad decided to permit darshan. This was followed, on 31 December, by a decision from the Lucknow bench of the Allahabad High Court, which ruled that since pictures of Lord Ram appeared in the Constitution, he was a constitutional entity. Therefore, the Court ruled, allowing darshan was not a partisan concession to one religious community.

Following the demolition, in December 1992, the Press Council received a query from the central government as to whether newspapers or magazines censured for communal writing could be deprived of government incentives such as advertisements. The Press Council was asked to recommend measures to be taken against erring news organs. Comprised of owners or managers of newspapers, the six-member body chose not to recommend any action against their own members. The Council decided that its existing moral authority was "quite effective" and that no further measures were needed to ensure the press's self-regulation. Instead, if a newspaper was censured twice within three years, the information would be forwarded to the Cabinet Secretary and the Chief Secretary, at central and state levels respectively, for "appropriate" action.[169]

Narasimha Rao's concern was to prevent the VHP from getting the political credit for building the temple. Accordingly, he argued for setting up a "non-political," i.e., Congress-approved body overseeing the temple construction. In June 1993, the Congress succeeded in getting major religious leaders to meet in Sringeri and call for a "non-political" trust to build the temple.[170] This meeting was held just two days after the VHP's Ram Janmabhumi Trust met at Hardwar, and announced that a fresh movement would be launched if the government did not return the land in about four months' time. Following the center's coup, the VHP postponed its movement; its own attempts to woo the monks' and mendicants' allegiance having failed.[171]

In the November 1993 Assembly elections, a scheduled caste, backward caste, and Muslim coalition combined to win the largest total of seats in U.P., long the center of gravity of Indian politics. Although the BJP slightly increased its vote tally over the 1991 elections, there was one party fewer in the elections this time; only three major parties contested in 1993, as opposed to four in 1991. The BJP also lost power in the three other states where it had ruled prior to the demolition, winning only in Delhi, where Assembly elections had not been held for over twenty years, and, eventually, in Rajasthan, after brokering agreements with other parties. A substantial number of backward castes, principally Yadavs, had shifted away from the BJP, and with the consolidation of the lower-caste and the Muslim vote, the BJP was effectively sidelined.

The BJP took comfort in the fact that it polled 35.7 million votes, ten million more than the Congress had won, out of the 98 million votes cast, and one hundred more seats.[172] Unquestionably, it represented an irreversible decline in Congress hegemony, but the BJP's claim to power was at the same time fundamentally altered as well. What it had fought hard to avoid and deny, namely lower castes as a separate voting bloc, was now definitively a major political force in its own right, and a potential spoiler of any claims to Hindu unity. Advani, in a note sent from Pipri Jail to the National Executive Meeting, philosophized that the setback suffered in the election was a setback for the party, but that its ideology of cultural nationalism was gaining more and more adherents. As measured by votes cast, this was perhaps true, but at the same time, the winds had shifted significantly, decentering the political field and introducing new forces whose interplay would forever complicate the dream of a Hindu nation.

This chapter has examined the Ram Janmabhumi campaign from the outside as it were, in terms of the reportage of the series of maneuvers carried out at Ayodhya, their repercussions in the capital, and the ways in which these reflected the stances of the press. A discursive shift occurred in the late 1980s, I have argued, as Hindutva became an overarching framework for thinking about economy, polity, and society together. It was not the only one available, but offered itself as the most powerful alternative to the effect Nehruvianism had exercised on the political imagination. This chapter has considered the initial phases of that shift, and marks its partial and turbulent character. The reconfiguration of the relationship between the vernacular and the language of command, reflected in the confusion and alarm of the English language press, was one way of indexing the realignment of political forces, and the emergence of a new language of politics and a new rhetoric of political mobilization. The Ram Janmabhumi movement was itself predominantly a Hindi language movement, but one that showed the influence of leaders who developed their strategies with a multilingual society in mind. The task of understanding such a movement dramatized the social distance between English and Hindi language presses, and showed that their respective codes of interpretation did not mesh with each other and had scarcely attempted to do so in the past.

   Coverage of the Janmabhumi movement was marked by a sense of cultural intimacy on the part of the Hindi language press, as opposed to the perspective exhibited in the English language press, which on the whole viewed the movement as a threat to peace and stability. A belief in the transparency of political power underlay the English language press's conception of itself as capable of speaking on behalf of the nation at large. Neither its colonial nor its post-Independence experience permitted the Hindi language press to share quite the same assumption. A popular religious nationalist movement challenged the English language media's complacency about its own cultural centrality. Underlying this complacency was an assumption of the propriety of the cultural order imposed by the state, and an acceptance of state authority as the leading developmental agency. The Ram Janmabhumi movement spoke in many voices, but among other things it asserted the right to kill, rendering unmistakable its challenge to the state's monopoly on violence, and underwriting its claim to state power. If various sections of the press, English and Hindi language both, had reservations about this last claim, it is the distance that the English language press maintained from popular exhortations to political mobilization, and the relative closeness of sections of the Hindi language press to such mobilizational rhetoric that must be highlighted.

What was critical was that English language news values were state-centric, following a colonial heritage, and reflecting the perspective of an elite business class that depended on the patronage of the developmentalist state. As such, English language news tended to require a certain distance from indigenous culture as a way of asserting its authority. A law-and-order perspective on the movement consequently became predominant.[173] Thus, when the state itself failed to fulfill its role in maintaining order, as the sangh parivar's violations of the law became more frequent and demolition became inevitable, the English language press was unable to construct coherent narratives about the state's passivity or collusion. Hindi language news values, by contrast, tended to be more "society-centric": more diverse in the social composition of its audience, and thus more hybrid in the sources of authority it could appeal to. This reflected not only the more anti-colonial heritage of an indigenous language press but also the remove at which it existed from the center of state power.

The social distance between the Hindi and the English language press itself became a strategic resource for Hindu nationalists, however. For the English language news, the Ram Janmabhumi movement appeared as a monolithic and often dangerous force, in the image of its sponsoring ideology of Hindutva. In contrast, Hindi news coverage presented a heterogeneous picture, culturally more intimate and politically more self-conscious. The resulting notoriety provided its own prestige to the campaign in the Hindi press, acknowledging its national significance and the scope of the resources marshaled for and against it. At the same time, the gap between the coverage of the campaign in the English and the Hindi press provided crucial camouflage for the mobilization, as it made it difficult for news stereotypes of Hindu nationalism to change, whose strategies were often pragmatic and expedient rather than fundamentalist.

The Ram Janmabhumi movement became prominent in a historical conjuncture where television could present the image of a society that was at one with itself, as I suggest happened with the Ramayan broadcast. But if the BJP and its allies perceived the possibility of Hindu unity here, what this overlooked was the means through which any attempts at unification had to proceed. Even as Hindu nationalists exploited the interpretive differences across a split public in their project of seizing power, what became clear was rather the odds against such unity: political challenges provoked by Hindu supremacism (lower-caste and other), and the insecure nature of the commitment Hindutva relied on, given its new technologies for securing political affiliation. What resulted instead was a deeper awareness of the mutual differences between the English and indigenous language print cultures that had together anchored the institution of a single field of representation.

This is obviously not an argument for distinguishing between essential features of the respective languages, or between a sympathetic Hindi press and a hostile English language press. It is, rather, an argument about the new context created by television, against which pre-existing institutional and cultural differences take on a new importance. Thus I have attempted in this chapter to highlight the productive nature of a split public that consumed Hindutva's message and participated in its incitements to violence against Muslims, while the latter had been targeted as subjects with questionable commitments to the Indian nation.

The apparently steady spiraling of tension and confrontation in the campaign can be seen, by comparison with the analysis in the introduction and the first three chapters, as no natural sequence of occurrences, but rather as developing against a structured set of possibilities and contradictions. The split public, reinforced by the media, created a political problem and a political opportunity simultaneously. The awareness of each on the part of the other, necessarily partial and distorted in the context, created a cognitive dissonance available for political mobilization. It was through the indefinitely multiplied dissemination from media institutions to their audience that the split public achieved its existence, and came to recognize itself as an English language and a Hindi language public respectively. For each of these, the crucial problem appeared to be in the other half, and for each, unity presented the answer, but each perceived the matter of unity in a different way. If the Janmabhumi movement was publicity-conscious and devised schemes for enhancing its media exposure, this was a two-way process, as the media itself shaped the kinds of openings available for the campaign to utilize.

The effect of the BJP's publicity campaign was to dramatize the incongruity of world-views that went into making a Hindu public, and rendering it a problem that could no longer be evaded, even if their own Hindu supremacist solution was deeply problematic. It was not only Hindutva's solution that was problematic, but as well the path chosen to arrive there. These tactics included capitalizing on the new idioms of consumption circulating in the public sphere, public relations campaigns stressing deeply primordial sentiments of hatred against a Muslim "other" that were sustained by a warped vision of Indian history, and arguments about bureaucratic incompetence and the failure of post-independence development. The comment made by a fifteen-year-old schoolgirl in conversation, "I am tired of Ram. I want a new name," revealed the kinds of problems that such a purely symbol-driven approach must run up against. Redefining a religio-ritualistic set of beliefs into a single-point message to maximize its acceptance, the BJP's media-driven strategy was designed to capitalize on the possibilities instituted by a national visual regime, translating symbols familiar in one arena into new demands in the cultural and political arenas. The half-life of symbols in those other arenas, however, tended to be shorter than of those in the realm of religion. This meant that there was a lack of proportion between the fickle and inconstant supporters the BJP could create for itself, and the vaulting character of the party's political ambitions. Not ideological coherence then, so much as the speed and deftness with which an unwieldy support base was orchestrated, in a series of spectacular and violent performances, was crucial in Hindutva's path to power. In the next chapter I elaborate on this point, to show the variety of mobilizational strategies that created both a Muslim threat and Hindu invincibility, satisfying various fractions of Hindutva's supporters while helping to recruit new ones to the cause.

CHAPTER 5

Organization, performance, and symbol

Social movements tend to be considered as unitary objects, so that if they have a single, definable goal, their motivation too is often thought to be simple, even singular, as in "the ideology" of a movement. In the case of Ram Janmabhumi, the means for imputing singularity of motive were readily available. Given the religious character of the actors, the arguments, and the symbols, the motive seemed self-evidently "religious," implying, then, a religious ideology. The Ram Janmabhumi movement itself was often described as an instance of "communalism," inspired by "communal" ideology. Against such a monadic view, it is important to stress that movements are systems of action, coordinating a multiplicity of beliefs and intentions.[1] While movements may have an ideology, these are usually produced for specific purposes, as strategic representations resonating with particular publics. What is necessary then is to map different accounts, views, and reflections of the movement and comprehend the manner of their mutual articulation. There has been a failure to recognize the variety of appeals made and intentions subsumed, and the often wide gaps between these. As Bourdieu has pointed out, an elementary relativism suggests that no single viewpoint could offer a comprehensive account of any object; the idea of a sovereign perspective, affected by those at higher levels of society, is hence open to this criticism. The related error here is that of intellectualism, substituting the observer's relation to the object for the object's relation to its activity, in this case the imputation of an ideology which defines the movement.[2] Examining actual practices permits a detailing of parts without presuming their identity in advance, and thus discloses contradictions that may be instrumental to the movement's functioning.

Although it did not begin with such a plan in mind, the Ram Janmabhumi movement's success in attracting support across society led its instigators to conceive of it as an unconventional route to political power. The championing of religious symbols immediately gave its claim distinctness; behind it lay a series of improvised maneuvers mobilizing a range of elements within Hindu traditions, apparently united through political ideology but in fact cohering through careful orchestration in a bid for power. The simulation of continuity with earlier forms of Hindu nationalist expression was misleading at the level of the movement's content, although important to its appearance. Hitherto, organized Hindu communalism had avoided the use of specific religious content, both out of piety to its modernist ideals and for fear of dividing its ranks.[3] The failure to recognize this shift has confused perceptions of the Janmabhumi movement.

The Hindu nationalists' deployment of different kinds of propaganda, circulating around and weaving between religious and political registers, pointed to a segmented public rather than a homogeneous one. The signs of this circulation and shuttling, even if collectively perceived, did not add up to a single collective understanding. The chief symbol of the movement, Ram, was itself polyvalent, as an androgynous, high-caste dark-skinned renouncer-king, friend of the high and the low, and lately appearing as man and child as well. The VHP and its allies presented their demand variously as merely for a Ram temple, as asserting the right of Hindus and retrospectively punishing Muslims, as a symbol of the appropriate path of national development, and as a precursor to constitutional reform. Symbol and propaganda were joined in performance, overseen through organizational means.

Highlighting the practice of the movement draws attention to its fabricated rather than primordial character, and to the contested and contradictory nature of its claims. Emphasizing artifice and risk points to the gaps and slippages in what is otherwise a totalizing narrative of communal menace, and highlights zones of weakness in what often appeared to be a Hindu nationalist juggernaut. Needless to say, our sympathies are not provoked by this intuition of vulnerability, nor our aesthetic sense gratified by the elaborate artifice in the movement's making. If a series of makeshift stratagems was aimed at symbolically uniting Hindus, it was through violence that the most dramatic and perhaps the most effective links were established. Violence served to exaggerate the movement's density and force, concealing the chinks between its different sections, and masking the confusion that would otherwise inevitably arise from the profusion and variety of its symbols. But if violence lent the movement a certain credibility and distinction, in the end its reliance on force marked the movement's limits. Thus on the one hand there was the demonstrated inability of the Hindu right to actually confront and tackle state power, as opposed to staging feints and sham defiance. The BJP's tame response to the dismissal of its state governments following the December 1992 demolition was a case in point.[4] On the other hand, even if physical violence could be aimed carefully at Muslims, there was a certain amount of spillover in riots that could at times rebound onto the riots' organizers. Tired of business losses due to riots and to the curfews following them, traders in Kanpur, U.P., for instance, hitherto loyal BJP supporters, made their support conditional, just prior to the 1993 Assembly elections: if the party created riots or any other trouble, the traders would boycott the polls.[5]

In any case, violence was beyond question built into the Hindu right's arsenal of methods.[6] We can broadly characterize two intersecting but distinct levels of aggression, rhetorical and physical, at work in pincer-like fashion, attempting to force closure on the gaps in Hindutva's narrative and to pluck out and expel its "others." This was no insignificant part of the performance of the Ram Janmabhumi movement. At the rhetorical level, the means included pamphlets, posters, wall-writings, slogans, and speeches, championing Hindu pride in various ways, threatening to difference in implicit and explicit ways, and demanding a rigid conformity that could extend to the minutiae of personal interaction; thus a popular sticker that read, *Hello nahin, Jai Shri Ram kaho* (Don't say "hello," say Victory to Lord Ram!). At the other end were far more chilling slogans, such as *Katua jab kata jayega to Ram Ram chillayega* (When the katua [the circumcised] is killed, he will cry out the name of Ram), and *Babar ki santaan/Jao Pakistan ya Qabristan* (Children of Babar/Go to Pakistan or to the graveyard), intending to extinguish the very existence of Islam as a distinct faith.[7]

For example, the December 1990 riot in Khurja, in western Uttar Pradesh, was preceded by more than two weeks of fireworks and bombs exploding every night all over town, while taped cassettes reproduced, over loudspeakers, Sadhvi Rithambhra's inflammatory speeches calling for action, and the soundscape of civil war, with heart-rending screams, gunfire and other noises. Pamphlets distributed earlier asked all supporters of Ram to blow on their conches or to beat on metal plates at a specific time, during the festival of Ramnavami, a few weeks prior to the December 15 riot. Rumors of a planned riot were sufficiently strong that huge amounts of money were wagered on the precise day they would begin, with local estimates of the total sum varying from eight to fifteen lakhs of rupees.[8] Cassette tapes played in Agra under cover of dark, over stereos in Maruti-Suzuki cars, during the November 1989 riots there, began with "Allah-ho-Akbar," and "Jai Shri Ram," followed by shouts of *bachao bachao* (help, help!) and *maaro-maaro* (kill, kill!).[9]

In Ayodhya itself, the VHP sought to transfigure a traditional place of pilgrimage into one in which every significant space pointed to the centuries-long struggle Hindus had allegedly waged to build the Ram Janmabhumi temple. Thus guidebooks on Ayodhya, sold in the town's numerous stores, commemorated not its several hundred temples and mosques but the firings of 30 October and 2 November 1990, when the central government unleashed an allegedly brutal reign of terror on Hindu pilgrims. The photographs showed bodies of wounded and slain activists, streets that were claimed to have been "flowing with blood," including one that was renamed Shaheed Marg, Martyrs' Street. When VHP activists offered to show visitors the sights of Ayodhya, it was these modern-day battle scenes that were shown, with a running commentary on the lengthy history of the Hindus' sufferings for their cause.[10] When kar sevaks were asked to explain their involvement in the building of the Ram temple, they invoked the sacrifices made by Hindus over several centuries as justification.[11] The VHP thus sought to suffuse the space of Ayodhya with a putative history of violence, thus leading even relatively pacifist supporters of the Ram temple campaign to conceive of yet more violence as serving a just cause.

The second, intersecting physical level of violence included both spatial and bodily strategies, the encroachment of both public and private spaces, and assaults on the physical persons of Muslims. Thus there was a melding together of signs and spaces in systematic ways.[12] In addition to aural and visual crowding of the entire milieu, most towns and cities across northern India witnessed a massing of Hindu crowds and the expansion and elaboration of Hindu rituals, with processions such as the numerous yatras, and new congregational exercises such as the *maha-aarti*[13] and the VHP's karseva, hitherto an exclusively Sikh activity. At times, the cumulative result was akin to living in the claustrophobic interior of a total environment, where every body and every word, every building and every activity, was fashioned as relay and transmitter of a single set of meanings.[14] Physical violence was an extension of this principle of occupation. Riots were, of course, their principal manifestation. The extensive presence of the VHP in the districts and blocks most affected by riots, up to the panchayat[15] level, and the proximity of rioting to shila yatra or rath yatra processions in the vicinity, have been recorded, as have repeated attacks on Muslim neighbourhoods by crowds with the same leaders.[16] The policy of the

VHP to cultivate local level police and administrative support, and the correspondingly extensive involvement of police forces at all levels of riots, from the initial rumor-mongering and instigation, to looting and repeated armed attacks, is also relevant here.[17] The formation of Hindu militias such as the Bajrang Dal and the Durga Vahini is one aspect of the display of aggression, and its harnessing of youth militancy.[18]

The administration of violence was, more crucially, enabled by the cultivation of "fighting castes" by the RSS, in the Valmiki and Khatik communities.[19] On an individual level, the display of bellicosity was intended to remake the allegedly weak and effeminate Hindu character; at a collective level, the show of aggression was meant to signal a united community on the ascendant as well as to intimidate any critics. Yatras carried out during the Ayodhya temple mobilization, such as the shila yatra and the rath yatra, were invariably periods when riots broke out, although organizers appear to have taken care to avoid the immediate vicinity of the processions. The Hindu right's success in terrorizing Muslims was meant to imply both the growing strength and passion of the Hindu community and the ability of the VHP and its allies to channel this strength.[20] The mobilization of crowds then seemed to require the spilling of blood, confirming the deep division between the communities and bringing doubters and dissenters closer to the flock.

PERFORMING THE MOVEMENT

A senior RSS leader illuminated an important aspect of their strategy with regard to the Ayodhya temple movement: "Beliefs never have rationale or logic. The Ram Janmabhumi in Ayodhya is a symbol."[21] Symbols can thus form meeting grounds for a range of different actions, or terms on which a variety of plans and transactions can converge. They may be invoked and displayed insistently, expressing an urge for unity that the symbol itself helps realize. There may be a contagion of incitement as one group after another observes the correlation between symbol and uprising, and constructs its own causation between the two, attempting to aggregate large numbers to one's cause, as well as out of the desire to be part of a larger movement. Movements may be characterized by deep, shared beliefs, but those are not the grounds on which reliable mobilization can be extended from region to region. That work has to be done by organization, through the labor of drawing people out, training and regulating their actions, and steering the whole through some determinate series of deeds, with definite ends in view. Symbols can serve to indicate these ends, although they may not exhaustively explain them; they may form part of the narratives through which these several aspects of organizational work are done.

If we describe the power of the symbol as "religious" or "sacred," as it arguably was in the Janmabhumi movement, it is political work that lifts the symbol out of the spaces of ritual life and into salience in the public domain, persuading or compelling disparate groups to enact their concern for the issue. Thus for instance the organizations, the pamphlets, the threats and intimidation of Muslims and others, which comprised the *labor* of engaging with and shifting the symbol out of its customary realm into one of urgency and popular concern, were coordinated by local VHP, Bajrang Dal, and other branches of the sangh parivar. "In a popular movement, it is necessary to assign work to the people, to keep them moving," Nanaji Bhagwat, Central Secretary of the VHP told me.[22] A series of activities then helped sustain the movement's unity, beginning with the shila pujan and yatra, and proceeding to the kalash yatra, where the holy bricks were replaced by ashes of the activists slain in October–November 1990, which were taken around and worshipped, and the Ram Jyoti yatra, where a flame replaced the ashes, and the *paduka yatra*, where wooden sandals replaced the flame, and so on.[23] They served to keep the machinery of the organization active and battle-ready in between the periods of kar seva, giving the impression of a mission that, despite all the political vagaries at the center, had its own force.

The paduka yatra was a device that the VHP came up with to cover the waiting period while kar seva was postponed, prior to the final demolition. When Bharat, the new heir to the throne appointed in deference to the wishes of his stepmother Kaikeyi, asks Ram to take back the throne, Ram refuses. He does not wish to disobey a parent's command, and vows to complete his fourteen years in the forest. Bharat, chagrined, asks him for his paduka, wooden sandals, so that he can place them on the throne to represent Ram in his absence. The story has come to symbolize the marvelous self-abnegation of both brothers, and the exemplary character of kingly rule in Ram Rajya. The VHP's Paduka Pujan was a message to the cadre to wait, as did Bharat for the return of Ram, and at the same time be ready for the ultimate goal of construction of Ram Janmabhoomi temple. In the paduka yatra, the VHP made 12,000 "replicas" of sandals consecrated by saints at Nandigram, and sent them to each of 550,000 villages for worship.[24]

Detailed plans for local involvement were made. Bhagwat, speaking at a closed-door meeting of the VHP preparatory to the *shila yatra* mobilization, stressed the need to involve each Hindu, each household, to arouse the feeling of a personal stake in the outcome. Regarding the transport of the shilas, fourteen- and fifteen-year-old boys would be chosen, each boy successively carrying the shila on his head for one or two hours. Thus each of them could get involved. Ten to twelve boys were to be selected from each village, on the basis of the concentration with which they performed exercises at the RSS's daily drill. For two to four weeks preceding the *yatra*, mental preparation for the task was to be ensured through proper instruction. The security of the shila yatra could be provideed by four boys from the Bajrang Dal, armed with sticks. These boys would also have to be prepared for a similar period of consciousness-raising. Those with the most strength, or who were good at judo-karate or wrestling, could be chosen for the purpose. In tribal areas, expertise at archery could be the criterion. If fifteen or twenty boys were selected at first and trained, eventually all the boys in the locality would want to get involved, Bhagwat predicted. A one month-long preparation in the village would offer ample scope for publicizing the movement. The Ram shila from the village would be taken around, soliciting contributions from each household, with coupons ranging from one and a quarter to five, and ten rupees being offered. The shila would be brought to the *prakhand* (*prakhand* being a unit with a population of 100,000), where fifty to one hundred shilas would be gathered. A *mahayagna* (great sacrifice) would then be conducted at this center, and at 7,000 such centers across the country. For this purpose, Sri Ram Mahayagna Samitis (committees) would be formed at each locality.

Bhagwat explained the symbolism of the Ram shilas. In an earlier era, when the force of asuras, or demons, was felt across the land, Sri Ram shilas were used to build the Ram Setu bridge, that in the Ramayan had been used to cross into the rakshasa kingdom of Lanka. Through the medium of the Ram Setu, the task of winning over the demons with the force of the gods was enabled. The Ram Shilas were for the construction of the Ram temple in Ayodhya. But at the present time, various kinds of demonic forces are visible everywhere, Bhagwat said. This activity could inspire people, and bring the strength of the gods on their side to defeat demonic forces, and so win an epochal victory for the nation.[25] In the shila puja scheme, it was decided that *upakhandas*, units of 2,000 people, would each bring a shila and send it to Ayodhya. Out of 345,800 such units in the country, puja was held at nearly 300,000 places; over 109 million participated, and contributions amounted to nearly eighty-three million rupees, according to VHP figures.[26]

Bhagwat indicated how the pedagogical aspects of the organization were interlaced with its mobilizing aims. The aim was to involve "all sections of society," he said, holy men and women but also local people, tribal organizations in tribal areas, youth organizations, and so on. There would be three or four exhibitions on India's history and culture, which included pictures of the scientific achievements of the past, to arouse a sense of pride in the people, he explained. The exhibitions would be presented in the assembly hall rented for the Hindu rituals, and then taken out on a procession. The VHP thus created simple programs that could be reproduced in different localities with little expertise, generating over the course of a few days a reliable turnout of school children and college goers as well as of older, more orthodox and ritually inclined people. Cumulatively, the results added substance to the more political elements of the movement, and helped extend its base.

Although the public impression generated by these large numbers was of a seamless Hindu movement, there is some evidence that caste configurations were preserved during the mobilization. This was the case, for instance, in Berasia, Madhya Pradesh. Berasia falls within Bhopal *tehsil*[27] according to official classification, but Bhopal has a relatively high percentage of Muslims; as a Hindu dominated town, Berasia was therefore placed by the RSS instead in Vidisha *tehsil* instead, arguing its greater cultural compatibility to that region. The RSS maintained a strong presence locally, and proved its ability to mobilize substantial numbers. The *tala kholo divas* (the day the mosque's locks were opened) was celebrated in Berasia as an anniversary. For instance, the *Ekatmata yatra* (Unity Pilgrimage), which was described here as the *Ganga jal yatra* (Ganges Water Pilgrimage), drew between fifty and sixty thousand people from surrounding villages, and the shila pujan drew a similar number.[28] A local RSS member listed the leaders of the organizers of the shila puja in Berasia. They were all well to do upper-caste businessmen, lawyers, or politicians, and all supporters or members of the RSS. The Ram shila yatra departed from the Talayya temple in Berasia, owned by members of the Agarwal and Maheshwari trading communities. During the shila yatra mobilization here, although members of the backward castes participated, caste taboos were observed; for example, there was no inter-dining amongst them. There were limits to mobilizing the women too. The Durga Vahini, which was the women's equivalent of the Bajrang Dal, groomed for "protection" for the movement, was limited here to prayer and singing, because, it was explained, the local women were "uneducated."

If mobilization had its limits due to existing social divisions, those more proximate to the issue at the movement's root might be presumed to have been drawn to it, with propinquity overcoming barriers of caste. Residents of Ayodhya themselves, however, could see VHP leaders and activists at close quarters and determine for themselves the differences between regular worshippers and the new visitors. As a result they had a keener sense than most of the theatrical character of the politics being staged. I will try to give some sense of the dense, shifting array of signs occupying Ayodhya during an especially hectic period, the July 1992 kar seva shortly before the final demolition in December 1992.[29]

In July 1992, kar seva at Ayodhya resumed, accompanied by loud and angry rhetoric from the VHP, and the media were full of the news. The contrast between perceptions in Delhi and in Ayodhya was instructive. With acquaintances in Delhi, the news that I was visiting Ayodhya provoked apprehension or alarm, and I was warned to travel only in groups, and to be very careful. One senior journalist told me I could be roughed up by the *lumpen* there. The dominant image was one of imminent danger. But there was another kind of response I encountered in Delhi, one of enthusiasm and respect for the auspicious venue of my mission. At the enquiry clerk's at the New Delhi railway station, amid the press and hubbub of jostling customers, I was rewarded with a beatific smile when I asked where I could get tickets for my destination. Earlier, the autorickshaw driver had beamed at me when he learned where I was going; it was as though I had lifted myself above other mortals by my disclosure. He did not ask why I was going or what I was going to do there: I could only be doing "good work," it seemed. Approaching our destination the next morning on the train, the ticket examiner was asked if, after Faizabad, the train would stop at Ayodhya, a mere 8 km. away. But of course, he protested – if it did not stop at Ayodhya, where would it stop? Ram Janmabhumi is famous across the globe, he said. This was a distinct, worldly accent on the theme, one referring to publicity rather than to piety as proof of significance, but here too there was no sense of anything amiss in Ayodhya.

It seemed as though the fervor of the movement grew as one moved away from Ayodhya, and receded as one approached it. From the rallying point of the Hindu mobilization, not passion but cynicism and suspicion dominated. Talking to Ayodhya and Faizabad residents, what was most striking was the distrust and scorn on view. When I asked residents if they performed kar seva, some answered yes or no, but more often I was greeted with a sardonic comment or a witticism. Oh yes, I am going to do kar seva, one worker replied, in exaggerated tones that mocked the question. "To do one's own work is the best kar seva. These people are making fools out of us," said a fruit vendor, dismissively. The whole thing is a *natak* (play), a number of people exclaimed.

The road from the main thoroughfare to the Janmabhumi area is a half-mile long, narrow and winding. The VHP had timed its July kar seva to coincide with the pilgrim rush of the thirteenth-day Jhula festival of July–August,[30] so a combination of VHP propaganda and more customary pilgrim fare was to be found. It was, of course, the design of the VHP precisely to insinuate its rituals into the spiritual calendar of Hindu pilgrims. In addition to the shops selling *tulsi malas* (rosary necklaces), sugar crystals, calendars, and incense, and the sweetmeat and tea stalls found in any north Indian temple town, there were also itinerant vendors, magicians, and fortune-tellers of the kind common in fairs. There were shamans selling potions and powders, and men with clairvoyant birds, either parrots or sparrows with clipped wings, that could pick out the card that contained your history. Fortune-tellers dominated the exhibits, interestingly, and some maintained a battery of modern appliances to assist them, including clocks, ammeters, and voltmeters, and in one case, a stethoscope. Visitors thus passed from one form of mummery to another, and so to the Ram Janmabhumi.

Sitting at a teastall behind the Babri Masjid, in the rain shadow region of the VHP so to speak, one could get a different sense of the Ram culture that pervaded the town. Ram Chander, who ran the shop with his old aunt, offered an interesting mix of perspectives on the commotion in the village. The VHP was conducting a *nautanki*, he said, mere theater. Everybody wants the temple to be built, he asserted. Was he prepared to sacrifice for its construction? His answer was unhesitating. Yes, he said. But the stories he told were bitingly sarcastic about the power relations within the movement. He saw a deep division between the *neta lok*, the leaders, and the *garib lok*, the poor. Although many people repeated accounts of the police firing on kar sevaks as validating the struggle to build the temple, Ram Chander was scornful of such accounts. The police and the movement leaders were united, in his view – it was the poor that suffered. "The police told the thief: Go and loot! And then they arrested him. That's the story here," he said. Several people had died or were wounded in the firing, of whom there was no news whatsoever because they were poor. But in the case of two of them, the Kothari brothers, their stories were told in posters and in cassettes and widely distributed, because their father was affluent. Where are the poor people who died, he asked.[31]

During the kar seva of October 1990, there had been considerable local involvement. Chief Minister Mulayam Singh Yadav's imposition of curfew during the Kartik festival period had allowed the VHP to portray the government as hostile to Hindus and partial to Muslims, and there was widespread sympathy for those who opposed the law at this time, and huge numbers of people had been drawn into Ayodhya to volunteer. During subsequent mobilizations however, local support dwindled and turned sour. A number of factors contributed to residents' cynicism. In Ayodhya, the VHP did its best to bypass locality altogether. The local supply of volunteers could never have met their needs in any case, and karsevaks were brought in from far and wide. After the BJP government came to power in U.P., a "Karsevakpuram" was set up, with makeshift arrangements for visiting activists, complete with kitchens. Provisions were brought in from outside the area using their own suppliers and sidestepping local merchants.[32] The regular flow of pilgrims avoided Ayodhya during the times when kar seva was on, ensuring that local businesses looked on the VHP with disfavor. Since Ayodhya was a temple town, subsisting largely on pilgrim traffic, the economic dislocation caused by the VHP was severe.

Local perceptions of the activists and the VHP leaders fed the hostility as well. For instance, it was said that the Janmabhumi movement leaders never worshiped at the Ram Lalla deity that they were ostensibly so concerned about, and that they drank liquor and ate meat. The sense of underlying aggression and militancy in the movement was alien to prevailing notions of religiosity. This was something clearly discernible in the salutation devised by the VHP, "Jai Shri Ram." It has been noted that greeting formulas in South Asia tend to be tied to religious affiliation.[33] The introduction of Ram in words of greeting was itself no innovation. The formula was in fact a modification of an existing greeting; villagers and townspeople might greet each other, Jai Ram ji ki, or Jai Siyaram, the latter name referring to his consort Sita as well. For the most part, the words were spoken softly. Beginning with an emphasis on "Jai," and continuing onto "Ram," the words would taper off into a quiet intonation that was almost a mutter, in relatively peaceable mutual acknowledgment or recognition. A sample greeting might be: JAI Ram ji ki. In the VHP form, the words were sanskritized, with the colloquial Siyaram giving way to the more formal Shri Ram. Karsevaks uttered the words loudly and defiantly, as a quasi-military salute rather than as a greeting or a shared prayer. So that now, it would be rendered: JAI SHRI RAM! The clear enunciation of each word and the high pitch of their utterance indicated not an invocation of conventional sentiment, but rather the statement of an explicit difference from convention or the emergence of a new one. The expectation of having the statement repeated in return signaled not greetings returned so much as the acknowledgment of this difference. Those whom I encountered uttering this cry were usually young men, dressed relatively fashionably in baggy trousers and shirts, and often adorned with saffron bands around their foreheads or arms. Being greeted in this way, one was immediately put on trial, in a sense, for they expected a reply. And in replying, one became aware of the loudness of the report, either by the effort required to match it or by one's failure to do so. In socio-linguistic terms, the difference in the VHP greeting marked dialectal variation rather than register variation, highlighting not *use*, but the *user*, as belonging to a different social group.[34] One college lecturer said that the locals were now afraid to utter the greeting: the meaning was no longer theirs, it had become inflected with alien intonations.[35] This was only the most superficial level of a presence that some residents described as highly coercive.

One customer at the teashop, who was something of a local wag, hailed a passer-by, "Jai Shri Ram!" When the passer-by failed to respond, he chided him, "*Prem se bolo,* Jai Shri Ram!" (Say it with love, Jai Shri Ram!). "I'll hit you with this bucket!" the man retorted. "First pay me for the twelve cups of tea you've had at my shop!" As part of a set of terms not in local use, its invocation was already a ploy. Joking with the VHP vocabulary thus served as a release. As a fat Brahmin was spotted walking toward the shop, another customer remarked, "*Dekho aa gaya Ram ka sasura*" (Look, there comes Ram's [expletive]).[36]

All politics is local, it is often said. Unless one understands the concrete relations of power at the site where political events occur, one cannot perceive how they develop or change. But here was a "movement" where the locals were often keenly aware of the staged and artificial character of the performance, whether they were Hindu or Muslim, and whether they believed in the temple or not. The program of the temple movement clearly could not have acquired the influence it did without the sanctifying force of publicity. We may observe here that mass mediated publicity inverts the meaning of "gravity" in its usual sense. An issue may acquire "gravity" when it is most widely disseminated, but by virtue of this fact, the smallest number of people have any direct knowledge of the events or are in a position to verify its seriousness. If the gravitational field around an object is strongest in its immediate vicinity, the opposite may be true of mass mediated events. Thus cynicism and suspicion towards the VHP was intense in Ayodhya and Faizabad, whereas in New Delhi these places signaled an exception to political corruption, not a confirmation of it.

YOKING SYMBOLS AND PROPAGANDA

The alternate blending and separation of religious and political appeals, and the oscillation between them, often seemed to presume that one or the other appeal was illegitimate. Thus in Parliament, Advani declared, "I am a simple political worker. I am not from the field of religion."[37] Sometimes, he had to belabor the point, as in the following speech in New Delhi: "Don't be under the misconception that I have become religious. I am a politician. Nowadays people tend to misunderstand me. If by mistake I wear saffron like him [pointing to a nearby sant] I don't know what people will think."[38] Or again, "this [the rath yatra] is a crusade against pseudo-secularism and minorityism which I regard as a political issue."[39] Nevertheless BJP campaign videos showed Advani posing on stage with a crown, such as those worn by religious heads, with a discus like Krishna, and with bow and arrow like Ram; and he and Murli Manohar Joshi posed for photo opportunities doing *puja* before a sacrificial fire.

In the "political" arena – in Parliament, in the capital city, in press conferences, and in meetings with politicians – Advani's message became a strictly political message: the Janmabhumi movement was about "pseudo-secularism," about the path in which the country was going, and the need to elect a new party into power. In the districts, and on the yatras, the message was couched as a religious rather than a political one – crowds were told explicitly that the rath yatra was not about getting votes. The calculation was a delicate one. The religious appeal would draw crowds to them, a portion of whom might reward the BJP precisely for its professed disregard for mere political gain and vote for them, while some might take them at their word and treat it as a religious issue entirely. Depending on who asked the question, they would explain that by religion they meant politics, or vice versa.

There was a strategic submergence and deployment of the boundary between religion and politics, as the campaign shifted across different regions of society. What varied were two factors: the orientation of the boundary vis-à-vis the audience, that is, whether the idiom of discourse was religious or political, and the prominence attributed to the boundary. What did it mean to talk of such a boundary? Through its invocation, they acknowledged the existence of modern politics and secular government, but at the same time addressed different perceptions of it: as required simply to liberate the birthplace and worship the Ram idol, as corrupt and in need of wholesale change, or as needing a strong unifying ideology. We can trace three major registers of the propaganda. In the first, the boundary between religion and politics is slight if not altogether invisible – the right of political parties to champion devotional causes is treated as self-evident. Here religion and politics are intertwined, then, although it is the religious rather than the political idiom that predominates. The involvement of the BJP and its allies is made evident, with their aim being not to secure power as such, but to use their power to worship Ram Lalla and express their devotion to the temple.

A primary medium for this religio-political mode of propaganda was the audio tape. A Unesco-sponsored study in the "developmental" benefits of audio-cassettes in India endorsed them unequivocally: they were simple to operate, they transcended literacy, allowing learners to choose their own pace, they offered a quick way to elicit responses and feedback, they could be highly specific to local cultures, and they encouraged audience participation.[40] It was the Hindu nationalists that most prominently capitalized on these benefits, however, building on a consumer market for cassettes that grew rapidly during the 1980s. The spread of inexpensive cassette technology dramatically changed popular music culture in India, in terms of its sheer volume, its quality, the range of styles available at any given place, as well as in the expanded configurations of its production, distribution, and consumption.[41]

The cassette boom followed on the heels of the expansion of the consumer market beginning in the late 1970s. With the big companies' concentration on the national market, the way was open for smaller entrepreneurs to develop more regionally-based tastes, which proved to be the preference of the overwhelming majority of consumers. Cassettes began to be sold not only in up-market consumer stores, but also in the stalls of street vendors dispensing betel nut, groceries, and fruits. With low overheads, small companies were able to make local musical traditions commercially viable; at the same time, they often survived by means of using film melodies and other cinematic sound effects.[42]

Music has been an obvious vehicle for grassroots social mobilization, in a society where print literacy was limited and prevailing traditions included extensive repertoires of folk song and dance, and traveling performers. Thus the Bundeli *aalha* and the Bhojpuri *birha* folk genres played their part in the struggle for independence, while the Arya Samaj used bhajans to propagate its messages of Hindu reform. However, where the use of music was didactic and not merely for entertainment, it was invariably through live performance. Recorded music was either classical, with devotional or courtly themes, or was from commercial films, which tended to avoid explicitly political issues for fear of censorship or market fragmentation. With the dominance of recorded film music in popular settings, music with explicit social and political themes has been scarce in India, in contrast with popular music in some other societies, such as reggae in the Caribbean and elsewhere, punk rock in Britain, or rap music in the U.S. In this context, the spread of cassette technology has broken through the oligopolistic control of the film and recording industries, and enabled more decentralized grassroots initiatives to become prominent. The advantage they offered was utilized to the hilt in the Ram Janmabhumi movement.

Here, audiocassettes using regional dialects such as Avadhi, Bhojpuri, and Maithili were extensively used, often in songs based on film tunes. Made in catchy melodies with devotional lyrics, they were interspersed with spoken commentary, providing a capsule account of events in the movement, or providing the benefit of the narrator's erudition to listeners. For instance, it might be explained that Shiva, Krishna, and Ram were actually all the same, or that Ram and Rahim were really synonymous. In this way, listeners of diverse persuasions were urged to join, although it is not clear to what extent Muslims would have been drawn in. The narrator/singer presented the compositions as already popular songs that he was merely reproducing for the public benefit; at the same time, the tune to which the song was to be sung was often announced in the introduction. Although the idiom and flavor of the performance were predominantly local, listeners were reminded of their membership in a larger composite culture.

Ram Avtar Sharma sang the songs in the cassette most widely distributed and heard, one titled *Jai Sri Ram*. Sharma is a singer of Haryanvi origin who earned his reputation as a popular singer of *rasiya*, a Braj genre of romantic-erotic songs – his *Meri chhatri ke neeche* (the chorus of which translates, Will you join me under my umbrella?) was a runaway hit in 1989.[43]

Sri Ram's temple has become a question of honour for all devotees. But the Bharatiya Janata Party, the Vishwa Hindu Parishad and the Bajrang Dal have taken the vow to liberate Ram Janm Bhoomi. Listen to how Sri Ram's devotees are singing new songs on the *dholak* and the *majira* everyday these days.[44] Listen! In this devotional song one village woman is telling her husband, "Let me go with you to Ayodhya, where Sri Ram temple is being built." And what is she saying? Listen:

> Come Come, Oh devotees
> Come running to Ram's temple,
> At His feet the world turns,
> He kindly watches over everyone,
> Friend of devotees
> I will seek His blessing, I will go to Ayodhya [*Mein darshan paungi, Ayodhya jaungi*] (rpt)
> . . .
>
> And devotees! Haridwar, Mathura, Kashi,
> In all these holy places,
> Some call him Kanha some Bhola[45]
> But it is the same
> Whether you call him Ram or Rahim.
> . . .
>
> We swear by Ram,
> We shall build Ram temple *there* [*Mandir wahin banayenge*].
> We shall show how to solve this Ram Janma Bhoomi issue.
>
> The world turns at God's feet,
> Ram, your creation is fathomless
> Your temple is across Saryu,
> Ram's creation is fathomless

[In conversational tone:] In the next song, the devotee is mad [with passion] for Ram. There is no place he hasn't looked for Ram. In the end when he couldn't find Ram, this is what he says:

> I am in love with Ram,
> Lord it has happened so often
> But where were you I kept on looking?
> In Mathura, in Kashi, in Gokul, in Jhansi
> For so long I've been singing Your praise,
> . . .

God, where haven't I searched?
I am crazy for you
Even then I couldn't get a glimpse of you.
Ram, this has happened to me so often (rpt)
. . .

This was far and away the most often heard song, booming from
loudspeakers all over Ayodhya during the height of kar seva, and sold in
cassettes at virtually every store in town. What appears as militant fervor
in the VHP's urban propaganda is here transformed into a religious
passion that knows no worldly limits or constraints. It is, moreover, not
presented as the address of a religious or political figure, but instead
presented as already belonging to the domain of popular discourse. The
singer is therefore only providing a rendition of something he has
overheard, and the audience is receiving but an echo of what is already
reverberating around them, by this account. Presumably in the interest
of reaching women as well as men, the song presents the feelings of a
woman, although it is presented as a *man's* report. Here we can see some
of the fault-lines in the public the VHP seeks to create, one where
unknown men have the right to make a general address, but women
may perhaps not claim the same right, although they may be invoked as
source. The song addresses its listeners in the second person singular:
although a crowd is being gathered, it is as individual devotees that the
audience is addressed.

Another song by Sharma names particular leaders and dwells on
their piety and devotion:

> Oh, witness the miracle of Shri Ram's *Kamandal* [monk's bowl]
> Oh, the BJP's dream was fulfilled
> Kalyan Singh[46] made our government
> What flowed in his heart made itself heard
> . . . Advani, Atal, Joshi and Singhal have also arrived
> Throwing themselves at Ram's feet
> They have shed tears
> They have made their vow for the idol
> We will put our life at stake for you
> Even after losing everything
> We will make your temple.[47]

There is a clear allusion to the Mandal reservations issue, but the BJP's
victory here belongs to the order of the marvelous rather than the
mundane. The ends of power are merely to illuminate the glory of god,
in this conception. Politics is merely an exercise in piety and devotion

here, expressing the fantasy of Ram Rajya, of a righteous and god-fearing ruler. The political gamble of the temple movement is thus transformed into the religious self-sacrifice of its leaders, summoning audiences to join in this selfless act.

Some of the appeals to mobilize offer prospects of flirtation and fun, and seek to be reassuring, although in ways that might have been disquieting to some.

> Oh, Lucknow's buffoonery
> attracts my heart
> Oh, Lucknow's buffoonery attracts my heart
> Oh, Ballia's language, Lucknow's blouse attracts me
> Oh, Mau's buffoonery attracts me
> Oh, even if sister-in-law is dark she looks good.

> And –
> In the Villages they said
> Oh, village elders and kids said we are friends, and we crack jokes,
> Oh there is no firing now, come on brothers
> 6 December was decided as the day of kar seva
> Bells and conch were sounded throughout the country
> Come Durga Bahini, come together, now there is no firing.[48]

Bhakti traditions tend to regard the soul as feminine, and so bestow a feminine persona on the male, likening his feelings to those of Radha for Krishna. The *rasiya* genre of romantic and erotic songs is androcentric in its portrayal of sexual relations, to say the least, with its accounts of male–female interaction dominated by the man's lecherous motives and the woman's coyness or resistance. But this is complicated by its bhakti influence, and makes gender boundaries more fluid than they may appear at first sight. In most of the cassettes distributed by the VHP, the addressee of the songs was male, and on occasion showed hints of the kind of lechery common in *rasiya*, as above. But the interweaving of devotional themes suggests at the same time a hybridity of interpretive style.[49] In the above cassette we have an explicit attempt to cajole and wheedle villagers into joining the VHP's expedition. This cassette was released when the BJP was in power in U.P., in 1991–92, combining the promise of merriment with an assurance of safety. Several kar sevaks I spoke to in July 1992 admitted that the government had brought them, in fact, on a free pilgrimage tour as it were.

The second register of the Ram Janmabhumi propaganda was again religious, but here the idiom opposes the political; presented as irredeemably corrupt. The boundary between the two is thus starkly prominent in this case, and divides the forces of good from the forces of evil. The speeches of Sadhvi Rithambhra illustrate this case.

Among the most powerful of Hindu nationalist orators are three prominent female leaders, Vijayaraje Scindia, Uma Bharati, and Sadhvi Rithambhra, who appear at odds with the patriarchal values espoused in most campaigns. The substantial presence of women as militant Hindu activists, in the Durga Vahini, the Rashtriya Swayam-sevika Samiti, the BJP's Mahila Morcha, as well as the VHP, points to the inculcation of an affirmative identity, one that emphasizes the value of women's participation in public life. At the same time, the traditional roots and obligations of such an identity are emphasized, so that obedience to the family and subordination to its injunctions overrides other commitments. Their display of female militancy suggests righteous violence that draws on notions of the pure woman as the sanctum of Hindu tradition. At the same time, the massing of female recruits serves to signal Hindu nationalist extension into the home, and thus implicitly into the very heart of Hindu society.[50] The speeches of Sadhvi Rithambhra offer a dramatic instance of female militancy on display, while typifying the movement's rhetorical transactions between purity, aggression, and a firmly patriarchal ordering of society.

Sadhvi Rithambhra (b. 1968) became involved in politics with the opening of the Babri Masjid in 1986. One newspaper write-up described her work as akin to that of the sage Vishwamitra, who in the Ramayan brought other sadhus together to destroy the forces of evil.[51] Within the BJP praise was more qualified. "She is not responsible for what she says," Uma Bharati informed me, "but she has a good voice." So good was her voice, in fact, that she became, via cassettes, the most widely heard demagogue in the VHP stable, through studio-produced cassettes that allowed her to sustain an intensity of emotion that a live performance could not have accomplished.[52]

Victory to ever true Dharam, to Vedic Dharam, to Mahavir Swami, to Lord Buddha, to Banda Bairagi, to Guru Govind Singh, to martyred Kar Sevaks and to Mother India. The character of Lord Ram inspires us to raise the voice of struggle againt every Ravan, against every Rakshas who is a violator of humanity. The so called secular people are unceasingly asking Hindus to remember Hindus' heritage. They ask Hindus to follow the path of Hindu culture. Mullah Mulayam Singh of Uttar Pradesh also says, "Hindus defend your heritage." I say, it is not our heritage to be beaten, to let wives and daughters be raped and sit quietly like eunuchs. Our culture, our heritage tells us to answer every Ravan in the manner of Ram. Our God Krishna doesn't tell

Gita at Kurukshetra to ask Arjun to leave the battlefield. Instead the 18th chapter of the Gita has been told to fortify Arjun's will to fight, [when he was] wanted to leave the battlefield. Our culture says that the one who commits injustice is not as [big] a sinner as the one who bears injustice. Our culture inspires us to follow in the steps of Maharana Pratap, Chhatrasal, Chhatrapati Shivaji . . ., Guru Govind Singh. We have considered the life of disrespect as lower than death, we have considered the life without self-respect as lower than death. We have considered a life without self respect as worse than death. That is why we don't fight shy of sacrificing our life for our self-respect and dignity. We have shown on 30 October and 2 November that vows taken from the platform of VHP are not empty political rhetoric, all of Hindu society fulfills it by sacrificing lives. We are not afraid of death. And the Hindu who is afraid of death, and for his personal gain tries to turn away from truth, I think, is no Hindu. Because Hindu culture isn't a language of death, but it is a tonic of immortality at the time of birth . . .

Beginning with a series of invocations meant to appeal across caste and sect, with the first invocation an explicitly brahminical one, she launches immediately into a call for aggression against evil and injustice. Religion, culture, and tradition combine to make one insistent demand – that Hindus prove their manhood, protect the women under their care, and thereby redeem themselves. Religion, culture, and manhood are telescoped together in a highly charged metonymy, so that they stand or fall together. The equation of the loss of *izzat*, respect, with death, uttered sonorously and repeated again and again with slight variations, produces a cumulative effect of considerable emotional force. Using misogynistic images to tap into male anxiety, she promises the greatest form of release as the ultimate glory. The accidental deaths of 30 October and 2 November 1990, from the Ayodhya firings, are declared proof of the VHP's commitment, in an inevitable but nevertheless compelling and powerful falsehood.

Look around you in the world, more shrouds are sold than *langot*.[53] This is the mentality of this country's political leaders. People are killed in riots and these leaders measure who got killed and whose vote they will get. Which party will benefit by whose killing? What an unfortunate and tragic period this country is passing through! Today the holy men of India are marching on the roads with the flag of the movement started by VHP. So called secular people, the shifty politicians pretending to secularism, without morality and religion . . . those people are agitated and squirming that India's sadhus are joining politics. The sadhus' work is to unite the country, and to divide the country is the politicians' job . . . Look at the dirty intentions of political leaders, they conspire to buy India's holy men with money. I get phone calls all the time, letters are sent [saying]: "Ritambhara Ji – How many lakhs will you to take to remain quiet?" I have told them, "I was born in the tradition of Sadhus" . . . I will never go among people to ask for votes. But I will surely say that till Hindus don't awaken politically, till the Hindu vote is not polarized, no power on earth can free Hindus from the period of disrespect and killings. [You must] accept this bitter truth in this country.

Rithambhra dwells on the themes of respect and revenge, honor, loyalty, and injured manhood. Her audience seems to be middle class in its aspirations if not in its actual economic standing. For example, she constructs at one point a scenario where the listener is a scooter rider who is insulted and wishes revenge; at another point, she asks the audience to postpone their intended purchase of a TV, VCR, or a Maruti car in the interests of the movement. Even if the majority of her audience neither possessed scooters nor were in a position to buy such goods, clearly these items belonged in its universe as desirable possessions. Here the differences can be noted from the address of Ram Avtar Sharma or Dwarka Singh Yadav, who focus on piety and enjoyment, but not through the medium of material possessions.

The emotions Rithambhra draws on are a blend of older feudal themes of honor, belonging to a hierarchical society based on rank, with more modern and typically petty bourgeois feelings of *ressentiment* – the outraged self-respect of lower middle-class men unable to assert themselves as they used to, and responding to the fierce competitive pressures of the marketplace with frustration. The pervasiveness of this sense of indignation and resentment, mounting to rage, and the diffuse targets she offers for it – raging from corrupt politicians and unpatriotic Muslims, to raped women, bad traffic, and rude drivers, are drawn together, repeatedly and emphatically declared to be the reawakening of a long dormant identity, of Hinduness. Rithambhra assumes a thoroughly cynical and disenchanted audience when it comes to politics. She is careful, therefore, to construct the VHP as a society of holy men, outside politics but attempting to remedy its deficiencies. The time has come, she suggests, when it is no longer possible to ignore the defects of politics – drawing on religion, it is necessary to fight evil-doers. As a *sadhvi*, her motives, like those of the *sadhu samaj* (society of saints) accompanying her, are irreproachable, and the success of her mission indisputable.

The first set of messages declares a chiefly religious task outside the ambit of politics, although sponsored by a political party. In contrast, Rithambhra, representative of the VHP's stable of orators, places the task of cleaning up politics as the central mission before Hindu society. Here religion shifts from being the *object* of action to serving as the *means* by which the objective is accomplished, and the *guarantee* that it will be honestly done, given the purity of the leaders and the power of the Hindu tradition. Those undertaking this activity empower themselves, as they enact their faith and their masculinity both, at the same time restoring the honor of their society. The obsessive repetition of the name Hindu, and its equation with all desirable qualities, point to the channeling of identity questions into one all-absolving answer. The ballads and folk songs, in comparison, are notably devoid of any notion of empowerment or personal transformation; devotion and worship simply reaffirm faith and continue age-old customs.

The third register of Hindu nationalist propaganda saw the most self-conscious use of religion and religious symbolism, and its subordination to a more explicitly political argument. Here Janmabhumi became a question of Hindu identity, which in turn was defined as a matter of cultural sovereignty and political equity. As with Rithambhra, the choice of Janmabhumi as an issue was symbolic of larger matters, but the gap between immediate task and overall mission elongates, becoming more a matter of calculation and reckoning, even as the rousing oratory allows emotion to take over reason. Thus census figures and proportional representation were brought into discussion. If Hindus, being 80 percent of the population (or 85 or 90 percent: the figure varied) could not have their sentiments respected in their own country, then this would clearly be undemocratic. Democracy in all the VHP's arguments is firmly by the numbers, with little room allowed for debate by a plausible minority. To refrain from exercising Hindu will, then, disclosed an exaggerated fear of minorities, mainly Muslims, who had to be reminded of their limited numbers. Politicians who cultivated such vote banks betrayed the majority. Hindus, whose tolerance was the product of a great culture, were being unfairly disadvantaged. The nobility of their traits was reinforced by the habit of submission, engendered by centuries of alien rule, first Muslim, then British. True freedom would consist in acknowledgment of Hindu identity, and the era of independence could then truly be said to begin, with prosperity becoming an assured prospect thereafter. Hindu identity ultimately functions in no less magical a fashion here than in Rithambhra. But what is promised becomes more abstract and encompassing even as the emotional charge decreases. If the VHP speaker promised *izzat*, restored manhood and a purified and strengthened society, BJP intellectuals foresaw success as guarantee of democracy, restorative of cultural pride and solution to economic failure.[54]

Not resentment so much as a reinvigoration program was noticeable here, the promise of redemption of an unrealized dream, of a strong and prosperous India. It was in striking this register that the BJP could say, for instance, that Janmabhumi was not about the temple, nor was it about religion – it was, rather, about the "wrong path" followed by the Nehruvian regime since independence. The issue that the BJP was campaigning for, then, was to return the country to its roots, to rid itself of its debilitating minorityism, and to question its British-imposed habit of suppressing its own genius as it struggled to live up to an alien "secular" image of the nation. What was most prominent here was the sense of a failed national project, and the desire to rectify it, in a fairly self-conscious instrumentalist use of religion for the purpose. Thus a rank-and-file VHP worker in Ayodhya described Lord Ram as a national symbol, adding that symbols were essential for the success of anyone's efforts. Also striking here was the candor about the political pedagogy being undertaken. As the abstraction of the political propaganda increased, the reflexive awareness demanded of supporters was also greater. By showing Ram in a solitary pose, plucked out from the context of his customary companions in traditional portraiture (his brother Lakshman, his wife Sita, and his devotee Hanuman), the power of the symbol to inspire audiences was increased, he explained.[55] An RSS activist, author of the most inflammatory wall-writings in Ayodhya, declared that he would depict Ram with a machine gun if he thought it necessary; the proof of a symbol's power was in what it was able to achieve in practice.[56]

To recall the account of Hindu nationalist strategy offered by an RSS member in Berasia, Madhya Pradesh, the aim of the Ram temple campaign was to bring the uneducated and the educated together in one movement. The uneducated were religious-minded, he said, and required education in a nationalist way of thinking.[57] This was a rough and summary way of referring to the variety of modes of appeal used in the mobilization. Here we can distinguish between the discursive character of support for movements from the *effects* of such discourses, developed and shaped in the practice of politics, and manifesting as "retail Hindutva" consumers, Hindu vote banks, kar seva volunteers, mosque demolition squads, and anti-Muslim rioters. It was in performance that political lines were drawn, as people cast their lot with one side or another in electoral, ideological, and indeed life-or-death battles. Undergirding all three registers was the figure of the Muslim as spoiler, hostile to Hindu religion, disloyal to the country that gave him or her birth, and holding politicians ransom to their vote bank. The Muslim as the internal enemy gave all three views a certain structure and stability, by depositing onto one pole all the contradictions and disaffections generated at the other.

The relentless focus on the single theme of the Ram temple could not have occurred without protests in Hindutva's ranks, and demands for a more ample political vision. Glimpses of such dissonance were occasionally discernible, if only afterwards. Thus, for instance, participants at a 1994 VHP-sponsored national Hindu women's conference, Hindu Mahila Sammelan, were critical of the fact that organizers had rejected demands to take up other issues, and insisted that the Ayodhya temple would be the sole focus of the Hindu nationalists. Some of the proposals they had made to the national organizers of the VHP had included: attention to some of the many derelict temples in their own region, Kanyakumari District in Tamil Nadu; a focus on women's issues; and programs of at least a few minutes in regional languages other than Hindi during the conference itself. All these suggestions had been ignored, they claimed.[58] We may assume that Hindutva encompassed many such currents of criticism, which it had to overcome through the sense of urgency created by its political mission, the use of short rather than long periods of gestation between its component campaigns, and Hindu nationalists' own superior access to the means of communication.

If nationwide television created a new visual regime, the strict controls imposed on it by virtue of state regulation meant that oppositional media had to use other media: print, audio, and direct communication, in addition to video. The range and variety of media utilized in the Ram Janmabhumi movement revealed its political sophistication, and pointed to Hindu nationalists' ability to exploit the complexities of a given cultural terrain to maximum effect. Through cassettes, the regional press, and privately circulated media such as pamphlets, posters, and video, forms of address could be utilized that were not viable in more established national media. For instance, brazen summons to militancy in newspapers attracted the censure of the Press Council, operating as it did under nostrums of objectivity. Rhetorics of devotion and of mobilization could thus complement more conventional propaganda with a degree of intimacy unmatched by anything the national press could offer, accommodating dialectal variation, regional idiom, and local events. Further, the more decentralized and market sensitive print and audio media operated within the footprint of larger media, of the national press and of television, and helped to intensify Hindutva's reach within a given area. In this way a variety of arguments and forms of appeal were stitched together through political performance, in a succession of campaigns that hammered relentlessly on a single theme, albeit one that telescoped out onto an entire spectrum of contemporary debates.

To understand the dispersed and mediated character of the Ram Janmabhumi movement requires examining the coordination of multiple efforts across a range of locations, from the kar seva in Ayodhya to the far-flung districts of the VHP's mobilizational work, to the U.P. press corps and the Delhi-based media, from the machinations of the Congress Party to the benign or active cooperation of police and administrative personnel. No single location study can reliably convey how these numerous parts came to be orchestrated together. The next chapter examines the links of the Vishwa Hindu Parishad of America with its parent organization, and presents an argument for its inclusion in understanding the workings of the movement. It affords an object lesson in the disjunctive discourses holding the movement together, in its assessment of Non-Resident Indians' expatriate nationalism, and of the strikingly different reasons the latter may have for espousing the cause of a strong Hindu nation.

CHAPTER 6

Hindutva goes global

For three days beginning on 21 September 1995, an extraordinary series of stories appeared in the news, about the elephant-headed god Ganesh. They began in Bombay, but were soon coming in from Leicester, Toronto, Chicago, and Edison, New Jersey. Offerings of milk to the deity in Bombay were disappearing before the eyes of worshippers, according to news reports. News photographs depicted spoonfuls of milk underneath the divine proboscis, which wondrously came to life before the temptation of devotees' offerings. Corporate executives and businessmen were quoted testifying to the authenticity of the miracle, and the price of milk shot up in Bombay and in much of Maharashtra, from fifteen to forty rupees a liter and more, becoming unavailable in many places. Stories began to be reported from London, Washington, D.C., and New York, of lactophilic Ganesh idols placated by transnational throngs of milk-bearing supplicants. Subsequent reports included interviews with scientists declaring that the phenomenon was merely an instance of capillary action, as liquid was drawn up along tiny surface fissures. The disclosure may have interrupted the deity's feeding frenzy, although the news cycle for freak events would not have lasted much longer than a few days in any case.

That there were individuals across the globe, prepared for whatever reason to attribute supernatural significance to the minor movements of matter was hardly novel. How did it become news? The story originated with Ganapati idols in Mumbai soon after a regional Hindu chauvinist party, the Shiv Sena, had come to power in the state of Maharashtra. Building on a tradition that had begun with Tilak's Ganapati festival, the Shiv Sena had continued to identify itself with the deity. If the genesis of the rumor was familiar in its causes, *viz.*, reporters flattering a new regime, its spread indicated the existence of an international community of sorts, whose members were determined to marvel at the same miracles and augur through the same omens. Jay Dubashi expressed it as follows: "It shows how close the Hindu community is when it comes to things that affect its identity, even closer than the Internet . . . not only to each other but also, to their Gods. This is something nobody but a Hindu understands." The insistence on the name of the Hindu community suggests that credulity here may have been a tacit way of registering identity. Collective willingness to perceive a miracle may have been the most significant aspect of the event, as Dubashi himself suggested: "A miracle is a miracle. Even if it is not a miracle, it is still a miracle in the eyes of those who see it."[1]

In 1993, nine months after the demolition of Babri Masjid, a conference labeled "Global Vision 2000" was held in Washington, D.C. by the VHP of America. Although the VHP was banned in India for its role in the destruction, several leaders were allowed to leave the country with the assurance that a purely cultural event was to be held, marking the centenary celebration of Swami Vivekananda's 1893 address to the World Parliament of Religions in Chicago. Few of the leaders wasted time in making their intentions clear. Member of Parliament Uma Bharati made it a point to denounce liberal Hindus who disagreed with the Hindu right's militancy: "To those of you who say you are ashamed to be Hindus, we want to tell you: *we* are ashamed of *you*. After December 6, the tiger has been let out of the cage." The conference was attended by over 5,000 Indians, most of them settled in the United States. Then-BJP President Murli Manohar Joshi declared to a cheering audience that 6 December 1992, the day of the demolition, was "the most memorable day" of his life, and that it inaugurated a new phase of Indian history. When Uma Bharati shouted out, "*Kaho garv se, hum Hindu hain*" (Say it with pride, we are Hindu), the Landover Capital Center echoed as the crowd repeated, "*Hum Hindu hain, hum Hindu hain.*"[2]

Condemning "Global Vision 2000," novelist Shashi Tharoor wrote in the *Washington Post* on "the peculiarly vicious fanaticism of expatriates." Like many other observers, Tharoor saw the endorsement of Hindu fanaticism as symptomatic of Indian political culture in the United States. He went on to make a connection between extremism and expatriates *tout court*, explaining their politics as resulting from a compound of frustration (as minorities in the U.S.) and guilt (at having "deserted the motherland"). The "American ethnic mosaic" was nowadays "full of imported bigotry," Tharoor argued, and Indian Americans were now competing with the "Fidelios of the foreign fringe," such as the "Muslim fundamentalists" trying to blow up New York.[3] The xenophobia Tharoor generously enacted on behalf of "America" was a mirror image of the organic conception of politics he criticizes. "Look under your feet. You will not find gnarled growths sprouting through the soles," writes Rushdie in *Shame*, in one meditation on belonging, as he protests his adaptibility to new environments. "Roots, I sometimes think, are a conservative myth, designed to keep us in our places."[4] The *power* of conservative myths however, is not to be underestimated, affecting even a professed "liberal Indian" like Tharoor.

Until a strong nationalist party rules India, and brings the country power and international prestige, Indians abroad will not get the respect they deserve, the President of the VHP of America declared in a 1994 speech commemorating slain Hindu militants.[5] The Hindu nationalist Bharatiya Janata Party, or Indian People's Party, is the natural candidate for such a task, he explained, since it draws on Hindu culture and upholds a program of aggressive national regeneration. If all politics is local, identity politics is no different. In order to improve their local image and conditions, Indians in the U.S. may support a militant nationalist party *at home*. Expatriate nationalism thus has a social basis different from that of its adherents in the homeland. Religion becomes a way of asserting cultural difference from the majority in the U.S. without an overt political emphasis. Simultaneously, faith and worship help to gloss over variations amongst expatriates, of language, sect, and region. The identity that is secured takes its place in a liberal vision of affirmative action, equal opportunity, and multiculturalism, accommodating other groups while making a claim for the distinction, indeed uniqueness, of Hindus.

THE FIGURE OF THE "NRI"

For many years, the most significant work of the VHP (Vishwa Hindu Parishad, or World Hindu Council), founded in India in 1964, was establishing numerous units outside India. The VHP of America has been registered since 1970, and regular meetings had begun as early as 1969, just five years after its founding in India. Its growth during the 1990s has been rapid.[6] Over half their work is in Bal Vihars or Children's Education Programs and in youth camps. The VHP also publishes literature on the "Hindu way of life," arranges seminars and lecture tours for visiting spiritual figures, provides family counseling "with a Hindu outlook on life," and operates social service projects mostly in India. In addition to these activities, which mainly tend to be episodic in nature, the VHP promotes a network of contacts and affiliations with other Indian religious and social organizations in the U.S., and often their own members may occupy prominent positions in these other organizations. Thus its influence extends well beyond its enrollment.

Importantly, it also serves as a channel of funds for VHP organizations in India, collected in the guise of charitable donations in the U.S. The United Way, for a while, had a donor choice agency code (#015546), so that tax-deductible contributions could be made to the VHP of America. The VHP had also signed up with AT&T's Rewards Program, in which customers could direct a portion of their monthly long-distance bill to an approved organization. Lobbying by activist groups ceased both efforts. Unofficial sources in the RSS and VHP in India indicated the amounts of donations were substantial, but they are, understandably, hard to estimate. For its part, the VHP periodically denied that Non-Resident Indians made an important financial contribution to activities in India, but their own literature acknowledged the flow of funds to projects in India and elsewhere. The Seva (Services) Project of the VHP claimed to have disbursed over $1.25 million during 1979–90 in various VHP projects, in India and in the U.S. This was probably too low an estimate. For instance, Congress (I) general secretary Kedarnath Singh alleged, in 1990, that the VHP had acquired Rs. 7 billion rupees for the Ram Janmabhumi temple, of which Rs. 2 billion had come from the U.S.[7] Their promotional literature noted, "The Parishad units in every state of Bharat (India) provide a unique link to serve many needy and deserving children of Mother Bharat." All VHP projects in India were on the "approved" list for funding. Although the centers in India receiving expatriate funds were always listed as performing social services, e.g., schools and medical centers, Hindutva propaganda was also considered a service by the VHP, as they "saved" lower castes and tribals from conversion by Christian and Muslim missionaries.[8]

Estimates of donations for the Global Vision 2000 Conference in Washington, D.C. itself ranged from half a million to five million dollars, with the official souvenir listing nearly $200,000 in confirmed donations. This support was used to enormous effect in militant campaigns back home, in terms of the dollars and pounds sterling that flowed in, as well as in the prestige of multinational support. For instance, in Ayodhya, at the VHP office, bricks for the Ram temple from abroad were enshrined prominently in a glass case, and each exhibit was labelled. Those from the far-flung villages of India were left in anonymous piles.

Among the parties contesting the 1996 general elections, the BJP was the only one to mention Indians living abroad in its manifesto's list of concerns. The party is sensitive to the advantages of having allies abroad, such as the VHP and the Overseas Friends of the BJP, a New York-based organization formed at BJP leader L. K. Advani's suggestion. The President of the VHP of America, Dr. Yashpal Lakra, estimated that there were sixteen million Indians living outside India, earning between $24 and $46 billion annually. Even if a small percentage was sent back "and was utilized properly," it would be of benefit, he said.[9]

In the early 1970s, the Indian government acknowledged the existence of an Indian diaspora and at the same time declared a kind of claim on Indians living beyond national boundaries, defining the term Non-Resident Indian, or NRI. The NRI has come to signal a kind of hybrid Third World power defined in the negative, with the shift from non-aligned to non-resident signaling perhaps the depleted possibilities available following the Cold War. Simultaneously avowing origin and denying location, "NRI" symbolizes the disjunct power of its referent. Their education and affluence, coupled with their claims of identity as Indians, rendered NRIs an apotheosis of the Indian middle class, exemplifying what "Indians" could achieve if they were not hampered by an underdeveloped society and an inefficient government. Thus "Indianness" came into its own, finally, but its being elsewhere was crucial to this achievement. The NRI is hardly a role model, however. If nothing else, middle-class resentment of their wealth alone ensures this; in addition, there is indignation at the differential rights awarded to NRIs. In the latter view, NRIs get representation without taxation, neatly inverting the problem of the American War of Independence. Dispersed in their presence and yet concentrated in their power, ubiquitous and yet elusive in owning responsibility, NRIs invite metaphorical description in the way they encapsulate contemporary flows of money and desire.

The Foreign Exchange Regulations Act of 1973 defines the term. If a citizen of India lived abroad for the purpose of carrying on a business or vocation, but declared his intention to stay in India for an indefinite period, then that person would be considered a Non-Resident Indian. The 1973 Act also introduces another concept, namely a "person of Indian origin," one that is effectively synonymous with and at the same time greatly expands the meaning of the term "NRI." A person is held to be of Indian origin if she or he had at any time held an Indian passport, or if either of their parents or grandparents was an Indian and a permanent resident in undivided India at any time. A wife of a person of Indian origin would be deemed to be of Indian origin too, although a husband would not receive this privilege. A person of Indian origin holding a foreign passport would thus be entitled to all facilities available to non-resident Indian citizens.[10] In popular parlance as well as in the numerous investment guides published, "NRI" is used as the term designating both these categories. NRIs would be allowed to deposit money in special accounts set up at competitive, guaranteed rates of interest for the depositors that would, at the same time, make scarce foreign exchange available to Indian government coffers. And both these eminently interested activities could be sanctified under the guise of a shared origin and culture. Thus the author of one guide to financial planning for NRIs writes:

Our civilisation going back to 5000 years and more has received many philosophies, cultures and religions, and has also given out many to others . . . Overseas Indians today are a broad class devoted and owing their heritage to the mother country. They have made good fortunes and also have acquired high technological capabilities. Even as they are eager to contribute to the development of the mother country, the country also wants to and can utilise their vast resources, finance and technology and experience. We are proud of them and they should be proud of us as well.[11]

We cannot miss the tacit negotiation going on here: if NRIs had finance capital, what "India" could offer in exchange was cultural capital, and the reassurance of genuine mutual belonging. Expatriate nationalism such as the VHP's drew on and referred back to this presumed commonality. One of the organization's volumes, *Hindus Abroad*, bears the sub-title "Dilemma: Dollar or Dharma," hinting at a similar transaction on the sangh parivar's part.[12]

Indian emigrants are few relative to the population at home; the number is estimated at fifteen million, with about one million in the U.S. However, overseas Indians have loomed large in the Indian public eye. We can tentatively date this new importance with the East African Indian exodus in the late 1970s, and the sympathetic coverage received by them in the press. India does not forget her sons and daughters even when they live abroad for generations, Amitav Ghosh wrote recently. He cited the case of Indians fleeing Uganda, some of whom sought, and received, Indian government help in being resettled. There was no link of obligation between the government and the refugees they chose to help – the latter had forsaken their Indian passports and in many cases had ceased speaking any Indian language. Ghosh suggests that the link was indeed not a material one, but existed in the imagination, one that survived mere worldly change.

This indissoluble connection is symbolized in the figure of the NRI. As V. Balasubramaniam points out in his *Guide to NRI Investment*, residence is normally crucial in a number of ways: to establish legal standing, to substantiate claims to citizenship, and so on. If the definition of Indian is independent of residency and even citizenship, there remains the quite old-fashioned test of blood and race – in this case, descent from Indian citizen(s). But even this could be waived in the case of non-Indian wives (but not husbands). So there was, willy-nilly, some notion of an Indian essence, albeit a gendered essence, that surpassed any positive definitions, one that was indifferent to vicissitudes of time and place.

The Hindu right weekly, *Organiser*, had this caustic observation to make about the prosaic interests behind this affinity of imagination:

Pandit Nehru told Indians in Burma to merge among the Burmese and forget about retaining Indian citizenship or heritage. At that time the Indian treasury was full. Today borrowing has gone on for a long time, so they are discovering Indians everywhere. Who is an NRI? It is being said that anyone, but anyone, who had at one time or another held an Indian passport . . . is entitled to all the "benefits" accorded by the State Bank of India with the patronage of the Government of India.[13]

The *Organiser*'s reference to Nehru is characteristically unfair; he was far from indifferent on the question of how Indians were treated abroad, and his refusal to advocate involvement in politics back home was nothing if not prudent.[14] But the location of the NRI phenomenon in the realm of financial interest is precise. After the oil boom and the movement of Indians to the Gulf countries, substantial amounts of foreign exchange began to flow into India. Between the mid-1970s and the mid-1980s the amount repatriated by semi-skilled and unskilled workers in the Gulf countries surpassed the foreign exchange deposited in bank accounts by Indians in the U.K. and the U.S., by about 50 percent: Rs. 14,000 crore versus Rs. 9,000 crore.[15] The money from the Gulf came without strings, and there was no question of the money returning abroad: it came to stay, regardless of interest rates or other inducements. NRI money from the West was deposited into external accounts, and the government announced that the accounts, as well as the interest earned, would be fully repatriable. Several inducements were and are offered to NRI investors. Deposits are exempt from wealth tax, and the interest earnings are exempt from income tax. Deposits of one year or more earn interest at rates significantly higher than domestic deposits and than the interest accrued by rupee accounts in international markets.

Several analysts pointed out that NRI money was "hot money" and thus an unstable cushion for the government to rest its borrowing on. In 1986, for instance, total foreign exchange holdings totaled around Rs. 7,000 crore, worth less than four months' imports, and NRI deposits totaled Rs. 9,000 crore. If NRIs had to choose between their money and their country, there was little doubt how they would act; the danger, therefore, was imminent. Indeed, in 1991, this was exactly what happened, and the foreign exchange balance went into the negative in June and again in September that year. Meanwhile, economist Ashok Mitra estimated that Gulf remittances could increase substantially, perhaps by as much as 50 percent, if the government took the trouble to provide incentives to remitters there. But the eyes of bureaucrats and politicians were turned further West, preventing such a policy from being formulated.[16] The NRIs who were targeted by the VHP were those in Europe and the U.S., the advance guard of the Indian twenty-first century, and friends and relatives of the governing classes.[17]

SYNDICATED HINDUISM: CRAFTING IDENTITY ACROSS DIVERSITY

An inclusive "syndicated Hindu" identity, even if asserted, exists mainly at the level of political ideology. As lived practice, it could not emerge all at once, given the relatively embedded systems of belief already in place. Here the international context of the VHP is influential. Relatively open-ended practices of religious identification have developed among immigrant communities over time, in what Raymond Brady Williams has described as "ecumenical Hinduism," developed in response to the pressure of a new environment and the desire to reproduce some form of community identity.[18] Bearing the burden of their difference from the majority society, religion has tended to become a site of syncretist cultural rather than sectarian religious expression.

Temple-building is perhaps its most visible expression. Building temples has traditionally been a crucial site of conflict between rival contenders for status and power, and has represented more than merely the spiritual genius of communities. Inden has argued that political struggles were often carried out in a ritual symbolic domain, and that the construction of temples was one arena in which, for instance, worshippers of Shiva and of Vishnu defied each other's claims to eminence.[19] Today, in India, dominance over Muslims and other minorities is an important object of much temple-building. In the U.S. the assertion of a minority community carries a different meaning.

In an era of multiculturalist politics, locating and instituting cultural difference becomes important in defining key markers of class and ethnic groups. For Indians, religious practices are often used to express distinction, in a kind of reformulated Orientalism, becoming a site of cultural rather than exclusively religious expression. While temple building has been the main method of such expression, conflicts between different sects and creeds have not been in the forefront of activity in the U.S. Thus several temples host deities from the north as well as the south, although such juxtaposition would not be found within the same structure in India. A recently inaugurated temple in the Dallas area calls itself the Hindu Unity temple, as if to highlight the novelty of the experiment being carried out: eleven deities from different regions or traditions are installed side by side there. The most spectacular result of such syncretist efforts, however, can be found in the case of the Ram temple movement itself.

The VHP's plan for the Ram temple in Ayodhya presents it as a symbol to restore national honor and signal the greatness of Hindu civilization. The proposed temple has a design incorporating a *shikhara*, a dome in the north Indian style; there are also two *gopurams*, domes in the south Indian style, although these are only a quarter of the shikhara's height. Such syncretism is without precedent in Indian temple architecture, and is cast as an explicitly political gesture by a largely north Indian-led Hindu right to their South Indian constituents. However new in India, such syncretism had an earlier expression in Livermore, California. The Shiva–Vishnu temple, two hours East of San Francisco, a large structure planned in 1977 and completed in 1986 on four acres of land, has both a shikhara and a gopuram, and exhibits a syncretism that to my knowledge is not present in temples existing at this time in India. The prominence of the temple in South Asian itineraries in the East Bay, and the volume of traffic between the West Coast and India suggest that syncretist efforts by immigrants abroad may offer models for nationalist efforts at crafting homogeneous "syndicated" identities at home. Such newly crafted models may serve as symbolic means of materializing the unity of a diverse community.

The liminal status of first generation Indians as immigrants inflects their expatriate nostalgia with a peculiar poignancy; "home" gains in brilliance as a constellation of memories drawing closer emotionally even as it recedes in time. "India" becomes a touchstone of their identity, assuring them of a place where they truly belong, or once belonged. It is ritual that best exemplifies the need here, with its deliberate enactment of repetitive, sanctified tasks whose monotony in performance belies the fullness of their evocations. The content of rituals as well as the ways in which they are enacted, and the means by which people's cultural, religious, and national identities (all of which are not necessarily distinct in their minds) are renewed, are adjusted, of course, to their changed circumstances.

Timings of sacred rituals and festivals are adjusted for the convenience of working people, so that major events are inserted into the American secular calendar rather than the Hindu calendar, with celebrations occurring on weekends, Labor Day, Thanksgiving Day, and other such holidays. With daily observance of ritual seldom possible, festival days acquire a disproportionate importance, and relatively minor festivals may be promoted to a new significance. The distinctness of sacred locations in India is recreated in the U.S., reading new meanings into topographical formations here. Pittsburgh, for instance, the location of the Venkateswara temple, is described in a statement issued by the temple committee as standing at the confluence of three rivers, the Allegheny, the Monongahela, and the (there) subterranean Ohio river to form a site fit for a place of worship. This of course draws on the importance of Prayag, near Benares, where the Ganga, the Yamuna, and the underground Saraswati river meet. Penn Hills, the precise location in the Pittsburgh area, is seen as being akin to the seven hills of Tirupati in India, where the most well-known Venkateswara temple stands.[20]

Transplanted to the West, there is unavoidably a new self-consciousness in ritual practices, as the difficulty of their recreation poses the question of the reasons involved. Vasudha Narayanan has noted some characteristic reformulations in the process. Idol worship and other pagan rituals are re-described as symbolic enactments of ideas more congenial with American Christianity. Thus, although diverse interpretations may exist with respect to particular traditions, one set of meanings is put forward, rewriting aberration and heresy as new forms of already known principles. Thus idol worship is described as secretly having more abstract forms of contemplation as its aim; burning camphor is thought to represent a symbolic cleansing of the self before learning from the guru; cow dung is said to have antiseptic properties, as also *vibhuti* (cowdung ash), and so on. At the same time, there are substantial infusions of scientific management and of therapeutic, self-help culture as well. A workshop demonstrating "Vedantic principles of self-enquiry" may be described as "a supreme stress management program spiritual workshop" and a *vratam*, a ritual pledge generally performed by women, may become "human resource management."[21] Of a piece with these processes is the syncretism of diverse currents in religious beliefs and rituals, so that deities not usually juxtaposed in the same temple in India, for instance, may be so installed in the U.S.

Rather than rejecting the realm of worldly affairs, or the knowledge applicable to them as represented in science, the version of spiritualism here is eminently pragmatic in its concerns. Every effort is therefore made to justify Hindu practices in terms of science, and indeed of modern management, and therapeutic culture as well.[22] Hindu spiritualism is seen as providing a necessary counterweight to the ills of a materialist society and, at the same time, as redeemable by the standards of that society itself. Such reformulations are by no means different from what these immigrants' counterparts in India might find congenial, as English-educated well-to-do professionals. In the U.S. however, lay people form the intermediaries between temple priests and the larger public. The priests themselves, usually traditionally trained in India, tend to lack the English language skills that would enable them to serve as public liaison. With a largely professional laity serving to manage religious affairs and liaise with a larger public, therefore, the tendencies are reinforced for Hindu practices more explicitly to become accoutrements in the care of the modern self.

On the face of it, expatriate support of far right Hindu nationalist politics at home is anomalous. Indians in the U.S. are, for the most part, prosperous and highly placed, although they are relatively new entrants in the country. Indian immigrants in the early part of the century, Punjabi farm workers for the most part, were also nationalist, but worked in conditions that were different in important respects, in a sharply contrasted historical moment. Discriminated against, and subject to racial attacks from whites, the Gadar Party they formed sent a band of armed revolutionaries to India to foment a war of liberation. When they went on demonstrations in the U.S., a cry that frequently

erupted was *firangi maro*, strike down foreigners![23] The contours of
nationalist politics appeared more fluid then, and summoned a very
different kind of engagement from its proponents, who in this case also
had little to lose. Indians today have one of the highest incomes of any
ethnic group in the United States, and the most education.[24] When they
have demonstrated the archetypal immigrant virtues in America, of
hard work, thrift, and material success, their ostensible identification
with extremist politics in India should give us pause. It can be explained
with quickly formulated notions of guilt, frustration, and political irresponsibility, but more careful attention is required to the specific contradictions they bring to and mobilize in their new locations.

Discussion of nationalism has tended to be scarce in debates on
ethnicity in the U.S., signifying the extent to which affiliation with
"American" nationality has been considered normative. Immigration
rather than the nation has been at the center of scholarly discussion,
with "assimilationist" and "pluralist" perspectives marking the poles of
this discussion in the 1960s and 1970s. "Assimilationists" held that the
salience of ethnicity diminished as immigrant populations aged genera-
tionally.[25] Those who argued from a "pluralist" perspective, on the
other hand, pointed out that ethnic identity was clearly persistent.[26]
Ethnic identity could be maintained by second and later generations in
ways different from the more cohesive, segregated community forms
displayed early on. By the 1970s, the persistence of ethnicity was generally acknowledged, although scholars were divided as to the importance they should accord to it: whether to consider it artificial and
insubstantial, or to give it genuine salience. Herbert Gans, in an influential essay, argued that ethnicity was largely "symbolic," and a leisure-
time identification, one that had little bearing on material outcomes in
people's lives.[27] Mary Waters confirmed earlier findings that people *chose*
ethnic identities, and the choices they made could vary from one time to
another. Ethnicity here was tied up with yearnings for community life.
But there were those who *could* not choose, but were given ethnicities
independent of their will, such as African-Americans. Ethnicity was
hardly a leisure-time luxury for them, she pointed out.[28]

Ethnicity for whites and ethnicity for non-whites, then, are two
different things. For the one group, it expresses choice and desire, for the
other, compulsion. It is this intimation of necessity that leads many
whites to project fantasies of community, of "deeper," "richer" culture,
onto non-whites, who somehow belong more "naturally." While Asians
have been dubbed as the "model minority," often earning degrees and

dollars at rates greater than those of whites themselves, the price of this success has been a tacit agreement not to rock the boat, and to consent to the existing racial hierarchy. As writer Shawn Wong has said, for minorities in America, silence wins love.[29] "Model minority" may ostensibly refer to Asian-Americans, but the unspoken reference is to African-Americans; it is they who are the "model" and archetype of the "minority": dark, unassimilated, and perhaps unassimilable. Referring in 1835 to "southern Americans" or those who are today classified as "Hispanics," Tocqueville wrote that they had two active passions that made them isolate themselves: the fear of resembling the Negro and the fear of falling below the level of whites.[30] Today, for many minorities, the "melting pot" still means striving towards an unattainable "white-ness" and fleeing an ever-threatening "blackness." Other racial minori-ties are not potential allies so much as threats of the taint of blackness they desire to escape.

In a country where bumper stickers saying "fourth generation native" are a claim to distinction, African-Americans, most of whom are at least fifth generation, might only provoke amusement if they sought to distinguish themselves on this score. Not only the forced character of their immigration influences this different reception, but a particular kind of cultural filter as well. Africans have for centuries been inter-marrying with non-African immigrants in the U.S., as they have in other societies such as in the Caribbean and in South America; most thus have ancestors who came of their own will, like other Americans. While numerous names may be used elsewhere to distinguish between an array of racial mixtures, in the U.S. there are only two: black and white. They obviously refer to essentialized notions of race rather than to the actual variety existing. Where do Indians fit in this schema?

Different politics are shaped by different histories: if Indians abroad experience racism, the kinds of racism they are exposed to, and the ways in which they inflect them, vary considerably. Indian immigrants to Britain came in the shadow of empire, with a culture of white colonial supremacy lingering even as colonial power itself receded. Like African-Caribbean immigrants they performed mainly low-paid, semi-skilled jobs. In spite of different experiences of racism and different issues they organized around, there were enough similarities in class and status that linkages could be formed in political coalitions, with "black" being used as a label of collective empowerment in the wake of the Black Power movement in the U.S.[31] An explicitly political relationship to the major-ity community could emerge, then, in a way that the very different experience of South Asians in the U.S. made less likely. Immigrant communities were much more cohesive and durable in the U.K., with social and geographic mobility being relatively limited. The arrival of Indians from East Africa in the 1970s, who were more upwardly mobile in their aspirations, has changed the profile of the community to some extent, with much more immigrant "success" occurring now. Strong community relationships endure, however, in a more hostile racial environment than that of the U.S.[32]

In the U.S., in contrast, most immigration has been relatively recent, occurring well into the era of decolonization, from 1965 onwards. The 1965 Immigration Act, which made historic expansions in quotas and abolished all explicit national discrimination, was the beginning of sizeable immigration from India.[33] This was just a year after the Civil Rights Act, part of a series of responses by a Democratic administration to enormous social unrest and powerful social movements, protesting against an empty rhetoric of American democracy. Michael Omi and Howard Winant have called the period of the 1950s and especially the 1960s a "great transformation" of the political landscape in the U.S., with a sea change in collective identities and political norms, due partly to racially-based movements.[34]

Most Indians now in the U.S. arrived after these movements had won their victories. Although they profited substantially from them, they did not necessarily identify with the participants in those struggles.[35] Coming in for the most part as "highly skilled professionals," their class and caste backgrounds usually pre-disposed them to view their privileges as a matter of right, and as one more confirmation of the merit that had brought them to America. Reinforcing the competitive individualism of these aspiring technocrats was a variety of factors in U.S. society. With the reach of mainstream society much greater than in Britain, community networks were more loose and informal, and more an occasion for socializing than a force for socialization. A more middle- to upper-middle-class status, residential spread in the suburbs, much stronger pressures to assimilate exerted in the schools, combined with other forces to progressively bleed Indians of most ethnically distinctive traits, especially from the second generation onwards. Few children speak an Indian language at home, for instance, a tendency reinforced by Indian parents who are mostly college-educated and fluent in English.[36] These forces for assimilation meant that Indians tended to identify with whites rather than work out distinct identities in their new environment. Dark-skinned themselves, most of them brought with them prejudices against black skin which were not always readily intelligible to African-Americans.

First generation Indians frequently employ metaphors of caste as a convenient way of referring to the interwoven manifestations of race and class in the U.S. Thus the U.S. is often described as a caste society, with African-Americans at the bottom and Indians above them. Just as the untouchables in India are converting to Islam to try and avoid discrimination, one Indian remarked, the blacks in this country are converting to Islam too. Just how far above African-Americans Indians do stand is, of course, a constant source of anxiety. Anecdotes about Indians' racial prejudices abound. But I have a story of my own. I was once accosted at a bar, late at night, by two quite tipsy African-Americans. One of them said to me, "Hey, you there!" I returned his greeting. He got straight to the point. "You're black, aren't you? Just like us?" I said that I was. His friend intervened, "They're black, just like us, but they act like they're better."

How do whites perceive Indians?, a visitor from India asked a group of Indians at a party. "Better than blacks" was the answer. As the constant point of reference, the proximity to blacks is reinforced even while desiring more distance. Such difference as they assert from them is bought with effort, by earning enough money to live in white neighborhoods, for instance, and sending their kids to white-dominated schools; without that effort, they would slide into the same pool, they fear. With job security in industry a thing of the past, and even senior employees liable to be laid off, Indians are acutely sensitive to their vulnerability. One VHP member in Los Angeles, trying to express what a catastrophe had befallen a pregnant teen who was turned out of home by her Indian parents, said, "This society will place them in the same status as blacks in the space of an eye wink."[37] Rather than allow her to go into any state or church-subsidized centers, which would presumably have had a large percentage of African-Americans, the VHP came to the rescue.

"Blackness" has, for most Indians, connotations of evil and sin at least as explicit as in the English language. Most Indian identities have contradictions which, if latent at home, become more prominent in the U.S. Mostly of upper-caste, and of middle- or upper-class origin, Indians in the U.S. are little prepared to be positioned as the Other. Such encounters, when they occur, may provoke memories of experiences at home that have not always been "figured out." The assertion of caste hierarchy usually carries with it the imputation of racial superiority, of "Aryan" versus "non-Aryan" for example. The viability of these claims of racially based caste difference need not detain us here; it is enough to indicate that essential differences are believed to underlie caste divisions.[38] With centuries of inter-mixture, however, the resulting physical similarity of castes at opposite ends of the hierarchy is extremely threatening to notions of caste purity, especially in the relative anonymity of urban environments. "Black brahmins," for instance, always run the risk of being thought of as low caste; as such, few are immune to the stigma of untouchability. The anxiety that accompanies the assertion of caste identity is, then, often considerable. Yet cultural defenses available seem limited and do little to address the underlying problem of arbitrarily asserted superiority. At least at present there have been few moves to re-inflect the notion of "blackness" in more positive, inclusive ways.[39]

Coming to the U.S., Indians are confronted with the return of the repressed: the blackness they deny at home now threatens to encircle them, as the category with which American society understands them. Even if Indians insist on being called "brown," the plea *not* to be called "black" is what is most audible. They aspire towards whiteness; in fact several early immigrants from India argued that they were actually Caucasian and succeeded in obtaining citizenship, until a Supreme Court judge ruled that Indians were not "white."[40] Denied full acceptance into white society, they assume a deliberately blurred perception of their relationship to the majority society, acknowledging their difference only in inclusivist terms, and evading their marginality.

Fear, inhibition, and a sense of their political weakness have combined to divert substantive political expression of Indians as a community in the U.S.; perhaps their material success is their reward. But success pursued in individual rather than collective terms has made it harder, not easier, to address issues they face as minorities. For a variety of reasons, then, they are often reluctant to identify discrimination as such when they encounter it. Being members of a relatively successful group, the competitiveness between individuals makes discussion of racism amongst them difficult: to raise the issue may be read as making an excuse for failure rather than as a description of a real social problem. With the independence struggle only a dim memory, there is little experience of collective oppression they can draw on to understand what they face in the U.S. Indeed, when racial violence targets Indians, their responses often stress their difference from the victims and deny any common identity, in a typical variant of minority pathology. The much-publicized case of the "Dotbusters" illustrates this tendency.

The beating of several Indians and the killing of at least one man in the vicinity of Jersey City, New Jersey in 1987 were by themselves not sufficiently newsworthy to warrant the attention of the major media. Only when "hate literature" appeared in letters and pamphlets, signed by "the Dotbusters," filtered through, did the media find a "newsworthy" symbol. (The group was later discovered to have all of two members, white men in their early twenties.) While the local Indian community staged rallies to demand protection, residents of Jersey City spoke of being ignored by more affluent Indians.[41] The wider Indian community never drew attention to these incidents of racial violence as indicative of their minority status in the U.S.

Jersey City, which is "the home of the Statue of Liberty" ("and her name Mother of Exiles," in Emma Lazarus's words) has the largest concentration of Indians in the United States. Described in *India Today* as "perhaps the closest thing to an Indian ghetto in the U.S.," most professional Indians refer to it with delicate disapproval. Gujaratis, many of them from East Africa, dominate its Indian population of 13,000, and most are employed in the service sector, including shopkeeping and real estate; most of the remainder commute to jobs in New York City.[42] More prominent members of the Indian community live in *south* New Jersey, as one of them pointed out to me.[43] They saw the visitations of violence in Jersey City as part of a karma they did not share. The events came at a time when black-versus-white tensions were unusually high. Affluent Indians no doubt had little desire to draw undue attention to themselves. One second generation Indian student, a member of the Hindu Students' Council (whose parent organization is the VHP of America), said he had taken a course with an Indian professor where it was explained that the victims of the Jersey City violence were different from the skilled professional "first generation" immigrants. They were less skilled "second generation" immigrants, the poor relatives and country cousins of the first generation with different attitudes to work and achievement. For a meritocratic audience of aspiring professionals raised in America, this explanation was enough to provide closure to that story.[44] It would make little difference to this response to argue that the man killed was a Citicorp manager in New York City, and that two of the people most badly beaten were medical doctors, and that none of these people were "sponsored immigrants." Nor would it matter to argue that it was the prosperity and industry of Jersey City Indians that brought them such unwelcome attention, not their failure to succeed on American terms.

SELF-MAKING AND IMMIGRANT CULTURES IN THE U.S.

One of the things Indians abroad tend to idealize most as a national cultural distinction is the strength of their family relationships, and the extent to which individuals define themselves in terms of their families. It is American couples who demand to get divorced at the drop of a hat, in this view, whereas Indians stick it out through thick and thin; it is in American families that parents and children go their separate ways, whereas an Indian family hangs together. In fact, the family tends to bear the brunt of the pressures of adjustment to the new environment. Marital tension and wife abuse are serious problems, and South Asian women's shelters are to be found near most major concentrations of Indians in the U.S. At the same time, many parents may find their children becoming strangers to them. The commonsense way of understanding what is certainly a more complex process is usually in terms of an inadequately "Indian" upbringing. It is an issue that often makes Indians look homeward longingly as an idealized site of acculturation, one where patriarchal authority in the family is relatively unquestioned.

RSS General Secretary H. V. Seshadri, writing in the *Organiser*, noted that for "Hindus" in the West (declining to use the term "Indians," per RSS custom), the crisis of parental authority over the children resulted in the most crucial challenge posed to Hindu values. Deploring the interference of the language of rights in bringing up children, he described it as a "cultural and spiritual crisis," expressing regret that physical punishment "even by parents" could not be administered without fearing legal reprisal.[45] Seshadri's dismay notwithstanding, his identification of the core problem is one most Indian parents in the U.S. would agree with.

The acculturation process for immigrants has always been a rapid and severe one with "individualism" serving as the shorthand description for the many forces involved as well as for their outcome. Ronald Takaki has argued, for instance, that the "iron cage" of individualism has been one of the crucial cultural constructs used to break down immigrant community relationships, by constituting the rational, autonomous individual as sovereign.[46] We have already mentioned some of these forces: English-speaking, middle- to upper-class professionals who are in many respects attuned to individualistic aspirations do not tend to form cohesive ethnic communities in which to raise their children. But this discussion would be incomplete without considering some aspects of the wider social and historical context in the U.S.

Since Tocqueville, the pervasiveness of American individualism has been a subject of discussion by social critics. Tocqueville understood individualism as a "calm and considered feeling" which inclined people to attend to their own interests and well-being, and so withdraw from the larger society. He saw this as an outcome of social equality and material prosperity, leading people to be able to fend for themselves. As a result of their self-sufficiency, people began to imagine that their destiny was in their own hands; this led, over the short term, merely to "damming the spring of public virtues," but in the long run merged into "the blind instinct of egoism."[47] Robert Bellah *et al.* have written that individualism lies at "the very core" of American culture. The ethic of "finding oneself" acknowledges the pain involved in such a distancing from family and friends but upholds the necessity of doing so, in a collective "pursuit of loneliness." If in some societies the family or the larger community forms the theater in which important phases of socialization occur, in the U.S. the stage for those processes is the individual.[48]

Sacvan Bercovitch offers an analysis that captures the characteristic contradictions of this process. He describes the ways in which, in the U.S., the Puritan project of self-fashioning, deeply identified with the larger project of empire building, was influential in one form or another since the seventeenth century. He indicates the lasting rhetoric of self-making as heroism, requiring individual will and imagination, that was at the same time something like a civic virtue and a national mission. The allegory of America as the promised land remains constant, he points out, although expressed variously over time. What was a purifying wilderness for Cotton Mather became, for Emerson, the redemptive frontier of the West. Bercovitch sees a persistent tendency in the culture to link self and social assertion with the moral assurance of a "self-proclaimed people of God." As a powerful national–cultural force, it has combined claims of fostering individual freedom with the paradoxical ability to direct that freedom into the reproduction of a relatively homogeneous culture, one which exacts a high degree of conformity and is capable of mobilizing unanimity of will in a short period of time. Rather than crystallize the Puritan ideology into a singular set of values, then, we can better understand it through its ability to enclose antithetical terms in a dynamic tension. It exerts its power by narrativizing contradictory forces into one form of fabulation, in characteristic mythic fashion.[49]

The issue of race becomes immediately obvious as an underlying theme in the enactment of the Puritan will. The takeover of what was declared to be "empty land" from the native Americans and the calm consignment of a whole people to the detritus of history, the establishment of an institution whose effects permeate society to this day, namely slavery, both of these acts were of fundamental importance in the establishment of "America" and testify to a deep belief in racial superiority as, in part, anchor and foundation stone in the project of American self-making. How then do non-whites inhabit such a self? In her interviews with white women in Northern California, Ruth Frankenberg found there was a persistent denial of substance to their culture; people often referred to it as "no culture." Respondents spoke of "the formlessness of being white," and of the unmarked nature of "whiteness" leading to anonymity.[50] The distinction of being unmarked, however, represents the privilege of a dominant culture that names others without having to identify itself, as Frankenberg points out. Whiteness appears then as the underlying basis on which all are evaluated and graded, and as the highest point of assimilation in a melting pot society. We may describe this as a blanking out of the normative core of an ostensibly plural culture. White immigrants are always already assimilated, then, even if they have just arrived. It is non-white immigrants, for instance, who get asked if they are going back; it is these "hyphenated Americans" who are asked which country they are "from," into the second generation and beyond.

The metaphors whites use have a wider historical significance here. The terms "color," "diversity," "richness," applied to the Other, as opposed to "white," "formless," "no culture," point to what is perceived as a more attenuated and empty atmosphere in which the self has its moorings. Bellah *et al.* discuss the notion of an "empty self," one that recognizes no ground of values to base its choices on other than the preferences of the self itself.[51] Ruth Frankenberg calls whites' accounts of their culture "thin descriptions," recalling Geertz's suggestion for *thick* description as the preferred means of analyzing culture.[52] Whites tend to perceive the flux and turbulence of a world where "all that is solid melts into air" as a predicament peculiarly theirs, in a project of modernity authored by and addressed to themselves.

If whites are at the "center," whether described in positive or in negative terms, then how do non-whites negotiate their position? As actors in an alien narrative of modernity, what choices might they make beyond marginality and imposture? In one variant of Hindu nationalism there is a characteristic response, which is to invert difference, and to present progress instead as originating from themselves, in a kind of historical subterfuge: "Hindu science" emerges as the visionary manifesto of modernity, even if it fell into disuse and disrepair thanks to alien invaders, primarily Muslims. Identity formation in the U.S., however, is indelibly marked by race. This is of course clearest in those whose formative years were spent in this country. I will quote a series of excerpts from an interview with a second generation Indian, Shyam Mudgal, born and raised in the U.S., and an active member of the VHP of America's students' wing, the Hindu Students' Council.[53]

I think deep inside I believe I'm strongly Hindu. That doesn't inhibit me from doing most things I want . . . What's important is understanding what an *atman* is, what *moksha* is, what the law of *karma* is . . . Hinduism is very consistent with science, so there's less of a dichotomy.

The multiple hesitations: "I think," "deep inside," "I believe," culminate in a defiant flourish: "I'm strongly Hindu." We can observe the splitting of the self, performed to acknowledge the otherness of a heathen culture in the received vision of modernity. The inner self is not described in the same language; the authority of a sacred tongue is invoked, making allusions that assert rather than deny otherness.

I identify with being an American completely . . . I don't think there is any conflict if you understand what the actual philosophical process of being a Hindu is . . . Sometimes there are traditions which it seems like you have to follow. Like going to the temple for instance. You have to understand why this is only a tradition and doesn't have a deeper significance . . .

The vigor of the assertion suggests the force of will required to be American, just as the more hesitant invocation of Hinduness indicates an unbudgeable insufficiency of nature. Again the implication of conflict and again the swift denial. Although Hinduness is "deep inside," its resolution is referred to an abstract level, rather than as something that needs to be worked out in practice. Thus traditions are described as "only" traditions, with no commitments entailed. What then does Hinduness mean?

We've even tackled social issues. We explain how all of mankind is one family. You can find reasons in Hinduism to get involved in social work. We're just using Hinduism as a driver force to get involved in daily life. Not in a fundamentalist way. But just to be proud of being Hindu. Subconsciously it gets instilled in us too, because of the media, that Hinduism is very primitive.[54]

Mudgal finally refers to marginality, although he exonerates the larger culture by condensing bias into the media, familiar villains in a blameless society. The reference is still not directly to race, but religion is fungible with it here. Addressing the problem of identity emerges as the key to the Hindu Students' Council's method. The cultural work he describes is not the task of oppositional signifying practice, however. There is little acknowledgment of the prolonged and extensive labor required to engage with, shift, and transform existing deep-rooted identities. Nor is such transformation intended, clearly, even though there is an allusion to the subconscious.

Where initially Hinduness was something deep inside, now it appears outside as a propulsive force impelling an already constituted self. "We're just using Hinduism" comes as an admission of strategic appropriation that begins from and returns to the field of American culture, not "in a fundamentalist way" but "just to be proud." All that is required is a better attitude, perhaps, but addressed merely at that level, there is a contradiction that remains, between being American and asserting Hindu identity. The "primitivism" of the latter sits ill with the modernity of quotidian life, leading to a splitting of the self and to denial, to a hectic criss-crossing between invoking a secret identity and domesticating it as already-known, as merely a useful tool. The contradiction is "resolved" in the mode of American self-fashioning, as an ongoing effort of individual will and imagination. Failure in the effort will be taken as an individual failure, without the wider culture intervening in explanation.

For first generation immigrants, home is a place bearing all the burden of the difference unresolvable in their new environment. It thus offers an identity crucial to recuperating a sense of self challenged by experiences of racial exclusion. Inhibitions in the expression of marginality in the U.S. tend to solidify their sense of the identity being repressed, and make it less fuzzy and plural, more unitary, heavy, and substantial. If for them, forming links with political parties at home is an outcome emanating from these issues, the next generation faces a somewhat different set of problems. Without their own memories of home to attach themselves to, first generation immigrants are rendered as means of "re-membering," as experiential links with the native land. Racial marginalization is experienced, and often denied, by both groups. Nevertheless a disjuncture remains between them, as the crucial loci of their early, formative years tend to be different. And this is only one of a series of disjunctures we can trace in the process of mapping the circuits of expatriate nationalism.

In the summer of 1997, I had the opportunity to attend a three-day camp conducted by the Hindu Swayamsewak Sangh.[55] Although the HSS has existed in the U.K. and elsewhere for many years, it is a relatively recent entrant to the U.S., most likely in the early 1990s. Yet its growth has been quite rapid. One senior member estimated that there were over 150 shakhas (branches) in the tri-state area alone, i.e., New York, New Jersey, and Connecticut, with an average weekly attendance of between fifteen and twenty at each. He attributed the increase to three factors: the ascension of the BJP to power at the center in India; the large number of software engineers coming into the country annually,[56] especially in the wake of efforts to tackle the "millennium bug"; and perhaps most importantly, the entry into the U.S. of a number of dedicated RSS activists who were also software engineers, and who were recruiting large numbers of new members.[57]

An earlier generation of immigrants, arriving from the Presidency Colleges and national institutes of technology, usually having spent several years and sometimes their entire lives in one of the metropolises, tended to be relatively well schooled in the modes and mores of modern, professional life. The sometimes lengthy experience of graduate school within the U.S. was usually a transformative experience as well, as students encountered the often diverse intellectual currents within a university setting, as well as people from different parts of India and the rest of the world.[58] A substantial percentage, up to about half of the most recent wave of immigrants, however, have diplomas in computer programming acquired over a short period of time (sometimes no more than three months, but more often one or two years), and come from a far greater spread of cities and towns than before, many of them from small towns in the Indian hinterland.[59]

A combination of different kinds of activities was provided in the camps. Most importantly, there was an experiential form of bonding, with members participating together in a variety of activities, structured as well as improvisational. The practice of engaging in relatively unquestioning, cooperative forms of activities were held to build solidarity; such activities are in fact part of the secret of members' loyalty to the sangh. But lest it lapse into mere self-indulgence, this was leavened by physical discipline as well as pedagogical activity, a combination of drill and lecturing. In shakha activity in India, discipline was in fact the dominant motif, with blind obedience to the leader being inculcated. Organizing well-paid professionals in the U.S. is another matter however; the stern RSS discipline was noticeably soft-pedaled at the camp I attended, with frequent apologies being made for such regimentation as

there was. For the 10 percent or so who were involved in the actual
organizing, the camp was extremely hard work, with little sleep and
endless chores; the remainder of the participants were more or less
enjoying a free ride, in this respect.

There were about a hundred and fifty people in all, comprised of
three groups: young male software engineers; a smaller number of older
professionals, mostly men; and a still smaller number of children of the
latter group and of other sangh sympathizers who had dropped them off
for the weekend. The few women present were there with their husbands, or they were teenagers. The young men were from a range of
medium-sized cities and smaller towns, such as Coimbatore, Davan-
gere, Faizabad, Hubli, and Indore. The latter represented a different
phase of immigration, responding to the enormous growth of the software industry beginning in the 1980s, drawing not only from the usual
reservoirs of educated professionals in the metropolises (which are,
except for New Delhi, all coastal cities), but reaching beyond to the
hinterland.[60] This was also a new phase of globalization, due to the
improvement of transnational links, with representatives of companies
headquartered in small towns in India, and having branch offices in
New York or San Jose. Imagine a company based, say, in Rajkot,
Gujarat and New York, completely skipping the usual metro office in
Mumbai or Delhi. According to one estimate, at any given time, there
are about 2,000 Indian entrepreneurs touring the U.S., hawking ré-
sumés collected from software engineers back in India, and seeking
contracts for data processing, mostly from accounting firms such as
Arthur Andersen as well as from communications companies such as
AT&T.[61] As a result, there are imports funneling into the U.S. from
hitherto little-exposed strata of Indian society, completely bypassing the
usual socialization of the bigger cities. In these hinterland regions, after
years of grassroots effort, Hindu nationalism now circulates within the
commonsense of the upper-caste, educated strata, with few other ideologies available to compete with it. It is not surprising, then, that with
improved communications, they should be more evident. The sangh
offers to these small-town aspirants to the upper middle classes a way of
being modern. It blends familiar signs of auspiciousness and authority
with a martial sternness that seems appropriate for the new work culture
they seek to absorb. In this sense, the sangh can be seen to capitalize on
the Nehruvian absence of a cultural policy, mediating modernity for the
small-town upper castes.

Participants at the camp were grouped roughly according to age and sex, and there were about a dozen groups of as many members each. The camp schedule consisted of general assemblies and collective exercises, including salutes to the bicornuate saffron flag, games and martial arts, lectures and prayer, and mealtimes. A sixty dollar fee covered the cost for each person; I later learned that HSS members paid about a third more, subsidizing what was meant as a recruiting venture. Lots of food and games and good company were meant to prepare a memorable experience, and a positive association with the sangh. One participant observed that the camp was like a seminar held by Microsoft, in the profusion of the offerings of food and drink. The asceticism of the sangh in India was not being reproduced here, it was clear.

There was a good deal of recitation and chanting of slogans and mantras, which blended into each other. People sitting in neat rows, repeating after the incantator of the moment – *Jai Bharat Mata Ki, Jai Bhavani Jai Shivaji* (Victory to Mother India, Victory to Bhavani, Victory to Shivaji), would be exhorted to shout ever louder. There was a trace of embarrassment on some faces at having to do this. But the speakers were for the most part mild in their approach; only two of four main speakers mentioned the sangh, and the tone was soft rather than hectoring, respecting the audience's right to disagree. There were martial arts exercises, with sticks, where we were taught how to strike one's opponent on the head. Later, as we passed the older men's group, I heard the leader tell them, you can really hit them wherever you can, between the legs preferably.

There was an "Upanishadic management consultant," K., who spoke to an avid crowd of engineers at the camp. He applied the insights of the Upanishads to management. Reality is shaped in our minds, he explained; we have to understand how our own minds create our knowledge, to behave towards others with compassion and respect, and always leave open the possibility of being wrong. As he wound up, one of the young engineers had a question. The idea of giving respect to others was a good one, he said. But what if it was required to retaliate or strike back at them? Respect, the consultant replied smoothly, comes from the Latin word meaning to look again, to re-evaluate. It represented a striking change of tone. The RSS old-timers beamed. Not for nothing was K. a management consultant. More than that, one suspected, here was the age-old figure of the wily Brahmin, able to bend his philosophy to the patron's convenience.

There was a pretty teenager who danced a number from the film *Rangeela* (Colorful) at the final evening's entertainment. She appeared to be a skillful dancer, but she wore a capacious *shalwar kameez* that completely hid her body, although the dance and the music suggested a provocative intent. It made for a curiously abstract experience. No doubt the audience was hardly an appropriate one for the occasion; indeed, she perhaps felt required to look restrained, so that even when she heaved her bosom, her face was completely expressionless.

The "Madanlal Dhingra" group, named for a terrorist patriot in the independence movement, was the teenagers' group. On the last evening, they put on a "slide show," compered with gawky élan by a pre-med student. Two boys held a sheet up, and behind it, several youths arrayed themselves in various postures. "Since we are Indian, and family is such a big part of Indian life," they presented a "3-D slide show" of their visits to family in India. The show focused on the shock of seeing cows on Indian streets, being overfed at relatives' houses, the stench of Indian bathrooms, being chased by something "my father has warned me against – *goondas*," being deserted by the girls because they couldn't fight the goondas, finally being killed on the streets of India! And, "because we're Hindu, we believe in reincarnation," the final frieze showed them striking extravagant postures of defiant return. Their use of images was interesting, as a way of handling discrepant realities and of describing a society they preferred to see from the outside, their Hindu identity itself appearing as an after-thought rather than as a felt attitude. The show seemed to confirm that difficulty the second generation had in fitting themselves into the spirit of the camp, so that even when they tried to assert their belonging, they only underlined their inability to relate to it.

With a combination of companionship, counseling, and exercise, woven together with spiritual discourse and Hindu nationalist history, the camp sought to provide a set of intellectual and bodily practices framing the process of class and cultural mobility for upwardly aspiring individuals. Thus there was a strong endorsement of traditional authority while subtly inflecting it with rationalist approaches to personal problem-solving in modern urban life. One participant, from Faizabad in Uttar Pradesh, told me he had only heard negative things about the RSS when growing up, and only after coming to the U.S. had he really come to know them, and to see what "brainwass" [*sic*] it was. Not only the affective bonding provided by the camp, but also the ways in which it made sense of a changing landscape for new arrivals made the "negative things" secondary or even perhaps justified them.

The kind of nationalism immigrants express is a product of their circumstances as well as the outcome of a specific form of association. While expatriate nostalgia and yearning for an idealized community may grow in response to alienation and frustration abroad, the specific ways in which they manifest are not already given. Rather, they are dependent on meanings selectively mobilized and articulated by the VHP and its affiliates. Not only improved communication is important here, but *selective* communication: to reproduce the relationship between disparate locations, it is crucial that the different branches of the VHP *maintain* their differences, so as to retain their affiliations and their recruiting ability within each location.[62]

The constituents of the VHP of America are mostly English-educated professionals and managers, whereas their counterparts in India have a far wider class spread, with a much higher percentage of lower middle-class members. Most of the differences between the two branches can be understood in the light of these more fundamental divergences. The former are relatively well-settled, and shun any association with oppositional politics in the U.S. itself; the understandings of the VHP circulating in their literature emphasize values and education, and highlight their contributions to social work.

For Mudgal and most other Indians who like him were born in the U.S., the Hindu nationalist politics of the VHP seem distant, a concern more of the first generation than of their own. For Mudgal, such politics do inform commonsense understanding of Indian society: he has tried to interest second generation kids in the "one or two issues" he has been involved in, like Kashmir and Ayodhya, but he finds they simply get "overwhelmed" by the alienness of the subject. His real involvement will be with fortifying Hindu identity in the U.S., he expects, through extending the reach and character of organizations like the Hindu Students' Council. Such an incompatibility of interests portends a generational split between organizations, clearly, with first generation immigrants maintaining and reproducing political affiliations with Indian organizations, and subsequent generations involved with their own, more U.S.-centered, concerns.

Few parents are equipped to deal with the qualitatively different problems faced by growing children in the U.S. compared to, say, in India. If the family is treated as a "haven in a heartless world," immigrant parents have a special come-uppance awaiting this fiction, as children tend to distance themselves in their attempt to cope with the contradictions between their upbringing and the demands of the larger society. The problems manifest themselves variously: uncommunicative, rebellious children, declining performance in school, lack of ambition, and dating. The determination of symptoms is gendered, as are the means of their redressal: it is a problem when *boys* are not ambitious, and when *girls* want to date. In any case, the children's rejection of patriarchal authority is often the moment of the most profound cultural crisis for first generation immigrants; their relationships with their own parents, and their culture, become more idealized the more they contemplate their alienation from their children.

It is here that the VHP's contribution came in, as members tell the story, with its unique emphasis on the irreplaceability of a Hindu cultural identity, understood as a national identity. Numerous VHP members asserted that the moment of recognition for parents of their alienation from their children was the moment when their "Indianness" finally struck them as an inescapable fact which they had to acknowledge and work with: the accumulated problems stemming from repressed contradictions could no longer be ignored. For our part we may understand this as the recognition by the VHP of a prime mobilizational opportunity specific to the U.S. Youth camps and Sunday school programs were instituted as means of providing "community support" for parents' acculturation efforts.

The most important task, as then-VHP President Mahesh Mehta saw it, was to let the children know that even outside their own families, they could find communities of selfless and caring individuals. The perception of selflessness was obviously critical in the VHP's securing its hold. Creating the equivalent of an extended family of uncles, aunts, and cousins proved successful not only as a live and accessible reference to consolidate children's sense of identity. Even if the children did not become quite as vociferously "Hindu" as their counterparts in India, the VHP refrained from making it an issue. The emphasis was on helping members blend into U.S. society. "We don't want to create any tension in their minds," Mahesh Mehta pointed out.[63] What the organization gained was not only the participation of the parents, but larger numbers to parade before the public, as with the Global Vision 2000 Conference (see above), where over half of the more than 5,000 participants were U.S.-born teenagers, far removed from the politics of Ayodhya. They had been assembled for a parallel youth conference (which, many of them protested, was boring and nothing like their youth camps) but adduced to the audience total.

A comparison of promotional literature from the VHP of India with its U.S. counterpart will illustrate some differences between the two. In *Vishwa Hindu Parishad: Samagra Darshan* (Vishwa Hindu Parishad: A Comprehensive View), Moropant Pingale writes in the Foreword:

Vishwa Hindu Parishad Hindu Samaj ki pratinidhik sansthan hai. Isme vishwa bhar mein phaile sabhi varnon aur sabhi vargon ke Hindu ek hi ichcha, ek hi asha aur ek hi aakanksha se sammalith hue hein ki Hindu samaj, Hindu dharm aur Hindu sanskriti, jiski vijai dundubhi kabhi vishwa bhar mein gunjthi thi . . . phir se apne poorv sthar par pahunch kar purani unchai ko chu le. Dusre shabdon mein hamara desh Bharat punah vishwa ke samaksh apni gurdan unchi kar ke "aham brahmosmi" . . . ka sandesh de kar vishwa bandhutva ka path padhaye.

[Vishwa Hindu Parishad is the representative organization of Hindu society. All castes and all classes of Hindus throughout the world unite in it with one desire, one hope, and one aspiration: that Hindu society, Hindu religion and Hindu culture, the drums of whose victory used to resound throughout the world . . . will once again reach the heights it occupied. In other words, our country Bharat once again should lift its head up in front of the whole world and, offering the message "I am Brahman" . . . teach the lesson of universal fraternity.][64]

The sweeping claims, expressed in short, repetitive, ringing phrases, summon the image of drum rolls accompanying a tremendous, ongoing march of people, with all the rhetorical force of a manifesto or a declaration of war. And indeed Pingale goes on to expound the familar theme of a divided Hindu society, weakened by centuries of Muslim rule and by discriminatory quotas and legislation instituted by vote-hungry politicians, at long last facing the prospect of unity and strength. Reunited and reinvigorated, it would hereafter emerge as winner in every struggle it encountered. The militancy and the Hindu supremacism of Pingale's rhetoric are unmistakable, the boldness of his claims breathtaking.

VHP Samagra Darshan (VHP: A Comprehensive View) begins its elaboration of the organization's activity with a discussion of *dharmacharyas* (spiritual teachers), and relies heavily on the mobilizing power of these traditional religious leaders to create their own base. The claim of the VHP to represent all of Hindu society is mediated and reinforced through the image of saffron-clad renouncers: since these gurus have always been Hindus' spiritual leaders, it is claimed, their union under the aegis of the VHP clearly demonstrates the representative nature of the organization. By the same token, the mass membership is required to entrust and delegate power to the gurus, and to follow orders from them.[65] Such a requirement is not imposed on the membership of the VHP of America, although they do delegate power to the parent organization in a sense, by virtue of sending large amounts of money for VHP social service projects.[66] The *Dharam Sansads* or Parliaments of Religion that the VHP convenes periodically in India would be unlikely to exert the same kind of authority in the U.S. The first *Sansad*, held in New Delhi in 1984, brought together 558 religious preachers from seventy-six different sects. In the U.S., the appearance of swamis tends to be on an individual rather than a collective basis, helping, for instance, to create an evening of Hindu experience. Any suggestion that decision-making power be delegated to them is likely to be considered extraordinary.

More secularized messages are seen as appealing to English-educated professionals in the U.S., as this representative statement of the VHP of America suggests:

Parishad is the International organization of Hindus, which has branches in many countries. All these sister organizations cherish the same Hindu ideal of Unity and exhibit the same Concern for the Welfare of the Humanity [*sic*]. Dedicated Parishad members practice the highest Hindu ideal of World is a one Family [*sic*] – *Vasudhaiva Kutumbakam* . . . Parishad promotes sincere practice of the time tested Hindu cultural and spiritual values, so we can enrich the American society [*sic*]. They drive [*sic*] an eternal inspiration through a live Contact with Mother Bharat . . . Platform of the Parishad provides expression to concerns like preserving rich spiritual, cultural Hindu heritage and creating positive identity and confidence in the Children . . . Parishad invites the serious minded leaders of American society to join hands in enhancing a better understanding.[67]

The VHP's goal of social and political organization of Hindus in India is replaced here by more abstract, humanitarian concerns. The stated aim is to contribute to the host society, but with a reminder of the VHP's far-flung concerns. The emphasis on creating confidence in children suggests that the "rich cultural heritage" by itself is inadequate for this purpose, and hints at the minority status that the second generation has to overcome. The familiar VHP declaration of the world as one family takes on a different meaning in this context: it is not the condescension of a majority community towards its inferiors, but the appeal of one more precariously situated, and requesting "serious minded" leaders to hear them out. Although Mother Bharat is invoked, the basis of the appeal is the organization's engagement with American society, albeit through the medium of Hindu values.

Dr. Yashpal Lakra, president of the VHP of America, explained the orientation to American values as natural and expressive of a deep affinity: "American justice and equality is almost identical with the way we think. If you think of the Bill of Rights, or of Jefferson's thinking, it is so akin to the Vedantic way of thinking." Whereas Islamic countries united legal and religious authority, in the U.S., the Constitution was not a Christian one, he pointed out. This was anticipated in Hindu thought, with its universalism and tolerance.[68] In this understanding, characteristic of Hindu nationalist argument, Hindu thought had the power both to assert and deny its existence at the same time, to be religious and secular at once. The celebration of American pluralism was thus implied to be really an observance of Hindu tradition, with the kind of conundrum beloved of RSS dialecticians. The abstract character of these assertions suited the VHP's U.S.-based constituents, for whom India was more palatable as idea than as reality: "Every time they go to India," Dr Lakra said, "they feel disgusted – they see the dirty streets and the dirty bathrooms. They don't want to identify with India. But they can take pride in Hindutva." Hindutva was offered as a substitute for India, then, with the VHP screening out issues deemed inappropriate for one reason or another.

Thus while support for the Ram temple in Ayodhya was sought, with ceremonies consecrating shilas or "sacred bricks" taking place in thirty-one cities in the U.S., the VHP's support for the promotion of indigenous companies over multinationals found no mention in the U.S. The *swadeshi* agitation to protest the presence of foreign companies in non-essential areas, given an uncertain endorsement by the BJP, but popular with VHP constituents in India, represented a powerful current of economic nationalism, but one that found little favor with Indians in the U.S., who tended to support liberalization.[69] A consistent Hindu nationalist position would have implied support for swadeshi politics; the VHP prefered to emphasize those issues that resonated in the context of the U.S., which led to a more selective choice of issues. If those in the subcontinent were impelled to live in India as it was, those abroad were free instead to imagine it as it might have been.

Hindu nationalism articulated a genteel multiculturalist presence in the U.S. with militant supremacism in India. The VHP of America

trumpeted Hindu culture as both a contribution to America's multiculturalist experiments and as an example of successful multiculturalism in
itself. This helped raise funds and secure prestige for the movement in
India. Those who supported the VHP in the U.S. might think of the
largely urban lower middle-class membership of the VHP in India as a
reservoir of Hindu nationalist sentiment that authorized their own. But
the differences could be enormous. Whereas family-based programs
were central to the VHP of America, in literature on the VHP in India
there was relatively little discussion of the family in India, given its
absence on the list of "social problems" current in India. The VHP of
America's professions of women's equality contrasted strikingly with the
VHP of India's denunciations of abortion and birth control as "insults to
motherhood."[70] The All India Women's Conference held by the VHP
in New Delhi in 1994 represented its belated attempt to address
"women's issues," and such initiatives are nascent. Celibate men and
women occupied most of the important positions in the VHP, harking
back to the Hindu right's notion of an ascetic (then exclusively male)
priesthood of nationalist fighters.[71] Similarly, Indian participants in
VHP-staged protests against GATT and multinational companies
might be surprised to know, for instance, that the VHP of America sees
no contradiction in emphasizing its loyalty to the U.S., and that its
members view GATT as part of a welcome process of liberalization. For
those in India, the VHP of America operated rather as a sign of the
VHP's far-flung reach, of the durability of "Hinduness" even amidst the
seductions of the West, and, not least of all, as a welcome source of a
strong currency.

Hindu nationalism, in its expatriate and indigenous forms, manifested a whole chain of differences constitutive of its collective organization. Indian immigrants' assertion of Indian/Hindu identity were
indissociable from their experience of racial marginalization in the
U.S.[72] They could have substituted religion for race, but regional and
national loyalties were usually still salient. In any case, they tended to
form syncretist organizations to enable both therapeutic enactments of
belonging and sites for the acculturation of their children as well.[73] The
politics they espoused centered on concerns in their new location even
when looking homewards with an aggressive Hindu nationalism. Second generation Indians in the U.S. for their part forged ways of "inte-
grating" into white-dominant society that could be answered by the
VHP's Hindu emphasis. They may have assumed the first generation's
political attitudes; at the same time, and perhaps more importantly, they

aspired to a culturally congenial way of asserting identity while avoiding the issue of race. Finally there was a much wider spectrum of people in India, who despite their militant, nationalist, and anti-U.S. politics, were likely to sense an affirmation of their politics from international support and certainly from international financial assistance.

The term "Hindu" itself thus enfolded a striking array of uses. We might say that it was more overtly aggressive and aspiring to hegemony in India, and more explicitly cultural and syncretic in the U.S. In fact, the distribution was not so neat. The meanings of "Hinduness" that were in dominance in India were political, although there were a number of other expressions it took, residual and emergent both, that were at variance with those political meanings. Residual meanings included older devotional and spiritual understandings of the term, and newer connotations taken on by the word encompassed more fluid and shifting identities based on consumption practices. In the U.S., those aspects of being "Hindu" that were predominant were, I suggest, more ecumenical, even if resonances of distinction and exclusiveness were their inseparable subtext. Seen in this way, the significance of Hinduness in one context appeared as a constitutive counterpoint to its significance in the other. If the word Hindu absorbed these multiple meanings into itself, its power and mystery increased rather than diminished, as the range and diversity of its effects testified.[74]

The transnational circuits of "Hindu nationalism" are a salutary reminder of the scope and variety of what is now called "globalization." With increased flow of information, centers of financial and political power that earlier would have been obscure to peripheral regions of control are now visible and more intelligible – or so those optimistic about globalization argue.[75] Viewed thus, "the global" becomes an autonomous level of analysis situated at the cutting edge of history, and the significance of the "local" is perceived only where circuits of global "flows" are interrupted.[76] Against this view, I would argue that complete transparency does not result, nor does universal homogenization follow, from increased transnational flows. While the image of "flow" highlights the fluidity of the processes involved, what it refers to is a series of symbolic translations across diverse locations rather than mechanistic movement along inert channels of passage.

The emphasis on translation highlights the irreducibly cultural character of transnational circuits of exchange. Those in some segments may be unaware of the surplus accrued in other segments from "goods" they help produce or circulate. Even when they are, their "awareness" may express locally rooted understandings whose "translation" into other segments preserves a certain incompleteness. Links of opaqueness as well as of transparency articulate disparate contexts in a global network of exchange. When people are restricted, however, cultures will always remain more local than global. Those favorably positioned in transnational networks may utilize the disjunctures represented in such circuits, thereby reinforcing structures of uneven economic and social development. Elucidating these new modes of mobilization is preliminary to developing creative political responses to them.

Conclusion

Former Prime Minister V. P. Singh, deriding the Hindu nationalist Bharatiya Janata Party in an April 1991 campaign speech, said, "Who are you to give us Ram? He belongs to all of us. Have you become Ram's sole agent? Have you made him a party member?"[1] V. P. Singh put his finger on the strategic nature of the Hindutva program, and the extent to which it was an advantage that belonged to the first-comer. Once this advantage had been seized, however, it changed the context for other political parties. Opposed as V. P. Singh may have been to the BJP, he could only argue that other parties too could claim Ram. If he protested against the BJP's presumption in "giving" Ram to the people, this only registered that the identification between deity and party had succeeded, at some level.

I have suggested that the growth of Hindu nationalism took place at a specific historical moment: the hiatus between a long period of Indian National Congress hegemony and an emerging dispensation characterized by the importance of the non-committed vote, and a newly salient "split public." There was the expectation that a "national party," one with a more or less countrywide base, would succeed the Congress. As a political party, the BJP had arisen in the shadow of the Congress Party, and for a long time had accepted its marginal role in Indian politics. Accordingly, the BJP, like its predecessor the Jan Sangh, served mainly to articulate the interests of the small town trading and professional classes who tended to be marginalized in the developmental plans of the Congress. It was only from the late 1980s onwards that the BJP came to express a national vision, designed consciously as an alternative to the Congress, and thus presenting itself as a possible successor to it. This was a new development, emerging in important respects against the past of the Hindu nationalists.

This political situation crystallized in conjunction with economic liberalization, in which state controls on economic growth were held

responsible for what the business-dominated press and Hindu nationalists perceived as a sense of national failure. The private sector's own
inability to become competitive after four decades of protection and
subsidies was exonerated in the process. Instead, business classes and the
people as a whole came to be positioned together as victims of a
misconceived political arrangement, now dubbed "Nehruvianism."
The BJP's claims of a new and triumphant nationalism seemed plausible
to middle and business classes seeking a viable political vehicle for their
ascendant fortunes. A party that had scarcely ever occupied office (the
1975–77 Janata government being its only substantive experience at the
center) appeared to them to be untainted by the Congress's post-
independence record. And the aggressive ideology of Hindutva resonated well with the harsh view the rich and the aspiring classes expressed
of how the nation should develop.

By the 1990s, Nehruvianism amounted to a set of principles observed
largely in the breach rather than an active working policy. Presenting it
as a symbol of moribund domination, the BJP sought to restructure the
existing political language to summon a new arena where it would
occupy center stage. It appeared as if the economy had acquired a
metaphorical status and could signal the prosperity or malaise of society
as a whole. Meanwhile, it was the sphere of culture whose deficiencies
could be precisely calibrated, it seemed, where social intervention could
be productive, directing people to adopt the most appropriate kinds of
behavior and thought.

In this environment, I have argued, Hindu nationalism participated
in a new currency of images, building on possibilities that arose in the
wake of economic liberalization and national television. If the Congress
Party used television to consolidate its Hindu vote and to profit from a
growing consumer market, Hindu nationalists deftly joined both efforts,
and in the process strengthened the relationship between politics and
Hindu identity. In this effort, the growth of audio-visual and print
media, and the increased production and distribution of consumer
goods in their wake, made possible a host of new recruiting methods.
Using these new avenues of communication also meant, however, that
the kind of political space the Hindu nationalists crafted was not necessarily the primordial space of the Hindu community projected in much
of their rhetoric.

The crucial term in nationalism's restructured political language was
"Hindutva," meant to exemplify the singular truth of the nation, long
covered over due to the fear of alien rulers and the compromises of weak

politicians. The Birthplace of Ram movement insisted on the right of the Hindu majority to demolish a mosque in the name of Lord Ram, and to erect a temple in its place. This act of creative destruction would unite a fragmented nation, the BJP claimed, and re-establish the greatness of a now-humiliated people. The impression of a nation united and unconquerable was a crucial aspect of Hindutva's force. The BJP's "battering Ram" approach understood political power to follow from a kind of property right in religious identity, asserted through public participation and consumption. What this indicated was a general expansion of the range of instrumentalities for political assertion, even as the particular modes chosen sought to narrow the available public space. But the very breadth of the appeal could undo its advantage, as other claims on Ram surfaced, and the arbitrariness of the initial ploy became evident.

The self-conscious use of symbolism involved in the Ram Janmabhumi campaign did not mean that it was simply a manipulated event. A range of issues condensed to form a broad-based movement, as I have argued, although its leaders kept it rigidly focused on advancing a more limited agendum of winning electoral power. Perceiving it merely as a degradation of politics is mistaken, although the Ram temple movement was undoubtedly violent and destructive. Rather, it signaled a new phase of politics, wherein a different relationship between communication and public participation was made possible by three factors: the growth of new media; the expansion of the market; and the legitimation crisis of political authority. The Hindu nationalists' mission was opportunistically refashioned to make use of all three factors. In the Ram Janmabhumi issue, the BJP found a set of symbols to dramatize the availability of new modes of popular expression, capitalizing on the Congress's reluctance to challenge it head-on, and so generating a seemingly unstoppable momentum in its own favor.

Despite the apparent binding power of Hindutva, there was no simple unity that participants in the Ram Janmabhumi movement as a whole could be self-conscious about. The mobilization represented a careful coordination of diverse strands of activities designed to maximize support across different social groups. Hindu nationalists saw their own effort as one of bringing the uneducated and the unpoliticized into the national mainstream through an instrumental use of religion, although they themselves accused their political opposition of subordinating religion to worldly ends. As an ideology of cultural unity under a strong state, Hindutva offered private industry the prospect of a pro-business regime with firm labor discipline, while preparing the nation for its long-deferred greatness. As a militant anti-Muslim program, it cemented together sections from the backward and upper castes by a program of aggression and hatred towards an increasingly endangered minority. As a utopian and nostalgic vision, it galvanized rural and small town populations, long deprived of a nationally intelligible language with which to make their political frustrations heard. For the most politically indifferent, it offered the simplest and most unexceptionable of challenges: to right a historic "wrong," and to honor Lord Ram with a temple. Detailing the various parts of Hindu nationalism, I have thus sought to engage with Hindutva as a contradictory and internally inconsistent phenomenon rather than taking literally its monolithic claims of strength.

In the assembly elections of November 1993, the limited caste basis of the BJP's support base was exposed. Backward Class swing votes, polarized by the debates around the Mandal Commission's reservations award, moved out of the BJP's electoral coalition. Lower castes began to assert themselves in numbers that changed the balance of power decisively in north India. The BJP had claimed to be a national party, but stood revealed as still a regional party with national ambitions, ready to forge alliances with the most ideologically diverse partners, including the lower caste Bahujan Samaj Party (Party of the Majority) in U.P. and the left-of-center Samata Sanghathan (Equality Party) in Bihar. Eventually, the chief legacy of the Hindu nationalists may have been not upper-caste domination so much as the introduction of methods that helped politicize such domination. What emerged was an era of more competitive politics and more fluid electoral alignments, and the realization that no single party could any longer dominate the country.

The BJP's attempt to establish sovereignty thus resulted, paradoxically, in the implosion of their claims about an undivided Hindu national family. For the time being at least, in the words of V. P. Singh, "nation is coalition." The Hindu vote has splintered between numerous parties; at the same time the BJP itself shows the stresses of its rapid expansion. Thus backward-caste sections of the party have broken away to form a separate party in Gujarat, and are at loggerheads with its upper-caste segment in Uttar Pradesh, to take only the two most prominent examples.[2] The BJP's strategy of allying with strong regional opponents of the Congress Party, as in Tamil Nadu and in West Bengal, serves the short-term purpose of defeating electoral rivals at the state level, but undermines its claims of ideological coherence, and opens itself to political contestation.[3] If part of the BJP's appeal during the Ram temple campaign had been the sense that it was a relatively untested product,[4] it increasingly takes on the familiar shades of other political parties, faction-ridden, unable to deliver on promises or secure effective governance, and unlikely to inspire deep commitment.

After it finally occupied office for a relatively extended period beginning in March 1998, the BJP showed itself to be far weaker than its aggressive political postures might have suggested. It has proven incapable of keeping its coalition partners in line, ready to abandon its political positions in order to ensure a longer lease of life in office, and unable to define the political field in terms of its own professed ideology. In the immediate aftermath of its ascent, we could observe an inability to negotiate a position and sustain it against the opposition of other parties. Instead the party appeared to take non-negotiable stances, and to engage in unilateral attempts to shift prevailing agenda, either by bureaucratic fiat or by force.[5] Failing this, it enacted the most opportunistic forms of bargaining and the most abject capitulation in order to stay in power.[6] On the whole, the weak and vacillating character of the BJP and its leaders' inability to command their own followers dispelled the image of a forceful party about to put its stamp on history.

Nevertheless, the Hindu nationalist campaign's disintegration products themselves have an extended half-life, and themes of Hindutva infuse into more and more spheres of life even as its sponsors' credibility wavers. That is, if the efforts of the BJP and its allies have had only a partial and uncertain effect in the political field, it is in the social and cultural realms that their influence continues to grow and develop.[7] This can be witnessed at regional, national, and international levels of practice. At the regional level, the caste-based composition of political opposition clearly leaves room open for the more expansive political vision of Hindu nationalism, endowed as it is with myths and customs that, after all, for centuries have served to encompass the most glaring inequalities. The upwardly mobile aspirations of scheduled and backward castes may be advanced by lower-caste coalitions, but the hegemony of upper-caste ideologies, although contested, cannot vanish so soon. The relative nascency of lower-caste political formations in the north, and their greater dependence on a smaller base of leadership, as against the Hindu nationalists' own relative experience and their reserves of cadre strength at the grassroots parties, contribute to Hindutva's continuing ability to strike up coalitions at this level. Nationally, the persistence of Hindutva is a symptom of the political vacuum at the center following the decline of the Congress and its ethos of secular developmentalism. Finally, Hindu nationalism may emanate from the sense of affirmation Indian professional classes experience as they embrace the opportunities flowing from transnational agencies eager to capitalize on a newly exposed domestic market. It may also operate in more cynical fashion, as Hindutva's excess of patriotic rhetoric helps compensate for the lack of safeguards against foreign exploitation, and the ascent of the *swadeshi* party signals only the descent into all-out freebooting.[8]

Hindsight permits the luxury of asking why the contradictions within the Hindu nationalist camp were not more clearly perceived before, and how the projection of a monolithic threat could have been sustained for so long. The emergence of Hindu nationalist politics in the 1980s and 1990s was typically described by critics in terms of a degeneration of an erstwhile secular dispensation, and the abandonment of responsible political behavior, not only by politicians but also by large sections of voters as they allowed themselves to be swayed by communal sentiments. The lengthy moratorium on politics outside the fold of the Nehruvian state and the dominant electoral parties predisposed elites to perceive new political issues as threats to order rather than as challenges to their understanding. In any case, the failure to perceive the many levels at which Hindu nationalism simultaneously operated, that were below and beyond the domain of politics per se, e.g., social, cultural, and religious propaganda, would have made any merely political response inadequate. In this process, the instigation of communal riots to polarize society and to define the Hindu–Muslim axis as a life or death question was a powerful means of sealing the interpretive gaps in Hindu nationalist rhetoric. As more and more riots provoked a widespread demand to impose law and order, it became even harder to see through the confusion deliberately cultivated as a means of political advancement.

Against the cries of Hindu fundamentalism, BJP leader L. K. Advani's disclosure of his party's attempt to woo the "non-committed vote" indicated a different conception of this phenomenon, one marked by a widening of the electoral space and a new awareness and deliberation on the part of voters.[9] Relating the BJP's growth to this new set of opportunities, he pointed to the judicious exploitation of voter psychology, while capitalizing on the Congress's weakness. In a climate of electoral uncertainty, Advani indicated the importance of choosing a winner over seeking a convincing or even a substantially different political vision. Far from auguring an unreconstructed subcontinental version of German fascism, the BJP was, in its own way, tapping into the newly mobile affiliations of voters, and had to plan for the possibility that these votes could swing out of its camp just as easily as they swung in.

If the era of Nehruvianism witnessed a national consensus on economic development, liberalization too was advanced in a similar fashion, with a surprising amount of unanimity across political parties, and with little debate despite its negative consequences. If Hindu nationalists subsequently excoriated Nehruvianism for its elitism, the irony is that they helped usher in an era of more arbitrary and authoritarian state policy, although in fact politics drew closer to popular aspiration in language if not in substance: by all accounts, a process of democratization and political decentralization was set in motion. This paradox, unexplained in most accounts of the process, can only be understood, I suggest, if we consider the means by which nationalism gained ascendancy, in its reliance on media and markets, and more broadly in new methods of political mobilization. The significance of this contradiction, I have argued, goes beyond the rise or fall of different political parties, and signals the reconfiguration of politics following the institution of a new mode of communication, specifically, television.

HOW HAS TELEVISION CHANGED THE CONTEXT OF POLITICS IN INDIA?

I have referred to the distinctive effect of television, bringing together two flows of time, the time of the image and the time of viewing, in one communicative event. Although a commercial institution, television produces the effect of a free and unconditional viewing experience, and insinuates a sense of costless social intimacy: the presence of a stream of ongoing communication lends itself to viewers' imaginative participation without necessarily enfolding them in networks of dependence. Audiences may thus enjoy watching even if they are critical of the content. Thus, although Doordarshan was a state-controlled monopoly, viewers who were often critical of the government nevertheless spoke approvingly of it. "It lightens the burden of the heart," said Rai Singh, a telephone lineman. "We go to the TV and 'open' it [*sic*]. It lightens our mental load."[10]

The perception of autonomy and of social affirmation is made available in the private space of media reception, and allows viewers to craft a distinct sense of personal sovereignty. This perception of sovereignty is not reducible to capitalist alienation. It belongs, rather, to a different if related systemic logic, that of the gift in its idealized sense, of unalloyed reciprocity and undemanding affirmation. At the same time, the ability to discreetly participate in a process of communication, without encountering the surveillance customary in social interaction, can provide a vantage point for critical reflection on society as a whole. It is through such experiences of autonomy allowed for by media reception that new political subjects may be made.

How these effects unfold in practice is uncertain, requiring investigation and careful historical contextualization. Doordarshan's creation of the mythological soap opera, incorporating many features of the developmental soap opera form that preceded it, turned out to be the genre form instrumental in crystallizing a distinct Indian televisual culture, and in amassing audiences that transcended the class limitations of a hitherto largely urban television audience. Choosing to violate a secularist taboo and broadcast a Hindu serial was only one of the Congress's many ineffectual attempts to address its crisis of legitimacy and widen its support-base, identifying itself with the glories of a mythical kingdom. In the event, the BJP was already identified with Hindu symbolism and hence in a much better position to make use of it.

The Ramayan serial served as a kind of flash point or moment of condensation, signaling a crisis of politics already evidenced in other ways, and offering audiences a familiar medium in which to share their perceptions. The telecast allowed deep divisions across society to be overlooked as viewers tuned in simultaneously to a narrative that, although in many ways new, claimed epic status. Audiences could conceive of the absence of a lost utopia, wherein a fantastic spirit of self-sacrifice made divisions of power and status irrelevant. This shared experience inserted into the spaces of daily life-images of a golden age that Hindu nationalism argued could be re-created, given sufficient political will. The private space of reception permitted critical reflection on these conceptions of the collectivity, drawing on metaphors and idioms that evoked wide identification.

Against an imagined oneness that reached across society, the print media spoke to audiences divided by language and culture. It was the more market-sensitive press, divided by language and stratified by class, that was crucial in making audience criticisms salient, while filtering them through media that were split between Hindi and English language presses. Carefully orchestrated plans of mass mobilization, united through image, rhetoric, and performance, gave decisive shape and focus to these expressions, resurrecting an old property dispute to extraordinary effect. Finally, global networks of Hindutva were important not only in generating capital and organizational resources, but also in helping catalyze the formation of mobilizational themes and imagery, which, in many ways, indigenous Hindu communities were too divided to inspire.

Retail Hindutva was manifest not only in the range of consumer objects made available to new supporters of Hindu nationalism, but also in the variety of consumption styles and the range of modes of aesthetic appropriation possible. It pointed to a greater energy and investment in securing popular participation. Its counterpart however was a greater confusion and violence in the public sphere, due both to the greater volume of participation and also to the more authoritarian character of state intervention, the latter itself partly justified by the former. The increase in popular participation reflected the chaos accompanying the enlargement of mass media reach, and its attendant reformulation of the relationship between political power and communication. Simultaneously this was accompanied by attempts to pre-empt germinating popular forces as their presence expanded in the public realm. The Ram Janmabhumi movement was an example of these countervailing tendencies, of popular expression and political containment.

Against the complex and unpredictable linkages I have detailed here, it should be noted that media studies typically treat audience accounts as the end point of their inquiry, assuming that theoretical elaboration should suffice to explain how these accounts fit together in a larger picture. As a result, scholars have tended to leave the contingency of media effects unexamined and unexplained in most critical arguments. Readings of texts or of audience response tend to be inserted into a prefabricated historical background, imported from already existing accounts, so that the crucial questions of how mediation occurs, between institution, text, and the wider context, are assumed or ignored. In failing to address these questions, the critical transformations actually wrought in the wake of the media tend to be missed, since they are theorized at a relatively high level of abstraction.

The extent to which Hindu nationalism expands its support base by a new and historically looser set of identifications, themselves built on a series of structured misperceptions, is missed in such abstract accounts. Or, if Hindutva is understood simply as a resurgence of popular expression accompanying mass media expansion, again; the internal incoherence of this support, expressed in my argument about multiple mediation through a split public, cannot be understood. Thus if, as some have argued, Hindutva is, *tout court*, the local face of globaliz-ation,[11] the reasons why it might at some point cease to be so elude such explanatory frameworks.

It is hazardous to try and predict how future political alignments may develop and what consequences might ensue from new configurations. It can be pointed out that following its ascent to power in 1998, BJP-led rule has been marked by gruesome carnage against underprivileged minorities, this time lower-caste and tribal Christians.[12] On the other hand, the level of communal violence under a BJP government has been substantially lower than that under the Congress, a party that continues to describe itself as the leading secular party. What this means, I suggest, is that the BJP still seeks to groom and cultivate its ideological rank and file, which remains its chief asset in relation to other parties. Violence, unfortunately, appears to be the swiftest and surest way to retain the loyalties of a cadre whose commitment could not otherwise endure their leaders' compromises. At the same time, the public posture of the party grows more cautious and reticent, more ostensibly inclusive and still dependent on a highly volatile and shifting base of non-committed voters. Here we can see the reflection of the party's political weakness against its continued and growing cultural acceptability. This contradic-tion takes expression in an increasingly instrumental use of Hindutva, as a rhetoric of religio-cultural triumphalism shielding a more blatantly unequal political dispensation. For the present, such a contradiction encapsulates the post-televisual character of Indian politics.

Thus the nuclear tests commissioned by the BJP in May 1998, only two months into office, seemed to function as a kind of technological quick fix, to lift a poor developing nation into the company of the world's leading powers. It was celebrated by Hindu nationalist activists as a return to a golden age of Vedic missile power, although with Pakistan rapidly following suit with its own nuclear tests, the BJP put a question mark against its own nationalist ambitions by reducing India to strategic parity with a country a fraction of its size. The week following the nuclear explosions, the Cabinet promptly passed central govern-ment counter-guarantees for four fast-track power projects in different states, assuring high returns to foreign investors even in the case of rupee depreciation. Simultaneously, a number of oil-exploration contracts and mining concessions were also awarded, mostly to U.S.-based com-panies. Shortly thereafter, the Exim Policy ushered in a substantial liberalization of consumer goods imports, which was surprising in the context of a substantial trade deficit and domestic recession. Finally, two hotly debated bills, relating to the Patents Act and to opening up the insurance sector to domestic and foreign business, were pushed through Parliament.[13] Taken together, the economic policy measures starkly contradicted the BJP's own stated pre-election position of "calibrated globalization," and served as an instructive complement to the party's nuclear posturing.

The new language of politics fashioned by Hindu nationalism was meant to be accessible beyond elites, restructuring the forms of public affiliation through a logic of commodification and thereby working around the contradictions of caste. Today, Hindu imagery circulates with a volume and velocity never witnessed before, and the BJP itself hovers around the center of the national stage, even if it does not dominate politics. If the large-scale entry of religion into national electoral politics represented the breaking of a powerful taboo, the shock of its arrival has dulled. Now it is in the consumer market that such imagery is most visibly present. If the BJP exaggerated the political consensus represented by popular acceptance of its temple campaign, themes of Hindu identity, in diluted form, have found a renewed presence in mass-mediated popular culture. Given the inability of a political consensus to form itself in the contemporary context, and the presence of interests too varied and too far apart to be bridged given the prevailing social forces, the excess mobilized by the BJP finds its way into civil society, to reside as a more thickly culturalized presence. Here it offers something like a compensation for the decline of older forms of public identity and armor against the increasing discontents of the political sphere.

An earlier vision of development foresaw the coming to self-consciousness of Indians who would discriminatingly draw from native traditions while building an independent society capable of taking on the West. Claims to an autonomous economy had of course to be qualified with liberalization, amidst the reliance on foreign capital and know-how, and the transformation of Indian businesses into the subsidiary branches of global enterprise. But even as structural reform and an increasingly open economy assure a dependent status for the country, nationalist pride reappears, albeit in more casual guise. If the Hindu nationalists advanced through market mechanisms, now the market itself advances through a greater sensitivity to the particularities of Indian culture, long neglected by businesses whose limitations of imagination reflected the then prevailing political consensus. Indigenous images offer new sources of meaning/value for businesses seeking to expand markets into previously untapped areas. They herald change, and simultaneously seek to address popular ambivalence towards change by providing reassurance of cultural continuity. New consumer identities are fashioned, championing local cultures and presenting the nation as coming into its own, paradoxically, amidst globalization.

If Hindu nationalism's cultural propaganda was in excess of what it could realize in terms of its political accomplishments, it was perhaps in the market that this propaganda took effect, albeit in diluted form, instanced in the kinds of appeals used to advance the sale of consumer goods. Indian business had grown in a protected economy, and operated with a limited conception of its market in terms of class and culture. Business's efforts were directed chiefly at creating an aesthetic for the consumption practices of the middle and upper classes; for the rest, the majority of the population, utility was favored over aesthetics. This was reflected, e.g., in the relatively slight expenditure on the promotion of goods for low-income consumers. Little effort was made to research and develop themes of indigenous or national culture as in themselves markers of product difference; multinationals, for their part, were not anxious to draw attention to their foreign origins either. In sum, businesses created an image of the market that, as could be expected, reflected the prevailing political and cultural balance of forces.

Hindu nationalism was critical in shifting this balance, cultivating as it did the vernacular language media, and emphasizing the alienness of a secular, English-speaking elite, and their hostility to popular faith. Although their intent was sectarian and anti-democratic, their thrust was effectively to make available a self-conscious popular aesthetic outside the realm of religion itself, where previously little effort had been exercised for the purpose.

Meanwhile the culture of an expanding market exercises its own influence on politics. Recall Hindu nationalist leader Pramod Mahajan's comment, signaling the nexus between marketing and political mobilization thus: "I think it is time we stopped shying away from words such as 'sell.' We must realize there has been a major revolution in communication." This points not only to the rise of market forces, but also to the metaphorical nature of the market, which now shapes the ways in which individuals conceive and assess choices. Markets also increasingly provide the terms in which politicians understand their constituents, who are rendered into audiences of the spectacle of politics. The relation between political authority and citizens simultaneously becomes more contractual and more coercive, as the demands of the economy predominate over earlier conceptions of the national good, thought to be achieved through state-led development. Politics increasingly becomes polarized between the assertion of individualized styles of enjoyment and self-expression on the one hand, and a more authoritarian character of rule on the other. Accompanying the shift towards a more technocratic understanding of politics was a greater self-consciousness about the means of politics. This process, in turn, promoted an increased awareness about culture itself, and about the hitherto taken-for-granted character of the symbols and practices comprising daily life.

Even in the absence of a Hindu nationalist domination then, we may have in India a Hinduized visual regime, evidenced for example in commodity consumption in daily life, acting as a kind of lower order claim than national identity and continuing to have a force in politics, albeit of a more dispersed, subtle, and less confrontational kind, in a kind of capacitance effect whereby social energy may be accumulated and stored via the allegiance to such images, to be put to use at some future moment, although in ways that would be hard to predict. The greater presence of consumption and of commodity images in public life as an aspect of larger political equations calls to mind a remark by Goebbels in one of his early writings, that politics is the plastic art of the state.[14] The possibilities and implications of the plastic arts, as Benjamin noted, increase tremendously with new reproductive technologies. At the same time, the politics that grow out of an aestheticized rather than a merely utilitarian approach assist in a mutation of the methods of political control, shifting away from massive state structures towards more decentralized forms. As individuals are exposed to the vagaries of the world market without the minimal buffers strong states used to be able to provide, an explosion of political conflict ensues, as different groups struggle to define new terms of identification and alignment. As earlier sources of authority become more and more difficult to sustain, what the ethical reference points of the new forms of politics will be remains to be determined.

Background to the Babri Masjid dispute

On 2 February 1986, then-Prime Minister Rajiv Gandhi, speaking on the occasion of Pope John Paul II's visit to New Delhi, declared, "India, a land of religion, believes in according equal reverence and respect to all faiths."[1] What the Pope understood from his words may not have been quite what Rajiv Gandhi had in mind. The latter had just completed a remarkable exercise in the practice of religious equality, placating the demand of a group of influential, conservative Hindus, to counterbalance a favor he had granted orthodox Muslim opinion the previous year.

Only the previous day, an extraordinary court judgment had been passed at his government's behest, favouring a Hindu rights lobby. Justice Krishna Mohan Pandey's judgment in Faizabad District Court declared the unrestricted right of worship for Hindus at a *mosque*, the Babri Masjid in Ayodhya. The judgment was passed with scarcely any comment on the voluminous litigation on the issue. For decades, Muslims had protested the encroachment of Hindu idols in their mosque, and against the closure of the structure. A year ago Gandhi had, with an Act of Parliament, over-ruled the Supreme Court's decision to order alimony payments for a divorced Muslim woman, Shah Bano. The Muslim community itself would decide on such matters hereafter, according to the Muslim Women's Bill that was passed. The decision created an unprecedented storm of controversy around issues of minority rights, and the political character of favors granted minority communities.[2] One favor for the Muslims, followed by one for the Hindus – equal reverence for both religions, in Rajiv Gandhi's distinctive understanding. This curious formula assumed the ability of the state to act as supreme arbiter while religious communities waited in line, a conception dangerously out of touch with the tempests of real politics, as Gandhi would soon find out. According to his former Home Minister, Arun Nehru, Rajiv Gandhi had, at the time, explained the sequence of his decisions as "tit for tat."[3] Subsequently, Arun Nehru himself accepted responsibility for the event, and the then-U.P. Chief Minister Vir Bahadur Singh was reportedly involved as well.[4] In any event, this was a move by the Congress Party, and only one of many bids it would make for its diminishing share of the "Hindu vote."

The process by which an obscure mosque in a relatively unimportant pilgrimage town became subject to the machinations of central ministers was hardly a straightforward one. From all indications, none of the movement's promoters had any inkling of the enormous power of the Ram Janmabhumi issue. It started out as a limited issue, *Tala Kholo Andolan* (Open the Locks Agitation), and an affair exclusively of the VHP. There were other issues that appeared far more important to the Hindu nationalists. Palliative measures aimed at lower castes occupied a central place in its efforts to win recruits. The numerous subsidiary organizations of the sangh performed various kinds of social services for underprivileged caste groups, to dissuade them from a confrontational approach to upper castes and win them over to the sangh. After the conversion of about fifty Dalits to Islam in Meenakshipuram, Tamil Nadu in 1980, such efforts were regarded as the cornerstone of the sangh's mission. Threats to the "integrity" of the nation in Assam, Kashmir, and Punjab, with separatist movements in each of those states, were the other main priorities. The Ayodhya issue was a relatively low-ranking one then, and in sangh literature was always mentioned alongside Benares and Mathura as but one of three holy towns "all Hindus" wished to "liberate." In each town there was a mosque that, Hindu nationalists alleged, encroached on a deity's birthplace, and so required demolition.

In Benares and in Mathura, the temples involved were major pilgrimage centers, drawing hundreds of thousands of pilgrims annually, and were part of an elaborate network of patronage relationships deeply rooted in those towns. For the RSS to politicize them in communal terms meant existing power structures would have had to be accommodated or overcome. Too much was at stake for existing, local vested interests to give way easily. Ayodhya was, in comparison a minor *teerth* (pilgrimage center) which had gained significance only in the eighteenth century. It drew fewer pilgrims from far-flung towns and cities than Benares or Mathura. Unlike Benares and Mathura, both of which had a mosque and a temple immediately adjacent to each other, on sites the Hindus claimed, the site in Ayodhya was occupied exclusively by a mosque, standing alone. And the symbol of

Ram itself, they would soon discover, was a mobilizing tool of enormous power.[5]

Adherents of the Ram Janmabhumi movement pointed to nineteenth-century British records, local legend, and Hindu elements in the mosque itself, in support of their claim that the mosque was built on the ruins of a grand Ram temple destroyed by Muslims. A widely circulated publicist arguing this was Justice Deoki Nandan Agrawal of the VHP, who in a pamphlet titled *Sri Ram Janmabhumi: Historical and Legal Evidence* (n.d.) swept aside any objections from those who might object to the centrality accorded Lord Ram: "Ram, Krishna and Shiva are the three deities worshipped by Hindus across the world, and all three symbolize our national aspiration of establishing Ramrajya," he wrote. With the attainment of Independence, and after the Partition of India, the country should have been declared a Hindu nation, but "large-hearted as we are," freedom of faith was allowed. However, the matter of Sri Ram Janmabhumi was one that was "a matter of National shame, and galling to the Hindu psyche." The "miscalled Babari Masjid" was not a mosque, he stated, as evidenced by the absence of minarets. Agrawal claimed to provide evidence that the building occupied the site of Ram's birthplace, while at the same time declaring that it was "an indisputable fact of history" and thus implicitly beyond a matter of evidence (p. 1). The temple was destroyed on the orders of the Mughal Emperor Babur, and a mosque built in its place in 1528, he claimed.

The VHP's claims became well-nigh the commonsense of a substantial section of the public by the early 1990s, by frequent repetition and all-too-scarce criticism. These claims involved several questionable assumptions. Firstly, the identification of present-day Ayodhya with the Ayodhya of the Ramayana was uncertain. The Buddhist city of Saketa, for instance, acquired the name of Ayodhya in the later Gupta period, and it was not certain the two referred to the same city. The claim that the Babri Masjid occupied the site of a Ram temple, most crucially, was at best uncertain. The most reliable source of evidence would have been archaeological, and while such evidence was offered in favor of Ram Janmabhumi, internal inconsistencies in the data and the lack of stratigraphical validity rendered these claims suspect at best.[6] Historical records during and following the period of the alleged demolition/construction (1528 C.E.) made no mention of any events relating to the claims. Virtually the entire corpus of textual evidence offered for the birthplace claim dated from the nineteenth century and relied on local legends, and were thus far from conclusive.

After the insurrection of 1857, such local legends increasingly began to be treated as fact by British chroniclers who found it convenient to affirm a systematic hostility between Hindus and Muslims. The source of these legends was unclear, but existing records of religious conflict in Ayodhya referred mainly to tension between Shaivite Sanyasins and Vaishnavite Bairagis. Hindu–Muslim conflict prior to the latter half of the nineteenth century centered on the Hanumangarhi temple, not on the Babri Masjid. A group of local Sunni Muslims charged in 1855 that the temple had replaced a mosque which had existed there earlier. The temple had been established by means of a grant from the Nawab of Avadh, Mansoor Ali. Subsequent investigations found that no mosque had existed there in the recent past, and that there may never have been one there. Nevertheless, a group of about 500 Muslims attacked in July 1855, to perform *namaaz* at the temple. The Bairagis, occupants of the temple, drew on local support of about 8,000 people, and turned back their attackers. They killed a large number of Muslims, followed the survivors to the Babri Masjid and captured it. No attempt was made to occupy the masjid, nor was any claim made on it, although accounts of the episode referred to it as the janmasthan (birthplace).[7]

The conflict over Hanumangarhi temple may have led to the spread of the Janmasthan story as a retaliatory exercise and as an attempt to check Muslim claims on the temple. The Nawab was considering building a mosque adjoining the temple to assuage the feelings of the Muslims, a move viewed with alarm by local Hindus.[8] At any rate, in 1857, following the Revolt, the head-priest of Hanumangarhi temple took over a part of the Babri Masjid compound and constructed a platform one hundred paces away from the mosque and to the east of it. Meanwhile Muslims prayed inside the mosque, entering from the north gate. Although a representative from the masjid filed a petition with the magistrate complaining of this encroachment, nothing appears to have been done about it. Similar petitions were filed in subsequent years. In 1885, permission was sought to construct a temple at the site of the *chabutra* (platform), which was described as the Chabutra Janmasthan. Citing objections from Muslims, the Deputy Commissioner of Faizabad dismissed the petition.

It was at this platform that worship was performed, and devotional songs sung, until the night of 22 December 1949. But in December 1949, an idol of the infant Ram in seated posture, Sri Ram Lalla Virajman, was forcibly installed by a group of fifty or sixty men who broke into the mosque. It was declared to be a miracle, and a Muslim constable's affidavit was produced to testify to the "flash of Divine Light" he saw inside the mosque before going into a trance, and awaking to find the idol installed and worship being performed. Although the issue of forcible dispossession of Muslim property was clear, and was stated before the courts, a series of complaisant judges overseen by a forgiving Congress state government, with Govind Ballabh Pant as Chief Minister, passed orders treating the idol's installation as a *fait accompli*. Muslim pleas that they were wrongfully being denied the right to worship at their own mosque were ignored. The property was placed in receivership, and Muslims were denied right of access to the mosque as a potential threat to the peace; Hindus were denied access as seemingly equal claimants to this privilege. The state abstained from filing any written statement in court declaring its stand, a situation that remained unchanged until the 1980s.

The issue was revived by a Congressman, Dau Dayal Khanna, Cabinet Minister from 1962–67 in Uttar Pradesh Chief Minister Chandrabhanu Gupta's government. He wrote a letter to then Prime Minister Indira Gandhi on 23 May 1983, demanding a solution to the "problems" of Ram Janmabhumi, Krishna Janmabhumi (in Mathura) and Kashi Vishwanath Mandir. He demanded that the "disputed sites" in these towns be returned to Hindus. In Nainital, Khanna held a meeting where he reiterated his demands. He contacted the RSS after this, and on 6 March 1984, a large general meeting was convened at which former Prime Minister Gulzarilal Nanda and Professor Rajendra Singh of the RSS were present. Khanna met with RSS chief Balasaheb Deoras also, and the RSS decided to support the cause at this time.[9]

On 19 December 1985, a high-level delegation from the VHP had met with then-U.P. Chief Minister Vir Bahadur Singh (Cong-I), threatening "grave problems" if the mosque was not unlocked by 8 March the following year. The delegation included two former high court judges and three top retired civil servants, all from the U.P. cadre.[10] Subsequently, the Ram Janmabhumi Sangharsh Samiti (People's Committee for the Restitution of Ram's Birthplace), formed two years earlier in 1984, gave the government a deadline of 8 March 1986. According to their ultimatum, if the lock on the mosque gates was not removed by then, they would break it themselves. This was conveyed by sadhus and sants comprising the Samiti on 19 January 1986 at Lucknow to Vir Bahadur Singh.

On 1 February 1986 the District Judge in Faizabad, Krishna Mohan Pandey, passed the order to have the locks on the Babri Masjid's inner courtyard gate opened after its having been sealed for thirty-six years, in response to a petition by advocate Umesh Chander Pandey. Litigants who had been involved in disputes over the mosque for decades were denied a hearing. The petitioner, in contrast, was not a party to any of the numerous suits pending in the case.[11] The application was first made on 28 January 1986, in the court of the Munsif of Faizabad, Harishankar Dubey. The Munsif had refused to hear the application without evaluating the court records, maintained at Lucknow. Pandey then appealed to the District Judge in Faizabad on 31 January. The order was passed the very next day and the mosque was opened within hours. Doordarshan television crews were at hand, and the opening was broadcast to a national audience.[12]

Both *The Indian Express* and *The Times of India* welcomed the verdict. According to an article in *The Times* the next day: "For centuries the local Muslims have *claimed* that the Ram Janma Bhumi is in fact the 'Babari Mosque,' named after the first Mughal invader who established a dynasty. *However*, the predominant Hindu majority has been *asserting* that this was originally the site of a 9-storey temple which was desecrated by the fanatic Muslim emperor who ordered a domed mosque to be raised in its place in a show of imperial arrogance [*sic*]" (emphasis added).[13]

In a contentious judgment, the District Judge reduced the entire communal dispute to the issue of "security," not of the legal property of the Wakf Board, or of Hindu–Muslim relations, but of the idols. No document on record existed under which the locks were placed, he declared, and there were other means of maintaining order, such as an armed police guard. The locks were declared to be "an unnecessary irritant to the applicant and other members of the community," and an "artificial barrier between the idols and the devotees." It was clear that "the members of the other community" (i.e., Muslims) were not going to be affected "by any stretch of the imagination" if Hindus worshipped at the mosque (described as "the premises" in deference to the Hindu right's view that the Muslims had no claim to it).[14]

The judgment meant that the trespass of the Ram Lalla idols in December 1949, admitted at the time by the U.P. government as "a wrongful act . . . imperilling public peace" was effectively being endorsed by the state. The District Judge, in his seven-page verdict, declared that there was "no justification for retaining the locks" and that there were "other ways to protect the idols and maintain law and order besides closing the gates" – these, it turned out, included prohibitory orders in the entire city and the deployment of armed police contingents in all sensitive areas.[15] The issue, of course, was not the "security" of the idols but of the mosque. Mohammad Hashim, in his petition of 3 February challenging the District Judge's order, charged that "from some time the members of the other community are determined in any way to finish the very building itself."[16] But nothing came of it. Why it was considered simpler to restrict movements on the whole city and station battalions of policemen rather than leave two padlocks on the mosque gates had, of course, to do with political rather than juridical or security concerns. Explaining these concerns involves a sharp break from the above case of trespass to another legal dispute, this time over alimony, modest in appearance but momentous in implications.

Principal among the reasons for opening the Babri Masjid gates was the felt need to cultivate the Hindu vote, to counterbalance the consolidation of Muslim opinion witnessed the previous year during the Shah Bano affair. The agitation following the Supreme Court decision in April 1985 in the case of *Ahmad Mohammad Khan v. Shah Bano Begum and others*, the biggest ever launched by Muslims after Independence. At issue was the right of a divorced Muslim woman to claim alimony. The repayment of the wife's dower, plus three months' maintenance, is the extent of the husband's legal obligation under existing personal law. Shah Bano had filed her claim under the Criminal Procedure Code, as other Muslim women had successfully done before her, and had won her case in the District Court in 1979 and subsequently, on appeal, in the Madhya Pradesh High Court. In the Supreme Court verdict, which was also in her favor, Justice Y. V. Chandrachud made several observations derogatory to Muslim Personal Law. His implication was that the judiciary had to save Muslim women from their men, since Islamic law was uncivilized. The judgment provoked rage from Muslim leaders, who led processions and marches with thousands of people in major cities. The Congress Party at first upheld the judgment as a sign of their commitment to secularism. When it became clear that Muslim leaders were steering votes away from the Congress, then Prime Minister Rajiv Gandhi made an about face and supported a February 1986 bill favoring Islamic law rather than the Criminal Procedure Code for divorced Muslim women. The Minister of State for Home Affairs, Arif Mohammed Khan, resigned in protest at the government's *volte-face*. The Muslim Women (Protection of Rights on Divorce) Bill made it virtually impossible for divorcees to get legal guarantees of maintenance, but the Muslim revolt against the Congress subsided. The bill provoked protest not only from progressive Muslims, but from liberal and conservative Hindus as well, each for their different reasons. Already reeling from a wave of communal riots, the Muslim community for its part closed in. Liberal and conservative critiques became united in Muslim perception as communal, and as desirous of imposing Hindu authority on minorities in the guise of secular legal rights.

Hindu conservative opinion responded with condemnations of Islam, and demanded the imposition of a uniform civil code.[17] Muslim rejection of the Supreme Court judgment was seen as traitorous to the Constitution, and claims of preferential treatment of Muslims began to be used for Hindu assertion. A former Kerala Chief Minister and a Congressman, C. Achutha Menon, declared that a uniform civil code was more urgently needed than any economic reforms regulating monopoly business or foreign trade. Once a common civil code was founded, communal fissures would close and caste differences too would die a natural death, he declared.[18] This argument was harnessed to that of the Ram temple movement. A mistaken conception of secularism lay at the root of the country's disunity, it was claimed, and this was the tolerance shown toward a minority's dreams of defunct imperial glories, by a Hindu majority too long used to subordinating itself. The Shah Bano case was one example, and the Babri Masjid was another. In the latter case, the VHP argued, "the Hindus," a self-evident community, in their view, with the VHP as their equally self-evident spokespersons, had lost their patience with the government's inability to erase this record of humiliation by alien invaders.

Notes

INTRODUCTION

1 For an event-history of the movement, see, e.g., S. Gopal, ed., *Anatomy of a Confrontation: The Babri Masjid–Ram Janmabhumi Issue* (New Delhi: Viking Penguin, 1991), and Asghar Ali Engineer, ed., *The Babri Masjid Ramjanmabhumi Controversy* (New Delhi: Ajanta, 1991).

2 I draw from Claude Lefort the idea that one society can be distinguished from another in terms of its *regime*, i.e., the manner of the shaping of human coexistence. The institution of a new visual regime thus involves a process of the reconfiguration of politics and the reshaping of the public; it simultaneously presents a technology for the perception of social relations and for *staging* them before society at large. Claude Lefort, "The Permanence of the Theologico-Political?" in *Democracy and Political Theory*, tr. David Macey (Minneapolis: University of Minnesota Press, 1988), p. 217.

3 On the whole I prefer the terms Hindu nationalism and Hindu nationalists to "the Hindu right," and this is not only because "the Hindu left" is a negligible quantity. The historic pact between the left and the right in the nationalist movement meant that the left was mostly coopted into the developmental project of the state in post-independence India. Partly as a result, oppositional politics has focused on definitions of the state itself, i.e., in contestation over the nation form. Hindu nationalism, as an oppositional movement, has thus included both left and right perspectives, although the latter is undoubtedly dominant. By Hindu nationalist I refer here mainly but not exclusively to the Bharatiya Janata Party (Indian People's Party, or BJP) and its affiliates. Considerable sections of other parties, notably the Congress, were also complicit in latent or patent forms of support for the cause of moving away from the earlier secular compromise, and in promoting the cause of the Ram temple movement, to name only the most prominent event of this period. (See below for further discussion.)

4 Hindutva is also used as the name for the family of organizations who define their common agenda in terms of Hinduness. Thus the name designates the complex of political and social organizations including the Bharatiya Janata Party, the Rashtriya Swayamsewak Sangh, the Vishwa Hindu Parishad, and affiliated organizations (see below).

5 By the words "politics" and "the political" I do not refer exclusively to any specific realm within society, such as that of the electoral or the public sphere, since the words must also grasp the principles through which such realms are designated as political in relation to other "nonpolitical" realms, such as the religious or the social. The religious and the political realms have obviously occupied the same territory for most of human history. In modern democracy, they are institutionally separated, but tend to constantly borrow from each other's vocabulary, since both claim the authority to prescribe behavior appropriate for the good of society, although in different ways. In democracy, the source of this authority is the people themselves, and any representation of this authority is particular, incomplete, and ephemeral. Consequently, any definition of politics or of the political requires constant correction, and is continuously subverted and reworked.

6 Here I consider commercial television as emblematic of the work of television in capitalist society.

7 Todd Gitlin, *The Whole World Is Watching: Mass Media in the Making and Unmaking of the New Left* (Berkeley and Los Angeles: University of California Press, 1980), p. 3.

8 Raymond Williams, *Television: Technology and Cultural Form* (New York: Schocken, 1975), p. 89.

9 *Ibid.*, p. 90.

10 Williams' own analysis, however, distinguishes between the *true* flow and what *appears* as the flow, "the published sequence of programme items" (p. 90), and thus misses the multiple flows that television brings together. Arguing that the distinguishing characteristic of the flow is the fact of its being planned, he identifies audience experience as well as a flow insofar as it is an effect of this planned flow (pp. 95–96). He thus takes the concept literally and misses its most productive insights, I suggest.

11 Richard Dienst utilizes an important distinction, one between the "time of the image" and the "time of viewing," in *Still Life in Real Time: Theory After Television* (Durham: Duke University Press, 1994), pp. 58–59. Mary Ann Doane has written that television's greatest ability is to be there – both on the scene and in your living room. Mary Ann Doane, "Information, Crisis and Catastrophe," in *Logics of Television: Essays in Cultural Criticism*, ed. Patricia Mellencamp (Bloomington and London: Indiana University Press and British Film Institute, 1990), p. 238. According to traditional notions of time and space, as Samuel Weber points out, television can be neither fully here nor fully there; it is rather "a split or a separation that camouflages itself by taking the form of a visible *image*. That is the veritable significance of the term 'television *coverage*': it covers an invisible separation by giving it shape, contour and figure." See Samuel Weber, "Television: Set and Screen," in *Mass Mediauras: Form, Technics, Media*, ed. Alan Cholodenko (Stanford: Stanford University Press, 1996), p. 120.

12 Marshal McLuhan, *Understanding Media: The Extensions of Man* (London: Routledge and Kegan Paul, 1964).

13 Claude Lefort, *The Political Forms of Modern Society: Bureaucracy, Democracy, Totalitarianism*, ed. John B. Thompson (Cambridge, Mass.: MIT Press, 1986).

14 Pierre Bourdieu, *The Logic of Practice*, tr. Richard Nice (Stanford: Stanford University Press, 1990), p. 107. My invocation of Bourdieu here is not without misgivings. See below.

15 Marcel Mauss, *The Gift: The Form and Reason for Exchange in Archaic Societies*, tr. W. D. Halls (New York: W. W. Norton, 1990).

16 Here we can recollect the arguments of Jurgen Habermas, about the intimate space of bourgeois domesticity, and its freedom from instrumental and market relationships, that laid the foundation for the possibility of the public man, who engaged in rational-critical dialogue. I suggest that, while such gendered, bourgeois relations may anchor the development of rational-critical sensibilities, Habermas is in fact elaborating on aspects of the communicative logic of print capitalism, by identifying it with a particular phase of West European history. This logic becomes clearer with electronic capitalism, I suggest. See his *Structural Transformation of the Public Sphere: An Inquiry into a Category of Bourgeois Society*, tr. Thomas Burger with Frederick Lawrence (Cambridge: MIT Press, 1989).

17 See Appadurai's *Modernity at Large: The Cultural Forms of Globalization* (Minneapolis: University of Minnesota Press, 1986), p. 3.

18 See *ibid.*, p. 8.

19 See Habermas, *The Structural Transformation*; Lefort, *The Political Forms of Modern Society*.

20 Ernest Gellner, *Nations and Nationalism* (Oxford: Basil Blackwell, 1983).

21 See chapter four for further discussion.

22 During the 1980s, overall newspaper circulation increased by approximately 140 percent. Between 1988 and 1992, Hindi dailies increased in audited circulation by 35 percent, from 2.6 million a day to more than 3.2 million a day. Robin Jeffrey, "Indian-Language Newspapers and Why They Grow," in *Economic and Political Weekly*, 18 September 1993, pp. 2004–2011. Cited in Charu Gupta and Mukul Sharma, "Communal Constructions: Media Reality vs. Real Reality," *Race & Class*, vol. 38, no. 1, 1996, p. 3.

23 Trotsky's formulation was a revision of the Comintern's statement on uneven development as the law of capitalist growth. He was opposed to the view that there could be "socialism in one country," and condemned this as "a social-patriotic blunder." Against this view, Trotsky argued that the uneven development in different countries was a combined process and called for an internationalist response. See his *The Third International After Lenin*, 4th edn., tr. John G. Wright (New York: Pathfinder, 1996), pp. 23–91.

24 Bourdieu mentions the "great number of things that I was able to find in [Gramsci's] work only *because* I hadn't read him" (emph. orig.). See *In Other Words*, 1990, p. 27.

25 See, e.g., Pierre Bourdieu, *Homo Academicus*, tr. Peter Collier (Cambridge: Polity Press, 1988); Antonio Gramsci, *Selections from the Prison Notebooks*, ed. and tr. Quintin Hoare and Geoffrey Nowell-Smith (New York: International Publishers, 1971), p. 185.

26 Pierre Bourdieu, *The Logic of Practice*, tr. Richard Nice (Stanford: Stanford University Press, 1990), p. 122.

27 Note that the gift exists in opposition to capital, and as a negation of it, as a form of exchange that symbolizes expenditure and distribution rather than accumulation. Nevertheless, this very activity can help to reproduce and accumulate symbolic capital.

28 I am grateful to Robert N. Bellah for helping me to see the force of this point.

29 Karl Marx, *Capital*, vol. 1, tr. Ben Fowkes (London: Vintage Books, 1977), pp. 125–163.

30 Stuart Hall, "Encoding/Decoding," in Stuart Hall *et al.*, eds., *Culture, Media, Language* (London: Hutchinson, 1980).

31 Important discussions of media reception study include David Morley, *The Nationwide Audience: Structure and Decoding* (London: British Film Institute, 1980); David Morley, "The Nationwide Audience: A Critical Postscript," *Screen Education*, no. 39, 1981; David Morley, *Family Television* (London: Comedia, 1986); Janice Radway, *Reading the Romance* (Chapel Hill: University of North Carolina Press, 1984); Ien Ang, *Watching Dallas: Soap Opera and the Melodramatic Imagination*, trans. Della Couling (London and New York: Methuen, 1985); John Fiske, *Television Culture* (London: Methuen, 1987); James Lull, ed., *World Families Watch Television* (Newbury Park, Calif.: Sage, 1988); Ellen Seiter *et al.*, *Remote Control: TV Audiences and Cultural Power* (London: Routledge, 1990); Jon Cruz and Justin Lewis, eds., *Viewing, Reading, Listening: Audiences and Cultural Reception* (Boulder, Colo.: Westview Press, 1994). An ethnographic study of television audiences notable for its sensitivity to issues of race, nationality, and religion, is Marie Gillespie's *Television, Ethnicity and Cultural Change* (London and New York: Routledge, 1995). For discussion of Stuart Hall's encoding/decoding model, see Justin Lewis, "The Encoding/Decoding Model: Criticisms and Reflections on Developments for Research on Decoding", *Media, Culture and Society* no. 5, 1983; and "Reflections upon the Encoding/Decoding Model: An Interview with Stuart Hall", in Cruz and Lewis, *Viewing, Reading, Listening*, pp. 253–274. For a general discussion on the premises of critical media studies, see Todd Gitlin, "Who Communicates What to Whom, in What Voice and Why, About the Study of Mass Communication?" *Critical Studies in Mass Communication*, no. 7, 1990, pp. 185–196.

32 The metaphor of reproduction is a useful but beguiling one. It contains the injunction to be mindful of the activity that goes to make and renew social structures, of the importance of recruiting people for the purpose. But reproduction is not a treadmill, and what is renewed is not necessarily the same day after day. In the incremental shifts and movements lie all the

facts of politics and history. The term is more useful at a much higher level of abstraction, as in reproducing a structured set of social relations, or a given mode of production. In empirical inquiry, however, "reproduction" serves instead as a disclaimer, and as a reassurance of the need to look no further.

33 Daniel Lerner, *The Passing of Traditional Society: Modernizing the Middle East* (Glencoe, Ill.: The Free Press, 1958). Stephen Greenblatt, in his discussion of the same section of Lerner's book, focuses on the rhetoric of Lerner's argument, and suggests that avowing empathy was a way of denying the Western interests at work in this process, which is of course true. Here I am interested in why this argument was plausible, and how it might have failed. See Greenblatt's *Renaissance Self-Fashioning: More to Shakespeare* (Chicago: University of Chicago Press, 1980), cited in Talal Asad, *Genealogies of Religion: Discipline and Reasons of Power in Christianity and Islam* (Baltimore: Johns Hopkins University Press, 1993), p. 14.

34 For a critical discussion of the modernization approach, see J. S. Valenzuela and A. Valenzuela, "Modernization and Dependency: Alternative Perspectives in the Study of Latin American Underdevelopment," in *Comparative Politics*, vol. 10 (4), July 1978, pp.537–538.

35 John R. McLane, *Indian Nationalism and the Early Congress* (Princeton, N.J.: Princeton University Press, 1977), p. 271.

36 Bipin Chandra Pal, *The New Spirit* (Calcutta, 1907), pp. 200–205, cited in Charles Heimsath, *Indian Nationalism and Hindu Social Reform* (Princeton, N.J.: Princeton University Press, 1964), p. 324. See also Partha Chatterjee, "The Nationalist Resolution of the Woman's Question," in Kumkum Sangari and Sudesh Vaid, eds., *Recasting Women: Essays in Colonial History* (New Delhi: Kali for Women Press, 1989), pp. 233–253.

37 Partha Chatterjee, *The Nation and its Fragments* (Princeton, N.J.: Princeton University Press, 1993).

38 For a discussion of the affinity between nationalist and Hindu "communalists," see Richard Gordon, "The Hindu Mahasabha and the Indian National Congress, 1915 to 1926," *Modern Asian Studies*, vol. 9, no. 2, 1975, pp. 145–203; for a history of the development of Hindu nationalist consciousness following contact with British colonialism, see Kenneth W. Jones, *Arya Dharm: Hindu Consciousness in Nineteenth-Century Punjab* (Berkeley: University of California Press, 1976).

39 See Bernard Cohn, "The Command of Language and the Language of Command," *Subaltern Studies IV* (New Delhi: Oxford University Press, 1985), pp. 276–329.

40 To give a rough idea of the increase in the scale of violence, in 1954, there were eighty-four riots, in which thirty-four were killed and 512 injured; in 1985, there were 525 riots, in which 328 were killed and 3,665 injured. See P. R. Rajgopal, *Communal Violence in India* (New Delhi: Uppal, 1987), pp. 16–17 for a table of frequency and casualties of communal incidents between 1954 and 1985. And as mentioned above, one incident alone in December 1992,

the demolition of Babri Masjid, sparked riots which claimed victims exceeding those in any previous year since independence. From several years after 1993, however, the incidence of riots dropped considerably.

41 See Madhav Godbole, *Unfinished Innings: Recollections and Reflections of a Civil Servant* (New Delhi: Orient Longman, 1996), p. 412. The figures are from official sources, and hence liable to be underestimated.

42 See chapter one.

43 One was Delhi, where legislative assembly elections were being held for the first time, and where no metropolitan council elections had been held since 1983. (A Union Territory, which had been governed by a metropolitan council before the Centre took over in that year, Delhi was granted a legislative assembly with seventy seats and a chief minister in 1993.) The BJP won forty-nine out of seventy seats in Delhi. The other was Rajasthan, where the party won ninety-five out of 200 seats; in the previous elections in 1990, it had contested 132 and won eighty-five. In Uttar Pradesh the BJP's seats fell from 211 to 177, in Madhya Pradesh, from 219 to 117, out of a total of 320, and in Himachal Pradesh, its total dropped from forty-six to eight, in a house of sixty-eight seats. Yogendra Yadav, "Political Change in North India – Interpreting Assembly Election Results," *Economic and Political Weekly*, 18 December 1993.

44 Conversation held in Piparia, Hoshangabad Dt., Madhya Pradesh, 19 June 1994. I am grateful to Surajit Sarkar for making this conversation possible.

45 In this connection, see the discussion in the introduction to Partha Chatterjee's *Nationalist Thought and the Colonial World* (London: Zed Books for the United Nations University, 1986).

46 As Louis Dumont has suggested, the coinage of the word "communalism" suggests its similarity to "nationalism," with the nation held as the more appropriate object of loyalty over community. Louis Dumont, "Nationalism and Communalism," *Religion/Politics and History in India. Collected Papers in Indian Sociology* (Paris/The Hague: Mouton, 1970), p. 90. My redefinition of the word as religious nationalism follows the recent example of Peter van der Veer, *Religious Nationalism – Hindus and Muslims in India* (Berkeley: University of California Press, 1994).

47 E.g., Romila Thapar, Harbans Mukhia, and Bipan Chandra, *Communalism and the Writing of Indian History* (New Delhi, 1977).

48 See Gyanendra Pandey, *The Construction of Communalism in Colonial North India* (New Delhi: Oxford University Press, 1990). Sanjay Subrahmanyam has discussed the idealization of pre-colonial caste and communal relations in arguments of this nature as misleading. See his "Before the Leviathan: Sectarian Violence and the State in Pre-Colonial India," in Kaushik Basu and Sanjay Subrahmanyam, eds., *Unravelling the Nation: Sectarian Conflict and India's Secular Identity* (New Delhi: Penguin, 1996), pp. 44–80. For an argument that inter-religious conflict pre-existed colonialism, see C. A. Bayly, "The Pre-History of 'Communalism'? Religious Conflict in India, 1700–1860," *Modern Asian Studies*, vol. 19 (2), 1985.

49 See for example, *Constituent Assembly Debates* 7, pp. 815–883; cited in Robert
   D. Baird, " 'Secular State' and the Indian Constitution," in Robert D.
   Baird, ed., *Religion in Modern India* (New Delhi: Manohar, 1981), pp. 389–416.
50 We know, of course, that the presence of religion in public life scarcely
   begins with electronic capitalism, nor has it been confined to non-Western
   countries. Religion has played a part in the formation of nations in the
   East as well as in the West. Linda Colley has recently argued the centrality
   of Protestantism in the process of "forging" the British nation. Internally,
   inspiration was drawn from images of a chosen people building nothing
   less than another and a better Israel; the replacement of "Israel" with
   "Great Britain" in popular translations of the psalms, for instance, was
   considered unremarkable. See Linda Colley, *Britons: Forging the Nation
   1707–1837* (New Haven: Yale University Press, 1990), p. 30. Externally, an
   opposition to Catholicism and "popery" marked British distinction: unlike
   the French, they were a free, rational-minded people. In the U.S., Robert
   Bellah *et al.* have made an influential argument regarding the persistence
   of a Puritan ethical project, deeply identified with the larger project of
   nation-building. Here too the moral assurance of a "self-proclaimed
   people of God" demonstrated a characteristic ability to link self- and
   social-assertion. See *Habits of the Heart: Individualism and Commitment in
   America* (Berkeley: University of California Press, 1985). Colley argues that
   religion was in fact the crucial unifying force for nations both within and
   without Europe: *Britons*, p. 369.
   Theorists have generally been reluctant to identify religion with the
   nation; the latter is considered to belong to the realm of the modern,
   whereas religion tends to be understood in terms that put it on the opposite pole; indeed all too often, the only term available for its presence in
   public life is "fundamentalist." See, e.g., Ernest Gellner's *Postmodernism,
   Reason, Religion* (London: Routledge, 1992), where the only discussion of
   religion is in terms of Islamic fundamentalism. What this confirms is the
   difficulty in conceiving religion in relation to other elements in modernity,
   so that an ahistorical use of the term becomes more comfortable. The
   Oxford English Dictionary cites two etymologies for the word. Cicero connected it to *relegere*, to read over again; later authors traced it to *religare*, to
   bind. Modern authors have preferred the latter view, the dictionary notes,
   but Cicero's etymology deserves attention, emphasizing as it does interpretive rather than mechanical activity. The current preferred etymology
   stresses the integrative effect of religion, which is a modern view of the
   bases of premodern societies. In any case, the important question, I suggest, is how religious ideas and practices inter-relate with other ideas and
   practices, rather than simply ascertaining their presence or absence.
   What is defined as "religion" varies widely, and is conditioned by
   historical experience. If the separation of church and state in the West
   influences modern views of religion, before this development it was the
   church itself that determined where the boundary between "religious"

and "secular" lay. To speak of "religion" in the abstract is thus hazardous. See, in this context, Asad, *Genealogies of Religion*. Religion's prominence across the world is irrefutable, but it is difficult to argue in general terms about what this represents. One recent study concludes that it represents a refusal to accept the consequences of the Enlightenment, and is an attempt to re-politicize religion that goes beyond the defense of inherited privileges. Another study argues that religious resurgence forms a kind of ethico-philosophical counterpart to globalization. See, e.g., Roland Robertson, *Religion and Globalization* (Beverly Hills: Sage, 1995). My own interest, by contrast, is in the specific *uses* of religion, understood as flexible congeries of symbolic practices that may interbraid with nationalist discourse.

51 See in this context the discussion of secularism as a concept in Marc Galanter, "Hinduism, Secularism and the Indian Judiciary," *Philosophy East and West*, vol. 21, no. 4, October 1971, pp. 467–487 (rpt. in University of Chicago, Committee on Southern Asian Studies, Reprint Series No. 49).

52 In making this point, I am indebted to a talk given by Gyanendra Pandey, "Can a Muslim be Indian?" at the Department of South Asian Languages and Civilizations, University of Chicago, 12 May 1997.

53 Bipan Chandra, *Communalism in Modern India* (New Delhi: Vikas, 1984).

54 See, e.g., Sumit Sarkar, "The Fascism of the Sangh Parivar," *Economic and Political Weekly*, 30 January 1993; Aijaz Ahmad, "Fascism and National Culture: Reading Gramsci in the Days of Hindutva," *Social Scientist*, vol. 21, nos. 3–4, March–April 1993. Ahmad suggests that the "refounding" of the communist movement would help "the liberal centre in reconstructing those premises of Nehruvian social democracy and independent national development which is [*sic*] so much a target of the fascist attack today" (p. 66). Such a view does not engage sufficiently with what is new about contemporary communalism, and seems nostalgic in its wish to resurrect moribund political forces, whether liberal or left. A related, subsidiary perspective can be distinguished, one that points to the enduring organizational basis of the Hindu nationalist, ignored or underplayed in most previous accounts, in the Rashtriya Swayamsevak Sangh (National Volunteer Corps, or RSS). The view recognizes the range of organizational fronts created by the Hindu nationalist in contemporary times, and the sophisticated array of mobilizational tactics it has employed, particularly in the Ram Janmabhumi campaign. See, e.g., Tapan Basu *et al.*, *Khaki Shorts, Saffron Flags: A Critique of the Hindu Nationalist* (New Delhi: Orient Longman, 1994).

55 For example, Ashis Nandy *et al.*, writing about the Ram Janmabhumi movement "from the perspective of Hinduism" (p vii), state that there are no villains in their story. They appear to see it rather as part of a "proxy battle" to make Hindus and Muslims into citizens on the model of the European Enlightenment (p. ix). Such an abstract re-staging of events magnifies the very power professedly opposed, so that the critique risks

self-subversion. See Ashis Nandy *et al.*, *Creating a Nationality: The Ramjanmab-humi Movement and the Fear of the Self* (New Delhi: Oxford, 1995).

56 Oskar Negt, "Mass Media: Tools of Domination or Instruments of Liberation? Aspects of the Frankfurt School's Communications Analysis," *New German Critique*, no. 14, Spring 1978, p. 63.

57 Nationalist discourse emerged through the consolidation of linguistic communities in "print capitalism," Benedict Anderson has argued. Nationalist politics became sharpened in a rational, secular public sphere, with its ideals based on horizontal relationships of citizenship rather than vertical ones of feudal loyalty, in this argument. It was in the abstract, homogeneous space created by print-commodities that a new community relatively free of traditional duties and obligations could be forged, if only in imagination. The question then is how the context of electronic capitalism might affect nationalist expression. See Benedict Anderson, *Imagined Communities: Reflections on the Origin and Spread of Modern Nationalism* (London: Verso, 1983). See also in this connection, Karl W. Deutsch, *Nationalism and Social Communication* (Cambridge, Mass.: MIT Press, 1966); Ernest Gellner, *Nations and Nationalism* (Oxford: Basil Blackwell, 1983).

58 I adopt this argument from Dipesh Chakrabarty, "Marx After Marxism: History, Subalternity and Difference," *Meanjin*, vol. 52, no. 3, 1993, pp. 421–434.

59 See, e.g., Mary Ryan, "Gender and Public Access: Women and Politics in 19th Century America," in Craig Calhoun, ed., *Habermas and the Public Sphere* (Cambridge: MIT Press, 1992); Nancy Fraser, "Rethinking the Public Sphere: A Contribution to the Critique of Actually Existing Democracy," in Bruce Robbins, ed., *The Phantom Public Sphere* (Minneapolis: University of Minnesota Press, 1993); and Oskar Negt and Alexander Kluge, *Public Sphere and Experience: Toward an Analysis of the Bourgeois and Proletarian Public Sphere*, tr. Peter Labanyi *et al.* (Minneapolis: University of Minnesota Press, 1993).

60 Here I am thinking, e.g., of the work of Nancy Fraser, e.g., *Unruly Practices: Power, Discourse, and Gender in Contemporary Social Theory* (Minneapolis: University of Minnesota Press, 1989).

61 See Paul Brass, "The Rise of the BJP and the Future of Party Politics in Uttar Pradesh," in Harold A. Gould and Sumit Ganguly, eds., *India Votes: Alliance Politics and Minority Governments in the Ninth and Tenth General Elections* (Boulder, Colo.: Westview Press, 1993), p. 276.

I HINDU NATIONALISM AND THE CULTURAL FORMS OF INDIAN POLITICS

1 See chapter two for a discussion of the Ramayan telecast, including viewership figures.

2 BJP's White Paper on Ayodhya and the Ram Temple Movement (New Delhi: BJP, 1993), p. 31.

3 "Ram Shilas for Ayodhya," *Times of India*, 5 November 1989, p. 3. For discussion on the VHP, see below.

4 The Ramayan and the Mahabharat serials, which began in 1987 and 1989 respectively, inaugurated a host of mythological television programming that appears to have become a fixture on Indian television (see chapter two).

5 *Illustrated Weekly of India*, 22–23 December 1990, p. 11. The throne of Lucknow would presumably go to the winner of assembly elections in the state of Uttar Pradesh. The Mahabharat tele-epic followed the Ramayan, and was on the air through 1990. Like the Ramayan, but perhaps more so, it has as its defining element a war waged by its protagonists on behalf of truth and justice. The imagery is unintentionally ironic, because the protagonists in the Mahabharat win something like a Pyrrhic victory, fighting against members of their own family, and losing many from their own side as well in the process.

6 Interviewed by Ramkumar Bhramar in *Ayodhya ka Pathik* (Ayodhya's Traveler) (New Delhi: Radhakrishna Prakashan, 1993), p. 84 (translation from the Hindi). The Bajrang Dal is a loosely disciplined but widespread outfit of militant Hindu youth, largely Backward Class, formed under the supervision of the Hindu nationalists to "guard" Hindu temples and processions, mainly from Muslims. Its formation was an open declaration of the Hindu nationalists' preparation for communal violence.

7 Footage shot for *Dharm Yudh*, a Jamia Milia Islamia Mass Communication Institute (New Delhi) presentation, 1989. I am grateful to Saba Dewan and Rahul Roy for permission to view the footage.

8 See chapter two.

9 This altered language of politics occurred amid changes in the international context, with the world-wide liberalization and deregulation of markets, begun first in Britain in the late 1970s and subsequently in the U.S. and elsewhere, and occurring more gradually and unevenly in India, due to its relative insulation from the world economy and to the deadlocked character of the balance of political forces represented in the Indian developmentalist state. Michel Foucault provides an elegant model for analyzing the shift in the character of power involved with what he calls the "governmentalisation of the state," and the introduction of the economy as the state's overarching mode of perceiving and intervening within society. The circular, self-referential character of sovereign power begins to give way, without altogether relinquishing its place, to a form of power that aims at the most convenient arrangement of "men and things," and works towards the welfare of the population as its chief goal. Here the centralizing and totalizing character of modern power is complemented by a tendency to diffuse and scatter power, to achieve the practical end of maximizing the convenience of all. There is thus an economic logic that begins to structure state perception and intervention, to the point where the distinction between state and society is no longer a useful heuristic, and the "reasons of state" increasingly become the reasons of society as well, i.e., those that engender the most suitable and expedient disposition of the economy. See Michel Foucault, "Governmentality," in

Colin Gordon *et al.*, eds., *The Foucault Effect* (London: Harvester Wheatsheaf,
1991), pp. 87–104.

10 See in this connection Thomas Blom Hansen's book *The Saffron Wave:
Democracy and Hindu Nationalism in Modern India* (Princeton: Princeton University Press, 1999), which connects the growth of Hindu nationalism to an
ongoing governmentalization of the state and to larger processes of globalization.

11 Etienne Balibar, "The Infinite Contradiction," *Yale French Studies*, 88, 1995,
p. 160.

12 The first few paragraphs of this section have appeared in an earlier form in
an essay titled "Ram Janmabhoomi, Consumer Identity and Image-based
Politics," in *The Economic and Political Weekly*, 4 July 1994.

13 Raj Krishna, "Growth, Investment and Poverty in Mid-Term Appraisal of
Sixth Plan," *Economic and Political Weekly*, 19 November 1983, cited in T. J.
Byres, "Introduction: Development Planning and the Interventionist State
Versus Liberalization and the Neo-Liberal State: India, 1989–1996," in T. J.
Byres, ed., *The State, Development Planning and Liberalisation in India* (Delhi:
Oxford University Press, 1997), p. 16. The overall GDP growth rate between
1950 and 1989, 3.7 percent, is lower than that of all developing countries as a
group. See Meghnad Desai, *Capitalism, Socialism and the Indian Economy*,
Annual Export-Import Bank Commencement Lecture (Bombay: Exim
Bank, 1993). The Hindu rate of growth was believed to be low in terms of
population growth not only in the economy, but also in society. Here the
Muslim rate of growth is presented, by Hindutva, as alarming in compari-
son, and destined to render Hindus into a minority. Studies refuting this
myth include: Department of Social Welfare, *Towards Equality: Report on the
Status of Women in India* (New Delhi: Government of India, 1975); Kanti
Pakrasi, "Marriage System and Its Impact on Family Formation and
Family Planning," in P. Padmanabha *et al.*, eds., *Recent Population Trends in
South Asia* (New Delhi: Controller of Publications, 1987); Asha Krish-
nakumar, "Canards on Muslims: Calling the Bluff on Communal Propa-
ganda," *Frontline*, 12–25 October 1991, pp. 93–98. Cited in Mukul Sharma
and Charu Gupta, "Communal Constructions: Medial Reality vs Real
Reality," *Race and Class*, vol. 1, no. 38, p. 19.

14 Jay Dubashi, "Hindu Rate of Growth," *Organiser*, New Delhi, 9 June 1985,
p. 2. Viewing the term as unpatriotic, Dubashi writes: "I did not expect
socialists like Raj Krishna to play the British game and blame the apparent
stagnation of India's economy on the Hinduness of India" (*ibid.*). This
construction of Nehruvianism was crucial to the Hindu nationalists' self-
presentation as redeeming the failed promise of Indian independence. Such
an emphasis falsely implied that the Hindu nationalists had had a coherent
and distinct alternative to the Congress's economic policy. See in this
context Bruce Graham, *Hindu Nationalism and Indian Politics: The Origins and
Development of the Bharatiya Jana Sangh* (Cambridge: Cambridge University
Press, 1990). At the same time, it obscured the importance of a more

proximate period for the galvanization of the Hindu nationalists, namely the Emergency of 1975–77.

15 "The Eighties: A Decade of Change," in *Business India*, 11–24 December 1989, p. 52. By 1990, the growth rate would drop to a low of 1.5 percent, a rate that persisted through the period under review.

16 See T. L. Sankar and Y. Venugopal Reddy, "Red Herring of Privatisation," *Economic and Political Weekly*, 17–24 February 1990, pp. 407–408.

17 R. Nagaraj, "Macroeconomic Impact of Public Sector Enterprises: Some Further Evidence," *Economic and Political Weekly*, 16–23 January 1993, pp. 105–109.

18 Arun Ghosh, "Ideologues and Ideology: Privatisation of Public Enterprises," *Economic and Political Weekly*, 23 July 1994, pp. 1929–1931.

19 For instance, the *Financial Times* of London quoted a senior official of an international agency, saying that India would have no difficulty in achieving an 8–10 percent growth rate on a sustained basis. *Financial Times*, 11 October 1989, cited in Bimal Jalan, "Introduction," in Bimal Jalan, ed., *The Indian Economy – Problems and Prospects* (New Delhi: Penguin, 1993), p. ix.

20 C. T. Kurien, *Global Capitalism and the Indian Economy* (New Delhi: Orient Longman, 1994), p. 100. "Balance of payments" refers to all aspects of a country's transactions with the rest of the world, such as exports, imports, remittances, interest payments, aid receipts, and foreign loans. See Bimal Jalan, "Introduction," in Jalan, ed. *The Indian Economy*, p. xvii.

21 Most of the growth in industrial output during the 1980s was in consumer appliances, and the fastest growing category in the imports bill appears also to have been consumer goods. A substantial fraction of the external debt – which grew from $7.9 billion in 1975 to $20.6 billion in 1980, reaching $70.1 billion by 1991 – went on consumer goods. See Desai, *Capitalism, Socialism and the Indian Economy*, pp. 8–10.

22 Jalan, "Balance of Payments, 1956 to 1991," p. 190 and "Introduction," p. xvii, in Jalan, ed., *The Indian Economy*.

23 The exchange rate of the rupee was Rs.19.60 to US $1 on 31 March 1991. The rupee was devalued in July 1991 and a dual exchange rate system was introduced in March 1992. The official and "market" exchange rates of the rupee in terms of US dollars at the end of March 1992 were Rs. 25.90 and Rs.31.05 respectively. See Jalan, "Introduction," p. xi, footnote.

24 Kurien, *Global Capitalism and the Indian Economy*, pp. 96–97.

25 Pulin B. Nayak, "On the Crisis and Remedies," *Economic and Political Weekly*, 24 August 1991.

26 Raja Chelliah, "Growth of Indian Public Debt," in Jalan, ed., *The Indian Economy*, p. 200. On the significance of the debt trap for national sovereignty, see Amiya Kumar Bagchi, "The Crisis: Response and Consequences," in M. A. Oommen *et al.*, eds., *Crisis in India* (New Delhi: Khanna Publishers and the Indian Political Economy Association, 1995), pp. 92–105.

27 Or to quote Jagdish Bhagwati, "The cure is defined by the diagnosis." In J. Bhagwati and T. N. Srinivasan, *India's Economic Reforms* (New Delhi:

Ministry of Finance, Government of India, 1993), p. 71. Cited in T. J. Byres, "Introduction," in T. J. Byres, ed., *The State, Development Planning and Liberalisation in India* (Delhi: Oxford University Press, 1997), p. 26.

28 Sandeep Bhargava, "Industrial Liberalisation: Policy Issues at State Level," *Economic and Political Weekly*, 26 August 1995, pp. M117–M122.

29 Ministry of Finance, *Economic Reforms: Two Years After and the Task Ahead – Discussion Paper*, 1993, cited in Kurien, *Global Capitalism and the Indian Economy*, p. 103.

30 See P. J. James, *Nehru to Rao: Neocolonisation Process in India* (Quilon, Kerala: Mass Line Publications, 1995), p. 165.

31 See Report No. 14 of the Comptroller and Auditor General, 1992, Annexure III. Cited in James, *Nehru to Rao*, p. 165 fn.

32 A. M. "Calcutta Diary," *Economic and Political Weekly*, 19–26 December 1992, pp. 2679–2680.

33 Ashok Rudra, "Some Pre-Budget Predictions," *Economic and Political Weekly*, 8 February 1992, pp. 265–266.

34 Kurien, *Global Capitalism and the Indian Economy*, pp. 98–99.

35 Bagaram Tulpule, "All the Answers," *Economic and Political Weekly*, 17–24 July 1993, pp. 1489–1490. "Voluntary retirement" is a misnomer; workers are typically coerced into signing agreements and accepting nominal severance packages.

36 S. P. Gupta, *Liberalisation – Its Impact on the Indian Economy* (New Delhi: Macmillan, 1993), pp. 14–15, cited in Kurien, *Global Capitalism and the Indian Economy*, p. 120.

37 Measured at 1980–81 prices, it decreased from 58–59 percent to 48–49 percent; at current prices, it decreased by about half this amount. EPW Research Foundation, "National Accounts Statistics of India – 3: Private Final Consumption Expenditure, Public Sector Transactions and Divergences in Estimates," *Economic and Political Weekly*, 2 December 1995, pp. 3095–3108.

38 Kirit Parikh, ed., *Mid-Year Review of the Economy 1994–95* (New Delhi: Konark Publishers in association with India International Centre, 1995), p. 194.

39 Pulin B. Nayak, "On the Crisis and Remedies," *Economic and Political Weekly*, 24 August 1991, p. 1993. The Prime Minister himself repeatedly assured Parliament that national interests were not being subordinated to the IMF and the World Bank. He described the conditionalities in folksy terms: "If you go to a bank and ask for a loan to buy a buffalo, there will be someone to monitor if you are actually buying a buffalo or another animal." Cited in Narendra Reddy, "In the Leadership Role – The Dynamic Consensus," in Narendra Reddy *et al.*, *PV Narasimha Rao: Years of Power* (Har Anand, New Delhi 1993), p. 201.

40 Thus the fact that India had had a respectable rate of return on investment in its public sector for the first two decades of planning could not have been guessed. See Parthasarathi Shome and Hiranya Mukhopadhyay, "Economic Liberalisation of the 1990s: Stabilisation and Structural As-

pects and Sustainability of Results," *Economic and Political Weekly*, 18 July 1998, p. 1928.

41 My use of the term is partly informed here by Nicos Poulantzas, who understands a conjuncture as "the strategic point where the various contradictions fuse in so far as they reflect the articulation specifying a structure in dominance. It is the starting point from which it is possible in a concrete situation to decipher the unity of the structure and to act upon it in order to transform it. It bears at once on the *economic, ideological, theoretical* and (in the strict sense) *political*, which in their interrelation, make up a conjuncture." Nicos Poulantzas, *Political Power and Social Classes*, tr. Timothy O'Hagan *et al.* (London: New Left Books, 1973), pp. 41–42. I qualify what I regard as Poulantzas's overly rigid, structural definition of the term by drawing on Gramsci, who opposes it to a more long term conception, i.e., "situation." A conjuncture, for Gramsci, is comprised of immediate and ephemeral characteristics of the economic situation, and essentially constitutes "the economic cycle." It is thus a product of "ever-changing combinations" of circumstances. See Antonio Gramsci, *Selections from the Prison Notebooks*, ed. and tr. quintin Hoare and Geoffrey Nowell-Smith (New York: International Publishers, 1971), p. 177, fn. 79. I use the term differently from Gramsci, however, in treating apparently ephemeral circumstances as symptoms indicative of deeper structural processes.

42 *Times of India*, 17 September 1993. See, in this context, my "Thinking Through Emerging Markets: Brand Logics and the Cultural Forms of Political Society in India," *Social Text*, Fall 1999, pp. 131–149.

43 The support given by large corporate houses to the Shiv Sena, whose labor unions are used to disrupt picket lines and strike deals with management instead, is only one instance of the kind of links between the most "modern" segments of the ruling classes and Hindu nationalists. The Shiv Sena is a Hindu nationalist party prominent in Maharashtra, independent of the BJP but often allied with it during elections. In 1995, the Shiv Sena came to power for the first time in the state. Sainath notes that "very large corporate houses" in Maharashtra and elsewhere have been using the Shiv Sena to crush trades unions in their factories. The Reliance group, for instance, has systematically promoted the Bharatiya Kamgar Sena (BKS, or Indian Workers' Union), which is controlled by the Shiv Sena, in all its factories (P. Sainath, "Bombay Riots of December 1992: A Report," in Mehdi Arslan and Janaki Rajan, eds., *Communalism in India: Challenge and Response* [Delhi: Manchar Publishers, 1994], pp. 196–197). In Bombay alone, the BKS now control unions in over 900 companies, including Larsen & Toubro and Bajaj, five star hotels, private airlines, and prominent hospitals. Padmanand Jha and Lekha Rattanani, "The 'Evergreen' Saffron Union," *Outlook* (New Delhi), vol. 2, no. 39, 25 September 1996, p. 16. I do not suggest that the working class is not itself influenced by Hindu–Muslim rivalry. See the discussion of trade union organizers Vivek Monteiro and Meena Menon in "What Collapsed with the Babri Masjid: A Study of the Trade Union

Movement," in Madhushree Dutta, Flavia Agnes and Neera Adarkar, eds., *The Nation, the State and Indian Identity* (Calcutta: Samya, 1996), pp. 174–206.

44 This influential analysis has been made by Lloyd I. and Susanne H. Rudolph in *The Pursuit of Lakshmi: The Political Economy of the Indian State* (Chicago: University of Chicago Press, 1987), pp. 19–58. See also, e.g., Stanley Wolpert, "The Indian National Congress in Nationalist Perspective," in Richard Sisson and Stanley Wolpert, eds., *Congress and Indian Nationalism: The Pre-Independence Phase* (Berkeley: University of California Press, 1988), pp. 21–44; Richard Sisson and Ramashray Roy, "The Congress and the Indian Party System," in Sisson and Roy, eds., *Diversity and Dominance in Indian Politics, Vol. 1: Changing Bases of Congress Support* (New Delhi: Sage, 1990), pp. 17–34; and Myron Weiner, *Party Politics in India* (Princeton: Princeton University Press, 1957).

45 See, e.g., Sudipta Kaviraj, "Democracy and Development in India," in Amiya Kumar Bagchi, ed., *Democracy and Development* (New York: St. Martin's Press, 1995), p. 114; and Sudipta Kaviraj, "Indira Gandhi and Indian Politics," *Economic and Political Weekly*, 20–27 September 1986, pp. 1697–1708, esp. pp. 1703–1704.

46 Thus a party slogan for the BJP in the 1993 assembly elections went: *Sab ko parkha baar baar/Hum ko parkho ek baar* (You've given the others many a chance/All we ask is one chance).

47 Sudipta Kaviraj makes an argument about the vernacularization of political language in India, although in the abstract. He therefore does not dwell on the uneven character of this process, where vernacularization is constantly interrupted and undercut by the opposite tendency, of a more globalized accent being endowed on language even as it is being vernacularized. See Kaviraj's "Democracy and Development in India," p. 93. Kaviraj points to the "nearly impossible paradoxicality" of English language analysis of this phenomenon, which reintroduces the conceptual difficulties that vernacularization seeks to overcome. I discuss in chapter four how this paradox appeared as the contradictions of a "split public," that both registered and resisted this process of vernacularization.

48 See chapter five.

49 Gramsci adapted the term from the conservative thinker Vincenzo Cuoco (1770–1823), who used it initially as a negative conception, to refer to the absence of more active (and, in Cuoco's view, destructive) revolutionary change in the Parthenopian Republic of 1799 in Naples. Later, Cuoco's use of the term shifted from a descriptive to a prescriptive register, as he came to see "passive revolution" as precisely the mechanism of change required if the dangerous example of the French Revolution was not to be repeated. *Selections from the Prison Notebooks*, p. 59 fn. 11.

50 *Ibid.*, pp. 114, 120.

51 In this connection, see note 11 above.

52 D. R. Gadgil, *Planning and Economic Policy in India* (Poona: Gokhale Institute of Politics and Economics, 1972), p. xii.

53 Gadgil, "Socio-economic Situation in India," in *ibid.*, p. 305.

54 *Ibid.*, pp. 305–306.

55 Indeed, some of the foremost advocates of liberalization in India had earlier been steadfast proponents of a planned economy, e.g., the economist Jagdish Bhagwati. See for instance the discussion in Byres, "Introduction," in Byres, ed., *The State, Development Planning and Liberalisation in India*, pp. 8–10.

56 *Ibid.*, pp. 11–28.

57 *Ibid.*, p. 26. Byres cites Bernstein on the "critical double contradiction" of structural adjustment in this respect, with the state itself having to be the agent of its own withdrawal. See Henry Bernstein, "'Agricultural Modernisation' and the Era of Structural Adjustment: Observations on Sub-Saharan Africa," *Journal of Peasant Studies*, vol. 18, no. 1, October 1990.

58 Antonio Gramsci, *An Antonio Gramsci Reader*, ed. David Forgacs (New York: Schocken, 1988), pp. 267, 229.

59 The figure is an estimate from *Times of India*, 8 July 1977. A detailed social and political history of the Emergency remains to be written. For a vivid journalistic account, see Kuldip Nayar, *The Judgement: Inside Story of Emergency in India* (New Delhi, 1977).

60 All India Congress Committee, *Congress Marches Ahead – 12*, December 1975–May 1976, p. 203. Cited in Francine R. Frankel, *India's Political Economy, 1947–1977: The Gradual Revolution* (Princeton: Princeton University Press, 1978), p. 550.

61 J. S. Bright, *Emergency in India and 5 + 20 Point Programme* (New Delhi, 1976), pp. 40–43. Cited in Frankel, p. 555.

62 *Economic Survey* (New Delhi: Government of India, 1975–76), pp. 12–13. Cited in Frankel, p. 556.

63 Norman D. Palmer, "India in 1976: The Politics of Depoliticization," *Asian Survey*, vol. 17, no. 2, February 1977, pp. 167–168. It was in this Bill that the preamble to the constitution was revised to declare India a "Sovereign Socialist Secular Democratic Republic," where the 1950 document proposed to establish a "Sovereign Democratic Republic."

64 Thus although the population control program was the most notable success of the Emergency, with 3.7 million being sterilized in the first five months of the campaign alone, the backlash made any family planning measures suspect for long thereafter, and certainly helped defeat the Congress in the 1977 elections. In the urban "beautification" projects in New Delhi, about 700,000 may have been evicted and over 150,000 structures demolished. Norman D. Palmer, "India in 1976: The Politics of Depoliticization," *Asian Survey*, vol. 17, no. 2, February 1977, pp. 173–174.

65 See Lee I. Schlesinger, "The Emergency in an Indian Village," *Asian Survey*, vol. 17, no. 7, July 1977, pp. 633–634.

66 The interview was broadcast over American educational television on 21 September 1976. Cited in Palmer, "India in 1976: The Politics of Depoliticization," p. 160.

67 Schlesinger, "The Emergency in an Indian Village," p. 638.

68 K. Balagopal, "From *etatism* to Economic Liberalisation," in Oommen *et al., Crisis in India*, pp. 56–77.

69 They succeeded three times: in 1977, when the Janata Party defeated the Congress (I) after the Emergency; in 1989, when V. P. Singh's Janata Dal coalition edged out the Congress; and in 1996. The first two governments fell well before their term was up, the first lasting three years, and the second, a little over one year. The United Front coalition that came to power in the 1996 elections did so on the coat-tails of the Congress and could not act independently of it.

70 On the evolution of Indian party politics, see, e.g., Sisson and Wolpert, eds., *Congress and Indian Nationalism. The Pre-Independence Phase*, Sisson and Roy, eds., *Diversity and Dominance in Indian Politics*; Stanley Kochanek, *The Congress Party of India* (Princeton: Princeton University Press, 1968); Myron Weiner, *Party Building in a New Nation* (Chicago: University of Chicago Press, 1967).

71 The *Wall Street Journal*'s editorial, when Rajiv Gandhi presented his 1985 budget, was titled "Rajiv Reagan"! Cited in "The Budget: A Bold New Approach," *India Today*, 15 April 1985.

72 For a discussion of this point with respect to television, see chapter two. With respect to the anglophonic character of the state bureaucratic elite, Sudipta Kaviraj has noted that with the Nehruvian emphasis on planning, there was a major focus on English language "information" in the processes of state functioning; this represented a shift from the bilingual culture characterizing the nationalist movement. English came to seem the repository of real nationalism, rather than any of the vernaculars. And with economic development, there came a growing cultural differentiation, rather than homogenization, between dominant English language elites and vernacular "others." Attempts by the state at cultural engineering immediately lifted these tensions onto the larger political stage. See Sudipta Kaviraj, "Writing, Speaking, Being: language and the historical formation of identities in India," in Dagmar Hellmann-Rajanayagam and Dietmar Rothermund, eds., *Nationalstaat und Sprachkonflict in Sud und Sudostasien* (Stuttgart, 1992), pp. 25–65. For further discussion, see chapter four.

73 His brother Sanjay Gandhi had presaged the attack on the public sector in an interview given during the Emergency, where he had stated that it should be allowed to die a natural death. The press was instructed by Mrs. Gandhi to "kill" the interview after protests by the leadership of the Communist Party (India), who had supported the Emergency, but it had already been circulated. See Prem Shankar Jha, *India: A Political Economy of Stagnation* (Bombay: Oxford University Press, 1980), pp. 170–171.

74 This useful term, indicating the corporate character of apparently disparate Hindu organizations, is a coinage of Venkitesh Ramakrishnan, who reported on the Ram temple movement for *Frontline*.

75 The period immediately following Independence was in fact quietist only in relation to the Congress Party. As far as the sangh itself was concerned, it

involved a considerable amount of internal debate on how the tragedy of Partition could have befallen the country, and what the sangh might have done to prevent it. In response to demands for a wider political engagement, several organizations were started up, including the Akhil Bharatiya Vidyarthi Parishad, to organize students and teachers, the Hind Mazdoor Sabha to contend with workers, and perhaps most important of all, support for a new political party, the Bharatiya Jana Sangh, to emphasize Hindu issues before the electorate. It should be noted that the Jana Sangh was conceived by a well-known parliamentarian, Dr. Shyama Prasad Mookher- jee, who was not formally a sangh member.

76 The RSS claims not to maintain a membership register; hence no precise figures are available. See *Balasaheb Deoras with Delhi Newsmen in the Press Club of India*, 12 March 1979 (Delhi: Suruchi Sahitya, 1979), p. 31.

77 There are outfits of more recent development which play a part in this narrative as well, including the Bajrang Dal, mentioned above, and the Durga Vahini, which is its female counterpart. In discussing the Hindu nationalists here, I will focus for the most part on organizational and tactical developments. A detailed genealogy of their ideological and political forma- tion that places the Hindu nationalists alongside rather than against Con- gress nationalism remains to be written.

78 John R. McLane, *Indian Nationalism and the Early Congress* (Princeton: Prin- ceton University Press, 1977).

79 See, e.g., *Congress Bulletin*, September–October 1949, p. 15, and November– December 1949, pp. 2–3, for a report of the Congress Working Commit- tee's decision to allow swayamsewaks to enroll as members of the Congress, and subsequently, what amounted to a reversal of this decision, purportedly due to Nehru's influence. See the discussion in Bruce Graham, *Hindu Nationalism and Indian Politics* (Cambridge: Cambridge University Press, 1990) pp. 19–21.

80 *Sri Balasaheb Deoras Answers Questions* (Bangalore: Sahitya Sindhu, 1984), p. 31. In a 1979 press conference, Deoras cited a constitution the RSS had submitted to the Indian government during the ban on the RSS in 1948, which led to the lifting of the ban. "In that constitution," he said, "there is a clause – RSS as such has no politics but RSS swayamsewaks can individ- ually join any political party which does not believe in violence and which has no extraterritorial loyalty." See *Balasaheb Deoras with Delhi Newsmen in the Press Club of India*, 12 March 1979 (Delhi: Suruchi Sahitya, 1979), pp. 10–12. Deoras implies that the non-political status of the RSS was a matter of force of circumstances rather than a principled position on the part of the RSS. While his view clearly had much support, his predecessor Golwalkar was of a different opinion, and presumably held the organization back from overt political engagement until his death in 1973.

81 That militants armed with little more than crowbars were allowed to break through barricades secured by thousands of police and military personnel deployed for the purpose confirmed what Muslim voters had suspected for a

while. Subsequent elections saw the fragmentation of the "Muslim vote" that had long been a mainstay of the Congress, and led to a more pragmatic choice of candidates, in effect undermining a cardinal *raison d'être* of the Hindu nationalists.

82 Personal interview with Govindacharya, Madras, 25 May 1992.

83 Des Raj Goyal, *Rashtriya Swayamsevak Sangh* (New Delhi: Radhakrishna Prakashan, 1979), pp. 178–179.

84 One of the standard works on the RSS, *The Brotherhood in Saffron*, in fact defines it as Hindu revivalist in character, seeking to establish a notion of community derived from the *advaita vedanta*. See Walter K. Andersen and Shridhar D. Damle, *The Brotherhood in Saffron.The Rashtriya Swayamsevak Sangh and Hindu Revivalism* (New Delhi: Sage, 1987); Walter Andersen, "The RSS: The Spearhead of Hindu Revivalism," in Sisson and Roy, eds., *Diversity and Dominance in Indian Politics*, vol. 2, p. 220. A recent work on the Hindu nationalists explains the RSS's involvement in the Janmabhumi movement by, among other things, stating that Ram was central to the RSS project from 1925 onward. A 1971 quote from the RSS weekly, *Organiser*, "Let Muslims look upon Ram as their hero and the communal problems will all be over," is also cited as proof of the long-standing history behind the "seemingly spontaneous and popular contemporary [Janmabhumi] movement," as instanced by the day of its inauguration and of its naming, Vijaya Dashami and Ram Navami respectively. The former is the day when Ram concluded his epic battle against Ravan, representing the forces of evil, and Ram Navami is regarded as Ram's birthday. Tapan Basu *et al.*, *Khaki Shorts, Saffron Flags. A Critique of the Hindu Nationalists* (New Delhi: Orient Longman, 1993), pp. 12–13. This is however one of the best short studies on the subject. Other studies I have drawn from include Andersen and Damle, *The Brotherhood in Saffron*, J. A. Curran Jr., *Militant Hinduism in Indian Politics: A Study of the RSS* (New York: Institute of Pacific Relations, 1951), Goyal and Christophe Jaffrelot, *Rashtriya Swayamsevak Sangh, The Hindu Nationalist Movement and Indian Politics* (New Delhi: Viking, 1996).

85 H. V. Seshadri, "When the 'Hindu Heart' is Awakened," in *Organiser*, 27 May 1984, p. 9. The failure of this campaign to generate much support indicates an indifference regarding the prospect of diminishing numbers; this may suggest the "fuzziness" of the Hindu community, as opposed to the "enumerated" sense of it in the VHP's conception. I draw these terms from Sudipta Kaviraj, "The Imaginary Institution of India," *Subaltern Studies VII* (New Delhi: Oxford University Press, 1991), pp. 20–33.

86 The most well known of the other Hindu parties were the Hindu Mahasabha and the Ram Rajya Parishad, both known for their exclusiveness. The Mahasabha, which was founded in the 1920s but began to participate in politics under the leadership of V. D. Savarkar from 1937 onwards, was specifically restricted to Hindus. It not only condemned Pakistan but also the failure of the Congress to espouse the "Hindu" cause including reconversion of those believed to have been converted to other

religions. Its electoral impact was slight, and diminished before long. Many of the Mahasabha's members left to join the Jan Sangh after the latter was founded. The Ram Rajya Parishad, founded in 1948 by Swami Karpatri, favored a largely rural economy based on barter, and the prohibition of cow slaughter and of alcoholic drinks. See Bruce Graham, *Hindu Nationalism and Indian Politics: The Origins and Development of the Bharatiya Jana Sangh* (Cambridge: Cambridge University Press, 1990), p. 27.

87 For a useful discussion of the Jan Sangh's proximity to small industrialists and traders, and their difficulty in redefining their socio-economic policy when seeking new constituents, see Graham, *Hindu Nationalism and Indian Politics*, pp. 158–195. RSS chief Balasaheb Deoras effectively confirmed this diagnosis about the Hindu nationalists, when he confessed in a press conference, "[W]e have no economic policy." See *Balasaheb Deoras with Delhi Newsmen in the Press Club of India*, 12 March 1979 (Delhi: Suruchi Sahitya, 1979), pp. 24–25.

88 See Ghanshyam Shah, "The Upsurge in Gujarat," *Economic and Political Weekly*, Special Number, August 1974, pp. 1429–1454; John R. Wood, "Extra-Parliamentary Opposition in India: An Analysis of Populist Campaigns in Gujarat and Bihar," *Pacific Affairs*, vol. 48, no. 3, 1975, pp. 313–334.

89 Christophe Jaffrelot, *The Hindu Nationalist Movement in India: 1925 to the 1990s* (New Delhi: Viking, 1996), p. 262.

90 Among other things, the RSS played a significant role in the production and distribution of underground literature during the Emergency. An all-India weekly news bulletin, *Lok Sangharsh*, produced in English and in Hindi, and another local bulletin, *Jana Vani*, began to be produced in mid-July 1975. It was duplicated in ten centers in Delhi and distributed in the thousands in adjoining states. Opposition members' speeches in the emergency session of Parliament in July 1975 were printed in Hindi and English, as well as pamphlets about the RSS's role in the parliamentary and extra-parliamentary opposition at this time. *The Delhi News Bulletin*, started by the RSS a few months after the Emergency was imposed, was sent to all state capitals. The process was repeated at the district levels (*Organiser*, 28 May 1975, p. 5). RSS sympathizers in London set up a "Friends of India Society" at this time; the society soon became the "Friends of India International," with branches in 40 countries and with Subramaniam Swamy as president. A ten-week satyagraha was launched on 14 November 1975, in which nearly 100,000 participated. Indians all over the country offered themselves for arrest, Gandhi style, and 80,000 men were taken in – 15,000 in Karnataka, 9,000 in Kerala, 8,000 in Bihar, 8,000 in U.P., 5,000 in Delhi. The satyagraha was organized in 300 districts by the leaders of India's underground movement. Its object was not to bring down the government, since this was not considered a realistic objective, but to test popular opinion and the strength of their own power of mobilization (*Organiser*, 4 June 1977, p. 11).

Complicating this picture of the RSS's politicization, however, is the more conciliatory, even abject, attitude of RSS chief Balasaheb Deoras, evidenced in his placatory letters to Mrs. Gandhi from Yeravada Central Jail in Poona, pleading for a lifting of the ban on the RSS. Deoras promised that his organization would be at the disposal of the government "for national uplift" if this were done, and arrested RSS activists were freed. See letters dated 22 August and 10 November 1975, in *Justice Demands: Letters of RSS Chief*, n.d., pp. 1–10. Such a tactical and ingratiatory approach on the part of the Hindu nationalists' leadership was reproduced amply during the Ram Janmabhumi campaign as well. This suggests an organization narrowly intent on advancing its own cause rather than one aiming at popular empowerment as such.

91 It was under Deoras's influence that RSS people started their own newspapers like *Yugadharma* (Nagpur, Jabalpur, and Raipur), *Swadesh* (Indore, Gwalior), and *Tarun Bharat* (Pune, Aurangabad, Solapur, and Mumbai). Geeta Puri provides one of the few insightful discussions I have seen on the formative character of the mid-to-late 1970s for the Hindu nationalists. See her *Bharatiya Jana Sangh: Organisation and Ideology – Delhi. A Case Study* (New Delhi: Sterling Publishers, 1980).

92 The only writer I am aware of who has developed an argument along these lines is Geeta Puri, in her volume *Bharatiya Jana Sangh*. There is a period limit to her arguments, however, and it is not certain how she would have read, for instance, the Ram temple campaign in the light of her emphasis on a genuine democratization of the party.

93 The more pragmatic and less sectarian approach of the younger BJP leaders such as Govindacharya and Pramod Mahajan, for instance, can be understood in this context.

94 The Jan Sangh secured 3.1 percent of the votes in 1952, 5.9 percent in 1957, 6.4 percent in 1962, 9.4 percent in 1967, and 7.4 percent in 1971. The Janata Party obtained 41.3 percent of votes polled in 1977, and since the Jan Sangh obtained nearly one-third of the 295 seats, a rough estimate would place their share of the vote at 14 percent. This is justified by the fact that with the high degree of opposition unity at this time, the ratio of vote to seat percentages was about 1, using Eric da Costa's "multiplier ratio." In 1980, the Janata party won 19 percent of the votes, and, by a similar estimate, the Jan Sangh got about 6.3 percent of the votes. In 1984, the percentage of the votes won by the BJP was 7.4. Although in terms of the number of seats there was a fall back to 1952 levels, the vote percentage was roughly where it had stood in 1971. Although the party's vote base had been eroded, new voters had come in at the same time. For 1952–1989 figures, see David Butler, Ashok Lahiri, and Prannoy Roy, eds., *India Decides. Elections 1952–1991* (New Delhi: Living Media Books, 1989), pp. 74–90.

95 See Jay Dubashi, *The Road to Ayodhya* (New Delhi: Voice of India Publications, 1992). For the BJP's pro-liberalization statements before the Conference on Indian Industry, see *BJP Meets Indian Industry*, Bharatiya Janata

Party Publication no. 127 (New Delhi), p. 18 and *passim*. See also Satish Padmanabhan and Ranvir Nayar, with Nilanjan Dutta, "An Affair of the Purse: The BJP is the New Darling of Industrialists," *Sunday*, Calcutta, 21–27 February 1991, pp. 50–52.

96 The issue of indigenous enterprise, or *swadeshi*, endured as a contradiction for the BJP leadership, which was anxious to prove its pro-business credentials while reassuring its rank-and-file of its nationalist bona fides. A Swadeshi Jagran Manch (Swadeshi Awareness Organization) was formed to promote the issue (above), but, significantly, no prominent party organizers were delegated to it.

97 Thus in 1991 the BJP abstained in crucial votes in the Lok Sabha on motions against the government following the IMF loan. See Narendra Reddy, "In the Leadership Role – The Dynamic Consensus," in Reddy *et al.*, *PV Narasimha Rao*. See also Charan D. Wadhwa, *Economic Reforms in India and the Market Economy: Interface with the States; Bureaucracy; Business and Society* (New Delhi: Allied Publishers and the Economic and Scientific Research Foundation, 1994), p. 110. For the BJP's economic resolutions see *BJP Economic Resolutions*, Publication no. E/16/95 (New Delhi: Bharatiya Janata Party, 1995). It was in its February 1991 session in Jaipur that the party first formulated its comprehensive critique of the public sector and state planning; this was revised and extended as a critique of "the Nehru model" in its March 1992 meeting in Sarnath. See *BJP Economic Resolutions*, pp. 114–116 and pp. 121–125.

98 V. D. Savarkar, *Hindutva. Who is a Hindu?* (Poona, 1942), p. 102. The authors of *Khaki Shorts* mention Savarkar's endorsement of Hindu festivals and pilgrimages, and of the figure of Ram (p. 9), but the more relevant point is that Savarkar relied on none of these means in pursuing his political work.

99 M. S. Golwalkar, *Bunch of Thoughts* (Bangalore: Jagarana Prakashana, 1980), p. 24.

100 As the RSS expanded into areas under the influence of the Arya Samaj, idol-worshipping tendencies came under criticism. The prayer too was changed, from a mixture of Hindi and Marathi to Sanskrit. Goyal, *Rashtriya Swayamsevak Sangh*, p. 201.

101 Golwalkar, *Bunch of Thoughts*, pp. 514–515.

102 *Ibid.*, p. 666.

103 *Ibid.*, p. 23.

104 Every volunteer is expected to devote himself to sangh activities entirely, to forsake all personal ambition, and to fuse his individual personality within that of the organization. All members must try to attend *sharirik* at least once a day, i.e, physical exercise routines, comprised of calisthenics, simple drill, and games. The purpose of sharirik is to inculcate discipline and solidarity as well as physical fitness. This is held before dusk and at dawn, to enable more members to attend at least one session. The *shakha* is at the heart of the method the sangh has devised, purportedly to "carry the

nation to the pinnacle of glory." *RSS: Widening Horizons* (Bangalore: Sahitya Sangama, 1992), p. 14. In addition, there are weekly discussion
sessions, *charchas*, and bi-weekly lectures, called *baudhiks*. Through the local
units, the sangh supervises its members and their work, closely watching
and guiding individuals and fostering a sense of loyalty so that the mere
anticipation of sangh disapproval is enough to create steadfast discipline. A
high value is placed on the personal conduct and comportment of the
swayamsevak; each activist is meant to win the approbation of the society
around him, and serve as a center of attraction for others. Curran, *Militant
Hinduism in Indian Politics*, p. 46.

105 The paucity of vision, the focus on the organization as an end in itself, and
the absence of internal discussion or dialogue added up to a classically
sectarian enterprise. As such, the time scale of the RSS was purely internal
and without reference to larger events. Ex-member Des Raj Goyal records
an August 1947 discussion with Golwalkar when the leader was asked how
the RSS planned to meet the challenge of political independence, and how
the RSS's role would change. Golwalkar's answer is worth reproducing:
"Do you believe that the British will quit? The nincompoops in whose
hands they are giving the reins of government will not be able to hold on
for even two months. They will go crawling on their knees to the British
and ask them to kindly return. The RSS will have to continue its work as in
the past" (Goyal, *Rashtriya Swayamsevak Sangh*, p. 96). Apart from qualifying
any pretensions the sangh has to a history of anti-colonial politics, the lack
of political involvement evinced here confirms the impression of a deeply
self-absorbed organization, intent on pursuing its adopted method with no
reference to external changes. At the same time, there is record of internal
debates on the need for greater involvement, but it was a while before
those demands were realized. Thus, e.g., Bhishikar reports that the Partition came as a shock to activists, who were led to question the judgment of
the leadership. S. Bhishikar, *Samarpit Ek Adyan Utkat Chaitanya, Dr. V.V.
Pendse*, cited in Andersen, "The RSS: The Spearhead of Hindu Revivalism," p. 226.

106 Interview with RSS activist, Dr. Sharad Bhogale, Aurangabad, 12 February, 1997.

107 Raghunandan Prasad Sharma, ed., *Vishwa Hindu Parishad – Samagra Darshan (A Comprehensive View)* (New Delhi, n.d.), pp. 5, 32.

108 *Ibid.*, pp. 7–12.

109 *Ibid.*, pp. 5, 32.

110 *Ibid.*, pp. 9–10.

111 Hindu ritual, as a language between humans and gods, occurred in specific
performative contexts where certain kinds of expectations or interventions
were provoked and others excluded. Thus in the Ramayana, the rakshasa
king Ravana acquires divine powers through his spiritual austerities, but
disdains to ask for protection against mere mortals, and thus becomes
vulnerable to Rama. His brother Kumbhakarna has mispronounced a

word in his own prayers for superhuman strength, and is thus condemned to sleeping for six months in a year. The discussion by the VHP here stands out in contrast in its abstraction, and the recontextualization of ritual within commodity logic.

112 The shift of the Hindu nationalists towards an engagement with actually existing Hindu traditions may have come from at least three sources. Firstly, we have noted that Deoras was an activist leader who departed from the exclusive focus on character-building the RSS had taken until that time, and had no objection to organizing "traditional Hindus," who after all, he said, comprised "85 percent of society." He admitted the danger of obscurantism and superstition entering in along with the resort to ritual, and described it as a "delicate issue." But clearly, the costs of pursuing such a path were seen as affordable (*Sri Balasaheb Deoras Answers Questions* [Bangalore: Sahitya Sindhu, 1984], pp. 52–53, 7–8). In any case, such ambivalence was rare on the part of the sangh parivar. Secondly, the leader of the Ram Janmabhumi movement was Ashok Singhal, who was convinced of the importance of religious rituals in cementing Hindu society; he may have been the one most responsible for the wholesale ritualization of RSS mobilizing tactics. An RSS-sponsored hagiography of Singhal dwells on his orthodox, ritualistic upbringing, and his devotion to Vedic *sanskar*. The sight of the Kumbh and Mahakumbh Melas in his hometown of Allahabad, with its millions of pilgrims massing together, had impressed him deeply as a sign of Hindu ritual's power of congregation. He felt that the recitation of Vedas and the practice of rituals, with saints and mahatmas, would serve to awaken cultural pride in people, strengthen nationalist feeling, and offer a true introduction to the Hindu way of life. Ramkumar Bhramar, *Ayodhya ka Pathik* (Delhi: Radhakrishna Prakashan, 1993), pp. 55–56. Already an RSS activist, for a while he contemplated quitting the sangh to join the company of sadhus and become a sanyasi. After an exchange of letters with Golwalkar and discussions with Deoras and Rajendra Singh, he decided to stay in the sangh, but his attachment to the Vedas and to rituals was undiminished (*ibid.*, pp. 57–58). The *Kumbh Mela* is a bathing fair, held at Allahabad and Hardwar, once every twelve years, when Jupiter enters Aquarius (Kumbh) (Crooke and Enthoven, *Religion and Folklore in Northern India*, p. 43). Finally, the experience of the VHP abroad, in observing the effectiveness of religious ritual in bringing Indians across region and sect together, I argue in chapter six, was crucial.

113 G.-D. Sontheimer, "Hinduism: The Five Components and their Interaction," in G.-D. Sontheimer and Hermann Kulke, *Hinduism Reconsidered*. South Asian Studies 24 (New Delhi: Manohar, 1991), pp. 197–212. In a subsequent essay, Sontheimer mentions the shift from a hierarchical, reciprocal relation between brahminical and folk religions, to the disjunction and severance of folk religion in modern, middle-class conceptions, and its relegation to the status of "superstition." See "The Erosion of Folk Religion in Modern India: Some Points for Deliberation," in Vasudha

Dalmia and Heinrich von Stientencron, eds., *Representing Hinduism: The Construction of Religious Traditions and National Identity* (New Delhi: Sage, 1995), pp. 389–398. Hindutva unquestionably revives many elements of "superstition," in this respect, while reinserting them within a schema of political assertion. See chapter five for further discussion. The mobilizational methods listed here worked as self-evident, practical tactics, while the ideological arguments of the Hindu nationalists were discursive and argumentative. This corresponds to the relationship between brahmanical and folk Hinduism: while brahminical Hinduism eschews idolatry, at least theoretically, and tends to be the source of most official versions of the religion, folk religion makes little attempt to justify itself. G.-D. Sontheimer, "Bhakti in the Khandoba Cult," in Diana Eck and Françoise Mallison, eds., *Devotion Divine: Bhakti Traditions from the Regions of India. Studies in Honor of Charlotte Vaudeville* (Groningen/Paris: Egbert Forsten/Ecole Française d'Extreme Orient, 1991), p. 231.

114 M. P. Degvekar, "The Origin and Growth of Vishva Hindu Parishad," *Hindu Vishva*. VHP Rajat Jayanti Souvenir (New Delhi), August 1990, p. 13. In the Ekatmata Yatra or Unity Journey, prominently bedecked vans carrying a portrait of "Bharat Mata," Mother India, against the map of the Indian subcontinent, and a large vessel of Ganges water, covered more than 50,000 kilometers, bringing the message to small towns and villages of the unity of India; for a sum of money, people could also obtain small bottles of Ganga *jal* mixed with "holy water" from more proximate sources, thus appropriating for themselves a part of India's inter-relatedness. Little was heard in subsequent campaigns of Bharat Mata, or Ganges water. The idea of an outreach program to retail a concept, as it were, established a precedent for later use in the Ram Janmabhumi campaign. This is suggested in a VHP pamphlet: "The subsequent decision of the leading dharmacharyas [religious teachers] to construct a befitting mandir [temple] to Lord Sri Rama at the Janmasthan [Birthplace] followed as a logical sequel to the above." The "logical" connection between the two, otherwise quite different, campaigns was precisely that of retailing Hindu identity, I would argue. See Anon., *The Saga of Ayodhya* (Bangalore: Jagrana Prakashana Trust, 1990).

115 Santosh Ji Trivedy, "Festivals for National Integration," *Hindu Vishva*, VHP Rajat Jayanti Souvenir (New Delhi), August 1990, p. 77.

116 *Ibid.*, p. 78.

117 Gopalbhai Ashar, "The Role of Religious Anushthans [Ceremonies] in Social Integration," *Hindu Vishva*, VHP Rajat Jayanti Souvenir (New Delhi), August 1990, pp. 79–80.

118 See Swapan Dasgupta, "Hedgewar's Legacy – The Limitations of Elitist Hinduism", *The Statesman*, 1 April 1989; reprinted in the *Organiser*, 23 April 1989, p. 11, for an argument about the utilization of "popular Hinduism" by Deoras's RSS.

119 Address to the civil servants of the Government of India, 30 January 1993.

V. Narasimha Rao: Selected Speechs, vol. II: July 1992–June 1993 (New Delhi: Publications Division, Government of India, 1993), p. 90.

120 Jay Dubashi, "BJP's Unique Role," *Organiser*, 25 June 1989, p. 2.

121 On the political phenomenon of "Thatcherism," see, e.g., Stuart Hall's important work, *The Hard Road to Renewal: Thatcherism and the Crisis of the Left* (London: Verso, 1988). See also Bob Jessop *et al.*, "Authoritarian Populism, Two Nations and Thatcherism," *New Left Review*, no. 147, September/October 1984, pp. 32–60; Dennis Kavanagh and Anthony Seldon, eds., *The Thatcher Effect* (Oxford: The Clarendon Press, 1989); and Paul Q. Hirst, *After Thatcher* (London: Collins, 1989).

122 See, e.g., *This is What Swadeshi is About*, talk by S. Gurumurthy, All India General Secretary, Swadeshi Jagran Manch, delivered on 15 January 1994 (Madras: Vigil, 9 February 1994).

123 This argument was first made in my essay, "Ram Janmabhumi, Consumer Identity and Image-based Politics." *Kar seva* is a form of worship through work, performed collectively, prominent in the Sikh community but hitherto absent in Hindu worship. Its appropriation by the Hindu nationalists as a form of political activism follows its use by Sikh militants in the mid-1980s, though curiously this parallel has been little remarked. The term was adopted in a VHP meeting at Hardwar on 23–24 June 1990. Gopal Sharma, *Kar Seva se Kar Seva Tak* (Jaipur: Rajasthan Patrika Limited, 1993), p. 40.

124 What is interesting here is not only the deliberate linking together of activities conventionally imagined as separate, but also, and perhaps more importantly, the specific kinds of linkages being promoted, and the ways in which new routes are chosen for exercising claims on the public domain. Recent historical work has challenged assumptions about consumption as an activity following automatically upon the development of industrial production, or about mass consumption as having a merely emulative quality, as lower classes enacted their aspirations for the lifestyles of their economic betters. Consumption as a middle-class activity began not in the late eighteenth, or early nineteenth, or in the twentieth century, but in fact appears to antedate the rise of industrial capitalism and mass production, as for instance Chandra Mukerji has argued (in *From Graven Images: Patterns of Modern Materialism* [New York: Columbia University Press, 1983]). Indeed some of the derogatory connotations of the term can be explained in terms of the self-fashioning of a new middle class as "cultured," and hence untainted by the things of commerce. If, to Marxist orthodoxy, acquiring and celebrating possessions is objectionable, a revisionist perspective might require not a rejection of consumption practices altogether so much as inquiry into their precise character and variety, and their relation to other spheres of society. As consumer society becomes coterminous with society itself, the alternative to consumption is not resistance but death. The ability to consume and the choice of things consumed then offer a gauge of the distribution of power and the patterns of participation, that is, of the

nature and quality of citizenship available, and the benefits it makes possible.

125 Portions of this section have appeared in an earlier form in an essay titled "Communalism and the Consuming Subject," in *The Economic and Political Weekly*, 10 February 1996.

126 L. K. Advani interviewed in *The Economic Times*, 10 August 1993, p. 7.

127 The frequent shifts represent a number of important political developments, including an increased political assertiveness of backward castes, especially of newly rich sub-castes, notably Yadavs, Lodhs, and Kurmis, previously subordinated to the more prosperous among them, chiefly the Jats. For almost three decades now, OBCs have been an important political force in the north Indian countryside. But there are sharp gradations among them in social and economic status. At the top is the so-called "creamy layer" of Jats, Yadavs, and Kurmis; below them are the Hajjams, Nais, Dhanuks, Telis, and other caste groupings who are markedly poorer. These are two fairly disparate groups put into one category. Chaudhury Charan Singh led the movement for the advancement of the agricultural OBC castes, in terms of choice political posts, co-operative loans, subsidized seeds, fertilizers, and other such benefits. All of Charan Singh's schemes for land reforms favoured local dominant landed castes who, according to the the 1971 agricultural census, formed about one-third of the land-holding classes and owned about 70 percent of the land. These benefits were to be confined to the upper OBCs, and Charan Singh relentlessly opposed the inclusion of poor and marginal farmers in his redistribution schemes. The difficulties began alter Charan Singh's death, when Yadavs separated out from the coalition, refusing to submit to Jat leadership; Mulayam Singh Yadav emerged as the leader reflecting this impulse, forging a coalition between Dalits, Muslims and OBCs. See Meenakshi Jain, "Strange Bedfellows in Uttar Pradesh," *Times of India*, 25 September 1996, p. 14.

128 In fact, the Congress never achieved a majority of the vote, even while by common consensus it was the ruling national party, and oppositional parties responded to the national agenda as set by the Congress. Ironically, the first time the Congress won an absolute plurality of votes was in 1984, when the decline of the Congress was already well under way. See David Butler *et al.*, *India Decides*.

129 Personal interview, Girdhar Gopal Maheshwari, Berasia, M. P., 10 May 1994.

130 E.g., Balwant Rai Garg, *Sri Ramjanmabhumi Mandir: Ayodhya ki Rakt Ranjit Gaurav Poorn Gatha* [Sri Ramjanmabhumi Temple: Ayodhya's Blood-Soaked, Pride-Filled Story] (Ambala: Bharat Vidya Mandir, n.d.).

131 E.g., see Deoki Nandan, *Shri Rama Janma Bhumi: Historical and Legal Perspective* (New Delhi: Vishwa Hindu Parishad, n.d.). Also see *The Great Evidence of Shri Ram Janmabhoomi Mandir* (New Delhi: Vishwa Hindu Parishad, 1991).

132 For rethinking received perceptions of violence, Georges Sorel's *Reflections*

On Violence, tr. T. E. Hulme and J. Roth (London: Collier-Macmillan, 1950) is a salutary text.

133 The information that a majority of karsevaks were from the backward castes, disclosed by a senior official in the U.P. Police, confirms this view. R. Dharapuri, DIG U.P. Police, personal interview, Lucknow, 13 February 1994.

134 Jay Dubashi, "Who is a Hindu?" *The Telegraph* (Calcutta), 10 July 1990, reprinted in *The Road to Ayodhya* (New Delhi: Voice of India Publications, 1992), p. 6.

135 See chapter five.

136 Golwalkar, *Bunch of Thoughts*, p. 667.

137 Bourdieu discusses, in his essay "Opinion Polls: A 'Science' Without a Scientist," the troublesome phenomenon of the "don't knows," the nemesis and undoing of the poll-taker's craft, whose numbers, always embarrassingly high, are sought to be reduced, disguised, or explained away. Polling assumes an informed electorate that, by its concerted choices, forms the foundation of modern politics; indeed polling itself is meant to ensure the functioning of democracy. The increasing number of "don't knows" suggests a reverse movement: a growing number of people who are not acquiring the skills and competencies they are supposed to, and are steadily proceeding in the opposite direction, to all appearances. The "non-committed voter" is the "don't know" of Bourdieu's essay, seemingly devoid of the intelligence that would protect him or her from the illusions destined to lead her astray, as Advani is willing to acknowledge publicly. Pierre Bourdieu, *In Other Words: Essays Towards a Reflexive Sociology*, trans. Matthew Adamson (Cambridge: Polity Press, 1990), pp. 168–174. Sometimes s/he is identified as proof of the inability of prevailing political discourse to address issues of salience to voters, as E. J. Dionne, Jr. has argued in the case of U.S. politics. See E. J. Dionne, Jr., *Why Americans Hate Politics* (New York: Simon and Schuster, 1991), pp. 18–23. Bourdieu's own suggestion is that "the people" demonstrate a willingness to surrender their freedoms and submit to power. For him, the "don't know" masses await a tyrant; the infusion of knowledge, were it possible, could perhaps thwart despotism. For Dionne, a disenchanted public awaits a new political discourse before returning to the practice of citizenship at the polls: not just knowledge, but the "right kind" of knowledge is awaited, according to him. But to situate the problem of voters' knowledge as the key issue at stake displaces the heart of the problem, I suggest.

138 Walter Benjamin, "The Work of Art in the Age of Mechanical Reproduction," in *Illuminations*, ed. Hannah Arendt, tr. Harry Zohn (New York: Schocken, 1968), pp. 217–251.

139 *Ibid.*, p. 241.

140 In this discussion I am indebted to an essay by Samuel Weber. Weber argues for two distinct meanings of "aura," but I have found it more helpful to retain Benjamin's emphasis on a single term. See "Mass

Mediauras, Or: Art, Aura and Media in the Work of Walter Benjamin," in Samuel Weber's *Mass Mediauras: Form, Technics, Media* (Stanford: Stanford University Press, 1996), pp. 76–107.

141 Benjamin, "The Work of Art,", p. 243.

142 G. W. F. Hegel, writing in the *Encyclopedia*, cited in Claude Lefort, "The Permanence of the Theologico-Political," *Democracy and Political Theory*, tr. David Macey (Minneapolis: University of Minnesota Press, 1988), p. 214.

143 For details of the collusion of public sector officials in the 1992 stock market scam, see Gurudas Das Gupta, *The Securities Scandal: A Report to the Nation* (New Delhi: People's Publishing House, 1993), pp. 62–78.

144 Thus the popularity of the former Chief Election Commissioner T. N. Seshan, and of the former Bombay deputy municipal commissioner G. R. Khairnar, both bureaucrats famous for a swift and ready technocratic vigilantism, suggested one diagnosis of the problem. Incorruptible disciplinarians, ready to cut through due process and exercise arbitrary personal authority for the greater good of the public, were seen as the answer, one that pointed towards a stronger, not a weaker state; indeed there was the fantasy of a dictator present here.

2 PRIME TIME RELIGION

1 Field notes, Delhi Doordarshan Kendra, March–May 1989. I conducted interviews with Doordarshan producers, program executives, audience research officers, as well as senior administrative officers during this period. I am grateful for the friendship and assistance of several Doordarshan personnel, who must however remain unnamed here. I thank Satish Deshpande for suggesting this title, some years before this chapter was written.

2 The Virat Hindu Sammelan, founded by former Union Minister Dr. Karan Singh, envisaged as the solution to the Ayodhya conflict a Hindu temple that would surround rather than replace the Babri Masjid, presumably as a more peaceful means of containing the Muslim threat. The VHS remained little more than a series of occasional meetings and publications, however, supported by a salaried staff. Field notes, interview with Virat Hindu Sammelan official, New Delhi, Summer 1988.

3 See Asghar Ali Engineer, ed., *Babri Masjid-Ranjanmabhoomi Dispute* (New Delhi: Ajanta, 1990).

4 Writing in the early nineteenth century, Hegel was already critical of the growing tendency to conceive of religion as belonging exclusively within the realm of private life, rendering politics an independent entity:

It has been the monstrous blunder of our times to try and look upon these inseparables as separable from one another, and even as mutually indifferent. The view taken of the relationship of religion and the state has been that, whereas the state had an independent existence of its own, springing from some source and power, religion was a later addition, something desirable perhaps for strengthening the political bulwarks, but purely subjective in individuals: – or it may be, religion is treated as something without effect on the moral life of the state, i.e., its reasonable law and constitution which are based on a ground of their own.

G. W. F. Hegel, *The Philosophy of Mind*, tr. William Wallace (Oxford: The Clarendon Press, 1894), pp. 156–157, cited in Claude Lefort, "Permanence of the Theologico-Political?" in his *Democracy and Political Theory*, tr. David Macey (Minneapolis: University of Minnesota Press, 1988), p. 214.

5 See Binod C. Agrawal, *SITE Social Evaluation: Results, Experiences, and Implications* (Ahmedabad: Space Applications Center, 1981).

6 Raymond Williams has pointed out that it is a distinct characteristic of the televisual medium's development that the means of communication precede their content. See *Television: Technology and Cultural Form* (New York: Schocken, 1975), p. 25.

7 Thus the audience attracted by in-house programming was generally a fraction of that of the sponsored programs. For the five day (weekday) period 25–29 July 1988, the evening Hindi news, at 32.3 percent, averaged about half the ratings of sponsored serials, 59.2 percent. The corresponding figure for English news was 20.4 percent. The morning "Breakfast show" averaged 9 percent and the late evening "Sansad Samachar" (Parliament News) averaged 3 percent (Market Research Advisory Services figures). Many of the shows are subject to frequent changes and thus found it hard to develop a regular following. Even before commercially sponsored serials were launched, the mainstay of Doordarshan's programming fare was its offering of two to three films per week. Then I&B Minister H. K. L. Bhagat acknowledged that although the films might not be "of a high standard," they had to be shown. "If we stop showing films, people will shut off their TV sets," he explained, suggesting in effect that the remainder of the programming was namesake. Raminder Singh, "TV No Luxury: Bhagat," *Indian Express*, 22 June 1983.

8 See, e.g., Arvind Singhal and Everett M. Rogers, *India's Information Revolution* (New Delhi: Sage, 1989).

9 Portions of this section and of chapter three have appeared in an earlier form in my "Mediating Modernity: Theorizing Reception in a Non-Western Society," *Communication Review*, vol. 1, no. 4, 1996, pp. 441–469.

10 In this chapter, my discussion pertains to Doordarshan, the state-owned television system, for the period 1987–88. In 1992, state monopoly over television began to erode, with the entry of satellite television. Doordarshan itself introduced a second channel in 1993, DD2 Metro, to provide more entertainment for the urban audience. By linking through satellite the four terrestrial transmitters in the four metros (Bombay, Madras, Delhi, and Calcutta), DD2 Metro was available in forty-two cities; elsewhere a satellite dish was required. Dishes are maintained by local cable operators, and services provided for a monthly fee of between a hundred and a hundred and fifty rupees. Next to DD2 Metro, the most watched service is the Murdoch-owned STAR TV, followed by ZEE TV, owned by Subhash Chandra (originally from a grain-trading family), and a host of other cable

channels. In 1993, about 21 percent of TV households in towns with a population of 100,000 and above had cable TV. About three-quarters of these households had STAR. Frank Small and Associates, "Star TV Homes Penetration Study," *Thompson Pocket Reference to Media in India, 1993–94*, p. 44. Cable commands the most profitable segment of the market, and dominates newsmedia coverage, but its viewership is likely to remain in a minority for the forseeable future.

11 See Daniel Lerner's influential *The Passing of Traditional Society: Modernizing the Middle East* (Glencoe, Ill.: The Free Press, 1958), and Wilbur Schramm, *Mass Media and National Development* (Stanford, Calif.: Stanford University Press, 1964). A useful summary of the main criticisms of the modernization perspective may be obtained in Aidan Foster-Carter, "From Rostow to Gunder Frank: Conflicting Paradigms in the Analysis of Underdevelopment," *World Development*, vol. 4, no. 3, March 1976, pp.167–180; and in J. S. Valenzuela and A. Valenzuela, "Modernization and Dependency: Alternative Perspectives in the Study of Latin American Underdevelopment," *Comparative Politics*, vol. 10, no. 4, July 1978, pp. 537–538.

12 Karl Marx, "On the Jewish Question," in Robert C. Tucker, ed., *The Marx–Engels Reader* (New York: W. W. Norton and Co., 1978), p. 44.

13 H. K. L. Bhagat, quoted in *The Indian Express*, 22 June 1983.

14 Partha Chatterjee, "The National State," *The Nation and its Fragments: Colonial and Postcolonial Histories* (New Delhi: Oxford University Press, 1993), p. 219.

15 See Ronald Herring, *Land to the Tiller: The Political Economy of Agrarian Reform in South Asia* (New Haven: Yale University Press, 1983), pp. 38–39, for use of the term "embedded bureaucracy." Herring makes his argument with respect to the implementation of land reform in Palghat, Kerala. For examples of planning failures and political obstacles to overcoming them, see, e.g., T. N. Seshan with Sanjoy Hazarika, *The Degeneration of India* (New Delhi: Viking, 1995), Section I: The Crumbling Edifice, and Section II: Path to Nowhere.

16 Mehra Masani, *Broadcasting and the People* (New Delhi: National Book Trust, 1976), pp. 147–148.

17 The first concerted attempt to open up the broadcasting system was in 1978. The B. G. Verghese Committee Report commissioned by the Janata government recommended an autonomous National Broadcast Trust, Akash Bharati, on the lines of the recommendation by the 1964 A. K. Chanda Committee Report. The Janata government rejected the plan, and it was shelved. When the Janata Dal came to power in 1990, this was revived and a bill proposing an autonomous broadcasting institution, the Prasar Bharati Bill, which considerably watered down the Verghese recommendations, was passed in Parliament; it remains to be implemented. See T. K. Thomas, "Akash Bharati vs Prasar Bharati: A Comparative Study," in T. K. Thomas, ed., *Autonomy for the Electronic Media: A National Debate on The Prasar Bharati Bill* (New Delhi: Konark Publishers, 1990), pp. 105–121.

18 When B. V. Keskar became Minister for Information and Broadcasting in 1952, audience research was "nipped in the bud." Although surveys continued to be conducted, they were treated as confidential documents, and not incorporated into program evaluation. G. C. Awasthy, *Broadcasting in India* (Bombay: Allied Publishers, 1965), pp. 217–220. See also P. C. Chatterji, *Broadcasting in India* (New Delhi: Sage, 1991), pp. 87–88 (revised and updated edition).

19 This may be characteristic of state-controlled broadcasting. The director of the USSR State Committee for Television and Radio, for instance, in 1984, described television as "a mirror of the principles of the State." Vladimir Popov, cited in Terry Doyle, "Truth at Ten? Some Questions of Soviet Television," *Sight and Sound*, Spring 1984, p. 108. Cited in Stephen Heath, "Representing Television," in Patricia Mellencamp, ed., *Logics of Television: Essays in Cultural Criticism* (Bloomington, Ind. and London: Indiana University Press and British Film Institute, 1990), pp. 274–275.

20 1983 and 1987 figures from *Television India (Facts and Figures)*, Audience Research Unit, Doordarshan, New Delhi, October 1988, p. 13. 1994 figures from *The Economic Times*, 30 March 1994.

21 Masani, *Broadcasting and the People*, p. 148. This was at any rate the case until recently. The 1997 Broadcasting Bill permits private broadcasting within India, but the practical implications of this legislation remain to be seen. The legislation under which the government maintained a monopoly over broadcasting was the Telegraph Act of 1885, which forbade private systems of telegraphic communication and made provisions for state monopoly in respect to it.

22 Chatterji, *Broadcasting in India*, pp. 104–105.

23 Indira Jaising v. Union of India and Others. Writ Petition No. 1980 of 1986, Bombay High Court (Civil). Jaising's argument was that Doordarshan's decision to edit out her comments on the Muslim Women's Bill while retaining various other comments on women's issues that she had made was politically motivated. In the absence of supporting evidence, the argument was a bold one. I thank Ashish Rajadhyaksha for making a copy of this petition available to me.

24 "Doordarshan has no censorship right: HC," *The Indian Post*, 25 June 1986. See also N. L. Chowla, "Courts not suited to guide Doordarshan," *Times of India*, 6 August 1988, p. 7. In February 1995, the Supreme Court, adjudicating a dispute between the Cricket Association of Bengal and Doordarshan, ruled that the airwaves were public property and that the government had no right to a monopoly over them. The consequences of the ruling remain to be seen. Sevanti Ninan, *Through the Magic Window: Television and Social Change in India* (New Delhi: Penguin, 1995), pp. 26–27.

25 Field notes. See also Masani, *Broadcasting and the People*, e.g., pp. 159–160.

26 Sunil Mishra, "Remember the Audience," in Thomas, *Autonomy for the Electronic Media*, p. 78.

27 Awasthy, *Broadcasting in India*, p. 28.

28 Arvind Singhal and Everett Rogers, *India's Information Revolution* (New Delhi: Sage, 1989), pp. 90–91. On *Simplemente Maria*, see Henry Geddes-Gonzales, "Articulating Narrative Strategies: The Peruvian Telenovela," in Anamaria Fadul, ed., *Serial Fiction in the Latin American Telenovelas with an Annotated Bibliography of Brazilian Telenovelas* (Sao Paulo: School of Communication and Arts, 1993), pp. 50–54.

29 Arvind Singhal, Everett M. Rogers, and William J. Brown, "Entertainment Telenovelas for Development: Lessons Learned," in Fadul, *Serial Fiction*, p. 158.

30 Both Manohar Shyam Joshi, who wrote the screenplay for *Hum Log*, and S. S. Gill agree that the experiment was a failure. Personal interviews, New Delhi, August 1989. On the Indian soap opera form, see Veena Das, "On Soap Opera: What Kind of Anthropological Object Is It?" in Daniel Miller, ed,. *Worlds Apart: Modernity Through the Prism of the Local* (London: Routledge, 1995), pp. 169–189.

31 Manohar Shyam Joshi, personal interview, New Delhi, 14 June 1994.

32 The civil servant responsible for the decision, former Information and Broadcasting Secretary S. S. Gill, disclosed that he had made the decision unilaterally and without moving any paperwork to seek ministerial clearance in the matter. Personal interview, 18 June 1994, New Delhi. This is a procedural detail illustrating institutional culture; commercialization could not have proceeded without political approval. Subsequently, Doordarshan entered into an agreement with CNN to start a 24-hour news channel, which would be broadcast on the state's INSAT 2-B satellite. Ashish Mullick, "DD, CNN Pact to Start 24 Hr News Channel," *The Times of India*, 30 June 1995, p. 7.

33 Pranab Bardhan, *The Political Economy of Deveopment in India* (Oxford: Basil Blackwell, 1984), pp. 32–39; 73–74.

34 I use the names "Ramayana" and "Mahabharata" to refer to the narrative traditions of these epics; "Ramayan" and "Mahabharat" are the names of their television serial versions.

35 S. S. Gill, "Why Ramayan on Doordarshan," *The Indian Express*, 8 August 1988.

36 Gyanendra Pandey, *The Construction of Communalism in Colonial North India*. (Delhi: Oxford University Press, 1990).

37 Chatterji, *Broadcasting in India*, p. 134. On the making of a national Indian music on All India Radio, see David Lelyveld, "Upon the Subdominant: Administering Music on All-India Radio," *Social Text*, vol. 39, 1994, pp. 111–127.

38 H. R. Luthra, *Indian Broadcasting* (New Delhi: Publications Division, 1986), pp. 347–353.

39 U. L. Baruah, "Secularism in the AIR: Not Only the Voice of Hinduism," *The Statesman*, 2 November 1983.

40 *Ibid.*

41 For a discussion of Hindustani and its relative merits vis-à-vis Hindi, see David Lelyveld, "The Fate of Hindustani: Colonial Knowledge and the

Project of a National Language," in Carol A. Breckinridge and Peter van der Veer, eds., *Orientalism and the Colonial Predicament: Perspectives on South Asia* (Philadelphia: University of Pennsylvania Press, 1993), pp. 189–214. For a discussion of the debates on language policy in the Constituent Assembly, see Granville Austin, *The Indian Constitution: The Cornerstone of a Nation* (Oxford: Clarendon Press, 1966), chapter 12. See also B. Shiva Rao *et al.*, eds., *The Framing of India's Constitution: Select Documents* (New Delhi: Indian Institute of Public Administration, 1968), pp. 615–628.

42 Charles A. Ferguson, "Diglossia," in P. P. Giglioli, ed., *Language and Social Context* (Harmondsworth: Penguin, 1972), pp. 244–245; on Hindi diglossia, see Rakesh Mohan Bhatt, "Sociolinguistic Area and Language Policies," in Edward C. Dimock *et al.*, eds, *Dimensions of Sociolinguistics in South Asia. Papers in Memory of Gerald B. Kelly* (New Delhi: Oxford and IBH Publishing Co., 1992), pp. 47–69; Yamuna Kachru, "Impact of Expanding Domains of Use on a Standard Language: Contemporary Hindi in India," *Studies in the Linguistic Sciences*, vol. 17, no. 1, 1987, pp. 73–90. For a general discussion of post-independence language policy see Jyotirindra Das Gupta, *Language Conflict and National Development: Group Politics and National Language Policy in India* (Berekeley: University of California Press, 1970).

43 See Vasudha Dalmia, *The Nationalization of Hindu Tradition* (New Delhi: Oxford University Press, 1999).

44 E.g., see K. S. Duggal, *What Ails Indian Broadcasting* (New Delhi: Marwah Publications, 1980), pp. 51, 113, 139. An oft-repeated joke makes the point well. The news in Hindi tends to be preceded by the announcement, "Ab Hindi mein samachar suniye" (Now please listen to the news in Hindi), which, in the joke, is paraphrased as "Ab Samachar mein Hindi suniye" (Now please listen to the Hindi in the news). That is, most of the words were not within the comprehension even of Hindi speakers.

45 In contrast, the Hindi film industry has continued to use Urdu as the most reliable way to communicate, following the tradition of the Parsi theatre from which it emerged. Thus the Bombay industry, a fair percentage of whose writers and artists were Muslim, has succeeded in crafting films with more or less national appeal, forging an idiom that those across much of the country were able to share. See in this context Mukul Kesavan, "Urdu, Awadh and the Tawaif: The Islamicate Roots of Hindi Cinema," in Zoya Hasan, ed., *Forging Identities. Gender, Communities and the State* (New Delhi: Kali for Women, 1994), pp. 244–257.

46 Awasthy, *Broadcasting in India*, pp. 111–113.

47 An important historian of Indian broadcasting, H. R. Luthra, mentions three "exceptions" to the policy of secular broadcasting that prevailed until the mid-1980s: in Srinagar, Kashmir, near the Pakistani border in Jullundur, Punjab, and in Kohima, Nagaland (in the Northeast). In all three cases, the decision was taken by the central government. Srinagar used to broadcast recitations from the Koran before it came under central rule in 1954, and the broadcasts were continued as a "special case," in the attempt

to maintain Indian as opposed to Pakistani hegemony over the Muslim majority population. After the conflict with China in 1962, a station was set up in Kohima, and readings from the Bible were introduced on Sundays. In Jullundur, programming for Sikhs was introduced to counter similar programming aired by Radio Pakistan in the late 1960s. Luthra, *Indian Broadcasting*, 1986, pp. 346–353.

48 The seventy-eight episodes of the Ramayan started on 25 January 1987. At episode one, it drew a 24 percent rating, i.e., 24 percent of television households tuned in. Episode eleven crossed the 50 percent mark, and with Episode forty-one, the 70 percent mark was reached. By the end of the serial, the rating was in excess of 80 percent. Heavy viewers were more likely to be women. High frequency of viewership had a slight skew towards the 45 + age group. Lower income groups were more likely to be light viewers. The program that followed Ramayan in the Sunday morning slot, *Chand Sitare* (Moon and Stars), averaged a rating of 30 percent. As much as 98 percent of potential viewers had seen at least one episode. Of the total audience reached, 91 percent had seen more than twenty of the telecasts. More than half the audience reached had seen forty or more episodes (Indian Market Research Bureau Special Report: The Ramayan Phenomenon: An Epic Programme). The Mahabharata, televised subsequently, achieved yet higher ratings. The director of the Ramayan serial, Ramanand Sagar, was born Ramanand Chopra, in Lahore in 1917. At first, he worked as a journalist and at the same time acquired a degree in Sanskrit; later he would claim a degree in Urdu as well. Ramanand Sagar, "Director's Diary," *Star&Style*, 21 November–4 December 1986, pp. 66–69. Compare, e.g., Ashish Rajadhyaksha and Paul Willemen, *Encyclopaedia of Indian Cinema* (London and New Delhi: British Film Industry and Oxford University Press, 1994), p. 188. He achieved early fame with his *Diary of a TB Patient* (1942), and his novel about communal riots during the Partition, *Aur Insaan Mar Gaya* (And Man Died, 1948) became a classic. As a screenwriter in Bombay he established himself working on Raj Kapoor's *Barsaat* (1949), and went on to become a film-maker himself. A 1969 screen index describes his films as "characteristically Indian" but appealing to "world audiences" also. There is a picture of a youthful Sagar, in a rakishly tilted hat and dark glasses, the image of a cosmopolitan *auteur*. Peter Cowie, ed., *International Film Guide 1969* (London: Tantivy Press, 1969), p. 100. A row of hit films was followed by a series of indifferent ones, including *Charas* (Hashish, 1978), *Baghaavat* (Revolt, 1983), and *Romance* (1985). Doordarshan appeared as a reprieve. S. S. Gill described him as a friend from his Lahore days; the request to make a fifty-two part serial based on Ramayan was addressed directly from Gill to Sagar. S. S. Gill, personal interview, New Delhi, August 1989; see also Gill, "Why Ramayan on Doordarshan." In the process, the *auteur* underwent a transformation, appearing in saffron and beads in interludes in the Ramayan serial, extolling the glories of Hindu culture, and offering similar messages in VHP-staged events.

49 I thank David Lelyveld for making available a copy of Vijay Bhatt's *Ram Rajya* for my edification.

50 Gill, "Why Ramayan on TV."

51 The appearance of the TV star Arun Govil drew huge crowds who perhaps came to secure his blessings, but in the end elected V. P. Singh, the candidate of the opposing party, to Parliament. V. P. Singh, who had resigned as Defence Minister under Rajiv Gandhi's Prime Ministership, had had to resign his seat in Parliament under the new anti-defection laws that forbade switching parties. In the resulting by-election in Allahabad in September 1987, the Congress candidate Sunil Shastri, son of former Prime Minister Lal Bahadur Shastri, opposed Singh.

52 According to newspaper reports, Doordarshan rejected Sagar's first submission, and questions about the possibility of a communal fallout were raised, before a revised version was finally granted approval in 1986. Gill told me that Rajiv Gandhi had asked him about the desirability of airing a Hindu epic on television. Gill had reassured him, he told me, that a national epic could not produce an adverse reaction. Personal interview, 18 June 1994.

53 Romila Thapar, "Epic and History – Tradition, Dissent and Politics in India," *Past and Present*, vol. 125, November 1989, pp. 3–26.

54 M. M. Bakhtin, "The Problem of Speech Genres," in Caryl Emerson and Michael Holquist, eds., *Speech Genres and Other Late Essays*, tr. Vern McGee (Austin: University of Texas Press, 1986, p. 4.

55 Textual references to the epic, unless otherwise stated, are to the 1938 version published by the Gita Press, reissued several times since. See H. P. Poddar, *Sri Ramcharitmanas* (Gorakhpur, U.P.: Gita Press, 1938). Numbered references to the text refer to book, stanza, and the individual line within a stanza. For translation I have drawn on R. C. Prasad, *Tulasidasa's Shriramacharitamanasa* (Delhi: Motilal Banarsidass, 1990). For a recent work on the performative tradition of the Tulsidas epic, see Philip Lutgendorf, *The Life of a Text: Performing the Ramcaritmanas of Tulsidas* (Berkeley: University of California Press, 1991). For the Valmiki Ramayana I have relied on Chimanlal Goswami, ed. and tr., *Srimad Valmiki Ramayana* (Gorakhpur: Gita Press, 1973–1976), Pts. 1–3. For bibliographies on the Ramayana, see N. A. Gore, *Bibliography of the Ramayana* (Poona, 1943); H. Daniel Smith, *Reading the Ramayana: A Bibliographic Guide for Students and College Teachers – Indian Variants on the Rama Theme in English Translations*. Foreign and Comparative Studies, South Asian special publications no. 4 (Syracuse: Maxwell School of Citizenship and Public Affairs, Syracuse University, 1983); H. Daniel Smith, *Select Bibliography of Ramayan-related Studies*. Ananthacharya Indological Series no. 21 (Bombay, 1989). Recent scholarly work on the Ramayana includes Paula Richman, ed., *Many Ramayanas: The Diversity of a Narrative Tradition in South Asia* (Berkeley: University of California Press, 1991); Joyce Burkhalter Flueckiger and Laurie Sears, eds., *The Boundaries of Tradition: Ramayana and Mahabharata Performances in South and Southeast Asia* (Ann Arbor: University of Michigan Center for South and Southeast Asian Studies, 1990); Monika

Thiel-Horstmann, ed., *Ramayan and Ramayanas* (Wiesbaden: Otto Harasowitz, 1991). For an overview of Valmiki's text and scholarship on it, see the introductory essays to the seven-volume English translation from Princeton University Press, with Robert P. Goldman as its series editor (see, e.g., the essays in vol. 1: *Balakanda*, trans. Robert P. Goldman, 1984; vol. 2: *Ayodhyakanda*, tr. Sheldon I. Pollock, 1986; vol. 3: *Aranyakanda*, tr. Sheldon I. Pollock, 1991).

56 The central narrative of Valmiki's story tells of Prince Ram, born to King Dasaratha of Ayodhya, and his brothers Bharata, Lakshman, and Shatrughna. The brothers are brave, virtuous, and loved by all, but Ram is the noblest of them; being the eldest as well, he is nominated to the throne. Bharata's mother Kaikeyi, incited to jealousy by her maid Manthara, schemes to banish Ram to the forest for fourteen years and have her son replace Ram. Invoking two boons which Dasaratha had long ago promised her, she succeeds in getting Ram to obey her in the name of his father's honor, and out of filial piety. Ram's wife Sita, and his inseparable companion Lakshman, accompany him to the forest. There they abide until the demon-king Ravan, angered by the brothers' treatment of his flirtatious sister (and subsequently aroused by tales of Sita's beauty), kidnaps Sita and imprisons her in his island kingdom, Lanka. With the help of a monkey army led by Hanuman and Sugriva, Ram and Lakshman attack and overwhelm the hitherto invincible demon kingdom, killing Ravan. Victorious, they return to Ayodhya, where Bharata joyfully relinquishes the throne to Ram. Ram is crowned king, and a glorious period of peace, prosperity, and justice ensues, Ram Rajya, now seen as a Golden Age. In the last book of the Valmiki Ramayan, the Uttara kanda, hearing suspicions about Sita's fidelity during her year's captivity in Lanka, Ram decides that drastic action must be taken to preserve his reputation as a king. He banishes Sita to the forest, where, in Valmiki's hermitage, she raises twins, Lava and Kusha. Years elapse before Ram encounters them, and determines they are his sons. The twins are reunited with their father, but Sita chooses to return to the earth, whence she came, and where the earth goddess welcomes her.

57 Bimal Krishna Matilal, "Moral Dilemmas: Insights from Indian Epics," in Matilal, ed., *Moral Dilemmas in the Mahabharata* (Shimla: Indian Institute of Advanced Study with Motilal Banarsidass, 1989), p. 4.

58 See, e.g., V. Raghavan, *The Ramayana in Greater India*. The Rao Bahadur Kamalashankar Pranshankar Trivedi Memorial Lectures, South Gujarat University (1975), pp. 1–3.

59 V. Raghavan, ed., *The Ramayana Tradition in Asia*, 2 vols. (New Delhi: Sahitya Akademi, 1976).

60 Velcheru Narayana Rao, "A Ramayan of their Own: Women's Oral Tradition in Telugu" in Paula Richman, ed., *Many Ramayanas: The Diversity of Narrative Tradition in South Asia* (Berkeley: University of California Press, 1991), pp. 114–136.

61 Ramdas Lamb, "Personalizing the Ramayan: Ramnamis and Their Use of the Ramcharitmanas'" in Richman, *Many Ramayanas*, pp. 241–242.

62 In a letter written to a friend cited in Yogindranath Bose's biography of Dutt. Cited in Clinton Seely, "The Raja's New Clothes: Redressing Ravana in Meghanadavada Kavya," in *ibid.*, pp. 137–155.

63 See M. M. Bakhtin, "The Problem of Speech Genres," in *Speech Genres and Other Late Essays*, tr. Vern McGee, ed., Caryl Emerson and Michael Holquist (Austin: University of Texas Press, 1986), pp. 60–102. Bakhtin defines speech genres as relatively stable types of utterances defined by a stylistic range. In fact, we can characterize speech genres by the kinds of responses they evoke, as their form is intrinsically related to the dialogical nature of language. I simplify here, but the resulting clarification illuminates my argument as well.

64 See "Forms of Time and Chronotope in the Novel," in M. M. Bakhtin. *The Dialogic Imagination*, trans. Caryl Emerson and Michael Holquist (Austin: University of Texas Press, 1981), pp. 84–258.

65 Here I have drawn on but qualified Bakhtin's discussion in "Epic and Novel" in *The Dialogic Imagination*, pp. 13–21. Bakhtin exaggerates the inaccessibility of the epic in this essay in his wish to foreground the importance of the novel. Elsewhere he acknowledges that while all genres have elements of the archaic, these are constantly renewed. See M. M. Bakhtin, *Problems of Doestoevsky's Poetics*, ed. and tr. Caryl Emerson (Minneapolis: University of Minnesota Press, 1984), p. 106.

66 Bakhtin seems at times to assume a conventional division between mythic and modern thought, where the rise of the latter destroys the basis for the existence of the former. Elsewhere, however, Bakhtin notes that language is under the power of images of the kind that dominate myth, and these impede the free movement of its intentions, and constrain the range of meanings words can take on.

67 *Bhattikavyam*, tr. G. G. Leonardi (Leiden: E. J. Brill, 1972). Cited in Smith, *Reading the Ramayana*, p. 81. My discussion here is indebted to Smith's excellent text.

68 The concept of genre itself gains its currency in the nineteenth century, we may recall, with the commodification of print goods and the resultant need to codify successful "formulas" for maximizing sales. Ralph Cohen, "History and Genre," *New Literary History*, vol. 17, no. 2, Winter 1986, p. 203. The Russian Formalist approach attempts to clear a path in the welter of the resulting profusion of genres, in the process critiquing the classical notion of a serene cumulative development. See Jury Tynyanov, "On Literary Evolution," in Ladislav Matejka and Krystyna Pomorska, eds., *Readings in Russian Poetics: Formalist and Structuralist Views* (Ann Arbor: Michigan Slavic Publications, 1978).

69 For a useful argument on the importance of a pragmatic rather than a prescriptive use of the category of genre, see Adena Rosmarin, *The Power of Genre* (Minneapolis: University of Minnesota Press, 1985), esp. chs. 1 and 2.

70 On mythological soap operas, see Philip Lutgendorf, "Ramayan: the Video," *The Drama Review*, vol. 34, no. 2, 1990, pp. 127–176; Vasudha Dalmia-Luderitz, "Television and Tradition: Some Observations on the Serialization of the Ramayana," in Thiel-Horstmann, *Ramayana and Ramayanas*; Marie Gillespie, "From Sanskrit to Sacred Soap: A Case-study in the Reception of two Contemporary TV versions of the Mahabharata," in D. Buckingham, ed., *Reading Audiences* (Manchester: Manchester University Press, 1993), pp. 48–74; Purnima Mankekar, "Television Tales and a Woman's Rage: Nationalist Recastings of Draupadi's Disrobing," *Public Culture* 5, 1993, pp. 469–492; Angelika Malinar, "The Bhagavadgita in the Mahabharata TV Serial: Domestic Drama and Dharmic Solutions," in Vasudha Dalmia and Heinrich von Stietencron, *Representing Hinduism: The Construction of Religious Traditions and National Identity* (New Delhi: Sage, 1995), pp. 442–467; and Ananda Mitra, *Television and Popular Culture in India* (New Delhi: Sage, 1995).

71 See Robert Allen, *Speaking of Soap Operas* (Chapel Hill: University of North Carolina Press, 1985), pp. 137–138, and Jostein Gripsrud, *The Dynasty Years: Hollywood Television and Critical Media Studies* (New York and London: Routledge, 1995), pp. 163–164. Allen also mentions its didacticism, but this suggests an explicit pedagogy that is no longer found in most soaps. Thus when Televisa in Mexico broadcast educational soap operas, it was considered necessary to devise a new name for them: developmental soap operas.

72 49 percent of the total viewers were male, but only 43 percent of the heavy viewers were male. Among the light and medium viewers, males were 57 and 55 percent respectively. *The Ramayan Phenomenon: An Epic Programme* (Indian Market Research Bureau, 1990), p. 8.

73 Diana L. Eck, *Darshan: Seeing the Divine Image in India*, 2nd edn. (Chambersburg: Anima Books, 1985).

74 Mani Kaul, personal communication, June 1988.

75 Syed Shahabuddin, an energetic proponent of conservative Muslim interests, had called for a boycott of the Republic Day Parade to protest what he saw as Hindu hegemony, in the wake of the Supreme Court judgment in the Shah Bano case in 1985. See Zakia Pathak and Sunder Rajan, "Shahbano: The Social Text," *Signo*, vol. 14, no. 3, 1989, pp. 558–582. He went on to become head of the Babri Masjid Action Committee, leading the Muslim response to the Vishwa Hindu Parishad. Here Shahabuddin is being identified with narrow-minded bigotry.

76 Neerja Kuckreja Sohoni, "Mahabharata Gives Hindus a Common Identity," *The Times of India*, 14 September 1989, p. 3. Syed Shahabuddin was a member of the Babri Masjid Action Committee and was active during this time in trying to consolidate a "Muslim vote," as a means of resisting what he decried as the violence being done to the community.

77 Sheela Bhatt, "DD Gifts Rs 40 Lakh a Week to Sagar, Khan," *Indian Express*, 1 July 1996. *Shri Krishna* started out on a private video circuit after

being rejected by Doordarshan, and it received successive extensions on its contract owing to viewership. Then the serial was aired on Doordarshan's second channel, DD-2 in April 1996. In June, it was upgraded to DD-1, reflecting its rising earnings. From May onwards, it was also being dubbed in Tamil, Telugu, Malayalam, and Bengali. Ratnottama Sengupta, "Talking About Religion Isn't Communalism," interview with Ramanand Sagar, *Times of India*, 16 September 1996.

78 The description is in Saloni Zaveri, "Myths, Masti, Magic," *Sunday* (Calcutta), 11–17 August 1996, p. 35. *Akbar Birbal* was aired on Zee TV.

79 See note 3.

80 Advertisement in *India Today*, 15 September 1995, p. 191.

81 Thus Radheshyam advised the actor Bhogilal, who went on to become famous as Krishna in Kathavachak's Vir Abhimanyu:

> [I]f you do the part of Shri Krishna well, you will become famous, people will keep your photograph in their homes. This is exactly what happened . . . I advised Bhogilal, whenever you go on stage you should smile slightly, at all times. Whether it is the Gita Updesha or the scene of Arjuna making a vow to revenge the death of his son, or the lament of Subhadra and Uttara . . . Bhogilal did that; he kept this slight smile constant.

Radheyshyam Kathavachak, *Mere Natak Kal* (My Life of Theater) (Bareilly, 1957), pp. 56–57, cited in Anuradha Kapur, "The Representation of Gods and Heroes in the Parsi Mythological Drama of the Early Twentieth Century," Vasudha Dalmia and Heinrich von Stietencron, eds., *Representing Hinduism: The Construction of Religious Traditions and National Identity* (New Delhi: Sage, 1995), pp. 416–417. Arun Govil, the actor who played Ram in Sagar's serial, appeared to achieve similar results with this method.

82 Geeta Kapur, "Ravi Varma: Representational Dilemmas of a Nineteenth Century Indian Painter," *Journal of Arts and Ideas*, nos. 17–18, June 1989; Tapati Guha-Thakurta, *The Making of a New "Indian" Art: Artists, Aesthetics and Nationalism in Bengal, c1850–1920* (Cambridge: Cambridge University Press, 1992).

83 Rajadhyaksha and Willemen, *Encylopaedia of Indian Cinema*, p. 145.

84 See Thomas Elsaesser, "Tales of Sound and Fury: Observations on the Family Melodrama," *Monogram*, vol. 4, 1972, pp. 2–15.

85 E.g., this influential argument has been made by Peter Brooks in *The Melodramatic Imagination* (New Haven: Yale University Press, 1976). Brooks accords an overly expanded status to melodrama, however, making it symptomatic of modernity as such. He thereby departs from examining its distinctness as *a* genre, co-existing with *other* genres.

86 Ravi Vasudevan, "Addressing the Spectator of a 'Third World' National Cinema: The Bombay 'Social' Film of the 1940s and 1950s," *Screen*, vol. 36, no. 4, Winter 1995, pp. 305–324; "The Melodramatic Mode and the Commercial Hindi Cinema: Notes on Film History, Narrative and Performance in the 1950s," *Screen*, vol. 30, no. 3, 1989, pp. 29–52.

87 Here we can briefly note some relevant distinctions between film and TV studies, as a way of indexing the greater sensitivity of the latter to questions of social practice and historical context. Film studies' concerns about technology and the cinematic apparatus have led to arguments for the ways in which subjectivity and spectatorship converge to produce the filmic text's illusion of reality, and to theories of the subject's ability to signify himself or herself in language. Working from psychoanalysis and literary theory, it has tended to suppress inquiry into the socio-historical conditions and consequences of viewership for a more abstracted model of the subject and its interaction with the text. In the process, the specific material effects of the filmic technology were replaced with questions centered on the iconic status of the image and the effects thereof. Television was for a long time parasitic on earlier forms of content, such as musical shows, drama, public events and so on. It was technically inferior to the cinema, which preceded it, and yet soon gained over it because of the need for "a form of *unified* social intake," in Raymond Williams' words. See his *Television: Technology and Cultural Form*, p. 28. The technically more indistinct nature of the televisual text, and the different quality of the spectator's relationship to the text due to a more diffuse and distracted context of reception, lead to different emphases in scholarship. Hence the focus on more social and historical indices of texts and audience readings, over the medium's structuring of subjectivity as a reliable guide to television's effectiveness.

88 Bhakti: devotion.

89 Interview in *Sakal* (Marathi daily, Pune), 2 October 1987, p. 20, cited in G.-D. Sontheimer, "The Ramayana in Contemporary Folk Traditions of Maharashtra," in Thiel-Horstmann, *Ramayana and Ramayanas*, p. 117, fn 1.

90 Sagar, "Director's Diary," pp. 66–69.

91 Tulsidas's *Sri Ramcharitmanas* was cited as the chief source of the TV version of the story, followed by Valmiki's Ramayana.

92 Robert C. Allen has made this point about Hollywood soap operas. Allen, *Speaking of Soap Operas*, pp. 70–71.

93 For the first twelve episodes of the serial, I have used the English subtitles from the video that were available at the time of writing. Excerpts from subsequent episodes are my translations. I have relied on the two-volume transcription of the serial's text, *Ramayana: A TV Serial by Ramanand Sagar*, tr. Girish Bakhshi, ed. Tomio Mizokami (Osaka University of Foreign Studies, 1992). I thank Professor Mizokami for making these volumes available to me.

94 Bal Kand of *Ramcharitmanas*, stanza 1, line 12.

95 The General Secretary of the RSS, H. V. Seshadri, gave a speech which appears to have drawn from a similar source as this passage: "[T]he Hindu Nation has had the unique honour of sending out, whenever it became powerful and resurgent, not its predatory armies for aggression on others, but messengers of spirituality, culture, art and science who conquered the unknown lands on the strength of their intellectual, moral and spiritual

attainments." He goes on: "Now, after a lapse of several centuries, Hindus are bestirring themselves once again." Speech at VHP of USA conference, New York, 8–9 July 1984, in H. V. Seshadri, *Hindus Abroad. The Dilemma: Dollar or Dharma?* (New Delhi: Suruchi Prakashan, 1990), p. 27.

96 Valmiki Ramayana, Bala Kanda, verse 2, stanzas 36–37.

97 Mimi Vaid-Fera, "The Ramayan on Television," *Imprint*, October 1987, p. 9.

98 Rakshasas are colloquially understood as demons, and are portrayed as such in most versions of the Rama story. Literally, the term means protectors. The rakshasas represented forest-dwellers, and a way of life that was different from the city-dwelling inhabitants of Ayodhya.

99 Ramanand Sagar's Ramayan, episode two.

100 See R. C. Majumdar, Radhagovinda Basak, and Pandit Nanigopal Banerji, *The Ramacaritam of Sandhyakaranandin* (Rajshahi, Bihar: Varendra Research Museum, 1939). Cited in Smith, *Reading the Ramayana*, p. 83.

101 Episode seven.

102 Episode thirteen.

103 Episode nine.

104 Episode eighteen.

105 Episode nineteen.

106 This detail in the story, absent in Tulsidas, though found in most popular retellings, emphasizes not only Shabari's naiveté but her low birth as well. High-caste orthodoxy might consider such fruit polluted.

107 See chapter three.

108 Simran Bhargava, "Divine Sensation," *India Today*, 30 April 1987.

109 Allen, *Speaking of Soap Operas*.

110 See Gramsci's "Modern Prince," in *An Antonio Gramsci Reader*, p. 184.

111 Here the absence in the Congress of any genuine rank and file was telling. The resulting association of top leaders in any propaganda attempt left the party less able to insulate itself from criticism. The BJP itself tended to be more careful, using members ostensibly associated with different organiz-ations, the Bajrang Dal or the Vishwa Hindu Parishad, to make religious appeals, thereby usually protecting its top leaders. Some BJP Members of Parliament, however, such as Uma Bharati, were habitually militant in their statements.

112 Roland Barthes, *Mythologies*, selected and tr. Annette Lavers (New York: Hill and Wang, 1972), p. 112.

113 E.g., see *Illustrated Weekly of India*, August 1985; *Imprint*, November 1985. The view that religious sentiment is epiphenomenal and is liable to disap-pear, or ought to disappear, is of course widely prevalent. For discussion of my argument about a "split public," see chapter four.

114 See Bourdieu, *The Logic of Practice*, p. 122.

115 These arguments articulate with Foucault's notion of governmentality (see chapter one, fn. 9). The governmentalization of the state, as Foucault defines the term for Western Europe, involves a rationalization of state

functioning, as the state becomes less focused on its *raison d'état*, less inwardly oriented, maximizing instead its economy of power, as it becomes attentive to the most distant points of its application and the most convenient relation between means and ends. Governmentality is then not a specific form we should expect to have reproduced, but rather a logic of the devolution of power, that in the Indian context borrows from a language of community and tradition. These traditions were themselves, of course, complicit with a colonial sociology of knowledge and governance. On the colonial sociology of knowledge, see, e.g., Bernard S. Cohn, "The Census, Social Structure and Objectification in South Asia," in *An Anthropologist Among the Historians and Other Essays* (New Delhi: Oxford University Press, 1987), pp. 224–254; Nicholas B. Dirks, "Castes of Mind," *Representations*, no. 37, Winter 1992, pp. 56–78. For an argument on governmentality in the context of Hindutva, see Partha Chatterjee, "Secularism and Tolerance," *Economic and Political Weekly*, 9 July 1994, pp. 1768–1777.

3 THE COMMUNICATING THING AND ITS PUBLIC

1 H. N. Singh, "TV Culture Has its Lighter Side," *Patriot*, 5 March 1985.
2 " 'Raw Deal' to Opposition on TV," *Times of India*, 28 August 1989, p. 1.
3 *Ibid.*, pp. 1 and 7.
4 During the 1980s and early 1990s, many hundreds of women became victims to the phenomenon of "dowry deaths" fueled by the expansion of the consumer market, as the families they married into proceeded to squeeze dowries from one set of in-laws after another. This is primitive capital absorption in a distinct sense. The process of commodification may thus intensify existing tensions in ritual hierarchies, at least initially, as the scope of the market is extended. See Madhu Kishwar and Ruth Vanita, eds., *In Search of Answers: Indian Women's Voices from Manushi* (London and Totowa, N.J.: Zed Books, 1984).
5 E. Valentine Daniel, *Charred Lullabies: Chapters in an Anthropography of Violence* (Princeton: Princeton University Press, 1996), p. 209.
6 Dronvir Kohli, "*Unke T.V. Aur Hamara Doordarshan*," [Their T.V. and Our Doordarshan] *Navbharat Times*, 25 November 1986, p. 9.
7 Field notes, April–May 1988.
8 Amita Malik, "What Happened to the Backroom Boys," *Indian Express Weekend*, 5 October 1986.
9 E.g., in comments of viewers reported in the Delhi Doordarshan Kendra's Audience Research Unit qualitative survey, 22 and 23 February 1989.
10 " 'Raw Deal' to Opposition on TV," p. 7.
11 Names of all interviewees in this chapter have been changed.
12 A substantial underclass, it should be mentioned, may regard the television as utterly beyond its ken. Thus Mohammed Guddu, a rickshaw-puller in Kaynagar, pointed out: "It's difficult to even manage the bare minimum household expenses. Poverty is the biggest problem here. The first thing is

to . . . try and earn a living so that one can feed one's children. For us, children are our TV."

13 Cited in Pierre Bourdieu, "Marginalia – Some Additional Notes on the Gift," in Alan D. Schrift, ed., *The Logic of the Gift: Towards an Ethic of Generosity* (New York and London: Routledge, 1997), p. 231.

14 See in this context Rudolf Mrazek's essay " 'Let Us Become Radio Mechanics': Technology and National Identity in Late-Colonial Netherlands East Indies," *Comparative Studies in Society and History*, vol. 39, no. 1, 1997, pp. 3–33.

15 Stuart Hall, "Encoding/Decoding," in Stuart Hall *et al.*, eds., *Culture, Media, Language* (London: Hutchinson, 1980). Also see my Introduction for a discussion on Hall and on reception studies.

16 Oskar Negt, "Mass Media: Tools of Domination or Instruments of Liberation? Aspects of the Frankfurt School's Communications Analysis," *New German Critique*, no. 14, Spring 1978, p. 63.

17 Richard Dienst, *Still Life in Real Time: Theory After Television* (Durham: Duke University Press, 1994), pp. 58–59.

18 Viewers may *know* that they are gathered and sold to advertisers, but they remain capable of acting *as if* they did not know this, and *as if* they thought they were free in their viewing behavior. It is therefore incorrect to assume real individuals actually hold the opinions implied by their behavior. Belief is displaced onto things rather than embodied in persons, following Zizek's reading of Marx's argument on commodity fetishism; to make sense of the work of ideology here, we must introduce rather, the idea of the "subject supposed to believe" and the "subject supposed to know," on behalf of whom viewers then accept certain notions. See Slavoj Zizek, "The Supposed Subjects of Ideology," *Critical Quarterly*, vol. 39, no. 2, Summer 1997, pp. 39–59.

19 For a discussion of fantasy as a product of the blocked consciousness of proletarian experience, see Oskar Negt and Alexander Kluge, *Public Sphere and Experience: Toward an Analysis of the Bourgeois and Proletarian Public Sphere*, foreword by Miriam Hansen, tr. Peter Labanyi, Jamie Owen Daniel, and Assenka Oksiloff (Minneapolis: University of Minnesota Press, 1993), pp. 28–38.

20 On the antinomy of "classes" versus "masses," and for an attempt at thinking through some of the contradictions of mass politics, see Etienne Balibar, *Masses, Classes, Ideas: Studies in Political Philosophy Before and After Marx*, tr. James Swenson (New York: Routledge, 1994).

21 I interviewed 169 people in Delhi and in "Kaynagar," a few hours away, in June and July 1988, and March–August 1989. Most of the interviews were with individuals, but in some cases they were performed with small groups. The interviews lasted anywhere from fifteen minutes to two hours. Ninety were from low income neighborhoods, and seventy-nine belonged to middle- to high-income neighborhoods. For the most part, however, the people I interviewed had television sets, which put them in the highest quartile of the population. Even within this section the income range is

considerable, with residences varying from tiny one- or two-room tenements to large apartments. One hundred and twenty-two of my interviewees were in Delhi, and the rest in Kaynagar. My interviewees were selected through introductions I obtained to residents in each neighborhood, as well as through "snowball sampling," with one interviewee sometimes suggesting others I might talk to. Thirty-three were Muslims, seven of them in Kaynagar. Fourteen of the Muslims were from low-income neighborhoods, one of them in Kaynagar; seventy-six of the non-Muslim interviewees were low-income neighborhoods, eight of them in Kaynagar. Sixteen were women, of whom three were from low-income neighborhoods, all of the latter in Delhi. I spoke to only one Muslim woman, a worker in Delhi. I spoke to five Sikhs, all men in Delhi, one of them middle class. The names of all interviewees have been changed. All the interviews were performed in Hindi, unless otherwise mentioned, and tape-recorded and transcribed. Unless mentioned, the interviews are with Delhi residents. I also received seventy-three letters in response to a solicitation published in *The Times of India* (New Delhi) and in the Hindi language daily *Navbharat Times* (New Delhi), requesting Ramayan viewers to write and describe why they liked the show. Ien Ang bases her study *Watching Dallas* (1985), on an analysis of forty-two letters collected in this way. In the following letters, the notation "P" refers to those addressed to me personally; "D" refers to letters addressed by Ramayan viewers to Doordarshan, from a file of 328 letters which I was able to read. "E" and "H" denote the language of the letters, i.e., whether they were in English or in Hindi.

22 A similar ambivalence characterizes some early descriptions of television in the U.S. It was seen to help keep the man in the house and thus saved marriages; at the same time it could be regarded as "the other woman," taking the husband's attention away from where it might otherwise have gone. Lyn Spigel, *Making Room for TV: Television and the Family Ideal in Postwar America* (Chicago: University of Chicago Press, 1992), pp. 36–72.

23 Joshua Meyrowitz, *No Sense of Place* (New York and Oxford: Oxford University Press, 1985).

24 See, e.g., Marie Gillespie, *Television, Ethnicity and Cultural Change* (London: Routledge, 1995).

25 Paddy Scannell, "Radio Times: The Temporal Arrangements of Broadcasting in the Modern World," in Philip Drummond and Richard Paterson, eds., *Television and its Audience: International Research Perspectives* (London: British Film Institute, 1988).

26 E. P. Thompson, "Time, Work-Discipline and Industrial Capitalism," in *Past and Present*, no. 38, 1967, pp. 56–97.

27 *Ibid.* Simultaneously, daily time comes to be calibrated according to broadcasting schedules even for those who have yet to enter the world of work. An activist in a voluntary organization, Sushil Kumar, told me how village children he was working with were now fluent with fractions of time they had had no use for before: "At 8:40, this program comes on, they'll say, and

at 9:25, that program comes on. Before, they would use units of a half-hour at most."

28 Mimi Vaid-Fera, "The Ramayan on Television," *Imprint*, October 1987.

29 E.g., *Illustrated Weekly of India*, 8 November 1987.

30 Supreme Court lawyer Gobinda Mukhoty, interviewed in *The National Herald*, 7 August 1988.

31 Letter PE 14; emphasis original.

32 Letter PE 15.

33 Letter DE 246.

34 Letter DE 195; emphasis original.

35 Letter PH 20.

36 Letter PH 12.

37 Letter PE 12; interviews with Digamber Singh, Chandru, and D. S. Damle respectively.

38 E.g., interview with Arun Govil, *Illustrated Weekly of India*, 8 November 1987.

39 Tericot, a combination of terylene and cotton, is a kind of polyester.

40 For an ethnographic account of popular discourses of corruption in politics, see Akhil Gupta, "Blurred Boundaries: The Discourse of Corruption, the Culture of Politics, and the Imagined State," *American Ethnologist*, vol. 22, no. 2, 1995, pp. 375–402.

41 Ranajit Guha, *Elementary Aspects of Peasant Insurgency in Colonial India* (Delhi: Oxford University Press, 1983).

42 While the remaining interviews were performed in Hindi, this interview was in English.

43 The Red Fort in New Delhi, built by the Mughal emperors, is the center of celebrations of nationality, such as Republic Day and Independence Day.

44 Indian media studies has tended to be dominated by an often overly empirical approach, where investigation into audience responses is thought to be capable of arriving at truths about the character of public opinion, of popular beliefs underlying national ideologies, and/or of subaltern sentiments whose exclusion can be compensated by a method of enumeration. Such an approach ignores the process of representation as well as the phenomenological specificity inherent to the work of a given media technology. Any media institution exhibits certain irreducible constraints arising from the material and symbolic limits of a process of signification. For an excellent antidote to media-centric empiricism, see Mrazek, " 'Let Us Become Radio Mechanics.' "

45 In trying to understand the nature of the claim of being a "counterpublic," I am drawing, of course, on the arguments of Habermas in his *The Structural Transformation of the Public Sphere* (Cambridge, Mass.: MIT Press, 1989), since he presents the modal form of politicization against which historical variations tend to be assessed. Habermas offers an immanent critique of the term, contrasting the claims of the public sphere with its historical forms and its decline over time. The political task of the bourgeois public sphere, comprised of the rational-critical discourse of propertied, educated

men, became the regulation of civil society, in a relationship of working antagonism with the state (p. 52). This corresponded to the newly public relevance of the private sphere of society, with the privatization of the economy in the household (p. 19). However the languages of affect and sentiment expressed in the private sphere, which lay the groundwork for rational–critical discourse in the public sphere, are understood by Habermas as languages of purely non-instrumental character. As such, he evokes the political climate of a secular society, where the claims of religion to the public sphere have been contained. The contest between religion and the secular state over the domain of politics does need to be factored in, however, even if we acknowledge that the nature of the balance varies from society to society.

46 In her foreword to Oskar Negt and Alexander Kluge's *The Public Sphere and Experience*, Miriam Hansen discusses some nuances of the word "experience," *Erfahrung*, a term which in the political climate of the 1960s had acquired a critical and oppositional force. She places Negt and Kluge's usage of the term in the context of German critical theory, chiefly in the work of Walter Benjamin and Siegfried Kracauer, and suggests that the English and American resonances of its translation ("experience") may be misleadingly empiricist. Hansen suggests that *Erfahrung* is a concept that refers both to unmediated sensation and to the organization of such sensation, i.e., both having and reflecting on experience (Negt and Kluge, *Public Sphere and Experience*, pp. xvi–xvii). Thus the exclusion of experience from the concerns of the bourgeois public sphere would simultaneously deprive it of the mediation required to make it intelligible.

47 I am summarizing a longer argument Negt and Kluge make about the recovery of fantasy as being central to overcoming alienation. Fantasy, in their view, can be reconstructed to bring out the lineaments of alternative forms of consciousness denied articulation in the bourgeois public sphere. *Public Sphere and Experience*, p. 33.

48 The Cow Protection movement in U.P., which began in the late 1880s and continued for some years thereafter provides, I suggest, an example of a kind of indigenous counterpublic, in which town and country came together. The organization of the movement drew on networks of local support, from village headmen and chiefs, local landlords and traders. See John R. McLane, *Indian Nationalism and the Early Congress* (Princeton: Princeton University Press, 1977), pp. 271–331; Gyanendra Pandey, "Rallying Round the Cow: Sectarian Strife in the Bhojpuri region, c. 1880–1917," in Ranajit Guha, ed., *Subaltern Studies II* (Delhi: Oxford University Press, 1983), pp. 60–129; Sandria B. Freitag, "Sacred Symbol as Mobilizing Idedology: The North Indian Search for a 'Hindu' Community," *Comparative Studies in Society and History*, vol. 22, no. 4, October 1980, pp. 597–625; Anand A. Yang, "Sacred Symbol and Sacred Space in Rural India: Community Mobilization in the 'Anti-Cow-Killing' Riot of 1893," *ibid.*, pp. 576–596. See also Pandey, "Mobilizing the Hindu Community," in his *The Construc-*

tion of Communalism in Colonial North India (New Delhi: Oxford University Press, 1990), pp. 158–200.

4 A ''SPLIT PUBLIC'' IN THE MAKING AND UNMAKING OF THE
RAM JANMABHUMI MOVEMENT

1 See the op. ed. piece cited in chapter two, by the then Information and Broadcasting Secretary S. S. Gill.

2 This view was expressed, with slight variations, in letters PH 7, PH 9, PH 23, PE 17, and PE 20. See chapter three, note 21 for notation on letters.

3 News media claiming to be objective typically rely on state authority to define the boundaries of normality. Thus "order" is by far the dominant value in the news, as empirical studies of the news media suggest. See, in this connection., Herbert Gans, *Deciding What's News* (New York: Viking, 1976).

4 Here I focus only on Hindi and English language news coverage, and my choice is unavoidably selective. Clearly more research remains to be done, not only with more exhaustive analysis of the news in these languages, but as well in other indigenous language news of the period. I would argue, however, that the notion of a split public offers a powerful heuristic that can illuminate trends in other sections of the print public as well.

5 This understanding of news in Western Europe is offered in Habermas's *The Structural Transformation of the Public Sphere*, e.g., pp. 57–88. For an argument pertaining to the U.S., see Michael Schudson, *Discovering the News: A Social History of American Newspapers* (New York: Basic Books, 1978). Schudson, however, argues that it was the rise of a democratic market society in the 1830s, under Andrew Jackson's presidency, that saw the emergence of objectivity as a criterion of news judgment in the U.S. For influential analyses of the news, see the Glasgow University Media Group, *Bad News*, vols. 1 and 2 (London: Routledge and Kegan Paul, 1976, 1980); S. Cohen and J. Young, eds., *The Manufacture of News* (London: Constable, 1973); Stuart Hall *et al.*, *Policing the Crisis: Mugging, the State, and Law and Order* (London: Macmillan, 1978); Daniel Hallin, *We Keep America On Top of the World* (New York: Routledge, 1993); and Todd Gitlin, *The Whole World is Watching: Mass Media in the Making and Unmaking of the New Left* (Berkeley: University of California Press, 1980). Regarding news in India, scholarly literature is as yet limited, with the exception of Rajeev Dhavan's *Only the Good News: On the Law of the Press in India* (New Delhi: Manohar, 1987).

6 I should stress that rather than locating an essential set of differences between languages, I am arguing about discrepancy between news values in Hindi and English language print news. However, for an insightful discussion of the profound gaps in communication between English language and indigenous language speakers, see Aniket Jaaware, "The Silence of the Subaltern Student." Paper presented at the Subaltern Studies Conference, Hyderabad, 1993.

7 This is not true, however, of the national Hindi dailies, which are owned and operated by the English language dailies, and for the most part carry articles translated from the English. As a result, the latter newspapers, e.g., *Navbharat Times* and *Jansatta* (belonging to *The Times of India* and *The Indian Express* groups respectively) are therefore quite unrepresentative of regional Hindi newspaper culture.

8 Thus for instance, in the period 1987–1996, coinciding with the growth of the television audience from a few millions to close to 200 million, the overall circulation of newspapers has grown by approximately 140 percent. See Charu Gupta and Mukul Sharma, "Communal Constructions: Media Reality vs. Real Reality," *Race & Class*, vol. 38, no. 1, 1996, pp. 2–3 fn.

9 Thus Habermas writes of the "re-feudalization" that occurs as the public sphere becomes entirely absorbed into the production process and large corporations proceed to dominate the market. He quotes from H. Haftendorn to elaborate on a point: "Were one to see the sense of the radio and television transmissions of the *Bundestag* sessions in their providing the listener (or viewer) at the receiver with the opportunity for participation in the work of elected representatives, then one would have to conclude that radio and television are not adequate for this purpose; that instead, by biasing and distorting the debates, they represent a disruption of parliamentary work." Habermas continues: "Before the expanded public sphere the [Parliamentary] transactions themselves are stylized into a show. Publicity loses its critical function in favor of a staged display; even arguments are transmuted into symbols to which again one can not respond by arguing but only by identifying with them." *The Structural Transformation of the Public Sphere*, p. 206.

10 E.g., Habermas, *The Structural Transformation of the Public Sphere*.

11 Underlying this dismissal tend to be tacit assumptions about the liberal–rational character of a print public, composed of a relatively small, educated intelligentsia, and able to guard against the discontents of more broad-based popular forces. Such assumptions take for granted the privileges anchoring the existence of a print public, and lead to a dead-end of pessimism about future possibilities. Moreover, the view that the larger public enabled by radio and television can only represent a fall from the Eden of eighteenth-century English coffeehouses and Parisian salons is not one that could be widely shared, least of all in societies that cannot claim those histories as their own.

12 Episode one of the Ramayan achieved a TRP (Television Rating Point, or percentage of households tuning in with respect to the total number of television households) of twenty-four in the four "Metros," Bombay, Calcutta, Madras, and Delhi. By Episode seventy-eight, on 31 July 1988, this had reached eighty TRPs. In the words of the IMRB Special Report, "Sunday mornings, for the first time, became advertising prime time." Ramayan's successor, Chand Sitare, managed a meager average of about thirty TRPs "at the four Metro level" in its first two episodes. Viewership

was more often "light" in Madras and "medium" in Calcutta, as opposed to the "heavy" viewing predominant in Bombay and Delhi, but even at these levels the ratings set a record for the time. See Indian Market Research Bureau (IMRB), "The Ramayan Phenomenon: An Epic Programme," Bombay, 1989.

13 E.g., see the excerpts from *Aaj* (Varanasi) below.

14 S. K. Goyal and Challapathi Rao, *Ownership and Control Structure of the Indian Press* (Indian Institute of Public Administration), Appendix X.2; Second Press Commission of India, *Report of the Second Press Commission* (Delhi: Controller of Publications, 1982), vol. 2, ch. 3, p. 241. Goyal and Challapathi Rao note that their estimate of monopoly control is an underestimate, due to unavailable or incomplete information on individual owners, and their business and family ties. The Registrar of Newspapers of India (RNI) defines the term "Common Ownership Unit" (COU) as a newspaper establishment owning two or more news interest newspapers, at least one of which is a daily. Eighty-two COUs were identified in 1979, that published 210 newspapers out of the total of 645 in 1979. However the RNI treats different editions of the same newspapers as different economic entities, and so under-reports concentration; thus the *Indian Express* is treated as ten different newspapers, since it is published in ten different places in India, and so on. *Ibid.*, pp. 237–238, 241. See also vol. 2, tables II–V, pp. 238–242. For more recent remarks on the monopolistic trend in the newspaper business, see also *Press Council of India. Annual Report* (1 April 1991–31 March 1992), New Delhi, pp. 7–8. The Report notes the difficulty of specifying concentration of ownership given the inadequacy of the categorization in the information maintained by the Press Registrar, and the reluctance of the media themselves to respond to the Commission's requests for assistance.

15 *Press Council of India. Annual Report*, pp. 7–8.

16 For discussion, see *Report of the Second Press Commission*, vol. 1, pp. 139–163. With respect to periodicals, these figures were 12.31 and 7.09 respectively. The Report notes the difficulty of specifying concentration of ownership given the inadequacy of the categorization in the information maintained by the Press Registrar, and the reluctance of the media themselves to respond to the Commission's requests for assistance.

17 The Second Press Commission noted that on legislation that went against the interests of private business, such as the Companies Act, the Monopolies and Restrictive Trade Practices Act, the proposals of nationalization of the Imperial Bank and Life Insurance Companies in 1956, or the bank nation- alization plan in 1969, the economic interests of newspaper owners were consistent with the stand taken by newspapers. The newspapers "controlled by big business" by and large opposed the measures listed, it was noted. *Report of the Second Press Commission,* p. 146. A content analysis of English language reportage on economic and political issues, completed some years before the Second Press Commission was convened, expressed agreement with this conclusion. Sumanta Banerjee, *India's Monopoly Press: A Mirror of*

Distortion (New Delhi: Indian Federation of Working Journalists, 1973), pp. 83–86. The principal shareholders in *The Indian Express* are the Goenka family. The Sahu-Jains and their associated companies are the major shareholders in the Bennett Coleman Company, whch publishes *The Times of India*. Other leading English language dailies published in the capital include *The Hindustan Times*, owned by the Birla family, one of the country's largest industrial houses, and *The Statesman*, which is owned by Tata Sons Private Ltd., Martin Burn Ltd., Mafatlal Gagalbhai and Co. Ltd., and other industrial houses. *Report of the Second Press Commission*, vol. 2, Appendix X2.

18 *Constituent Assembly Debates* VII, p. 780, cited in Rajeev Dhavan, *Only the Good News: On the Law of the Press in India* (New Delhi: Manohar, 1987), p. 102. The latter volume offers a good discussion, indeed the only significant one to my knowledge, of the historical shifts in the relations between the press and the Indian state.

19 The point deserves qualification. Certainly in the West, the public sphere is an ambivalent category, theoretically a bulwark of democracy but in practical terms, a threat to order. The historical experience that informs the theory of the public is significantly different in formerly colonial countries, however, resulting in a much deeper ambivalence towards the term on the part of the state. Thus the theoretical sanctity of the public sphere is institutionalized in the constitutional protection granted to the press in countries like the U.S., contrasting with the absence of such safeguards in places such as India. I am indebted to Carin McCormack for this qualification.

20 The Press Council, established in 1966, abolished during the Emergency in 1976, and set up again during the Janata government in 1979, was designed as a body that would warn, admonish, and censure reprehensible reportage in the news media. By far the majority of complaints are registered by the government to harass newspapers, however. See Dhavan, *Only the Good News*, pp. 420, 430. In a survey carried out by the Second Press Commission, 332 out of 392 newspapers thought government policy was unfair in respect to the allocation of advertisements. *Report of the Second Press Commission*, p. 106.

21 The Diwakar Committee on Small Newspapers, 1966, had recommended the encouragement of small newspapers as an effective means of furthering communication.

22 See T. J. S. George, *The Provincial Press in India* (New Delhi: Press Institute of India, 1966), pp. 5–6.

23 Cited *ibid.*, p. 51.

24 See in this context the useful discussion of secularism as a concept in Marc Galanter, "Hinduism, Secularism and the Indian Judiciary," *Philosophy East and West*, vol. 21, no. 4, October 1971, pp. 467–487 (rpt. in the University of Chicago, Committee on Southern Asian Studies, Reprint Series No. 49).

25 Exceptions included *The Navbharat Times* in the Hindi press ("a group of committed Marxists there," in the words of one RSS leader) and *The Indian*

Express in the English press, and the latter emphatically so under Arun Shourie's editorship, which lasted until November 1990, and to a slightly lesser extent thereafter under Prabhu Chawla. Personal interview with Devendar Swaroop Agarwal, Director, Deen Dayal Upadhyaya Research Centre, New Delhi, 27 April 1994.

26 Thus the Indian Newspaper Society, in 1989, had 167 English language members (i.e., newspapers and periodicals), as against 161 Hindi language members. *INS Press Handbook* (New Delhi: Indian Newspaper Society, 1989), p. clxxix.

27 One confirmation appeared in the quantity of advertising. In a 1981 survey, the maximum space given to advertisements was in English language papers, 49 percent, with the figure still higher for the bigger papers. Hindi papers devoted a somewhat smaller amount of space for the same purpose, 34.7 percent, as against a general average of 39 percent. *The Times of India* devoted 60 percent of its space to advertisements, and *The Indian Express*, 55 percent. The First Press Commission had recommended that the quantum of advertisements should not exceed 40 percent of the total area.

28 See in this connection Braj B. Kachru, *The Alchemy of English: The Spread, Functions and Models of Non-Native Englishes* (Oxford: Pergamon Institute, 1986).

29 Relatively independent language formations, e.g., Avadhi, Bhojpuri, Chattisgarhi, and Maithili, were rendered into "dialects" subordinate to Hindi, rather than acknowledging the status of Hindi as itself derivative of these earlier formations, in the political project of constructing a national language. See in this connection Sadhna Saxena, "Language and the Nationality Question," *Economic and Political Weekly*, 8 February 1997, pp. 268–272. Here we may note in passing the importance of identifying Hindi exclusively with the Devnagari script, claiming a Sanskritic heritage for it and thereby seeking to ghettoize Urdu as a Muslim tongue. The Hindutva wave of the period under examination, it should be stressed, was most visible in the Hindi belt, although it was later revealed that large numbers of kar sevaks were dispatched from Andhra Pradesh as well.

30 It should be noted that a small number of journalists in English language newspapers, notably Swapan Dasgupta and Chandan Mitra, became vocal supporters of the BJP following V. P. Singh's implementation of the Mandal Commission recommendations in 1990, and specifically in response to Advani's rath yatra from Somnath to Ayodhya a few weeks later. (Arun Shourie, at the time editor of *The Indian Express*, had declared his sympathies a few years earlier, during the Shah Bano movement.)

31 The association between a Sanskritized Hindi language and Hinduized conceptions of Indian nationalism, and the prominence of this association in the Indian National Congress during the independence movement, lends particular importance to Hindi in the development of contemporary communalism. (On the Congress's advancement of Hindi against Urdu, see, e.g., J. E. Sanjana, "The Congress National Language," in *Caste and Outcaste* [Bombay: Thacker & Co., 1946], pp. 86–94.) The question of how the press

in other indigenous languages related to the topic is not thereby diminished, however: the growing stature of regional parties, as well of the BJP in non-Hindi speaking states, makes this clear. This remains a subject for future research.

32 The emphatic and insistent repetition on a unique and immoveable location clearly carried an affective force that went beyond merely factual claims. The demand to build at the birthplace and *not* elsewhere articulated with the larger Hindu nationalist claim of reaching to the past to set the future right, and gave the project a sense of concreteness. At the same time, to utter this demand was to protest against the existential trauma of dislocation. What Gaston Bachelard has written about the home may be applied to the notions of the birthplace expressed here: "[I]t is our first universe, a real cosmos in every sense of the word . . . [W]e travel to the land of Motionless Childhood, motionless the way all immemorial things are." *The Poetics of Space*, tr. Maria Jolas (Boston: Beacon Press, 1969), pp. 4–5. We cannot fail to notice the deep irony of the Hindutva project, which sought to abolish spatial distinctions within Hindu, indeed Indian society itself, but through an emphasis on the irreducible and the particular.

33 But on several occasions, BJP leaders showed their sympathy for a more hardline position, so that their identification with the so-called militants was asserted, even if at other times it was denied. Thus Advani publicly criticized the VHP for postponing kar seva at then-Prime Minister V. P. Singh's request (interview in *The Hindustan Times*, 23 September 1990). The criticism was disingenuous, since the BJP and V. P. Singh's Janata Dal had had an electoral alliance, and political expediency had governed decisions on the temple movement.

34 In making this argument about the use of English in India, I am indebted to Vivek Dhareshwar's "Caste and the Secular Self," *Journal of Arts and Ideas*, nos. 25–26, 1993, pp. 117–118.

35 The term "sanctioned ignorance," from Gayatri Spivak, refers to the larger structures of social power that endorse particular information as "knowledge" and occlude the rest as irrelevant or immaterial. See Sarah Harasym, ed., *The Postcolonial Critic: Interviews, Strategies, Dialogues. Gayatri Chakravorty Spivak* (London and New York: Routledge, 1990).

36 In this context, "Rahu and Ketu" refers to traditional foes. Rahu is the head of a mythological demon severed by Lord Vishnu, and its torso was later known as Ketu.

37 Prabhash Joshi, "Chunautiyon ke beech Khada Patrakar" [Reporters Stand Between Challenges], in Jayaprakash Bharati, ed., *Hindi Patrakaritha: Dasha aur Disha* [Hindi Journalism: Condition and Direction] (New Delhi: Pravin Publishers, 1994), p. 15.

38 "The Great Suicide" by "Congressman," a byline which the magazine, *Mainstream*, explained was that of a leading figure in the Congress Party. The article has been declared as the work of Narasimha Rao in N. Ram, "A Tale of Two White Papers," (editor's column), *Frontline*, 21 May 1993, pp. 30–31.

39 Justices O. Chinappa Reddy, D. A. Desai, and D. S. Tewatia, *Citizens' Tribunal on Ayodhya. Judgement and Recommendations* (New Delhi, December 1993), p. 73.

40 "A Way Out in Ayodhya," *The Times of India*, 16 October 1990, p. 8. On the rath yatra, see Richard Davis, "On the Iconography of Rama's Chariot," in David Ludden, ed., *Making India Hindu* (Philadelphia: University of Pennsylvania Press, 1994).

41 N. Mukhopadhyay, "Whose God is it Anyway: Putting Rama Through Scrutiny," *Sunday Mail*, 2–8 July 1989, p. 2.

42 See the remark by S. P. Singh on the need for professionalism in "Who is Afraid of Hindi Journalism?" *Vidura*, New Delhi, vol. 29, June 1992, p. 15. On the "communal-minded" management of newspapers, see Asghar Ali Engineer, "The Press on Ayodhya Kar Seva," *Economic and Political Weekly*, vol. 26, no. 20, 18 May 1991, p. 1263.

43 The serpent that, according to mythology, holds up the world. See Crooke and Enthoven, *Religion and Folklore in Northern India*, pp. 63–64.

44 Abhinav Kautilya, "Tell Them Also the Importance of Ram," *Aaj*, Varanasi, 9 December 1990, p. 6.

45 Anandeshwar Prasad Singh, *Ulajh gaya hai mandir aur masjid masla* [Mandir and Mandal Issues are Entangled], Aaj, 22 November 1990, p. 6.

46 *Aaj*, Varanasi, 5 December 1990, p. 1.

47 *Ibid.*, 22 December 1990, p. 1. The Mandal Commission report, which recommended reservations for Backward Classes, was proposed to be implemented by the V. P. Singh government in order, among other things, to split the Hindutva vote; indeed it made public the repressed secret of Hindutva, that their members were not equal, and that until recently the majority had not even been considered Hindus. See for instance Gauri Viswanathan's discussion of the debates around B. R. Ambedkar's decision to convert from his "untouchable" status into Buddhism, in *Outside the Fold: Conversion, Modernity, and Belief* (Princeton: Princeton University Press, 1998), pp. 212–235. Marc Galanter provides an excellent discussion of the ways in which the Indian state has succeeded the British colonial state in defining caste. Unlike its predecessor, however, the Indian state is not only interested in classification and enumeration, but also in making citizenship available to "depressed" or "backward classes" not on the neutral terms typically associated with citizenship but on terms of what he calls compensatory discrimination. This then provides an altered context for politics, one that needs to be emphasized. See *Competing Equalities: Law and the Backward Classes in India* (Berkeley: University of California Press, 1984).

48 Virendra Singh, "The Press in India 1990–91," *Press and Advertiers' Yearbook, 1990–91* (New Delhi: INFA Publications, 1991), p. 4a.

49 BJP public relations coordinator Amitabh Sinha, personal interview, New Delhi, 27 April 1994.

50 L. K. Advani interviewed in *The Economic Times*, 10 August 1993, p. 7.

51 See editorials in *The Times of India*, 30 October and 1 November 1990.

52 The BJP's percentage of the vote had increased from 7.4 in 1984 to 11.4 in 1989 to 21 in 1991; simultaneously, it increased its seat total from two to 119, in a house of 543 in the Lok Sabha. Figures from Robert L. Hardgrave, Jr., "Alliance Politics and Minority Government: India at the Polls, 1989 and 1991," in Harold A. Gould and Sumit Ganguly, eds., *India Votes: Alliance Politics and Minority Governments in the Ninth and Tenth General Elections* (Boulder, Colo.: Westview Press, 1993), pp. 239–240.

53 Personal interview, New Delhi, 27 April 1994.

54 *Organiser*, 14 October 1990.

55 E.g., see the following *Times of India* articles by Swapan Dasgupta in 1990: "Invoking Ram to fight Mandal," 14 October, p. 12; "Journey to Ayodhya: Hindu Nationalism Comes of Age," 23 October, p. 8; "Post-Ayodhya Equations: Growing Irrelevance of Janata Dal," 5 November, p. 8.

56 The slogan was tested on respondents in a city, a town, and a village, and, with positive results, was commissioned for use in the election campaign, according to an interview with then cabinet minister I. K. Gujral. "Politics and Advertising," *Imprint*, New Delhi, November 1985, p. 29.

57 On the rise of Ramachandran in films and subsequently in politics, see M. S. S. Pandian, *The Image Trap. MG Ramachandran in Film and Politics* (New Delhi: Sage, 1992). On N. T. Rama Rao, see Joseph W. Elder and Peter L. Schmitthenner, "Film Fantasy and Populist Politics in South India: NT Rama Rao and the Telugu Desam Party," in Robert E. Frykenberg and Pauline Kolenda, eds., *Studies of South India. An Anthology of Recent Research and Scholarship* (Madras and New Delhi: New Era Publications and American Institute of Indian Studies, 1985), pp. 373–387. In 1986–87, N. T. Rama Rao lent his friend Ramanand Sagar costumes and sets from the belongings he had accumulated over a long career of acting in mythologicals, when Sagar filmed the Ramayan serial.

58 *India Today*, 15 January 1990, p. 43.

59 Amitabh Sinha, personal interview, New Delhi, 27 April 1994.

60 Noteworthy in this context are the attacks on reporters by activists in Ayodhya on 6 December 1992 (see below).

61 "Only BJP Has Moved Ahead." Interview with L. K. Advani by Manoj Joshi, *Frontline*, 20 July–2 August 1991, p. 35.

62 *Ibid.*

63 Raghunandan Prasad Sharma, ed., *Vishwa Hindu Parishad: Samagra Darshan* [Vishwa Hindu Parishad: An Entire View] (New Delhi, n.d.), pp. 50, 58.

64 L. K. Advani, personal interview, New Delhi, 2 June 1994.

65 Systematic exposure to media occurs only for a part of the population, perhaps less than half; for the rest it is more sporadic, and often indirect rather than direct. Video vans, popularized by J. K. Jain and Company in New Delhi, are used to deepen media reach. Although their first use in political campaigns was in 1985 by Devi Lal in Haryana, the idea has its genesis with government media. The Division of Audio Visual Publicity (DAVP) of the Information and Broadcasting Ministry ran mobile 16 mm

film units to take government propaganda into the rural regions. Covered with a three-sided mobile hoarding with pictures commissioned by the party, the arrival of the van itself tends to be something of a spectacle in villages. The van typically contains a video player, a generator, a screen which in some cases folds out to 20″ × 30″, an audio system and projector, and three sleeping berths. In the daytime, the van is used to announce the shows, which are confined to evenings. Posters, banners, and loudspeakers are used for publicity. In the case of commercial advertising, which the vans are used for in regular times, the workers in the van are responsible for all the outreach, and for maximizing audence turnout at each show. In political advertising, party workers run the show, and the van operators are more like technicians. Crowds range from 100 to 5,000, if sufficient organization has been done. In the 1993 assembly elections, the BJP rented 125 vans, of which twenty were equipped with large screens. The Congress had only fifty vans, but they were able to get local cable operators to show their films at prime time. Shalini Asthana, Director, and Rakesh Sharma, Manager, Operations, Jain Studios, personal interview, New Delhi, 19 May 1994.

66 L. K. Advani, personal interview, New Delhi, 2 June 1994.
67 My discussion of the BJP's media strategy is based on press coverage, which offers indirect testimony, and on interviews with journalists in New Delhi, Faizabad, Lucknow, and Varanasi conducted during March–June 1994 and June 1996.
68 Interview with S. P. Singh, Editor, *Navbharat Times,* July 1996.
69 *Frontline* cover photograph, 31 July 1992.
70 Chiranji Lal Purohit, *"Hindi jati ki patrakarita"* [Hindi journalism], *Saancha,* June–July 1989, cited in Charu Gupta and Mukul Sharma, "Communal Constructions: Media Reality vs Real Reality," *Race and Class,* vol. 38, no. 1, 1996, p. 4. For more discussion of this point, see chapter one.
71 Robin Jeffrey, "Indian-Language Newspapers and Why They Grow," *Economic and Political Weekly,* vol. 28, no. 38, 18 September 1993, pp. 2004–2011.
72 *A Preliminary List of Circulations Certified for the Six Monthly Audit Period,* Audit Bureau of Circulations, Bombay, 29 April 1989, pp. 1–7; 31 December 1992, pp. 1–8, cited in Jeffrey, "Indian-Language Newspapers and Why They Grow," p. 2009. Membership of the Audit Bureau of Circulations submits the circulation claims of newspapers to advertiser scrutiny, and permits sponsors and advertising agencies to assess the reach of ads published in a given daily and to plan their media budgets. Auditors of member newspapers provide the figures at six-month intervals, and these are checked against outside estimates periodically.
73 In the second half of 1990 alone, for instance, *Amar Ujala* added 32,000 copies to its sales. In the second half of 1992, audited circulation for seven *Aaj* editions in U.P. and Bihar rose by 41,000 copies; for four *Amar Ujala* editions, by 25,000; and for four *Dainik Jagaran* editions, by 18,000. Audit

Bureau of Circulations, 31 December 1992, p. 5, cited in Jeffrey, "Indian-Language Newspapers and Why They Grow," p. 2009.

74 See *Report of the Subcommittee Appointed by the Press Council of India on 8.11.1990 to Examine the Role of the Press on the One Hand and on the Other the Role of the Authorities in Dealing with the Press Relating to the Coverage of the Ramjanmabhumi-Babri Masjid Issue*, given at Thiruvananthapuram, Kerala, 21 January 1991. See also Singh, "The Press in India 1990–91," p. 4a.

75 Interview with Siyaram Yadav, *Aaj*, Varanasi, June 1996. The interviews in U.P. in June and July 1996 were performed by S. Ravindran, based on a schedule of questions I provided.

76 Uma Chakravarti *et al.*, "Khurja Riots 1990–91. Understanding the Conjuncture," *Economic and Political Weekly*, vol. 27, no. 18, 2 May 1992, p. 951.

77 Interview with Manoj Kumar Singh, Chief Reporter, *Aaj*, Varanasi, and General Secretary, Patrikar Sangh (Reporters' Association), Varanasi, June 1996.

78 "Who is Afraid of Hindi Journalism?" *Vidura*, New Delhi, vol. 29, June 1992, p. 15. The sources of reportage were sometimes surprising. Thus, for instance, many priests in the Ayodhya temples were reported to double as stringers for local Hindi papers. Shikha Trivedi, "Where Mahants Serve as Reporters," *Economic Times*, 4 November 1990, in Sharma and Gupta, "Communal Constructions," p. 4.

79 Prabhash Joshi, interviewed by Raj Kishore, "Mukhya Cheez Hai Apni Aazadi ko Banaye Rakhna" [The Important Thing is to Remain Independent], in *Patrakaritha ke Pehlu* [Aspects of Journalism] (Kanpur: Sahitya Sadan, 1988), pp. 75–91.

80 "Who is Afraid of Hindi Journalism?", p. 19.

81 *Press Council of India Annual Report* (1 April 1991–31 March 1992), New Delhi, p. 14.

82 "Who is Afraid of Hindi Journalism?", p. 15. *Aaj* was reported to be notorious in this regard, on one account going as far as charging for press cards. Interview with Arun Asthana, State Correspondent, *Amar Ujala*, Lucknow, June 1996.

83 Shiwaji Sarkar, "Stylebook of the Lathi," *Vidura*, New Delhi, September–October 1987, p. 3.

84 The point of this story is not to call for professionalism as panacea, but to criticize the situation-specific constraints in communication. When reporters internalize professional rules of journalism, they at the same time internalize the institutional constraints within which these rules can be exercised. Network news reporters, e.g., require little reminding of the apron strings of corporate sponsorship, and accepting these limits as given, they often feel unhindered in their professional duties. Meanwhile the news is increasingly influenced by the public relations departments of corporate and government offices. Professionalism may thus serve diverse ends, and is by itself no guarantee of transparency in communication.

85 Sri Krishna Singh, personal interview, Faizabad, 18 July 1992.

86 Interview with Ahsamul Haq, reporter, *Qaumi Morcha*, Varanasi, June 1996.

87 Interview with R. D. Satyendra Kumar, freelance journalist, Varanasi, 16 June 1996.

88 From *bachcha bachcha Ram ka, janmabhumi ke kaam ka* [every child of Ram [goes to] work for the janmabhumi [temple]. Prabhash Joshi, *Jansatta* editor, "*Chunautiyon ke Beech Khada Patrakar*" [Challenges Before Reporters], in Jaiprakash Bharati, ed., *Hindi Patrakaritha: Dasha aur Disha* [Hindi Journalism: Status and Prospect] (New Delhi: Pravin Publishers, 1994), p. 16.

89 *Ibid.*

90 Interview with Ajay Singh, U.P. State Correspondent, *Janmat* (Delhi), Lucknow, June 1996.

91 Interview with Rakesh Kumar, Principal Correspondent, *Swatantra Bharat*, Lucknow, June 1996. See also Ramaseshan, "The Press on Ayodhya" *Economic and Political Weekly*, 15 December 1990.

92 Interview with Vinod Pandey, News Desk, *Aaj*, Varanasi, June 1996.

93 Interview with Siyaram Yadav, *Aaj*, Varanasi, June 1996.

94 Interview with Ashish Bagchi, City Chief, *Dainik Jagran*, Varanasi, June 1996.

95 Interview with Ahsamul Haq, reporter, *Qaumi Morcha*, Varanasi, June 1996.

96 Interview with Shiv Kumar Shukla, ex-City President, Vishva Hindu Parishad, Varanasi, June 1996.

97 *Aaj*, 22 November 1990, p. 5.

98 Here Bakhtin's discussion of the ancient Greek "adventure novel of ordeal" is relevant. See "Forms of Time and Chronotope in the Novel" in *The Dialogic Imagination*, tr. Caryl Emerson and Michael Holquist (Austin: University of Texas Press, 1981), pp. 86–110.

99 See Achille Mbembe, "The Banality of Power and the Aesthetics of Vulgarity in the Postcolony," *Public Culture*, vol. 2, no. 2, Spring 1993, pp. 1–30.

100 My account here draws from the following sources: Gowri Ramnarayan, "To Ayodhya for Peace," *Frontline*, 27 August 1993; Praveen Swami, "Beyond Slogans," *Frontline*, 10 September 1993; Venkitesh Ramakrishnan, "Upstaging Hindutva," *ibid.*; Sadanand Menon, "On to Resist a Culture of Vandalism," *The Economic Times*, 14 August 1993; Upendra Baxi, "Sahmat's Secularism: Neither 'Short-Cut' nor 'Credit-card,'" *Mainstream*, 9 October 1993. Articles reprinted in *Muktnaad. Hum Sab Ayodhya. A Selection of Reports, Editorials, Discussion, Comments from the Press* (New Delhi: SAHMAT, 1994).

101 Then about US $80,000.

102 E.g., see Nikhil Chakravartty's critique in "No Short-Cut to Secularism," *Mainstream*, 18 September 1993.

103 Ketan Tanna *et al.*, "Playing the BJP's Game," *Sunday*, Calcutta, 29 August–4 September, 1993, p. 33.

104 For a sympathetic discussion of Sahmat that, however, appears to accept the BJP's criticisms fully, see Sudhanva Deshpande, "Sahmat and the Politics of Cultural Intervention," *Economic and Political Weekly*, vol. 31, no. 25, 22 June 1996, pp. 1586–1590.

105 In the summer of 1992, Uma Bharati predicted that, in the next elections, the BJP and the Congress would form a coalition government, but, she said, the subsequent government would be the BJP's alone. Personal interview, New Delhi, 1 August 1992.

106 See Appendix for background to the Babri Masjid dispute.

107 See G.-D. Sontheimer's discussion in "Religious Endowments in India: The Juristic Personality of Hindu Deities," *Zeitschrift fur vergleichende Rechtswissenschaft*, Stuttgart, vol. 69, no. 1, 1964, pp. 45–100.

108 Gopal Sharma, *Kar Seva se Kar Seva Tak* (Jaipur: Rajasthan Patrika Limited, 1993), p. 17.

109 *Aaj* was published simultaneously from Agra, Allahabad, Gorakhpur, Jamshedpur, Kanpur, Lucknow, Patna, Ranchi, and Varanasi. Combining all these editions, its average daily circulation during the period 1 January–30 June 1993 was 4,94,080. *The Times of India* had editions in Ahmedabad, Bangalore, Bombay, Chandigarh, Lucknow, New Delhi, and Patna. Its total daily circulation for the same period was 7,93,152. *The Indian Express* circulation figures are listed for six editions, for the following areas: Bombay–Pune–Nagpur, New Delhi–Chandigarh, Madurai–Vijayawada–Madras, Bangalore–Cochin–Hyderabad, Vizianagram–Coimbatore–Kozhikode, and Ahmedabad–Baroda. Average daily circulation for the above period totaled 3,42,692. Audit Bureau of Circulations, 1 January–30 June 1993, Bombay, pp. 16–17.

110 *The Times of India*, 28 October 1989, p. 11.

111 "Ayodhya Land Disputed: HC", *The Times of India*, 8 November 1989, p. 1.

112 Sharma, *Kar Seva se Kar Seva Tak*, p. 33; V. M. Badola, "Shilanyas peaceful," *The Times of India*, 10 November 1989, p. 24.

113 *Frontline*, 28 October 1989.

114 *The Times of India*, 18 October 1989, p. 23, and editorial, 21 October 1989, p. 16.

115 "Politicised Communalism," *The Times of India* editorial, 26 October 1989, p. 14. "Can Anything Be Done," *Indian Express* editorial, 7 November 1989, p. 8. In Bhagalpur alone, over 48,000 people were affected in riots that began on 24 October 1989 and continued for over a month, with an estimated 982 people killed and 259 seriously injured. A second round of killings took place in March 1990. *Recalling Bhagalpur: A Report on the Aftermath of the 1989 Riots* (People's Union for Democratic Rights, Delhi, February 1996).

116 *The Times of India* editorial: "Good Sense on Ayodhya," 10 November 1989, p. 12; S. C. Dixit quoted in V. M. Badola, " 'Shilanyas' peaceful," *The Times of India*, 10 November 1989, p. 1.

117 "An Important Announcement," editorial, *Indian Express*, 11 November 1989, p. 8. Photo spread p. 10. "Puja begins amid tight security," Sanjay Suri, *Indian Express*, 10 November 1989, p. 1.

118 *Aaj*, 6–10 November 1989.

119 The RSS floated an organization called *Aarakshan Virodhi Andolan* (Anti Reservation Struggle) to coordinate the movement. "BJP Hide and Seek on Mandal Report," *The Times of India*, 1 September 1990. Further, the BJP students' organization, the Akhil Bharatiya Vidyarthi Parishad (All India Students Organization), came out openly against Mandal as well, although its vice-president, Suraj Yadav, grandson of the author of the Mandal report, came out in support of it. *New Age* (Delhi), 9 September 1990, pp. 1, 14.

120 Hiranmay Karlekar, *In the Mirror of Mandal: Social Justice, Caste, Class and the Individual* (Delhi, Ajanta Publications, 1992), p. 4.

121 "Rathyatra by Advani to mobilise opinion," *Indian Express*, 13 September 1990.

122 "People tell me – why do you say these things? You are spoiling your image – it will have a bad effect," Advani disclosed. Personal interview, New Delhi, 2 June 1994.

123 Madhavkant Shukla, "*Ab Nahin Roknevali Hai Advaniji ki Rath Yatra*" [Now Advaniji's rath yatra is not going to be stopped], *Aaj*, Varanasi, 15 October 1990, p. 1.

124 "Advani's Juggernaut rolls on Midst Unbelievable Scenes," *Organiser*, 14 October 1990, p. 5.

125 Amitabh Sinha, personal interview, New Delhi, 27 April 1994. For similar details on the rath yatra, see Sharma, *Kar Seva se Kar Seva Tak*, pp. 46–49.

126 Kripashankar Shukla, "*Rath Yatra se Judi Hai Aprajey Jan Bhavna*" [Invincible Popular Feeling is Tied to the Rath Yatra], *Aaj*, Varanasi, 19 October 1990, p. 7.

127 Swapan Dasgupta, "Journey to Ayodhya: Hindu Nationalism Comes of Age," *The Times of India*, 23 October 1990, p. 8. Advani quoted in Dasgupta, "Invoking Ram to Fight Mandal," *The Times of India*, 14 October 1990, p. 12.

128 Speech by Advani at Nangloi in New Delhi, reported in "Tumultuous Welcome to Rath Yatra," *Indian Express*, 16 October 1990, p. 1. Advani interviewed by Chidanand Rajghatta, *The Times of India*, 20 November 1990, p. 9.

129 *The Times of India* editorial: "The successful Rath Yatra has . . . demonstrated that blind faith is too deep rooted to be wished away or beaten into submission . . . Unfortunately, such a powerful exhibition of Hindu feeling is fraught with danger." "A Way Out in Ayodhya," 16 October 1990, p. 8.

130 *Sunday Observer*, 13 October 1990, p. 1. Ram Manohar Lohia was a socialist leader and a critic of the Congress. Bal Thackeray was the founder of the Shiv Sena, a Maharashtra-based Hindu rightist party.

131 The role of Dixit is mentioned, and the kar sevak interviewed, in Anand Patwardhan's film, *Ram Ke Naam* [In the Name of God]. See also Nilanjan Mukhopadhyaya, *The Demolition: India at the Crossroads* (New Delhi: Indus, 1994), pp. 297–304.

132 Radhika Ramaseshan, "The Press on Ayodhya," *Economic and Political Weekly*, 15 December 1990, pp. 2701–2704.

133 "Wanted: The Healing Touch," *Indian Express* editorial, 1 November 1990, p. 8.

134 "Stop This Madness," *Indian Express* editorial, 3 November 1990, p. 8.

135 " 'Kar seva' to be intensified, says VHP," *The Times of India*, 3 November 1990, p. 1.

136 See *Report of the Subcommittee Appointed by the Press Council of India on 8.11.1990*, cited above. See also Singh, "The Press in India 1990–91," p. 4a.

137 *Aaj*, 19 October 1990, p. 3.

138 See the discussion of miracles and the rumors of invincibility in Shahid Amin's "Gandhi as Mahatma," in Ranajit Guha and Gayatri Chakravorty Spivak, eds., *Selected Subaltern Studies* (New York and Oxford: Oxford University Press, 1988), pp. 288–348.

139 For the examples of the "miracles," and the note on the introduction of evening editions at this time, see Ramaseshan, "The Press on Ayodhya."

140 Interview with Sharad Bhogale, Aurangabad, 28 January 1997.

141 Advani, interviewed in *Frontline*, 20 July–2 August 1991, p. 37.

142 *National Integration Council: Report of the Standing Committee*, 26 April 1992, p. 6.

143 Venkitesh Ramakrishnan, "The Demolition Game," *Frontline*, 8 May 1992, p. 26.

144 "Chavan Unhappy Over Security at Ayodhya Shrine," *The Hindustan Times*, 12 July 1992, p. 1.

145 E.g., "The inefficiency of the Central Government was manifested in Ayodhya during the visit of the NIC team on April 7. It was a virtual fiasco." Ramakrishnan, "The Demolition Game," p. 26.

146 "VHP body threatens countrywide stir," by Ratan Mani Lal, *The Times of India*, 5 April 1992, p. 11.

147 Venkitesh Ramakrishnan, "Climb-down in Delhi," *Frontline*, 9–22 November 1991, p. 17.

148 *Times of India* editorial, 15 July 1992.

149 Dilip Awasthi, "Ayodhya: The Final Countdown," *India Today*, 31 July 1992, p. 50.

150 Namita Bhandare with Sarat Chandra, "They're Back!" *Sunday*, 26 July–1 August 1992, p. 25.

151 The then-*sarsanghchalak* (supreme leader) of the RSS, Balasaheb Deoras, saw the Congress Party as a potential ally rather than a foe, and had good relations with Narasimha Rao. Then Joint General Secretary Rajinder Singh (appointed *sarsanghchalak* in 1993) described Narasimha Rao as "a very nice man." Interview with Rajinder Singh by S. K. Pande in *Frontline*, 15 January 1993.

152 Manoj Joshi, "Ayodhya Game Plan," *Frontline*, 14 August 1992, p. 4.

153 Dileep Padgaonkar, "Saving the Republic," *The Times of India*, 18 July 1992, p. 1.

154 "Dharm Sankat ki Sthithi" [The Condition of a Religious Dilemma], *Aaj*, 23 July 1992, p. 6.

155 *The Indian Express*, 20 July 1992, p. 8.

156 *The Times of India*, 2 December 1992.

157 "SC gives Kalyan Govt final chance," *The Times of India*, 28 November 1992, p. 1; "UP Govt Assurance to SC: Construction won't be allowed at site," *Sunday Times*, 29 November 1992, p. 1.

158 Mahesh Narain Singh, secretary of the Ramjanmabhumi Mukti Yagna Samiti, in *Sunday Times*, 29 November 1992, p. 1; President of the Ramjan-mabhumi Nyas, Parmhans Ramchandra Das in *Sunday Times*, 6 December 1992, p. 1.

159 Interview with Vinay Katiyar in *Telegraph*, 29 November 1992.

160 *Citizens' Tribunal on Ayodhya: Report of the Inquiry Commission*, New Delhi, 1993, p. 44.

161 "Ayodhya Mein Pratikatmak Karseva" [Symbolic Karseva in Ayodhya], editorial, *Aaj*, 2 December 1992, p. 6. Adjoining article: Vijaykumar "Madhu", Hindu Card Aur Muslim card Mein Ulajhi Rao Sarkar" [Rao Govt. entangled Amid Hindu card and Muslim card].

162 "NIC authorises PM to take any action on Ayodhya issue," *The Times of India*, 24 November 1992, p. 1.

163 Y. R. Tripathi, Principal, Saket Degree College, personal interview, Ayod-hya, 21 February 1994. See also *CTA: Report of the Inquiry Commission*, p. 91.

164 *CTA: Report of the Inquiry Commission*, pp. 99–100.

165 Madhav Godbole, *Unfinished Innings: Recollections and Reflections of a Civil Servant* (New Delhi: Orient Longman, 1996), pp. 360–365.

166 *Ibid.*, p. 412.

167 Venkitesh Ramakrishnan, "A Case Demolished," *Frontline*, 17 December 1993, p. 21.

168 *The Times of India*, 24 December 1992, p. 1.

169 *Press Council of India Annual Report* (1 April 1993–31 March 1994), New Delhi, p. 17.

170 These being the Shankaracharyas of Puri, Hardwar, Sringeri, and Prayag.

171 Venkitesh Ramakrishnan, "A Year of Shame," *Frontline*, 17 December 1993, p. 20.

172 *Election Analysis: BJP Polled One Crore Votes and Won One Hundred Assembly Seats More Than the Congress-I* (New Delhi: Bharatiya Janata Party [Central Office], n.d.), p. 2.

173 This was in keeping with a well-established inclination on the part of the news media. See Gans, "Symbolic Ethnicity," and Gitlin, *The Whole World is Watching*.

5 ORGANIZATION, PERFORMANCE, AND SYMBOL

1 Alberto Melucci, "The Symbolic Challenge of Contemporary Movements," *Social Research*, vol. 52, no. 4, Winter 1985, p. 792.
2 Pierre Bourdieu, *The Logic of Practice*, tr. Richard Nice (Stanford: Stanford University Press, 1990), pp. 27, 34.
3 The work that gave Hindu communal politics its best-known political manifesto was Savarkar's *Hindutva*, first published in 1923, two years before the founding of the RSS. Savarkar creates a philological foundation for a conservative and exclusivist nationalism, defined in terms of territory and faith. He begins by noting that the association between word and thing is often arbitrary: a rose by any other name would smell as sweet, he writes, quoting Shakespeare. The word "Hindu" itself is of Persian coinage, absent in ancient texts. Audaciously, Savarkar declares Hindutva to be the root word, prior to "Hindu" itself, signifying the qualities of fatherland and holyland both. Thus Lingayats, Sikhs, Jains, and non-Brahmins, even if recognizing other gods than Hindus, still had the origins of their faith within the country; thus the location of their temporal interests and their spiritual inclinations would be the same. There were exceptions, however, such as Sister Nivedita, who, although not of Hindu parentage, "*felt* she was a Hindu and that is, apart from all technicalities, the real and the most important test" (p. 107). Despite his invocation of Hinduness, Savarkar is not making an argument about for a religiously based politics based on religious belief per se, or on ritual; rather, his highly self-conscious approach to symbols and their uses has to be appreciated. See Vinayak Damodar Savarkar's *Hindutva* (Poona, 1942); also Dhananjay Keer, *Veer Savarkar* (London: Sangam, 1988). J. E. Sanjana suggests that the word Hindutva was coined by Bengali nationalist Chandranath Bose around the 1860s, in a work of that title. See Sanjana's *Caste and Outcaste* (Bombay: Thacker, 1946), p. 120.
4 Thus when the powers of the state were ultimately mobilized, the Hindu warriors were no match against it. (For example, the punitive dismissal of BJP-led state governments after the demolition in Gujarat, Himachal Pradesh, and Madhya Pradesh, over and above the dismissal of Kalyan Singh's government in Uttar Pradesh, could hardly be resisted by activists' might.)
5 Radhika Ramaseshan, "Changing Equations," *Pioneer*, New Delhi, 15 November 1993.
6 To provide nuanced and textured understandings of violence while engaging with the academic requirements of abstraction, and the epistemic violence it entails, is an important challenge that this brief section cannot do justice to. Different authors have addressed the problem; see, for instance, Veena Das, ed., *Mirrors of Violence: Communities, Riots and Survivors in South Asia* (New Delhi: Oxford University Press, 1990); Allen Feldman, *Formations of Violence: The Narrative of the Body and Political Terror in Northern Ireland* (Berkeley: University of California Press, 1991); Gyanendra Pandey, "In Defence of the Fragment,"

Representations, no. 37, 1992; Rajeswari Sunder Rajan, "The Subject of Sati: Pain and Death in the Contemporary Discourse on Sati," *Real and Imagined Women: Gender, Culture and Post-Colonialism* (London: Routledge, 1994).

7 A sample of wall-writings from Ayodhya, 22 July 1992: *Rakt denge . . . pran denge / Mandir ka nirman karenge* (We will shed blood, we will give our lives / We will build the temple); *Mehej jidh hai, masjid nahin* (It is mere obstinacy, not a mosque); *Balidani veeron ki bhumi / Khoon mangti taza re!* (The place of martyred heroes / is demanding fresh blood [sacrifice]).

8 See Uma Chakravarti *et al.*, "Khurja Riots 1990–91. Understanding the Conjuncture," *Economic and Political Weekly*, vol. 27, no. 18, 2 May 1992, pp. 951, 954, and VHP–UP and the Sriram Janam Bhumi Mukti Yagya, *Sriram Janambhumi ki Raksha Hetu*, c. March 1989, cited in *ibid.*, p. 964, fn. 10.

9 *Times of India* November 1989, cited in Manuel, p. 255. See also "A voice in the dark set Ghaziabad aflame," *Times of India*, 31 January 1991, p. 9, and "How a simmering cauldron was ignited," *Times of India*, 16 December 1990, p. 13, cited in Peter Manuel, *Cassette Culture: Popular Music and Technology in North India* (Chicago: University of Chicago Press, 1993), p. 281, fn. 26.

10 Conversations with Parmanand Mishra, VHP activist and field notes, Ayodhya, 16–22 July 1992.

11 Field notes, and interviews with Ms. Maharaji, from Sonbhadra, Kashi District, and with Mr. Ramesh, Ayodhya, 19 July 1992.

12 This followed an illustrious historical precedent. Following Hindu–Muslim riots in Bombay in 1893, Bal Gangadhar Tilak and other leaders in Poona worked to reorganize the annual Ganapati festival into a more far-reaching affair. Ganapati is the pot-bellied, elephant-headed deity who symbolizes pleasure and devotion, and accepts prayers for overcoming obstacles in popular traditions. Hindus were instructed to stay away from the Muslim festivities, and the musicians were given more and better paying work in the bands accompanying Ganapati processions. The Muslims had their Muharram procession, when they took out *tabuts*, decorated replicas of the tombs of the Prophet's grandsons martyred in the month of Muharram, and ritually immersed them. It regularly drew large numbers of lower-caste Hindus who joined in the public festivities, and the celebrations were only a few days before the Ganapati festival. In a move that foreshadowed later identifications of Hindutva with secularism, the Ganapati festival was declared to be *sarvajanik*. The word, literally "all people," is usually translated as "public," but the salient unit was understood not in terms of individuals, but of neighborhood and caste groupings, which typically converged. With localities free to devise their own verses and stage their own *melas*, there was a tendency to develop along the caste patterns that neighborhoods were shaped in. The Ganapati puja responded to the more fluid display of Muharram with *a rational ordering of space*, in three inter-related ways. There was a competitive attempt to fill a space now defined in volumetric rather than in ritual terms. Secondly, the identity of the groups was not relevant;

each participant thus contributed an identical increment irrespective of caste or status. Finally, in addition to participation, there was a further homogenization at the level of expression, in the design of a common symbol wielded together by the different groups. For more detail on the history of the Ganapati festival, see Richard Cashman, *The Myth of the Lokamanya. Tilak and Mass Politics in Maharashtra* (Berkeley: University of California Press, 1975), pp. 75–97, and Stanley A. Wolpert, *Tilak And Gokhale. Revolution and Reform in the Making of Modern India* (New Delhi: Oxford University Press, 1991 [1961]), pp. 67–70.

13 Aarti is the ceremonial adoration of a deity or an important personage, by the circular movement of a lighted lamp before the deity or person. The maha-aarti is a new congregational ritual used by the VHP in its attempt to define a Hindu public.

14 Field notes, Ayodhya, 18 July 1992.

15 Panchayat: village assembly composed of elected representatives.

16 People's Union for Democratic Rights, *Bhagalpur Riots*, Delhi, April 1990, p. 31.

17 *Ibid.*, p. 28.

18 To what extent they may have participated in actual rioting is not clear. Govindacharya, the BJP general secretary, described the Bajrang Dal as an urban middle-class phenomenon, and petit bourgeois in character [*sic*]. They would run away at the sign of a fight; it was the scheduled castes, the Valmikis, who would fight, he said. BJP General Secretary Govindacharya, personal interview, Madras, 22 June 1992.

19 S. R. Dharapuri, DIG U.P. Police, personal interview, Lucknow, 13 February 1994.

20 Asghar Ali Engineer, "The Bloody Trail: Ramjanmabhoomi and Communal Violence in U.P.," *Economic and Political Weekly*, 26 January 1991, pp. 155–159.

21 G. S. Sudarshan, RSS *boudhik pramukh*, or principal intellectual, interviewed by Pankaj Pachauri in *India Today*, 30 June 1989, p. 59. Slavoj Zizek has demonstrated that what counts as ground and what counts as conditions are ultimately contingent and exchangeable. How to escape this exchangeability of ground and circumstances? "The only way out of this impasse is therefore the intervention, at a certain point, of a tautological gesture . . . literally presupposing itself in its exteriority, in its external conditions." See *Tarrying With The Negative: Kant, Hegel and the Critique of Ideology* (Durham: Duke University Press, 1993), p. 147. There is thus no internal ground or potential, which is realized when a suitable set of external circumstances is achieved. The external relation of presupposing (whether it is of ground presupposing conditions or vice versa) needs then to be replaced by a pure tautological gesture in which the thing presupposes itself. Nothing new is discovered; there is rather the simple assertion of an already-present thing. This is the paradox of the nation finding its identity: the institution of a new identity is declared merely to be the re-institution of something pre-existing,

already there. Thus the name indicates the return of the thing to itself, and subsumes what may be rather different contents. Zizek discusses the example of the shark in Spielberg's film *Jaws*. Different interpretations may be put forth of what the shark signifies: the untamed world of nature, the threat of the Third World to the U.S. as symbolized in the small town in the story, or of the exploitative nature of capitalism itself. To argue precisely what fears are symbolized and what is not symbolized would be to misunderstand the way the film works, Zizek argues. The shark serves as a vessel containing diverse, free-floating, and possibly inconsistent fears. To say that it symbolizes them is misleading; rather it replaces them by causing fear to be focused on itself rather than on those other matters, even if it is those fears which feed its perception. Extending this argument to the figure of the Jew in anti-Semitism, Zizek points out that the name "Jew" provides no new information. Rather, it displaces information already present and unifies it in a new realm, one that is then declared as the ground, the Jewish conspiracy. Behind the several conditions of moral crisis, unemployment and inflation, scarcity of goods, etc., we then perceive the operations of the self-same cause or ground (pp. 146–149).

22 Nanaji Bhagwat, personal interview, New Delhi, 17 March 1994.
23 Ram jyoti yatra: procession or pilgrimage bearing lamps lighted in Lord Ram's name. Kalash yatra: procession or pilgrimage bearing ash-filled urn. Paduka yatra: procession or pilgrimage bearing wooden sandals.
24 R. C. Batura, "VHP takes a leaf out of Bharat's book," *Organiser*, 4 October 1992, pp. 9–10. In the 15 August issue of *Organiser*, the figure was 6,000 padukas (sandals).
25 Footage from the Media Storm Collective, New Delhi. I am grateful to Sabina Gadihoke and Sabina Kidwai for giving me access to the footage.
26 Nanaji Bhagwat, "Sri Ram Shilla Pooja Plan," *Hindu Vishwa*, August 1990, pp. 60–63.
27 Tehsil: administrative sub-division of a district.
28 This section is from personal interviews with S. C. Jain, Giridhar Gopal Gattani, and Giridhar Gopal Maheshwari, Berasia, 10 May 1994.
29 My visit was in the company of Kewal Kapoor and Shahana Bhattacharya. I am grateful to Venkitesh Ramakrishnan for his help during this visit.
30 *Fairs and Festivals as Seasonal Markets* (Bombay: Hindustan Thompson Associates, 1978), p. 157. The average attendance of the Jhula festival was estimated at 100,000 in 1978.
31 Ram Chander, personal interview, 22 July 1992. The father, Hiralal Kothari, was a Calcutta stockbroker who told me that although he felt the loss of his sons, it pleased him to know that people kept his sons' picture in their homes and worshipped them. Personal interview, Ayodhya, 22 July 1992.
32 I thank Venkitesh Ramakrishnan for pointing this fact out to me.
33 Charles A. Ferguson, "The Structure and Use of Politeness Formulas," *Language in Society*, no. 5, 1976, pp. 137–151.

34 Charles A. Ferguson, "South Asia as a Sociolinguistic Area," in Edward C. Dimock Jr. *et al.*, eds., *Dimensions of Sociolinguistics in South Asia. Papers in Memory of Gerald B. Kelly* (New Delhi: Oxford and IBH Publishing Co., 1992), p. 30. In this context, relevant work marking South Asian socio-linguistics as a field, in addition to the above volume, includes Murray B. Emeneau, *Language and Linguistic Area: Essays by Murray B. Emeneau*, ed. A. S. Dil (Stanford: Stanford University Press, 1980); Colin P. Masica, *Defining a Linguistic Area: South Asia* (Chicago: University of Chicago Press, 1976); Prabodh B. Pandit, *India as a Sociolinguistic Area* (Poona: University of Poona, 1972); Michael Shapiro and H. F. Schiffman, *Language and Society in South Asia* (Dordrecht: Foris, 1983).

35 Dr. Swaminath Pandey, interviewed by Shahana Bhattacharya, Kewal Kapoor, and Arvind Rajagopal, Ayodhya, 19 July 1992.

36 Field notes, Ayodhya, 21 July 1992. *Sasura* is an abusive term used between menfolk, derived from *sasur*, father-in-law.

37 7 November 1990 speech to Lok Sabha, printed in *Organiser*, 7 December 1990, p. 9.

38 *Eyewitness News* video news magazine, May 1991.

39 Advani interviewed in *The Times of India*, 20 November 1990, p. 9.

40 Sumanta Banerjee, *Audio Cassettes: The User Medium* (Paris: Unesco, 1977), pp. 47–48.

41 In this section, I have drawn extensively from the careful discussion in Manuel, *Cassette Culture*.

42 The indigenous cassette industry picked up momentum as the coating with magnetic oxide of polyester tape began in India on a large scale after 1984, along with local production of the molded shell, hubs, and rollers. In 1990, only about 18 percent of the tapes sold in India contained foreign components. Led by an energetic fruit stall merchant who diversified to form the T-Series company, by the mid 1980s cassettes conveyed 95 percent of all recorded music, and by 1991 India became the second largest producer of cassettes in the world, making about 217 million annually. Anil Chopra, "Magnetic Tape: To Import or Not to Import," *Playback*, December 1986, pp. 66–67, cited in Manuel, *Cassete Culture*, p. 75. Inderjit Badhwar, "A Supersuccess Story," *India Today*, 30 April 1987, pp. 110–112; Lincoln Kaye, "Flickering Fortunes," *Far Eastern Economic Review*, 1 September 1988, p. 51; Harini Swamy, "In the Big Music Bazaar," *Times of India*, 21 July 1991, p. 9; Simran Bhargava, "On a Fast Track," *India Today*, 15 January 1991, pp. 58–60, cited in Manuel, *Cassette Culture*, p. 62–63.

43 Manuel, *Cassette Culture*, pp. 196–197. I am grateful for Sanjay Kumar's help in translating the passages in this section.

44 Dholak: small drum played at both ends. Majira: small cymbals.

45 Colloquial names for Krishna and Shiva respectively.

46 Chief Minister of the BJP-led state government in Uttar Pradesh in 1990–91.

47 Dwarka Singh Yadav, *Ishwar Stuti* [Lord's Prayer], Rama Cassettes Production, n.d. The caste of the singer, whose name, Dwarka Singh Yadav, is

displayed on the case, suggests sensitivity to the post-Mandal era the tape was issued in.

48 *Ibid.*
49 Manuel, *Cassette culture*, pp. 204–207, 220.
50 On the women's organizations shaped by the Hindu right, see Tanika Sarkar, "The Woman as Communal Subject: Rashtra Sevika Samiti and Ramjanmabhoomi Movement," *Economic and Political Weekly*, 31 August 1991; Tanika Sarkar and Urvashi Butalia, eds., *Women and the Hindu Right: A Collection of Essays* (New Delhi: Kali for Women Press, 1995).
51 "Rithambhra is dedicated to protecting the country's honour," *Aaj*, Varanasi, 27 December 1990, p. 2. See also Kumkum Sangari, "Consent, Agency and Rhetorics of Incitement," *Economic and Political Weekly*, vol. 28, no. 18, pp. 877–880; and Basu *et al.*, *Khaki Shorts, Saffron Flags*, pp. 100–102.
52 The following extract is from an audio-cassette titled Sadhvi Rithambhra, purchased in Ayodhya in June–July 1992.
53 Loincloths, a symbol of *brahmacharya*, or ascetic manhood.
54 See, e.g., Jay Dubashi, "BJP's Unique Role," *Organiser*, 25 June 1989, p. 2; L. K. Advani in *The Economic Times*, 10 August 1993, p. 7.
55 Interview with Parmanand Mishra, Ayodhya, 19 July 1992.
56 Interview with Sathyanarayan Maurya, Ayodhya, 21 July 1992.
57 Interview in Berasia, Madhya Pradesh, 10 May 1994.
58 G. Sarojini and S. Rajamma, personal interview, Hindu Mahila Sammelan, New Delhi, 7 May 1994. For these participants in the VHP's conference, devotional fervor outweighed political conviction. Although they believed that the religious demands of Hindus took precedence over other concerns in India, or perhaps because of this fact, they had come to New Delhi only to proceed to traditional sites of pilgrimage, such as Hardwar and Rishikesh. Their attendance at the conference was only for the duration of a few hours. Ayodhya was not on their itinerary, as it happened.

6 HINDUTVA GOES GLOBAL

1 Jay Dubashi, "We Are So Close To God," *Hinduism Today*, vol. 17, no. 12, December 1995, p. 11.
2 Arvind Rajagopal, "An Unholy Nexus: Expatriate Anxiety and Hindu Extremism," *Frontline* (Madras), 10 September 1993.
3 Shashi Tharoor, "Growing Up Extreme: On the Peculiarly Vicious Fanaticism of Expatriates," *The Washington Post*, 25 July 1993, p. C5.
4 Salman Rushdie, *Shame* (New York: Alfred A. Knopf, 1983), p. 90.
5 Yashpal Lakra. Speech marking the fourth Anniversary of the 30 October 1990 firings at Ayodhya, India, in Hinsdale, Illinois, Vishwa Hindu Parishad of America, Greater Chicago Chapter, 30 October 1994.
6 For example, the organization was registered in forty states in 1998, up from chapters in only thirteen states in 1993.

7 Cited in A. G. Noorani, "Taxing Hindutva," *Frontline*, 9 April 1999, p. 106. Noorani points to a recent amendment to Section 80G of the Income Tax Act, that would extend the definition of tax-exempt "charitable" purposes to activities such as those of the VHP and its affiliates. According to another news report, in 1989 the VHP asked the Reserve Bank of India (RBI) permission to bring in hundreds of millions of rupees donated by its supporters worldwide for the Ram temple campaign. The RBI had objected that the VHP was a political organization, and had denied permission. Subsequently, according to Income Tax Commissioner Viswa Bandhu Gupta, large amounts had been brought into India in cash form with the help of illicit currency traders, or what in India are called hawala transactions. See Om Prakash Tiwari, "Where is the Missing File of the VHP?" *Rashtriya Sahara*, New Delhi, 6 February 1999. Tr. V. B. Rawat. Posted on South Asia Citizens Web, <aiindex.mnet.fr>. For an account of Vishwa Bandhu Gupta's notice to the VHP to furnish its return of income for 1990–91, and Finance Minister Madhu Dandavate's countermanding of Gupta's notice, see *Times of India*, 18 March 1990 and Noorani, "Taxing Hindutva."

8 In 1986, the amount of money sent by Christian and Muslim religious organizations, according to the estimate of Reserve Bank figures quoted in a VHP publication, was 4.38 billion rupees (then about $365 million), representing a dramatic increase from the 1977 figure of 735.9 million rupees (then about $98 million). Jaswant Rai Gupta, *Hinduon ka Dharmantaran Evam Videshi Dhan* [Role of Foreign Money in Conversion of Hindus] (New Delhi, n.d.), pp. 9–10.

9 Dr. Yashpal Lakra, personal interview, 4 May 1996.

10 T. V. Ramachandran, *Non-Resident Indians Investment Policy Guidelines and Procedures: A Compendium* (Bangalore: Puliani and Puliani, 1992), pp. 21–25.

11 V. Balasubramanian, *Indians Abroad. The NRI Syndrome* (Bombay: Business Book Publishing House, 1987), p. 1.

12 H. V. Seshadri, *Hindus Abroad – The Dilemma: Dollar or Dharma* (New Delhi: Suruchi Prakashan, 1990).

13 *Organiser*, 5 May 1991, p. 12.

14 E.g., see Hugh Tinker, *The Banyan Tree* (London and New York: Oxford University Press, 1977), p. 10.

15 Ashok Mitra, "Foreign Balances and the Class Divide," in *Cutting Corners* (Calcutta: Bookfront Publication Forum 1992), pp. 1–3.

16 *Ibid.*

17 Indians from the U.S. and Europe traveled to India to participate in a December 1990 meeting in Bangalore of the organization. Dr. Mukund Mody of New York and Mr. Narayan Swaroop Sharma of London led the delegations. See Vinod Ghildiyal, "NRI's 'mad rush' to join BJP's overseas unit," *Organiser*, 5 May 1991, p. 12.

18 The phrase is Raymond Brady Williams's. See his *Religions of Immigrants from India and Pakistan: New Threads in the American Tapestry* (Cambridge: Cambridge University Press, 1988), pp. 51–54.

19 Ronald Inden, *Imagining India* (Oxford: Basil Blackwell, 1990).

20 Vasudha Narayanan, "Creating the South Indian 'Hindu' Experience in the United States," in Raymond Brady Williams, ed., *A Sacred Thread: Modern Transmission of Hindu Traditions in India and Abroad* (Chambersburg: Anima Publications, 1992), pp. 160–163.

21 *Ibid.*, pp. 172–174.

22 For instance, references cited by Mahesh Mehta in an article entitled "Vivekananda's Message – Modern Perspective," included *The Life of Swami Vivekananda*, Fritjof Capra's *Tao of Physics*, and Stephen Covery's *The Seven Habits of Highly Effective People*. See *Hindu Vishwa*, vol. 21, no. 2, Global Vision 2000 Special Issue, 6 August 1993, p. 24.

23 Mark Juergensmeyer, "The Gadar Syndrome: Ethnic Anger and Nationalist Pride," in S. Chandrasekhar, ed., *From India to America: A Brief History of Immigration; Problems of Discrimination; Admission and Assimilation* (La Jolla, Calif.: Population Review Publications, 1982).

24 According to the 1990 Census, there were 890,000 Asian Indians in the U.S., of whom two-thirds were foreign-born. 65.7 percent of the males and 48.7 percent of the females had a bachelor's degree or higher. This compares with 43.2 percent for all Asian males and 32.7 percent for all Asian females, and 23.3 percent for all males and 17.6 percent of all females in the total population. The per capita income of Asian Indians in 1989 was $17,777 p.a., as against the national per capita income of $14,143 p.a. and the per capita income for whites of $15,687 p.a. Asian Indians were below only the Japanese (American) per capita income of $19,373 p.a. The poverty rate for Asian Indians in 1989 was 9.7 percent, below the 13 percent for the entire nation and the 14 percent for all Asians (Hmong, Cambodian, and Laotian accounting for a disproportionate percentage of the Asian poor). See *We the American . . . Asians*, U.S. Department of Commerce: Economics and Statistics Administration, Bureau of the Census, September 1993.

25 Michael Hechter, "Group Formation and the Cultural Division of Labor," *American Journal of Sociology*, vol. 79, no. 5, 1978, pp. 293–318. For an overview of the debate, see William L. Yancey, Eugene P. Ericksen, and Richard N. Juliani, "Emergent Ethnicity: A Review and Reformulation," *American Sociological Review*, vol. 41, no. 3, 1976, pp. 391–402.

26 Andrew M. Greeley, *Ethnicity in the United States: A Preliminary Reconaissance* (New York: Wiley, 1974).

27 Herbert J. Gans, "Symbolic Ethnicity: The Future of Ethnic Groups and Cultures in America," *Ethnic and Racial Studies*, vol. 2, 1979, pp. 1–20.

28 Mary C. Waters, *Ethnic Options: Choosing Identities in America* (Berkeley: University of California Press, 1990).

29 Shawn Wong, "Is Ethnicity Obsolete?" in Werner Sollors, ed., *The Invention of Ethnicity* (New York: Oxford University Press, 1989), p. 230.

30 Alexis de Tocqueville, *Democracy in America*, vol. 1, ed. J. P. Mayer, tr. George Lawrence (New York: Doubleday, 1969), p. 357.

31 See Avtar Brah, "Difference, Diversity and Differentiation," in James

Donald and Ali Rattansi, eds., *"Race," Culture and Difference* (London: Sage, in association with the Open University, 1992).

32 For a useful discussion of political consciousness among Asian Indian youth in Britain, see KumKum Bhavnani, *Talking Politics* (Cambridge: Cambridge University Press, 1991).

33 The 1965 Immigration Law still discriminates against persons from India since the quota for India is only 20,000 out of 390,000 (5.1 percent of the total), though India's population constitutes 15.3 percent of the world's population. Setting a flat rate quota system discriminates against the more populous countries, which are, by and large, non-white countries. See Chandrashekar, *From India to America*.

34 Michael Omi and Howard Winant, *Racial Formation in the United States from the 1960s to the 1980s* (New York: Routledge, 1986).

35 453,000 of the 890,000 Asian Indians in the U.S. in 1990, or over 50 percent of their population, arrived after 1980. *Statistical Abstract of the United States 1993*, Bureau of the Census, Department of Commerce, Table 18. For an essay that suggests that in the U.S., the term "post-Civil Rights" may stand in for what is termed "postcolonial" elsewhere, see Ruth Frankenberg and Lata Mani, "Crosscurrents, Crosstalk: Race, 'Postcoloniality' and the Politics of Location," *Cultural Studies*, vol. 7, no. 2, 1993, pp. 292–310. They use "post-Civil Rights" to signify the double articulation of, on the one hand, resistance to issues of white or Western dominance and, on the other hand, the rise of collective struggles for self-articulation.

36 According to the 1990 Census, only 14.5 percent of Indians spoke an Asian language at home, compared for instance to a figure of 65.2 percent for Asians as a whole.

37 Vijay Ruikar, personal interview, 28 August 1994.

38 It may be mentioned, however, that K. S. Singh, reporting on a comprehensive survey of communities in India by the Anthropological Survey of India, states that the variation *within* castes is often greater than that *between* castes: "[O]ur populations are derived from four racial stocks . . . [However], . . . [b]iologically, most of the Indians are a highly mixed people. We no longer talk of racial classification of Indian populations. Instead we now talk of morphological and genetic variations among populations which, it is stated, are more so within a community than between communities." In "The People of India, Culture and Communication," Paper presented at Ogilvy & Mather Workshop on Culture and Communication, Bangalore, 7–11 July 1994.

39 One instance I am aware of, of positive assertions of "blackness," is in Tamil cinema, with the actor Rajnikanth inaugurating a trend of dark-complexioned heroes who spurn the use of makeup; Vijayakanth and Bhagiyaraj are two other instances of successful heroes whose dark color is explicit. However, most heroes continue to be regarded as "fair." With heroines, the code is much more stringent, and there are only scattered instances of actresses who have broken the color bar.

40 Several Japanese and Chinese applicants were denied citizenship on the basis of the 1790 Naturalization Law, which limited the privilege to "free white persons"; after 1870, the privilege was extended to "aliens of African nativity or persons of African descent" as well. However, Indians were the only ones among Asians to be judged as members of the "European" race, being believed part of "the Mediterranean branch of the Caucasian family," and many courts granted Indians American citizenship. Observations by Justice George Sutherland in the judgment of the Supreme Court, in denying citizenship to Takao Ozawa (*Ozawa v. U.S.*) in 1922, offered the culmination of this trend. However, in the very next year, the same judge, in *U.S. v. Bhagat Singh Thind*, ruled that Indian nationals were ineligible for citizenship. Thereafter this avenue was closed to Indian nationals. Chandrasekhar, *From India to America*, pp. 19–20.

41 Pramila Patel and Yogesh Rawal, personal interview, 11 September 1994. Names of interviewees have been changed in this chapter, except those named as office holders.

42 Shekhar Gupta, "The U.S.: An Indian Nightmare. The Racist Dotbusters Go Berserk in Jersey City," *India Today*, 15 December 1987, pp. 125–126. *India Today* reports the Indian population of Jersey City as 13,000 in 1987, as opposed to the *New York Times*, which has a figure of 9,000. See Alfonso A. Narvaez, "Jersey City Indian Community Protests Rash of Racial Attacks," *New York Times*, 8 October 1987, p. B3. Since the racial attacks, however, many of the better-off Indians have moved to Edison, New Jersey, a more upscale locality.

43 Dr. Sujata Shah, personal interview, 2 September 1994.

44 Shyam Mudgal, personal interview, 31 August 1994.

45 H. V. Seshadri, "For the Hindus in the West, the Crucial Challenge is of their Children," *Organiser* (Delhi), 4 November 1984, p. 9.

46 Ronald Takaki, "A Dream Deferred: The Crisis of Losing Ground," in Ronald Takaki, ed., *From Different Shores: Perspectives on Race and Ethnicity in America* (New York: Oxford University Press, 1987), p. 250.

47 Tocqueville, *Democracy in America*, vol. 2, pp. 506–508.

48 Robert N. Bellah *et al.*, *Habits of the Heart: Individualism and Commitment in American Life* (Berkeley: University of California Press, 1985), pp. 142, 56–71.

49 Sacvan Bercovitch, *The Puritan Origins of the American Self* (New Haven: Yale University Press, 1975). Bercovitch stresses the mythic aspect of the Puritan cultural influence to the exclusion of the ways in which it was embodied in rules and practices, in the material functioning of social institutions. His argument stresses continuity with a nowadays unfashionable confidence: we could instead point to the gaps and discontinuities, the contradictions and transformations in the Puritan narratives.

50 Ruth Frankenberg, *White Women, Race Matters: The Social Construction of Whiteness* (Minneapolis: University of Minnesota Press, 1993), p. 197.

51 *Ibid.*, pp. 154–155.

52 *Ibid.*, p. 206.

53 This was one of fifteen interviews with Hindu Students' Council members conducted during August–October 1994.

54 Shyam Mudgal, personal interview, 31 August 1994.

55 Field notes, San Francisco, May 1997. The Hindu Swayamsewak Sangh is the foreign branch of the RSS, retitled to acknowledge its foreign membership, with the "national" component of the title dropped. The camp was in Loma Mar, California, and was held in May 1997. The HSS was founded in the early 1960s when a few activists from the Rashtriya Swayamsewak Sangh settled in the U.K.; it was formally launched on Guru Poornima Day, 2 July 1966. See *Sangh Sandesh*: Newsmagazine of the Hindu Swayamsevak Sangh (U.K.), vol. 6, no. 2, March–April 1995, p. 25.

56 The number of H-1B visa holders, i.e., workers with specialty occupations, the greatest part of whom are software engineers, admitted in 1996 totaled 20,239, out of a total of 36,999 non-immigrants admitted that year; this amounted to nearly 80 percent of non-immigrants admitted. Tables 3 and 40, *1996 Statistical Yearbook of the Immigration and Naturalization Service*, United States Department of Justice, pp. 32 and 114. The H-1B visa limit was increased from 65,000 to 115,000 from 1 October 1998 onward.

57 Vijay Gupta, Hindu Swayamsewak Sangh, telephone interview, 17 January 1999. A number of other VHP and HSS members reiterated what Gupta said.

58 It is the Indians who were born in the U.S. or came as children who form the bulk of the Hindu Students Council – broadly, the second generation, as I explain below. Coming after the first generation, we should note, were the family connections brought into the U.S. by these immigrants, spouses and siblings who then brought their own spouses and siblings. This second phase of immigrants typically arrived at a later stage of their lives, and were consequently unable to reproduce the success of their sponsoring relatives.

59 This is an estimate, based on conversations with several software engineers working in the U.S. I thank in particular Sambasivan Amarnath, P. S. Srikkanth, and Hari Reddy.

60 For a useful account of an Indian company providing large numbers of software engineers to U.S. companies, see the case study by Sanjeev Dheer, Brian Viard, and John Roberts, "Tata Consultancy Services: Globalization of Software Services," SM-18, Graduate School of Business, Stanford University 1995. India's software exports have grown at a rate of 53 percent per annum since 1985. *Ibid.*, p. 12.

61 Telephone interview, Sambasivan Amarnath, software engineer, Princeton, N.J., 5 February 1999.

62 This of course reinforces the discretionary power of the heads of the organization, but it would be crude to call this manipulation without conceding the extent to which each branch expresses interests distinctive to its position, even while coordination is achieved between the different branches. It should be pointed out, however, that non-resident Indians

have for decades been an important source of finances for the VHP's activities in India.

63 Interview with Dr. Mahesh Mehta, former president of the VHP of America, of Needham, Mass., 2 September 1994.

64 Moropant Pingale, *Prak-kathan* [Foreword] in Raghunandan Prasad Sharma, ed., *Vishwa Hindu Parishad: Samagra Darshan* [Entire View], (New Delhi, n.d.).

65 *Ibid.*, pp. 9–11.

66 See note 39 above.

67 Vishwa Hindu Parishad of America, Inc., pamphlet, n.d.

68 Dr Yashpal Lakra, personal interview, 4 May 1996.

69 Literature handed out at a VHP-organized conference carried quotes from nationalist leaders such as Gandhi, declaring the desire for foreign goods to be exactly like desiring another man's woman, and therefore detestable. Wall-hangings listed brand names of consumer goods made by foreign companies, with indigenous equivalents named against each. Some of the "indigenous" companies listed in fact produced goods in partnership with foreign companies, such as Tata's and Godrej, and other brands had recently been acquired by foreign companies, such as Campa Cola and Thums Up. But a note at the bottom urges the reader to locate products made by small, local companies in preference to using foreign goods, a statement that makes a clear political choice, and one that the VHP of America prefers to avoid. *Bahurashtriya Kampaniyon ke Vikalp ke Roop Mein Swadeshi Upbhokt Vastuon ki Suchi* [List of Indigenous Consumer Goods as Options Instead of Foreign Companies' Goods], n.d.

70 Swami Ramsukhdas, *Matrushakti Ghor Apmaan* [Grave Insult to Motherhood] (Gorakhpur, U.P.: Gita Press, 1993).

71 Uma Chakravarty, "Whatever Happened to the Vedic Dasi," in Kumkum Sangari and Sudesh Vaid, eds., *Recasting Women: Essays in Colonial History* (New Delhi: Kali for Women, 1989). RSS leaders' claims of celibacy are often contested by their critics, it should be noted; but the claims are taken seriously by Hindu nationalists themselves.

72 See Harold Isaacs, *Images of Asia* (New York: Basic Books, 1972); Sucheta Mazumdar, "Racist Responses to Racism: The Aryan Myth and South Asians in the United States," *South Asia Bulletin*, vol. 9, no. 1, 1989.

73 See Williams, *Religions of Immigrants from India and Pakistan* and Williams, *Sacred Thread.*

74 This paragraph owes its inspiration to Carin McCormack.

75 E.g., Roland Robertson, *Globalization* (London: Sage Press, 1990).

76 This model of globalization is but a little-reconstructed version of modernization theory, one where the residual category of "tradition" is replaced by "the local."

CONCLUSION

1 *Eyewitness News* video news magazine, May 1991.
2 The Gujarat breakaway faction, the Rashtriya Janata Party (National Peoples' Party), led by RSS old-timer Shankarsinh Vaghela, eventually merged with the Congress (I). See V. Venkatesan, "A strategic merger," in *Frontline*, 16 July 1999, pp. 42–43. In U.P., the BJP's Chief Minister, Kalyan Singh, a member of the backward castes, has been the focus of backward-caste disaffection within the party, and warring factions within the party are headed by senior and upper-caste BJP leaders such as Lalji Tandon and Kalraj Mishra. See, e.g., Venkitesh Ramakrishnan, "Simmering discontent," *Frontline*, 2 July 1999, pp. 41–42.
3 See, e.g., Michael Gillan, "BJP in 1998 Lok Sabha Elections in West Bengal," *Economic and Political Weekly*, 5–12 September 1998, pp. 2391–2395. In Tamil Nadu, the stormy alliance of the BJP with J. Jayalalitha's AIADMK (All India Anna Dravida Munnetra Kazhagam, or All India Dravidian Progress Party) was replaced, in early 1999, by a partnership with K. Karunanidhi's DMK (Dravida Munnetra Kazhagam). The DMK was of course founded as an atheist, anti-Brahmin party, and like its breakaway party, the AIADMK, professes a commitment to secular ideals. In the case of Maharashtra, the BJP's alliance with the Hindu chauvinist Shiv Sena Party has had its own share of tensions, with deep differences between the Sena's Maratha parochialism and the charismatic style of its supreme leader, Bal Thackeray, and the BJP's own grassroots organization, which is more Leninist in form if not in substance.
4 To recall a BJP campaign slogan from the November 1993 assembly elections, *Sab ko parkha baar baar, Hum ko parkho ek baar* (You've given the others chance after chance; All we ask is one chance).
5 The most prominent example here is of course the nuclear testing of 1998, which constituted a dramatic and in many ways disastrous departure from a decades-old policy of refusing the nuclear option. For discussion, see, e.g., the special section "Testing Times," *Economic and Political Weekly*, 30 May 1998, pp. 1295–1315, 1349–1352.
6 Thus key provisions of the BJP's program, such as the revocation of Article 370, guaranteeing special status to Kashmir, the building of the Ram temple at the site of the demolished mosque in Ayodhya, and the introduction of a uniform civil code applicable to all religious communities, have repeatedly been backgrounded to ensure the survival of its diverse electoral coalitions with former enemies, such as the Samata Sanghathan, the Janata Dal, the Bahujan Samaj Party, and so on.
7 However, in a dramatic sign of its growing acceptability in the electoral realm itself, the Supreme Court ruled in 1996 that an appeal to Hindutva in election campaigning did not express a political appeal based on religious identity, and thus did not violate the Representation of People Act, 1951, which forbade religious appeals in elections. The court argued that Hindutva

meant Indian culture, and did not apply specifically to Hindus. The long identification of Hindutva with a specific political party and program, and with a particular set of electoral practices was thus ignored, implicitly endorsing Hindu nationalists" own claims for their slogans. Prabhoo v. Prabhakar Kunte and Ors. AIR 1996 SC 11 113. The case involved accusations of corrupt electoral practice against Dr. Prabhoo, the Mayor of Bombay, and his agent Bal Thackeray. For discussion of this and related cases, see Brenda Cossman and Ratna Kapur, *Secularism's Last Sigh? Hindutva and the (Mis)Rule of Law* (New Delhi: Oxford University Press, 1999).

8 See, in this context, Jayati Ghosh, "The economic effects of the BJP," *Frontline*, 21 May 1999, pp. 100–102. For more general discussion on the consequences of unregulated dismantling of controls, see, e.g., S. S. Gill, *The Pathology of Corruption* (New Delhi: HarperCollins, 1998), and Dharmendra Bhandari, *Inviting the Invaders: India Inc. – For Sale* (Jaipur: Rashmikant Durlabhji, 1998). Bhandari was Consultant to the Joint Parliamentary Committee on Securities Scam.

9 Interview with L. K. Advani, *The Economic Times*, 8 September 1993.

10 See chapter three.

11 E.g., see Ashis Nandy *et al.*, *Creating a Nationality: The Ramjanmabhumi Movement and the Fear of the Self* (New Delhi: Oxford University Press, 1995).

12 See V. Venkatesn, "A hate campaign in Gujarat" and Praveen Swami, "A deadline in Maharashtra," in *Frontline*, 29 January 1999, pp. 107–112 and p. 113 respectively.

13 See Ghosh, "The economic effects of the BJP."

14 Cited in Philippe Lacoue-Labarthe, *Heidegger, Art and Politics: The Fiction of the Political*, tr. Chris Turner (Oxford: Basil Blackwell, 1990), p. 62. Lacoue-Labarthe gives as his source Paul de Man, "Hegel on the Sublime," *Displacement: Derrida and After* (Bloomington: Indiana University Press, 1983), but de Man's text does not mention Goebbels.

APPENDIX: BACKGROUND TO THE BABRI MASJID DISPUTE

1 *The Times of India*, 3 February 1986, p. 1.

2 See Zakia Pathak and Rajeswari Sunder Rajan, "Shah Bano," *Signs*, January 1991. See also Asghar Ali Engineer, ed., *The Shah Bano Controversy*, New Delhi, 1987.

3 In early 1986, the Muslim Women's Bill was passed to play the Muslim card; and then came the decision on Ayodhya to play the Hindu card. It was supposed to be a package deal. I knew it was a dangerous thing to do and I did not agree . . . When I asked Mr. Rajiv Gandhi who is showing the worship . . . at Ayodhya on Doordarshan two days after it was unlocked, he did not reply; he merely smiled and observed it was tit for tat for the Muslim Women's Bill." Interview with Arun Nehru cited in "The Babri Masjid – Ramjanmabhumi Question," in Asghar Ali Engineer, ed., *Babri Masjid – Ramjanmabhumi Controversy* (Delhi, 1990), p. 167.

4 Arun Nehru, "Appeasement policy has proved bane of the nation," in *Indian Express*, 3 January 1993, rpt. in *Shame Shame Pseudo Secularism* (Hyderabad: Jana Sandesh Publishers, 1993). The involvement of Vir Bahadur Singh was asserted by senior government sources.

5 It is reported that the RSS had prepared a document where the relative merits of launching agitations at the three sites were evaluated. The legal agreement between the Sri Krishna Temple in Mathura and the Idgah mosque abutting it (and believed to stand on the ruins of an older Krishna temple) was considered "very sound." Whereas an agitation in Ayodhya would, it was predicted, set off a massive Hindu consolidation all over the world, and in turn trigger an agitation in Kashi. See Venkitesh Ramakrishnan, "Saffron Offensive: 'Liberation Theology' of a Different Kind," *Frontline*, 8 September 1995, pp. 4–12.

6 Digs had been done in Ayodhya thrice, in 1955–56, in 1969–70, and in 1975. During the last of these digs, the Janmabhumi area was surveyed and claims were made that brick bases were found that could have been supports for stone pillars from the temple. However, the author B. B. Lal, retired Director General of the Archaeological Survey of India, made no mention of these bases in his original report on the survey (*Indian Archaeology – A Review*, 1976–77, pp. 52–53), and waited thirteen years to make the announcement in the RSS magazine *Manthan* (October 1990). The improbability that brick bases would have supported stone pillars contributed to the incredulity of professional archaeologists towards Lal's revisionist report. After the mosque's demolition, additional "evidence" was "unearthed" that Janmabhumi supporters welcomed as confirming their case. Here again, the absence of reliable contextual evidence and the fastening onto objects as proof in themselves distinguished what columnist Sukumar Muralidharan dubbed as "karseva archaeology." For a discussion of the debates, see D. Mandal, *Ayodhya: Archaeology After Demolition* (New Delhi: Orient Longman, 1993).

7 E.g., W. C. Benet, ed., *Gazetteer of the Province of Oudh*, 3 vols., vol. 2, p. 7, cited in K. N. Panikkar's "A Historical Overview" in S. Gopal, ed., *Anatomy of a Confrontation: The Babri Masjid–Ram Janmabhumi Issue* (New Delhi: Viking Penguin, 1991), p. 41. I have drawn my account from Panikkar, pp. 30–31 and from Sushil Shrivastava's *The Disputed Mosque: A Historical Inquiry* (New Delhi: Vistaar, 1991), pp. 44–45. For an ethnographic account of the bairagis in Ayodhya, see Peter van der Veer, *Gods on Earth: The Management of Religious Experience and Identity in a North Indian Pilgrimage* (New Delhi: Oxford University Press, 1989).

8 *Ibid.*, p. 32.

9 Gopal Sharma, *Kar Seva se Kar Seva Tak* (Jaipur: Rajasthan Patrika, 1993), p. 28. Sources who had quit the VHP confirmed that it was Dau Dayal Khanna who had revived the issue.

10 "Illegal Restriction of Ramjanmabhumi" – letter from J. R. Gupta, Office Secretary, VHP, New Delhi, in *Organiser*, 12 January 1986, p. 12.

11 Mohammed Farooq, son of Zahoor Ahmad, and Mohammad Hashim Ansari, who were involved in the case from 1951 onwards. Here I will briefly summarize the history of the legal disputes over Babri Masjid. In 1885 and in 1886, a Mahant Raghubar Das appealed successively before the Sub-Judge, Faizabad, the Court of the District Judge of Faizabad, and the Judicial Commissioner of Oudh, to construct a temple at the Ram Chabutra. The appeal was denied, on the grounds of its proximity to the mosque, and the absence of evidence that the plaintiff was proprietor of the land in question. Parmanand Singh, "The Legal History of the Ayodhya Litigation," in Vinay Chandra Mishra, ed., *Ram Janmabhoomi Babri Masjid. Historical Documents, Legal Opinions and Judgements* (Delhi: Bar Council of India Trust, 1991), pp. 29–31. Reprint of Special Issue of *Indian Bar Review*, vol. 18(2) 1991. In 1934, a Hindu–Muslim riot resulting from the killing of a cow in nearby Shajahanpur village, on Bakr-Id, led to an attack on the Babri mosque by Hindus. The mosque was repaired and reconditioned by a Muslim contractor at the expense of the British government. In 1936, the Commissioner of Waqfs instituted an inquiry under the U.P. Muslim Waqfs Act into the ownership of the property, and in March 1946, the mosque was declared Sunni property. In December of 1949, the idols were forcibly installed in the mosque; thereafter, the legal history of the dispute presents "an astounding scenario," in the words of one Member of Parliament (G. M. Banatwalla, "Babri Masjid-Ram Janambhoomi Controversy Analysed," in Mishra, *Ram Janmabhoomi Babri Masjid*, p. 79). The District Magistrate, K. K. Nayar, on being ordered by the Commissioner of Faizabad, Shyam Sunderlal Dar, to remove the idols, refused to do so. Instead he restrained them from coming near the mosque, and allowed four Hindu priests to perform aarti at the center of the mosque every day. (Nayar was subsequently made to retire. He later contested the Parliamentary elections as a Jan Sangh candidate, as did his wife, Shakuntala Nayar.) In the civil suit filed by Gopal Singh Visharad, the court did not address the issue of trespass, and only considered whether the right to perform prayers was to be free or restricted. An interim injunction was granted against the removal of the idols, and from interfering with the worship being carried on. (*Sri Gopal Singh Visharad vs. Zahir Ahmad & Others*. Order of Civil Judge, Faizabad, 3 March 1951, suit no. 2 of 1950.) On appeal by the Muslims the order was upheld by the Allahabad High Court, *vide* – judgment dated 26 April 1955. Suit no. 12 of 1961, filed on 18 December 1961 in the Court of the Civil Judge, Faizabad by the U.P. Sunni Central Board of Waqfs and eight Sunni Muslim individuals, was the only suit filed by Muslims, and it was made the leading suit. The relief it claimed was a declaration that the building in question was a mosque and its surrounding area a Muslim graveyard, and, if the court deemed it necessary, possession by removal of the idol and other objects of Hindu worship. This suit was pending. The existing arrangement contiued until 1 February 1986, when Umesh Chandra Pandey's petition led to an order to unrestricted worship

by Hindus at the mosque. (*Umesh Chandra Pandey vs. State of U.P. and 30 others. Civil Appeal no. 6 of 1986*, 1 February 1986.)

12 (1993) 1 U.P. Local Bodies and Educational Cases: Mohammad Hashim vs. State of U.P. and others, para 21.

13 Anand Sagar, "Ramjanmabhumi nurtures tension," *The Times of India*, 5 February 1986, p. 1.

14 Judgment of District Judge, Faizabad, Shri K. M. Pandey, 1 February 1986. In Engineer, *Babri-Masjid Ramjanmabhoomi Controversy*. S. K. Tripathi, Express News Service, "Hindus euphoric at unlocking of temple," *Indian Express*, 6 February 1986, p. 7. The presiding judge, K. M. Pandey, was appointed to the High Court in 1991. In a volume of his essays published by the RSS, his anti-Muslim prejudices are given free vent. See *Voice of Conscience* (Lucknow: Din Dayal Upadhyay Parkashan), 1996.

15 Sagar, "Ramjanmabhumi nurtures tension"; Tripathi, "Hindus euphoric at unlocking of temple."

16 Writ petition no. 746 of 1986, Mohammad Hashim vs. District of Faizabad. Cited in *Report of the Inquiry Commission, Citizens" Tribunal on Ayodhya*, 1993, p. 117.

17 In addition to its other fallout, the Shah Bano incident had the impact of rejuvenating debates on the Uniform Civil Code (UCC), which has been written into the Indian Constitution as a Directive Principle. The BJP has strongly pushed for a UCC, while taking as its model Hindu personal law, which is seen to be the most progressive. In the debate about UCC, women's groups have unfortunately been put in a position where their demands for women's legal rights and equality before the law resonates uncannily with rightist demands for a UCC. While feminists have been careful to distance themselves from the right, there is a debate raging within the community of activists about the strategic value of asking for equality before the law when the prevailing balance of forces allows such a demand to be hijacked by the right. At the same time arguments about the variations in customary law within Hindu communities, and the effects of colonial legislation on homogenizing laws relating to women (such as on widow remarriage, inheritance, and divorce) are utilized to point to the Hindu right's dismissal of these differences while championing the idea of a unitary Hindu understanding of womens' legal rights. Some activists have argued for a "reverse option" which would allow women to choose to return to personal laws so long as they do not go against women's fundamental interests. For select examples of these positions, consult: All India Democratic Women's Association, National Convention 9–10 December 1995, "Equal Rights, Equal Laws" (draft resolution), "Hindu Laws and Women," "Women and Muslim Personal Law"; "Civil Codes and Personal Laws: Reversing the Option" prepared by Working Group on Women's Rights, 18 November 1995; People's Union for Democratic Rights' response to "Civil Codes and Personal Laws: Reversing the Option," 22 December 1995; A. G. Noorani, "Civil code vs reform," *Frontline*, 23 February 1996;

Kumkum Sangari, "Politics of Diversity: Religious Communities and Multiple Patriarchies," *Economic and Political Weekly*, 23 December 1995, pp. 3287–3310, and 30 December, pp. 3381–3389. For material on the discourse around Muslim bigamy, and the attempts to "save" Hindu men who convert to Islam in order to undergo second marriages, see Flavia Agnes, "Hindu Men, Monogamy and Uniform Civil Code," *Economic and Political Weekly*, 16 December 1995, and Gitanjali Gangoli, "Anti-Bigamy Bill in Maharashtra: Wider Debate Needed," *Economic and Political Weekly*, 20 July 1996. Needless to say, these articles expose the Hindu right's interest in protecting the identity of the majority community, instead of engaging in a struggle for womens' political and economic rights.

18 Ram Jethmalani, "A Call for Sanity," *Indian Express*, 26 October 1985, rpt. in *The Shah Bano Case. Nation Speaks Out* (Bangalore: Jagarana Prakashana, 1986); C. Achutha Menon, "Uniform Civil Code Still a Hazy Concept," *The Hindu*, 27 August 1985, rpt. *ibid.*

Select bibliography

NEWSPAPERS

Aaj
Dainik Jagran
The Economic Times
Hindustan Times
The Indian Express
Janmat
Jansatta
Navbharat Times
New Age
The Organiser
Quami Morcha
Swatantra Bharat
Telegraph
The Times of India

REPORTS

All India Democratic Women's Association, "Equal Rights, Equal Laws," (draft resolution) National Convention 9–10 December 1995.

Bharatiya Janata Party. *Election Analysis: BJP Polled One Crore Votes and Won One Hundred Assembly Seats More Than the Congress-I.* New Delhi: Bharatiya Janata Party (Central Office), n.d.

BJP Meets Indian Industry. Bharatiya Janata Party Publication no. 127, New Delhi, 1993.

BJP's White Paper on Ayodhya and the Rama Temple Movement. New Delhi: BJP, 1993.

INS Press Handbook, New Delhi: Indian Newspaper Society, 1987–1993.

National Integration Council: Report of the Standing Committee, 26 April 1992.

People's Union for Democratic Rights, *Bhagalpur Riots*, Delhi, April 1990.

response to "Civil Codes and Personal Laws: Reversing the Option," 22 December 1995.

Press Council of India Annual Report (1 April 1993–31 March 1994), New Delhi.

Report of the Subcommittee Appointed by the Press Council of India on 8.11.1990 to Examine the Role of the Press on the One Hand and on the Other the Role of the Authorities in Dealing with the Press Relating to the Coverage of the Ramjanmabhumi-Babri Masjid Issue, given at Thiruvananthapuram, Kerala, 21 January 1991.

RSS: Widening Horizons. Bangalore: Sahitya Sangama, 1992.

Second Press Commission of India, *Report of the Second Press Commission*, Delhi: Controller of Publications, 1982.

Sri Balasaheb Deoras Answers Questions. Bangalore: Sahitya Sindhu, 1984.

We the American . . . Asians. U.S. Department of Commerce: Economics and Statistics Administration, Bureau of the Census, September 1993.

Working Group on Womens' Rights, "Civil Codes and Personal Laws: Reversing the Option," 18 November 1995.

SECONDARY SOURCES

Advani, L. K. "Preparing for the future," interview in *Frontline*, Madras, June 15–28, 1996, pp. 25–27.

Agnes, Flavia. "Hindu Men, Monogamy and Uniform Civil Code," *Economic and Political Weekly*, 16 December 1995, pp. 3238–3244.

Ahmad, Aijaz. "Fascism and National Culture: Reading Gramsci in the Days of Hindutva," *Social Scientist*, vol. 21, nos. 3–4, March–April 1993, pp. 32–68.

Allen, Robert C. *Speaking of Soap Operas*. Chapel Hill: University of North Carolina Press, 1985.

A.M. "Calcutta Diary," *Economic and Political Weekly*, 19–26 December 1992, pp. 2679–2680.

Andersen, Walter K. and Shridhar D. Damle. *The Brotherhood in Saffron. The Rashtriya Swayamsevak Sangh and Hindu Revivalism*. New Delhi: Sage, 1987.

"The RSS: The Spearhead of Hindu Revivalism," in Ramashray Roy and Richard Sisson, eds., *Diversity and Dominance in Indian Politics* (vol. 2). New Delhi: Sage, 1990.

Anderson, Benedict. *Imagined Communities. Reflections on the Origin and Spread of Nationalism*. London: Verso, 1983.

Ang, Ien. *Watching Dallas: Soap Opera and the Melodramatic Imagination*, tr. Della Couling. London and New York: Methuen, 1985.

Anon. *Angry Hindu! Yes, Why Not?* New Delhi: Suruchi Prakashan, 1988.

The Shah Bano Case. Nation Speaks Out, Bangalore: Jagarana Prakashana, 1986.

"Who is Afraid of Hindi Journalism?" *Vidura*, New Delhi, vol. 29, June 1992, p. 15.

The Saga of Ayodhya. Bangalore: Jagrana Prakashana Trust. 1990.

Appadurai, Arjun. "Patriotism and Its Futures," *Public Culture*, Winter 1993, pp. 411–430.

Asad, Talal. *Genealogies of Religion: Discipline and Reasons of Power in Christianity and Islam*. Baltimore: Johns Hopkins University Press, 1993.

Ashar, Gopalbhai. "The Role of Religious Anushthans [Ceremonies] in Social Integration," *Hindu Vishwa*, 1992, pp. 79–80.

Austin, Granville. *The Indian Constitution: the Cornerstone of a Nation.* Oxford: Clarendon Press, 1966.

Awasthy, G. C. *Broadcasting in India.* Bombay: Allied Publishers, 1965.

Bachelard, Gaston. *The Poetics of Space*, tr. Maria Jolas. Boston: Beacon Press, 1969.

Badhwar, Inderjit. "A supersuccess story," *India Today*, 30 April 1987, pp. 110–112.

Bakhtin, M. M. *The Dialogic Imagination*, tr. Caryl Emerson and Michael Holquist. Austin: University of Texas Press, 1981.

  Problems of Doestoevsky's Poetics, ed. and tr. Caryl Emerson. Minneapolis: University of Minnesota Press, 1984.

  Speech Genres and Other Late Essays, tr. Vern McGee, ed. Caryl Emerson and Michael Holquist. Austin: University of Texas Press, 1986.

Balasubramanian, V. *Indians Abroad. The NRI Syndrome.* Bombay: Business Book Publishing House, 1987.

Banatwalla, G. M. "Babri Masjid-Ram Janambhoomi Controversy Analysed," in Vinay Chandra Mishra, ed., *Ram Janmabhoomi Babri Masjid. Historical Documents, Legal Opinions and Judgement.* New Delhi: Bar Council of India Trust, 1991, pp. 29–31. [Reprint of special issue of *Indian Bar Review*, vol. 18 (2), 1991.]

Banerjee, Sumanta. *India's Monopoly Press. A Mirror of Distortion.* New Delhi: Indian Federation of Working Journalists, 1973.

Bardhan, Pranab. *The Political Economy of Deveopment in India.* Oxford: Basil Blackwell, 1984.

Barthes, Roland. *Mythologies*, selected and tr. Annette Lavers. New York: Hill and Wang, 1972.

Basu, Tapan *et al. Khaki Shorts, Saffron Flags: A Critique of the Hindu Right.* New Delhi: Orient Longman, 1994.

Batura, R. C. "VHP takes a leaf out of Bharat's book," *Organiser*, 4 October 1992, pp. 9–10.

Baxi, Upendra. "Sahmat's Secularism: Neither 'Short-Cut' nor 'Credit-card,' " *Mainstream*, 9 October 1993, pp. 11–15.

Bayly, C. A. *Local Roots of Indian Politics: Allahabad 1880–1920.* Oxford: The Clarendon Press, 1975.

  "The Pre-History of 'Communalism'? Religious Conflict in India, 1700–1860," *Modern Asian Studies*, vol. 19 (2), 1985, pp. 177–204.

Bellah, Robert N. *et al. Habits of the Heart: Individualism and Commitment in American Life.* Berkeley: University of California Press, 1985.

Benjamin, Walter. *Illuminations: Essays and Reflections*, ed. Hannah Arendt, tr. Harry Zohn. New York: Schocken Books, 1968.

Bercovitch, Sacvan. *The Puritan Origins of the American Self.* New Haven: Yale University Press, 1975.

Bhagwat, Nanaji. "Sri Ram Shilla Pooja Plan," *Hindu Vishwa*, August 1990, pp. 60–63.

Bhargava, Sandeep. "Industrial Liberalisation: Policy Issues at State Level," *Economic and Political Weekly*, 26 August 1995, pp. M117–M122.

Bhargava, Simran. "Divine Sensation," *India Today*, 30 April 1987, pp. 170–171.

Bhatt, Rakesh Mohan. "Sociolinguistic Area and Language Policies," in Edward C. Dimock, Jr., *et al.*, eds., *Dimensions of Sociolinguistics in South Asia. Papers in Memory of Gerald B. Kelly*. New Delhi: Oxford and IBH Publishing Co., 1992, pp. 47–69.

Bhavnani, KumKum. *Talking Politics*. Cambridge: Cambridge University Press, 1991.

Bhramar, Ramkumar. *Ayodhya ka Pathik* [Ayodhya's Traveler]. Delhi: Radhakrishna Prakashan, 1993.

Bourdieu, Pierre. *Homo Academicus*, tr. Peter Collier. Cambridge: Polity Press, 1988.

In Other Words: Essays Towards a Reflexive Sociology, tr. Matthew Adamson. Cambridge: Polity Press, 1990.

The Logic of Practice, tr. Richard Nice. Stanford: Stanford University Press, 1990.

Brah, Avtar. "Difference, Diversity and Differentiation," in James Donald and Ali Rattansi, eds., *"Race", Culture and Difference*. London: Sage, in association with the Open University, 1992.

Brass, Paul R. "Caste, Class and Community in the Ninth General Elections for the Lok Sabha in Uttar Pradesh"; "The Rise of the BJP and the Future of Party Politics in Uttar Pradesh," in Harold A. Gould and Sumit Ganguly, eds., *India Votes. Alliance Politics and Minority Governments in the Ninth and Tenth General Elections*. Boulder: Westview Press, 1993.

Brooks, Peter. *The Melodramatic Imagination*. New Haven: Yale University Press, 1976.

Burkhalter Flueckiger, Joyce, and Laurie Sears, eds. *The Boundaries of Tradition: Ramayana and Mahabharata Performances in South and Southeast Asia*. Ann Arbor: University of Michigan Center for South and Southeast Asian Studies, 1990.

Business India. "The Eighties: A Decade of Change," 11–24 December 1989, p. 57.

Butler, David, Ashok Lahiri, and Prannoy Roy, eds. *India Decides. Elections 1952–1991*. New Delhi: Living Media Books, 1991.

Cashman, Richard. *The Myth of the Lokamanya. Tilak and Mass Politics in Maharashtra*. Berkeley: University of California Press, 1975.

Chakravarti, Uma *et al.* "Khurja Riots 1990–91. Understanding the Conjuncture," *Economic and Political Weekly*, vol. 27, no. 18, 2 May 1992, pp. 951–965.

Chakravartty, Nikhil. "No Short-Cut to Secularism," *Mainstream*, 18 September 1993, p. 6.

Chandra, Bipan. *Communalism in Modern India*. New Delhi: Vikas, 1984.

Chatterjee, Partha. *The Nation and its Fragments. Colonial and Postcolonial Histories*. New Delhi: Oxford University Press, 1993.

Chatterji, P. C. *Broadcasting in India*. Revised and updated edition, New Delhi: Sage, 1991.

Chelliah, Raja. "Growth of Indian Public Debt," in Bimal Jalan, ed., *The Indian Economy – Problems and Prospects*. New Delhi: Penguin, 1993, pp. 78–95.

Cockburn, Alexander. *Corruptions of Empire*. London: Verso, 1988.

Cohen, Ralph. "History and Genre," *New Literary History*, vol. 17, no. 2, Winter 1986, pp. 117–142.

Cohn, Bernard. "The Command of Language and the Language of Command," *Subaltern Studies IV*. New Delhi: Oxford University Press, 1985, pp. 276–329.

Colley, Linda. *Britons: Forging the Nation 1707–1837*. New Haven: Yale University Press, 1992.

Cowie, Peter, ed. *International Film Guide 1969*. London: Tantivy Press, 1969.

Crooke, William and R. E. Enthoven. *Religion and Folklore in Northern India*. New Delhi, 1972.

Cruz, Jon and Justin Lewis, eds. *Viewing, Reading, Listening. Audiences and Cultural Reception*. Boulder, Colo.: Westview Press, 1994.

Curran, J. A., Jr. *Militant Hinduism in Indian Politics: A Study of the RSS*. New York: Institute of Pacific Relations, 1951.

Das, Veena, ed. *Mirrors of Violence: Communities, Riots and Survivors in South Asia*. New Delhi: Oxford University Press, 1990.

Das Gupta, Gurudas. *The Securities Scandal: A Report to the Nation*. New Delhi: People's Publishing House, 1993.

Das Gupta, Jyotirindra. *Language Conflict and National Development: Group Politics and National Language Policy in India*. Berkeley: University of California Press, 1970.

Dasgupta, Swapan. "Hedgewar's Legacy – The Limitations of Elitist Hinduism," *The Statesman*, 1 April 1989. [Reprinted in the *Organiser*, 23 April 1989, p. 11.]

Davis, Mike. *City of Quartz*. London: Verso, 1991.

Degvekar, M. P. "The Origin and Growth of Vishva Hindu Parishad,' *Hindu Vishva*. VHP Rajat Jayanti Souvenir, New Delhi, August 1990, p. 91.

Desai, Meghnad. *Capitalism, Socialism and the Indian Economy*, Annual Export–Import Bank Commencement Lecture. Bombay: Exim Bank, 1993.

Deshpande, Sudhanva. "Sahmat and the Politics of Cultural Intervention," *Economic and Political Weekly*, vol. 31, no. 25, 22 June 1996, pp. 1586–1590.

De Tocqueville, Alexis. *Democracy in America*, ed. J. P. Mayer, tr. George Lawrence. New York: Doubleday, 1969.

Deutsch, Karl W. *Nationalism and Social Communication*. Cambridge, Mass.: MIT Press, 1966.

Dewan, Saba and Rahul Roy. *Dharm Yudh*, a Jamia Milia Islamia Mass Communication Institute Video Presentation, 1989.

Dienst, Richard. *Still Life in Real Time: Theory After Television*. Durham: Duke University Press, 1994.

Dimock, Edward C., Jr., *et al.*, eds. *Dimensions of Sociolinguistics in South Asia. Papers in Memory of Gerald B. Kelly*. New Delhi: Oxford and IBH Publishing Co., 1992.

Dionne, E. J., Jr. *Why Americans Hate Politics*. New York: Simon and Schuster, 1991.

Dirks, Nicholas. "Castes of Mind," *Representations*, no. 37, Winter 1992, pp. 56–78.

The Hollow Crown. Ethnohistory of an Indian Kingdom. Cambridge: Cambridge University Press, 1986.

Donald, James and Ali Rattansi, eds. *"Race", Culture and Difference*. London: Sage, in association with the Open University, 1992.

Dubashi, Jay. "BJP's Unique Role," *Organiser*, 25 June 1989, p. 2.

"Hindu Rate of Growth," *Organiser*, 9 June 1985, p. 2.

Duggal, K. S. *What Ails Indian Broadcasting*. New Delhi: Marwah Publications, 1980.

Dumont, Louis. *Religion/Politics and History in India. Collected Papers in Indian Sociology*. Paris/The Hague: Mouton, 1970.

Eck, Diana L. *Darshan: Seeing the Divine Image in India*. 2nd edn. Chambersburg: Anima Books, 1985.

Elder, J. W. and Peter L. Schmitthenner, "Film Fantasy and Populist Politics in South India: NT Rama Rao and the Telugu Desam Party," in Robert E. Frykenberg and Pauline Kolenda, eds. *Studies of South India. An Anthology of Recent Research and Scholarship*. Madras/New Delhi: New Era Publications/American Institute of Indian Studies, 1985, pp. 373–387.

Elsaesser, Thomas. "Tales of Sound and Fury: Observations on the Family Melodrama," *Monogram*, vol. 4, 1972, pp. 2–15.

"TV Through the Looking Glass," *Quarterly Review of Film and Video*, vol. 14, nos. 1–2, 1992, pp. 5–27.

Emeneau, Murray B. *Language and Linguistic Area: Essays by Murray B. Emeneau*, ed. A. S. Dil. Stanford: Stanford University Press, 1980.

Engineer, Asghar Ali. "The Bloody Trail: Ramjanmabhoomi and Communal Violence in U.P.," *Economic and Political Weekly*, 26 January 1991, pp. 155–159.

"How Muslims Voted," *Economic and Political Weekly*, vol. 31, no. 21, 25 May 1996, p. 1241.

"The Press on Ayodhya Kar Seva," *Economic and Political Weekly*, vol. 26, no. 20, 18 May 1991, p. 1263.

Ed. *The Babri-Masjid Ramjanmabhumi Controversy*. Delhi: Ajanta Publication, 1990.

Engineer, Asghar Ali, and A. K. Narain. "Ganesa: The Idea and the Icon," in Robert C. Brown, ed., *Ganesh: Studies of an Asian God*. Albany: State University of New York Press, 1991.

Eyewitness News video news magazine, May 1991.

Fadul, Anamaria, ed. *Serial Fiction in the Latin American Telenovelas with an Annotated Bibliography of Brazilian Telenovelas*. Sao Paulo: School of Communication and Arts, 1993.

Feldman, Allen. *Formations of Violence: The Narrative of the Body and Political Terror in Northern Ireland*. Berkeley: University of California Press, 1991.

Ferguson, Charles A. "Diglossia," in P. P. Giglioli, ed., *Language and Social Context*. Harmondsworth: Penguin, 1972, pp. 232–251.

"South Asia as a Sociolinguistic Area," in Edward C. Dimock, Jr., *et al.*, *Dimensions of Sociolinguistics in South Asia. Papers in Memory of Gerald B. Kelly*. New Delhi: Oxford University Press and IBH Publishing Co., 1992, pp. 25–36.

"The Structure and Use of Politeness Formulas," *Language in Society*, vol. 5, 1976, pp. 137–151.

Foster-Carter, Aidan. "From Rostow to Gunder Frank: Conflicting Paradigms in the Analysis of Underdevelopment," *World Development*, vol. 4(3), March 1976, pp. 167–180.

Foucault, Michel. "Governmentality," in Colin Gordon *et al.*, eds., *The Foucault Effect*. London: Harvester Wheatsheaf, 1991, pp. 87–104.

Frankenberg, Ruth and Lata Mani. "Crosscurrents, Crosstalk: Race, 'Post-coloniality' and the Politics of Location," *Cultural Studies*, vol. 7, no. 2, 1993, pp. 292–310.

White Women, Race Matters: The Social Construction of Whiteness. Minneapolis: University of Minnesota Press, 1993.

Freiberg, J. W. *The French Press: Class, State and Ideology*. New York: Praeger, 1981.

Freitag, Sandria B. "Enactments of Ram's Story and the Changing Nature of 'the Public' in British India", *South Asia*, vol. 14, no. 1, 1991, pp. 65–90.

"Sacred Symbol as Mobilizing Idedology: The North Indian Search for a 'Hindu' Community," *Comparative Studies in Society and History*, vol. 22, no. 4, October 1980, pp. 597–625.

Frykenberg, Robert E. and Pauline Kolenda, eds. *Studies of South India. An Anthology of Recent Research and Scholarship*. Madras/New Delhi: New Era Publications/American Institute of Indian Studies, 1985.

Gadihoke, Sabina and Sabina Kidwai. Footage from the Media Storm Collective, New Delhi.

Gangoli, Gitanjali. "Anti-Bigamy Bill in Maharashtra: Wider Debate Needed," *Economic and Political Weekly*, 20 July 1996, pp. 1921–1925.

Gans, Herbert J. "Symbolic Ethnicity: The Future of Ethnic Groups and Cultures in America," *Ethnic and Racial Studies*, vol. 2, 1979, pp. 1–20.

Garg, Balwant Rai. *Sri Ramjanmabhumi Mandir: Ayodhya ki Rakt Ranjit Gaurav Poorn Gatha* [Sri Ramjanmabhumi Temple: Ayodhya's Blood-Stained, Pride-Filled Story]. Ambala: Bharat Vidya Vihar, 1988.

Geddes-Gonzales, Henry. "Articulating Narrative Strategies: The Peruvian Telenovela," in Fadul Anamaria, ed., *Serial Fiction in the Latin American Telenovelas with an Annotated Bibliography of Brazilian Telenovelas*. Sao Paulo: School of Communication and Arts, 1993.

Geertz, Clifford. *Negara. The Theatre State in Nineteenth-Century Bali*. Princeton: Princeton University Press, 1980.

Gellner, Ernest. *Nations and Nationalism*. Oxford: Basil Blackwell, 1983.

Postmodernism, Reason, Religion. London: Routledge, 1992.

Ghosh, Amitav. "The Diaspora in Indian Culture," *Public Culture*, vol. 2, no. 1, Fall 1989, pp. 73–78.

Ghosh, Arun. "Ideologues and Ideology: Privatisation of Public Enterprises," *Economic and Political Weekly*, 23 July 1994, pp. 1929–1931.

Gillespie, Marie. *Television, Ethnicity and Cultural Change*. London: Routledge, 1995.

Gitlin, Todd. *The Whole World Is Watching: Mass Media in the Making and Unmaking of the New Left*. Berkeley and Los Angeles: University of California Press, 1980.

Godbole, Madhav. *Unfinished Innings: Recollections and Reflections of a Civil Servant*. New Delhi: Orient Longman, 1996.

Goldman, Robert P. *The Ramayana of Valmiki, vol. 1: Balakanda*, tr. Robert P. Goldman. Princeton: Princeton University Press, 1984.

Goldman, Robert and Arvind Rajagopal. *Mapping Hegemony: Television News and Industrial Conflict*. Norwood, N.J.: Ablex, 1992.

Golwalkar, M. S. *Bunch of Thoughts*. Bangalore: Jagarana Prakashana, 1980.

Gopal, S. L., ed. *Anatomy of a Confrontation: The Babri Masjid–Ram Janmabhumi Issue*. New Delhi: Viking Penguin, 1991.

Gore, N. A. *Bibliography of the Ramayana*. Poona, 1943.

Goyal, S. K. and Challapathi Rao. *Ownership and Control Structure of the Indian Press*. New Delhi: Indian Institute of Public Administration, 1982, appendix X.2.

Gramsci, Antonio. *An Antonio Gramsci Reader*, ed. David Forgacs. New York: Schocken, 1988.

Selections from the Prison Notebooks, ed. and tr. Quintin Hoare and Geoffrey Nowell-Smith. New York: International Publishers, 1971.

Greeley, Andrew M. *Ethnicity in the United States: A Preliminary Reconaissance*. New York: Wiley, 1974.

Guha, Ranajit Guha. *Elementary Aspects of Peasant Insurgency in Colonial India*. Delhi: Oxford University Press, 1983.

Gujral, I. K. "Politics and Advertising," *Imprint*, New Delhi, November 1985, p. 29.

Gupta, Jaswant Rai. *Hinduon ka Dharmantaran Evam Videshi Dhan* [Role of Foreign Money in Conversion of Hindus]. New Delhi, n.d.

Gupta, S. P. *Liberalisation – Its Impact on the Indian Economy*. New Delhi: Macmillan, 1993.

Gupta, Shekhar. "The U.S.: An Indian Nightmare. The Racist Dotbusters Go Berserk in Jersey City," *India Today*, 15 December 1987, pp. 125–126.

Gurumurthy, S. *This is What Swadeshi is About*, [talk] All India General Secretary, Swadeshi Jagran Manch delivered on 15 January 1994, Madras: Vigil (A public opinion forum), 9 February 1994.

Habermas, Jurgen. *The Structural Transformation of the Public Sphere: An Inquiry into a Category of Bourgeois Society*, tr. Thomas Burger. Cambridge, Mass.: MIT Press, 1989.

Hall, Stuart. "Encoding/Decoding," in Stuart Hall *et al.*, *Culture, Media, Language*. London: Hutchinson, 1980.

The Hard Road to Renewal: Thatcherism and the Crisis of the Left. London: Verso, 1988.

"Reflections upon the Encoding/Decoding Model: An Interview with Stuart Hall," in Cruz and Lewis, *Viewing, Reading, Listening*, pp. 253–274.

et al. Policing the Crisis: Mugging, the State and Law and Order. London: Macmillan, 1978.

Haque, Mazharul, S.M. *What is News in India? A Content Analysis of the Elite Press.* Lanham: University Press of America, 1988.

Hardgrave, Robert L., Jr. "Alliance Politics and Minority Government: India at the Polls, 1989 and 1991," in Harold A. Gould and Sumit Ganguly, eds., *India Votes: Alliance Politics and Minority Governments in the Ninth and Tenth General Elections.* Boulder, Colo.: Westview Press, 1993, pp. 239–240.

Hechter, Michael. "Group Formation and the Cultural Division of Labor," *American Journal of Sociology*, vol. 79, no. 5, 1978, pp. 293–318.

Heimsath, Charles. *Indian Nationalism and Hindu Social Reform.* Princeton: Princeton University Press, 1964.

Herring, Ronald. *Land to the Tiller: The Political Economy of Agrarian Reform in South Asia.* New Haven: Yale University Press, 1983.

Hindustan Thompson Associates. *Fairs and Festivals as Seasonal Markets.* Bombay, 1978.

Hirst, Paul Q. *After Thatcher.* London: Collins, 1989.

Indian Market Research Bureau (IMRB). *The Ramayan Phenomenon: An Epic Programme.* Bombay, 1989.

Innis, Harold A. *The Bias of Communication.* Toronto: University of Toronto Press, 1951.

Empire and Communications. London: Oxford University Press, 1950.

Jaffrelot, Christophe. *The Hindu Nationalist Movement and Indian Politics.* New Delhi: Viking, 1996.

Jain, Meenakshi. "Strange Bedfellows in Uttar Pradesh," *Times of India*, 25 September 1996, p. 14.

Jalan, Bimal, ed. *The Indian Economy – Problems and Prospects.* New Delhi: Penguin, 1993.

India's Economic Crisis – The Way Ahead. New Delhi: Oxford University Press, 1991.

Jeffrey, Robin. "Indian-Language Newspapers and Why They Grow," *Economic and Political Weekly*, vol. 28, no. 38, 18 September 1993, pp. 2004–2011.

Jessop, Bob *et al.* "Authoritarian Populism, Two Nations and Thatcherism," *New Left Review*, no. 147, September–October 1984, pp. 32–60.

Jethwaney, Jaishri. *Impact of the Media and Election Campaigning Techiques on Delhi Women: Delhi Assembly Elections, November 1993.* Indian Institute of Mass Communication – Friedrich Ebert Stiftung, 1994.

Jha, Padmanand and Lekha Rattanani, "The 'Evergreen' Saffron Union," *Outlook* (New Delhi), vol. 2, no. 39, 25 September 1996, p. 16.

Jones, Kenneth W. *Arya Dharma: Hindu Consciousness in Nineteenth Century Punjab.* Berkeley: University of California Press, 1976.

Joshi, Manoj. "Only BJP has moved ahead" (interview with L. K. Advani), *Frontline*, 20 July–2 August 1991, p. 35.

Joshi, Prabhash. "Chunautiyon ke beech Khada Patrakar" [Challenges Before Reporters], in Jaiprakash Bharati, ed., *Hindi Patrakaitha: Dasha aur Disha* [Hindi Journalism: Condition and Direction]. New Delhi: Pravin Publishers, 1994.

Juergensmeyer, Mark. "The Gadar Syndrome: Ethnic Anger and Nationalist Pride," in S. Chandrasekhar, ed., *From India to America: A Brief History of Immigration; Problems of Discrimination; Admission and Assimilation*. La Jolla, Calif.: Population Review Publications, 1982.

Kachru, Braj B. *The Alchemy of English: The Spread, Functions and Models of Non-Native Englishes*. Oxford: Pergamon Institute, 1986.

Kachru, Yamuna. "Impact of Expanding Domains of Use on a Standard Language: Contemporary Hindi in India," *Studies in the Linguistic Sciences*, vol. 17, no. 1, pp. 73–90.

Kapur, Anuradha. "Deity to Crusader: The Changing Iconography of Ram," in Gyanendra Pandey, ed., *Hindus and Others: The Question of Identity in India Today*. New Delhi: Viking Penguin, 1993.
   "The Representation of Gods and Heroes in the Parsi Mythological Drama of the Early Twentieth Century," Vasudha Dalmia and Heinrich von Stietencron, eds., *Representing Hinduism: the Construction of Religious Traditions and National Identity*. New Delhi: Sage, 1995.

Kapur, Geeta. "Ravi Varma: Representational Dilemmas of a Nineteenth Century Indian Painter," *Journal of Arts and Ideas*, New Delhi, nos. 17–18, June 1989, pp. 78–92.

Karlekar, Hiranmay. *In the Mirror of Mandal: Social Justice, Caste, Class and the Individual*. New Delhi: Ajanta Publications, 1992.

Kavanagh, Dennis and Anthony Seldon, eds. *The Thatcher Effect*. Oxford: The Clarendon Press, 1989.

Kaviraj, Sudipta. "The Imaginary Institution of India," *Subaltern Studies VII*. New Delhi: Oxford University Press, 1991, pp. 20–33.
   "Writing, Speaking, Being: Language and the Historical Formation of Identities in India," in Dagmar Hellmann-Rajanayagam and Dietmar Rothermund, eds., *Nationalstaat und Sprachkonflict in Sud und Sudostasien*. Stuttgart, 1992, pp. 25–65.

Kaye, Lincoln. "Flickering Fortunes," *Far Eastern Economic Review*, 1 September 1988, p. 51.

Kesavan, Mukul. "Urdu, Awadh and the Tawaif: The Islamicate Roots of Hindi Cinema," in Zoya Hasan, ed., *Forging Identities. Gender, Communities and the State*. New Delhi: Kali for Women, 1994.

Kishore, Acharya Giriraj. "A Glimpse of the Ekatmata Yagna," *Hindu Vishwa*, Rajat Jayanti Souvenir, New Delhi, August 1990.

Kishore, Raj. "Mukhya Cheez Hai Apni Aazadi ko Banaye Rakhna" [The Important Thing is to Remain Independent], in *Patrakaritha ke Pehlu* [Aspects of Journalism]. Kanpur: Sahitya Sadan, 1988, pp. 75–91.

Kochanek, Stanley. *The Congress Party of India*. Princeton: Princeton University Press, 1968.

Kurien, C. T. *Global Capitalism and the Indian Economy*. New Delhi: Orient Longman, 1994.

Our First Five Year Plan. Madras, 1966.

Lamb, Ramdas. "Personalizing the Ramayan: Ramnamis and Their Use of the Ramcharitmanas," in Paula Richman, ed., *Many Ramayanas: The Diversity of a Narrative Tradition in South Asia*. Berkeley: University of California Press, 1991, pp. 235–255.

Larson, Gerald. *India's Agony Over Religion*. Buffalo: SUNY Press, 1995.

Lefort, Claude. *The Political Forms of Modern Society: Bureaucracy, Democracy, Totalitarianism*, ed. John B. Thompson. Cambridge, Mass.: MIT Press, 1986.

Lerner, Daniel. *The Passing of Traditional Society: Modernizing the Middle East*. New York: Free Press, 1958.

Lewis, Justin. "The Encoding/Decoding Model: Criticisms and Re-developments for Research on Decoding," *Media, Culture and Society*, no. 5, 1983, pp. 179–198.

Lichterman, Paul. "Thin Culture," *Media, Culture and Society*, vol. 14, 1992, pp. 421–448.

Lull, James, ed., *World Families Watch Television*. Newbury Park, Calif.: Sage, 1988.

Lutgendorf, Philip. *The Life of a Text: Performing the Ramcharitmanas of Tulsidas*. Berkeley: University of California Press, 1991.

Luthra, H. R. *Indian Broadcasting*. New Delhi: Publications Division, 1986.

Malik, Yogendra K. and V. B. Singh, *Hindu Nationalists in India. The Rise of the Bharatiya Janata Party*. Boulder: Westview, 1994.

Capital: A Critical Analysis of Capitalist Production, tr. Samuel Moore and Edward Aveling, ed. Frederick Engels. Vol. 1. Moscow: Progress Publishers, 1954.

The Eighteenth Brumaire of Louis Bonaparte. New York: International Publishers, 1963.

Marx, Karl. "On the Jewish Question," in Robert C. Tucker, ed., *The Marx–Engels Reader*. New York: W. W. Norton and Co., 1978.

Mandal, D. *Ayodhya: Archaeology After Demolition*. New Delhi: Orient Longman, 1993.

Manuel, Peter. *Cassette Culture: Popular Music and Technology in North India*. Chicago: University of Chicago Press, 1993.

Masani, Mehra. *Broadcasting and the People*. New Delhi: National Book Trust, 1976.

Masica, Colin P. *Defining a Linguistic Area: South Asia*. Chicago: University of Chicago Press, 1976.

Matilal, Bimal Krishna, ed. *Moral Dilemmas in the Mahabharata.*. Shimla: Indian Institute of Advanced Study with Motilal Banarsidass, 1989.

Mbembe, Achille. "The Banality of Power and the Aesthetics of Vulgarity in the Postcolony," *Public Culture*, vol. 2, no. 2, Spring 1993, pp. 1–30.

McLane, John R. *Indian Nationalism and the Early Congress*. Princeton: Princeton University Press, 1977.

McLuhan, Marshall. *The Gutenberg Galaxy: The Making of Typographic Man.* London: Routledge and Kegan Paul, 1962.

Understanding Media: The Extensions of Man. London: Routledge and Kegan Paul, 1964.

Mellencamp, Patricia, ed. *Logics of Television: Essays in Cultural Criticism.* Bloomington and London: Indiana University Press and British Film Institute, 1990.

Melucci, Alberto. "The Symbolic Challenge of Contemporary Movements," *Social Research*, vol. 52, no. 4, Winter 1985, pp. 789–816.

Meyrowitz, Joshua. *No Sense of Place: The Impact of Electronic Media on Social Behaviour.* New York: Oxford University Press, 1985.

Mishra, Vinay Chandra, ed. *Ram Janmabhoomi Babri Masjid. Historical Documents, Legal Opinions and Judgements.* New Delhi: Bar Council of India Trust, 1991.

Mitra, Ashok. *Cutting Corners.* Calcutta: Bookfront Publication Forum, 1992.

Monteiro, Vivek and Meena Menon. "What Collapsed with the Babri Masjid: A Study of the Trade Union Movement," in Madhushree Dutta, Flavia Agnes and Neera Adarkar, eds., *The Nation, the State and Indian Identity.* Calcutta: Samya, 1996, pp. 174–206.

Morley, David. *Family Television.* London: Comedia, 1986.

"The Nationwide Audience: A Critical Postscript," *Screen Education*, no. 39, 1981, pp. 3–14.

The Nationwide Audience: Structure and Decoding. London: British Film Institute, 1980.

Mukhopadhyay, Nilanjan. *The Demolition: India at the Crossroads.* New Delhi: HarperCollins, 1994.

Nagaraj, R. "Macroeconomic Impact of Public Sector Enterprises: Some Further Evidence," *Economic and Political Weekly*, 16–23 January 1993, pp. 105–109.

Nandan, Deoki. *Sri Rama Janma Bhumi: Historical and Legal Perspective.* New Delhi: Vishwa Hindu Parishad, n.d.

Nandy, Ashis, *et al. Creating a Nationality: The Ramjanmabhumi Movement and the Fear of the Self.* New Delhi: Oxford University Press, 1995.

Narayanan, Vasudha. "Creating the South Indian 'Hindu' Experience in the United States," in Raymond Brady Williams, ed., *A Sacred Thread: Modern Transmission of Hindu Traditions in India and Abroad.* Chambersburg, PA: Anima Publications, 1992, pp. 160–163.

Narayana Rao, Velcheru, "A Ramayan of their Own: Women's Oral Tradition in Telugu," in Paula Richman, ed., *Many Ramayanas: The Diversity of Narrative Tradition in South Asia.* Berkeley: University of California Press, 1991, pp. 114–136.

Nayak, Pulin B. "On the Crisis and Remedies," *Economic and Political Weekly*, 24 August 1991, pp. 1993–1997.

Nehru, Arun. *Shame Shame Pseudo Secularism.* Hyderabad: Jana Sandesh Publishers, 1993.

Ninan, Sevanti. *Through the Magic Window: Television and Social Change in India.* New Delhi: Penguin, 1995.

Noorani, A. G. "Civil code vs reform," *Frontline*, 23 February 1996, pp. 92–94.

Omi, Michael and Howard Winant. *Racial Formation in the United States from the 1960s to the 1980s.* New York: Routledge, 1986.

Omvedt, Gail. *Cultural Revolt in a Colonial Society: The Non-Brahman Movement in Western India 1850–1935.* Poona: Socialist Scientific Education Trust, 1976.

Padmanabhan, Satish, Ranvir Nayar, and Nilanjan Dutta. "An affair of the purse: The BJP is the new darling of industrialists," *Sunday*, Calcutta, 21–27 February 1991, pp. 50–52.

Pandey, Gyanendra. *The Construction of Communalism in Colonial North India.* New Delhi: Oxford, 1990.

"In Defence of the Fragment," *Representations*, no. 37, Winter 1992, pp. 27–55.

"Modes of History Writing: New History Writing of Ayodhya," 18 June 1994, pp. 1523–1528.

"Rallying Round the Cow: Sectarian Strife in the Bhojpuri Region, c. 1880–1917," in R. Guha, *Subaltern Studies II.* Delhi: Oxford University Press, 1983, pp. 60–129.

Pandian, M. S. S. *The Image Trap. MG Ramachandran in Film and Politics.* New Delhi: Sage, 1992.

Pandit, Prabodh B. *India as a Sociolinguistic Area.* Poona: University of Poona, 1972.

Panikkar, K. N. "A Historical Overview," in S. Gopal, ed., *Anatomy of a Confrontation: The Babri Masjid-Ram Janmabhumi Issue.* New Delhi: Viking Penguin, 1991.

Parikh, Kirit, ed. *Mid-Year Review of the Economy 1994–95.* New Delhi: Konark Publishers in association with India International Centre, 1995.

Pathak, Zakia and Rajeswari Sunder Rajan, "Shah Bano," *Signs*, vol. 14, no. 3, Spring 1989, pp. 558–582.

Patil, Sharad. "Democracy: Brahminical and Non-Brahminical," *Frontier*, Calcutta, 30 September–21 October 1995, pp. 42–46.

People's Union for Democratic Rights. *Recalling Bhagalpur: A Report on the Aftermath of the 1989 Riots.* New Delhi, February 1996.

Pingale, Moropant. *Prak-kathan* [Foreword], in Raghunandan Prasad Sharma, ed., *Vishwa Hindu Parishad: Samagra Darshan* [Entire View]. New Delhi, n.d.

Pollock, Sheldon I. *The Ramayana of Valmiki, vol. 2: Ayodhyakanda,* tr. Sheldon I. Pollock. Princeton: Princeton University Press, 1986.

Prashad, Vijay. "The Untouchable Question," *Economic and Political Weekly*, 2 March 1996, pp. 551–559.

Radway, Janice. *Reading the Romance.* Chapel Hill: University of North Carolina Press, 1984.

Raghavan, V., ed. *The Ramayana Tradition in Asia.* 2 vols. New Delhi: Sahitya Akademi, 1976.

Rajadhyaksha, Ashish and Paul Willemen. *Encylopaedia of Indian Cinema.* London and New Delhi: British Film Institute and Oxford University Press, 1994.

Raj Goyal, Des. *Rashtriya Swayamsevak Sangh*. New Delhi: Radhakrishna Prakashan, 1979.

Rajagopal, Arvind. "Ram Janmabhumi, Consumer Identity and Image-based Politics," *Economic and Political Weekly*, 2 July 1994, pp. 1659–1668.

"An unholy nexus: Expatriate anxiety and Hindu extremism," *Frontline*, Madras, 10 September 1993, pp. 13–15.

Rajan, Rajeswari Sunder. *Real and Imagined Women: Gender, Culture and Post-Colonialis*. London: Routledge, 1994.

Rajgopal, P. R. *Communal Violence in India*. New Delhi: Uppal, 1987.

Ram, N. "A Tale of Two White Papers," *Frontline*, 21 May 1993, pp. 30–31.

Ramachandran, T. V. *Non-Resident Indians Investment Policy Guidelines and Procedures: A Compendium*. Bangalore: Puliani and Puliani, 1992, pp. 21–25.

Ramakrishnan, Venkitesh. "Saffron Offensive: 'Liberation Theology' of a different kind," *Frontline*, 8 September 1995, pp. 4–12.

"Upstaging Hindutva," *Frontline*, 10 September 1993.

Ramaseshan, Radhika. "Changing Equations," *Pioneer*, New Delhi, 15 November 1993.

"The Press on Ayodhya," *Economic and Political Weekly*, 15 December 1990, pp. 2701–2704.

Ramnarayan, Gowri. "To Ayodhya for Peace," *Frontline*, 27 August 1993.

Reddy, Chinappa O., D. A. Desai, and D. S. Tewatia. *Citizens' Tribunal on Ayodhya. Judgement and Recommendations*. New Delhi: December 1993.

Richman, Paula, ed., *Many Ramayanas: The Diversity of a Narrative Tradition in South Asia*. Berkeley: University of California Press, 1991.

Robertson, Roland. *Religion and Globalization*. Beverly Hills: Sage, 1995.

Rosen, Philip, ed., *Narrative, Apparatus, Ideology*. New York: Columbia University Press, 1986.

Rosmarin, Adena. *The Power of Genre*. Minneapolis: University of Minnesota Press.

Rudolph, Lloyd I. "The Media and Cultural Politics," in Harold A. Gould and Sumit Ganguly, eds., *India Votes. Alliance Politics and Minority Governments in the Ninth and Tenth General Elections*. Boulder: Westview Press, 1993.

Rudra, Ashok. "Some Pre-Budget Predictions," *Economic and Political Weekly*, 8 February 1992, pp. 265–266.

Sagar, Ramanand. "Director's Diary," in *Star&Style*, 21 November–4 December 1986, pp. 66–69.

SAHMAT. *Muktnaad. Hum Sab Ayodhya. A Selection of Reports, Editorials, Discussion, Comments from the Press*. New Delhi: SAHMAT, 1994.

Sangari, Kumkum. "Consent, Agency and the Rhetorics of Incitement," *Economic and Political Weekly*, vol. 28, no. 18, 1 May 1993, 867–883.

"Politics of Diversity: Religious Communities and Multiple Patriarchies," *Economic and Political Weekly*, 23 December 1995, pp. 3287–3310, and 30 December 1995, pp. 3381–3389.

Sankar, T. L. and Y. Venugopal Reddy. "Red Herring of Privatisation," *Economic and Political Weekly*, 17–24 February 1990, pp. 407–408.

Sarkar, Shivaji. "Stylebook of the Lathi," *Vidura*, New Delhi, September–October 1987, p. 5.

Sarkar, Sumit. "The Fascism of the Sangh Parivar," *Economic and Political Weekly*, 30 January 1993, pp. 163–167.

    The Swadeshi Movement in Bengal, 1903–1908. New Delhi: People's Publishing House, 1973.

Sarkar, Tanika and Urvashi Butalia. 'The Woman as Communal Subject: Rashtra Sevika Samiti and Ramjanmabhoomi Movement," in *Economic and Political Weekly*, 31 August, 1991, pp. 2057–2062.

    Women and the Hindu Right: A Collection of Essays. New Delhi: Kali for Women Press, 1995.

Savarkar, Vinayak Damodar. *Hindutva*, 2nd edn. Poona, 1942.

Schramm, Wilbur. *Mass Media and National Development*. Stanford: Stanford University Press, 1964.

Seely, Clinton. "The Raja's New Clothes: Redressing Ravana in Meghanadavada Kavya," in Paula Richman, ed., *Many Ramayanas: The Diversity of Narrative Tradition in South Asia*. Berkeley: University of California Press, 1991.

Seiter, Ellen *et al*. *Remote Control: TV Audiences and Cultural Power*. London: Routledge, 1990.

Seshadri, H. V. "For the Hindus in the West, the Crucial Challenge is of their Children," *Organiser*, Delhi, 4 November 1984, p. 9.

    Hindus Abroad. The Dilemma: Dollar or Dharma? New Delhi: Suruchi Prakashan, 1990.

    "When the 'Hindu heart' is awakened," *Organiser*, 27 May 1984, p. 9.

Seshan, T. N. with Sanjoy Hazarika. *The Degeneration of India*. New Delhi: Viking Press, 1995.

Shapiro, Michael and H. F. Schiffman. *Language and Society in South Asia*. Dordrecht: Foris, 1983.

Sharma, Gopal. *Kar Seva se Kar Seva Tak*. Jaipur: Rajasthan Patrika Limited, 1993.

Sharma, Raghunandan Prasad, ed. *Vishwa Hindu Parishad: Samagra Darshan* [Vishwa Hindu Parishad: An Entire View]. New Delhi, n.d.

Shrivastava, Sushil. *The Disputed Mosque: A Historical Inquiry*. New Delhi: Vistaar, 1991.

Singh, Anandeshwar Prasad. "*Ulajh gaya hai mandir aur masjid masla*" [Mandir and Mandal issues are entangled], *Aaj*, 22 November 1990, p. 6.

Singh, K. S. "The People of India, Culture and Communication," Paper presented at Ogilvy & Mather Workshop on Culture and Communication, Bangalore, 7–11 July, 1994.

Singh, Parmanand. "The Legal History of the Ayodhya Litigation," in Vinay Chandra Mishra, ed., *Ram Janmabhoomi Babri Masjid. Historical Documents, Legal Opinions and Judgements*. New Delhi: Bar Council of India Trust, 1991, pp. 29–31. [Reprint of special issue of *Indian Bar Review*, vol. 18(2), 1991.]

Singh, Virendra. "The Press in India 1990–91," in *Press and Advertisers' Yearbook 1990–91*. New Delhi: INFA Publications, 1991.

Singhal, Arvind, Everett M. Rogers and William J. Brown. "Entertainment Telenovelas for Development: Lessons Learned," in Anamaria Fadul, ed., *Serial Fiction in the Latin American Telenovelas with an Annotated Bibliography of Brazilian Telenovelas*. Sao Paulo: School of Communication and Arts, 1993.

and Everett Rogers. *India's Information Revolution*. New Delhi: Sage, 1989.

Sisson, Richard and Stanley Wolpert, eds. *Diversity and Dominance in Indian Politics*. 2 vols. Berkeley: University of California Press, 1988.

Smith, Daniel H. *Select Bibliography of Ramayan-related Studies*. Ananthacharya Indological Series no. 21, Bombay, 1989.

Reading the Ramayana: A Bibliographic Guide for Students and College Teachers – Indian Variants on the Rama Theme in English Translations. Foreign and Comparative Studies, South Asian special publications no. 4, Syracuse: Maxwell School of Citizenship and Public Affairs, Syracuse University, 1983.

Sollors, Werner, ed. *The Invention of Ethnicity*. New York: Oxford University Press, 1989.

Sontheimer G.-D. "Bhakti in the Khandoba Cult," in Diana Eck and Françoise Mallison, eds., *Devotion Divine: Bhakti Traditions from the Regions of India. Studies in Honor of Charlotte Vaudeville*. Groningen/Paris: Egbert Forsten/Ecole Française d'Extreme Orient, 1991.

"The Erosion of Folk Religion in Modern India: Some Points for Deliberation," in Vasudha Dalmia and Heinrich von Stientencron, eds., *Representing Hinduism: The Construction of Religious Traditions and National Identity*. New Delhi: Sage, 1995, pp. 389–398.

"Hinduism: The Five Components and their Interaction," in Sontheimer and Hermann Kulke, *Hinduism Reconsidered*. South Asian Studies 24, New Delhi: Manohar, reprint, 1991, pp. 197–212.

"The Ramayana in Contemporary Folk Traditions of Maharashtra," in Monika Theil-Horstmann, ed., *Ramayana and Ramayanas*. Wiesbaden: Otto Harasowitz, 1991.

"Religious Endowments in India: The Juristic Personality of Hindu Deities," *Zeitschrift fur vergleichende Rechtswissenschaft*, vol. 69, no. 1, 1964.

Statistical Abstract of the United States 1993. Bureau of the Census, Department of Commerce.

Subrahmanyam, Sanjay. "Before the Leviathan: Sectarian Violence and the State in Pre-Colonial India," in Kaushik Basu and Sanjay Subrahmanyam, eds., *Unravelling the Nation: Sectarian Conflict and India's Secular Identity*. New Delhi: Penguin, 1996.

Swami, Praveen. "Beyond Slogans," *Frontline*, 10 September 1993, pp. 34–36.

Takaki, Ronald, ed. *From Different Shores: Perspectives on Race and Ethnicity in America*. New York: Oxford University Press, 1987.

Tanna, Ketan, *et al.* "Playing the BJP's Game," *Sunday*, 29 August–4 September 1993, pp. 28–33.

Thapar, Romila. "Epic and History – Tradition, Dissent and Politics in India," *Past and Present*, no. 125, pp. 3–26.

Tharpar, Romila, Harbans Mukhia and Bipan Chandra. *Communalism and the Writing of Indian History*. New Delhi, 1977.

Television India (Facts and Figures). Audience Research Unit, Doordarshan, New Delhi, October 1988.

Thiel-Horstmann, Monika, ed. *Ramayan and Ramayanas*. Wiesbaden: Otto Harasowitz, 1991.

Thomas, T. K., ed. *Autonomy for the Electronic Media: A National Debate on The Prasar Bharati Bill, 1989*. New Delhi: Konark Publishers, 1990.

Tinker, Hugh. *The Banyan Tree*. London and New York: Oxford University Press, 1977.

Trivedy, Santosh Ji, "Festivals for National Integration," *Hindu Vishva*, VHP Rajat Jayanti Souvenir, New Delhi: August 1990, p. 77.

Tulpule, Bagaram. "All the Answers," *Economic and Political Weekly*, 17–24 July 1993, pp. 1489–1490.

Tynyanov, Jury. "On Literary Evolution," in Ladislav Matejka and Krystyna Pomorska, eds., *Readings in Russian Poetics: Formalist and Structuralist Views*. Ann Arbor: Michigan Slavic Publications, 1978.

Valenzuela, J. S. and A. Valenzuela. "Modernization and Dependency: Alternative Perspectives in the Study of Latin American Underdevelopment," in *Comparative Politics*, vol. 10(4), July 1978, pp. 537–538.

van der Veer, Peter. *Gods on Earth: The Management of Religious Experience and Identity in a North Indian Pilgrimage*. New Delhi: Oxford University Press, 1989.

Religious Nationalism – Hindus and Muslims in India. Berkeley: University of California Press, 1994.

Vanaik, Achin. *The Painful Transition. Bourgeois Democracy in India*. London: Verso, 1990.

Vasudevan, Ravi. "Addressing the Spectator of a 'Third World' National Cinema: The Bombay 'Social' Film of the 1940s and 1950s," *Screen*, vol. 36, no. 4, Winter 1995, pp. 305–324.

"The Melodramatic Mode and the Commercial Hindi Cinema: Notes on Film History, Narrative and Performance in the 1950s," *Screen*, vol. 30, no. 3, 1989, pp. 29–52.

Vishwa Hindu Parishad. *The Great Evidence of Shri Ram Janmabhoomi Mandir*. New Delhi, 1991.

Vishwa Hindu Parishad of America, Inc. *Bahurashtriya Kampaniyon ke Vikalp ke Roop Mein Swadeshi Upbhokt Vastuon ki Suchi* [List of Indigenous Consumer Goods as Options Instead of Foreign Companies' Goods]. n.d.

Waters, Mary C. *Ethnic Options: Choosing Identities in America*. Berkeley: University of California Press, 1990.

Weiner, Myron. *Party Building in a New Nation*. Chicago: University of Chicago Press, 1967.

Williams, Raymond Brady, ed. *A Sacred Thread: Modern Transmission of Hindu Traditions in India and Abroad*. Chambersburg: Anima Publications, 1992.

Wolpert, Stanley A. *Tilak and Gokhale: Revolution and Reform in the Making of Modern India*. Berkeley: University of California Press, 1961.

Wong, Shawn. "Is Ethnicity Obsolete?" in Werner Sollors, ed., *The Invention of Ethnicity*. New York: Oxford University Press, 1989.

Yadav, Dwarka Singh. *Ishwar Stuti* [Lord's Prayer]. Rama Cassettes Production, n.d.

Yadav, Yogendra. "Political change in North India – Interpreting Assembly election results," *Economic and Political Weekly*, 18 December 1993, pp. 2767–2774.

Yancey, William L., Eugene P. Ericksen, and Richard N. Juliani. "Emergent Ethnicity: A Review and Reformulation," in *American Sociological Review*, vol. 41, no. 3, 1976, pp. 391–402.

Yang, Anand A. "Sacred Symbol and Sacred Space in Rural India: Community Mobilization in the 'Anti-Cow-Killing' Riot of 1893," *Comparative Studies in Society and History*, vol. 22, 4 October 1980, pp. 576–596.

Zaveri, Saloni. "Myths, masti, magic," *Sunday* (Calcutta), 11–17 August 1996.

Zizek, Slavoj. *Tarrying with the Negative: Kant, Hegel and the Critique of Ideology*. Durham: Duke University Press, 1993.

Index